THE ANABASIS OF ALEXANDER

THE ANABASIS OF ALEXANDER;

OR,

The History of the Wars and Conquests of Alexander the Great.

LITERALLY TRANSLATED, WITH A COMMENTARY, FROM THE GREEK OF ARRIAN THE NICOMEDIAN,

BY

E. J. CHINNOCK, M.A. LL.B, LONDON,

Rector of Dumfries Academy

GYAN

Published by

Gyan Publishing House
5, Ansari Road
Daryaganj, New Delhi-110002
Phone: 011-47034999, 9811692060
E-mail: books@gyanbooks.com

Distribution Network
gyanbooks.com
India, USA, Canada, UK, Australia, France

ISBN : 978-81-212-2243-3 (PB)
First Published, 1884

2nd Impression 2021

Printed at: Gyan Press, Delhi.

The
Anabasis of Alexander
Author: E. J. Chinnock

THE ANABASIS OF ALEXANDER;

OR,

The History of the Wars and Conquests of Alexander the Great.

LITERALLY TRANSLATED, WITH A COMMENTARY, FROM THE GREEK OF ARRIAN THE NICOMEDIAN,

BY

E. J. CHINNOCK, M.A., LL.B., LONDON,
Rector of Dumfries Academy.

London:
HODDER AND STOUGHTON,
27, PATERNOSTER ROW.
MDCCCLXXXIV.

PREFACE.

WHEN I began this Translation, more than two years ago, I had no intention of publishing it; but as the work progressed, it occurred to me that Arrian is an Author deserving of more attention from the English-speaking races than he has yet received. No edition of his works has, so far as I am aware, ever appeared in England, though on the Continent many have been published. In the following Translation I have tried to give as literal a rendering of the Greek text as I could without transgressing the idioms of our own language. My theory of the duty of a Translator is, to give the *ipsissima verba* of his Author as nearly as possible, and not put into his mouth words which he never used, under the mistaken notion of improving his diction or his way of stating his case. It is a comparatively easy thing to give a paraphrase of a foreign work, presenting the general drift of the original; but no one, unless he has himself tried it, can understand the difficulty of translating a classical Author correctly without omission or mutilation.

In the Commentary which I have compiled, continual reference has been made to the other extant authorities on the history of Alexander, such as Diodorus, Plutarch, Curtius, Justin, and Aelian; so that I think I may safely assert that, taking the Translation and the Notes together, the book forms a complete history of Alexander's reign. Much geographical and other material has also been gathered from Herodotus, Strabo, Pliny, and Ammianus; and the allusions to the places which are also mentioned in the Old Testament are given from the Hebrew.

As Arrian lived in the second century of the present era, and nearly five hundred years after Demosthenes, it is not to be expected that he wrote classical Greek. There are, however, at least a dozen valuable Greek authors of this century whose works are still extant, and of these it is a safe statement to make, that Arrian is the best of them all, with the single exception of Lucian. I have noticed as many of his deviations from Attic Greek constructions as I thought suitable to a work of this kind. A complete index of Proper Names has been added, and the quantities of the vowels marked for the aid of the English Reader. In the multiplicity of references which I have put into the Notes, I should be sanguine if I imagined that no errors will be found; but if such occur, I must plead as an excuse the pressure of work which a teacher in a large school experiences, leaving him very little energy for literary labour.

E. J. C.

DUMFRIES,
December, 1883.

CONTENTS.

PAGE

Life and Writings of Arrian 1
Arrian's Preface 6

BOOK I.

CHAP.

I. Death of Philip and Accession of Alexander.—His Wars with the Thracians 8
II. Battle with the Triballians 12
III. Alexander at the Danube and in the Country of the Getae 14
IV. Alexander destroys the City of the Getae.—The Ambassadors of the Celts 16
V. Revolt of Clitus and Glaucias 18
VI. Defeat of Clitus and Glaucias 22
VII. Revolt of Thebes (*September*, B.C. 335) . . 25
VIII. Fall of Thebes 28
IX. Destruction of Thebes 31
X. Alexander's Dealings with Athens 34
XI. Alexander crosses the Hellespont and visits Troy . . 36
XII. Alexander at the Tomb of Achilles.—Memnon's advice Rejected by the Persian Generals 38
XIII. Battle of the Granicus (B.C. 334) 41
XIV. Arrangement of the Hostile Armies 43
XV. Description of the Battle of the Granicus 45
XVI. Defeat of the Persians.—Loss on Both Sides . . 47
XVII. Alexander in Sardis and Ephesus 50
XVIII. Alexander marches to Miletus and Occupies the Island of Lade 52
XIX. Siege and Capture of Miletus 55
XX. Siege of Halicarnassus.—Abortive Attack on Myndus 58
XXI. Siege of Halicarnassus 61

CHAP.		PAGE
XXII.	Siege of Halicarnassus	63
XXIII.	Destruction of Halicarnassus.—Ada, Queen of Caria	64
XXIV.	Alexander in Lycia and Pamphylia	66
XXV.	Treason of Alexander, Son of Aëropus	68
XXVI.	Alexander in Pamphylia.—Capture of Aspendus and Side	70
XXVII.	Alexander in Phrygia and Pisidia	72
XXVIII.	Operations in Pisidia	74
XXIX.	Alexander in Phrygia	76

BOOK II.

I.	Capture of Mitylene by the Persians.—Death of Memnon	78
II.	The Persians capture Tenedus.—They are Defeated at Sea	80
III.	Alexander at Gordium	82
IV.	Conquest of Cappadocia.—Alexander's Illness at Tarsus	84
V.	Alexander at the Tomb of Sardanapalus.—Proceedings in Cilicia	87
VI.	Alexander advances to Myriandrus.—Darius Marches against him	89
VII.	Darius at Issus.—Alexander's Speech to his Army	91
VIII.	Arrangement of the Hostile Armies	94
IX.	Alexander changes the Disposition of his Forces	97
X.	Battle of Issus	99
XI.	Defeat and Flight of Darius	101
XII.	Kind Treatment of Darius's Family	104
XIII.	Flight of Macedonian Deserters into Egypt.—Proceedings of Agis, King of Sparta.—Alexander occupies Phoenicia	106
XIV.	Darius's Letter, and Alexander's Reply	111
XV.	Alexander's Treatment of the Captured Greek Ambassadors.—Submission of Byblus and Sidon	114
XVI.	The Worship of Hercules in Tyre.—The Tyrians refuse to admit Alexander	117
XVII.	Speech of Alexander to his Officers	120
XVIII.	Siege of Tyre.—Construction of a Mole from the Mainland to the Island	121
XIX.	The Siege of Tyre	123
XX.	Tyre Besieged by Sea as well as Land	124
XXI.	Siege of Tyre	127

CHAP. PAGE
XXII. Siege of Tyre.—Naval Defeat of the Tyrians . . 129
XXIII. Siege of Tyre 131
XXIV. Capture of Tyre 132
XXV. The Offers of Darius rejected.—Batis, Governor of Gaza, refuses to Submit 134
XXVI. Siege of Gaza 136
XXVII. Capture of Gaza 137

BOOK III.

I. Conquest of Egypt.—Foundation of Alexandria . . 140
II. Foundation of Alexandria.—Events in the Aegean . 142
III. Alexander visits the Temple of Ammon . . 144
IV. The Oasis of Ammon 147
V. Settlement of the Affairs of Egypt 148
VI. March into Syria.—Alexander's Kindness to Harpalus and his other early Adherents 150
VII. Passage of the Euphrates and Tigris 152
VIII. Description of Darius's Army at Arbela . . 154
IX. Alexander's Tactics.—His Speech to the Officers . . 157
X. Rejection of Parmenio's Advice 159
XI. Tactics of the Opposing Generals 160
XII. Alexander's Tactics 163
XIII. The Battle of Arbela 164
XIV. Battle of Arbela.—Flight of Darius 166
XV. Defeat of the Persians and Pursuit of Darius . . 168
XVI. Escape of Darius into Media.—March of Alexander to Babylon and Susa 170
XVII. Subjugation of the Uxians 174
XVIII. Defeat of Ariobarzanes and Capture of Persepolis . 176
XIX. Darius pursued into Media and Parthia 179
XX. March through the Caspian Gates 181
XXI. Darius is Assassinated by Bessus 182
XXII. Reflections on the Fate of Darius 185
XXIII. Expedition into Hyrcania 187
XXIV. Expedition against the Mardians 189
XXV. March to Bactra.—Bessus aided by Satibarzanes . 191
XXVI. Philotas and Parmenio put to Death 193
XXVII. Treatment of Amyntas.—The Ariaspians . 195
XXVIII. Alexander crosses the Hindu-Koosh . . 196

CHAP. PAGE

XXIX. Conquest of Bactria, and Pursuit of Bessus across the Oxus 199
XXX. Capture of Bessus.—Exploits in Sogdiana . 201

BOOK IV.

I. Rebellion of the Sogdianians 205
II. Capture of Five Cities in Two Days 206
III. Storming of Cyropolis.—Revolt of the Scythians 208
IV. Defeat of the Scythians beyond the Tanais . . . 210
V. Spitamenes destroys a Macedonian Detachment . 212
VI. Spitamenes driven into the Desert 214
VII. Treatment of Bessus 216
VIII. The Murder of Clitus 218
IX. Alexander's grief for Clitus 221
X. Dispute between Callisthenes and Anaxarchus . . 223
XI. Callisthenes Opposes the Proposal to honour Alexander by Prostration 225
XII. Callisthenes refuses to Prostrate himself . . 228
XIII. Conspiracy of the Pages 229
XIV. Execution of Callisthenes and Hermolaus . . . 231
XV. Alliance with the Scythians and Chorasmians . . 233
XVI. Subjugation of Sogdiana.—Revolt of Spitamenes 235
XVII. Defeat and Death of Spitamenes 237
XVIII. Oxyartes Besieged in the Sogdian Rock . . 239
XIX. Alexander Captures the Rock and Marries Roxana 241
XX. Magnanimous Treatment of the Family of Darius . 242
XXI. Capture of the Rock of Chorienes 244
XXII. Alexander reaches the River Cabul, and Receives the Homage of Taxiles 246
XXIII. Battles with the Aspasians 248
XXIV. Operations against the Aspasians 250
XXV. Defeat of the Aspasians.—The Assacenians and Guraeans Attacked 252
XXVI. Siege of Massaga 254
XXVII. Sieges of Massaga and Ora 255
XXVIII. Capture of Bazira.—Advance to the Rock of Aornus 257
XXIX. Siege of Aornus 260
XXX. Capture of Aornus.—Arrival at the Indus . . 262

BOOK V.

CHAP.	PAGE
I. Alexander at Nysa	265
II. Alexander at Nysa	267
III. Incredulity of Eratosthenes.—Passage of the Indus	269
IV. Digression about India	270
V. Mountains and Rivers of Asia	273
VI. General Description of India	274
VII. Method of Bridging Rivers	277
VIII. March from the Indus to the Hydaspes	279
IX. Porus obstructs Alexander's Passage	280
X. Alexander and Porus at the Hydaspes	282
XI. Alexander's Stratagem to get across	283
XII. Passage of the Hydaspes	284
XIII. Passage of the Hydaspes	285
XIV. The Battle at the Hydaspes	287
XV. Arrangements of Porus	288
XVI. Alexander's Tactics	290
XVII. Defeat of Porus	291
XVIII. Losses of the Combatants.—Porus Surrenders	293
XIX. Alliance with Porus.—Death of Bucephalas	295
XX. Conquest of the Glausians.—Embassy from Abisares.—Passage of the Acesines	297
XXI. Advance beyond the Hydraotes	299
XXII. Invasion of the Land of the Cathaeans	301
XXIII. Assault upon Sangala	302
XXIV. Capture of Sangala	304
XXV. The Army refuses to Advance.—Alexander's Speech to the Officers	306
XXVI. Alexander's Speech (*continued*)	308
XXVII. The Answer of Coenus	311
XXVIII. Alexander resolves to Return	313
XXIX. Alexander recrosses the Hydraotes and Acesines	314

BOOK VI.

CHAP.	PAGE
I. Preparations for a Voyage down the Indus	317
II. Voyage down the Hydaspes	318
III. Voyage down the Hydaspes (*continued*)	320
IV. Voyage down the Hydaspes into the Acesines	321
V. Voyage down the Acesines	323
VI. Campaign against the Mallians	324

CHAP.	PAGE
VII. Campaign against the Mallians (*continued*)	326
VIII. Defeat of the Mallians at the river Hydraotes	328
IX. Storming of the Mallian Stronghold	329
X. Alexander dangerously Wounded	331
XI. Alexander Wounded	333
XII. Anxiety of the Soldiers about Alexander	335
XIII. Joy of the Soldiers at Alexander's Recovery	336
XIV. Voyage down the Hydraotes and Acesines into the Indus	338
XV. Voyage down the Indus to the Land of Musicanus	340
XVI. Campaign against Oxycanus and Sambus	342
XVII. Musicanus Executed.—Capture of Patala	343
XVIII. Voyage down the Indus	345
XIX. Voyage down the Indus into the Sea	346
XX. Exploration of the Mouths of the Indus	348
XXI. Campaign against the Oritians	349
XXII. March through the Desert of Gadrosia	351
XXIII. March through the Desert of Gadrosia	353
XXIV. March through Gadrosia	355
XXV. Sufferings of the Army	356
XXVI. Alexander's Magnanimous Conduct	358
XXVII. March through Carmania.—Punishment of Viceroys	360
XXVIII. Alexander in Carmania	362
XXIX. Alexander in Persis.—Tomb of Cyrus Repaired	364
XXX. Peucestas appointed Viceroy of Persis	367

BOOK VII.

I. Alexander's Plans.—The Indian Philosophers	369
II. Alexander's Dealings with the Indian Sages	371
III. Self-sacrifice of the Indian Calanus	372
IV. Marriages between Macedonians and Persians	374
V. The Soldiers Rewarded	376
VI. An Army of Asiatics Trained under the Macedonian Discipline	378
VII. Navigation of the Tigres	379
VIII. The Macedonians Offended at Alexander	381
IX. Alexander's Speech	383
X. Alexander's Speech (*continued*)	386
XI. Reconciliation between Alexander and his Army	387

CHAP. PAGE

XII. Ten Thousand Macedonians sent Home with Craterus. —Disputes between Antipater and Olympias . . . 390
XIII. The Nisaean Plain.—The Amazons 393
XIV. Death of Hephaestion 395
XV. Subjugation of the Cossaeans.—Embassies from Distant Nations 398
XVI. Exploration of the Caspian.—The Chaldaean Soothsayers 400
XVII. The Advice of the Chaldees rejected 402
XVIII. Predictions of Alexander's Death 404
XIX. Embassies from Greece.—Fleet prepared for Invading Arabia 406
XX. Description of Arabia.—Voyage of Nearchus . . . 408
XXI. Description of the Euphrates and the Pallacopas . 411
XXII. An Omen of Alexander's Approaching Death . . 412
XXIII. The Army Recruited from the Persians.—Hephaestion's Memory Honoured 414
XXIV. Another Omen of Alexander's Death 417
XXV. Alexander Seized with Fever 418
XXVI. Alexander's Death 420
XXVII. Rumour that Alexander was Poisoned 421
XXVIII. Character of Alexander 422
XXIX. Apology for Alexander's Errors 424
XXX. Eulogy of Alexander 425
Index of Proper Names 429

ERRATA.

Page 3. Four lines from the bottom, for Anab. v. 1, *read* v. 5, 1.
Page 8. Note 1, for Diod., xix. 93, 94; *read* xvi. 93, 94.
Note 3, for Diod., xvi. 85; *read* xvii. 4.
Page 48. For Onares *read* Omares.
Page 108. (Note) for Zeph. i. 2; *read* 11.
Page 116. (Note) for *Paradise Lost*, viii. 18; *read* i. 446.

LIFE AND WRITINGS OF ARRIAN.

LIFE AND WRITINGS OF ARRIAN.

ALL we know of Arrian is derived from the notice of him in the *Bibliotheca* of Photius, who was Patriarch of Constantinople in the ninth century, and from a few incidental references in his own writings. We learn from Suidas that Dion Cassius wrote a biography of Arrian; but this work is not extant. Flavius Arrianus was born near the end of the first century of the Christian era, at Nicomedia, the capital of Bithynia. He became a pupil of the famous Stoic philosopher Epictetus, and afterwards went to Athens, where he received the surname of the "younger Xenophon," from the fact that he occupied the same relation to Epictetus as Xenophon did to Socrates.[1] Not only was he called Xenophon by others, but he calls himself so in *Cynegeticus* (v. 6); and in *Periplus* (xii. 5; xxv. 1), he distinguishes Xenophon by the addition *the elder*. Lucian (*Alexander*, 56) calls Arrian simply *Xenophon*. During the stay of the emperor Hadrian at Athens, A.D. 126, Arrian gained his friendship. He accompanied his patron to Rome, where he received the Roman citizenship. In consequence of this, he assumed the name of Flavius.[2] In the same way the Jewish historian, Josephus, had been allowed by Vespasian and Titus to bear the imperial name Flavius.[3]

Photius says, that Arrian had a distinguished career in Rome, being entrusted with various political offices, and at last reaching the supreme dignity of consul under

---

[1] Cf. Arrian (*Cynegeticus*, i. 4). [2] See *Dio Cassius*, lxix. 15.
[3] Cf. Josephus (*Vita ipsius*, 76).

Antoninus Pius.[1] Previous to this he was appointed (A.D. 132) by Hadrian, Governor of Cappadocia, which province was soon after invaded by the Alani, or Massagetae, whom he defeated and expelled.[2] When Marcus Aurelius came to the throne, Arrian withdrew into private life and returned to his native city, Nicomedia. Here, according to Photius, he was appointed priest to Demeter and Persephone. He died in the reign of Marcus Aurelius.

The earlier literary efforts of Arrian were philosophical. After the expulsion of the philosophers from Rome, by Domitian, Epictetus delivered his lectures at Nicopolis, in Epirus, where it is probable that Arrian was his pupil.

I. These lectures were published by Arrian, under the title of *Discourses of Epictetus,* in eight books, the first four only of which have come down to us. He tells us himself in the introduction to this work, that he strove as far as possible to preserve the very words of his teacher as mementoes of his method of reasoning and diction. Gellius (xix. 1) speaks of a fifth book of these Discourses.

II. He also compiled *The Enchiridion of Epictetus,* an abstract of the philosophy of Epictetus, which is still extant. This manual of the Stoic moral philosophy was very popular, both among Pagans and Christians, for many centuries.

III. Another work by Arrian, in twelve books, distinct from the above, is mentioned by Photius under the title of "*Ὁμιλίαι Ἐπικτήτου,*" or *Friendly Conversations with Epictetus.* Of this only a few fragments survive.

IV. Another lost work of Arrian on the life and death of Epictetus is mentioned by Simplicius in the beginning of his Commentary on the Enchiridion.

V. Besides editing these philosophical works, Arrian

---

[1] Cf. Lucian (*Alexander*, 2).

[2] See *Dio Cassius*, lxix. 15.

wrote many original books. By far the most important of these is the *Anabasis of Alexander*, or the History of Alexander the Great's Campaigns. This is one of the most authentic and accurate of historical works. Though inspired with admiration for his hero, the author evinces impartiality and freedom from hero-worship. He exhibits great literary acuteness in the choice of his authorities and in sifting evidence. The two chief sources from which he drew his narrative were the histories written by Ptolemy, son of Lagus, and Aristobulus, son of Aristobulus, both of whom were officers in Alexander's army. Other authorities quoted by Arrian himself were :—Eratosthenes, Megasthenes, Nearchus, Aristus, and Asclepiades. He also made use of Alexander's letters, which he mentions five times;[1] only once, however, quoting the exact words of the writer. The last authority which he mentions, is the *Royal Diary* kept by Eumenes, of Cardia, the private secretary of Philip as well as of Alexander, and by the historian Diodotus, of Erythrae. It is used by Arrian only once,[2] as it is by Plutarch.[3]

VI. The work named *Indica*, is a description of India, and was usually united in manuscripts with the Anabasis, as an eighth book. Though it may be looked upon as a supplement to the Anabasis, Arrian often refers in the one work to the other.[4] From this we may infer that the author wished the *Indica* to be considered a distinct book from the Anabasis; and from the remark in Anab. v. 1, it is clear that it was composed after the Anabasis. This book is written in the Ionic dialect, like the History of Herodotus and the Indica of Ctesias. The latter untrustworthy book Arrian wished to supplant

---

[1] See *Anabasis*, i. 10, 4; ii. 14, 4; ii. 25, 3; vi. 1, 4; vii. 23, 7.

[2] *Anab.*, vii. 25.

[3] *Life of Alexander*, chap. 76.

[4] See *Anab.* v. 5, 1; 6, 8; vi. 28, 6; *Indica*, 19, 21, 23, 32, 40 cc.

by his own narrative, principally based on the works of Megasthenes and Nearchus.

VII. Photius mentions among Arrian's historical works:—*The Events after Alexander,* in ten books, which gives the history of Alexander's successors. Photius (cod. 92) has preserved many extracts from this work.

VIII. *Bithynica* in eight books, a work often quoted by Eustathius in his commentaries to the Iliad and to Dionysius Periegetes. In regard to the contents of this book, Photius (cod. 93) says:—"The Bithynica commences from the mythical events of history and comes down as far as the death of the last Nicomedes, who at his death bequeathed his kingdom to the Romans, who had never been ruled by a king after the expulsion of Tarquin."

IX. *Parthica,* in seventeen books. See Photius (cod. 58).

X. *History of the Alani.* See Photius (cod. 93). Only fragments of this and the *Parthica* remain.

XI. Besides the large works, we learn from Photius (cod. 93) that Arrian wrote the biographies of the Corinthian Timoleon and of the Syracusan Dion. Lucian (Alex. 2), also states that he wrote the life of Tilliborus, the notorious robber of Asia Minor.

XII. A valuable geographical work by Arrian has come down to us, called "*Περίπλους πόντου Εὐξείνου,*" a description of a voyage round the coasts of the Euxine. This naval expedition was executed by him as Governor of Cappadocia. The Alani, or, Albani of the East, a tribe related to the Massagetae, were threatening to invade his province, and he made this voyage with a view of fortifying the most important strategic points on the coast. From section 26 of the Periplus we find that this voyage must have taken place about the year 131 or 132 A.D.; for the death of King Cotys II., noticed in that passage as just dead, is proved by Böckh's investigations to have occurred in 131 A.D. Two other geographical works, *The Periplus of the Red Sea* and *The Periplus of the Euxine*, formerly ascribed to Arrian, are proved to belong to a later date.

XIII. A work on *Tactics*, composed 137 A.D. In many parts this book agrees nearly verbally with the larger work of Aelian on the same subject; but Leo Tacticus (vii. 85) expressly mentions the two works as distinct.

XIV. *An Array of Battle against the Alani*, is a fragment discovered in the seventeenth century in the Description of his Battles with the Alani, who invaded his province, probably 137 A.D., as Arrian had previously feared.[1]

XV. A small work by Arrian on the Chase, forms a supplement to Xenophon's book on the same subject. It is entitled *Cynegeticus of Arrian or the second Xenophon the Athenian*.

The best editions of the Anabasis are the following:—The *editio princeps* by Trincavelli, Venice, 1535; Gerbel, Strassburg, 1539; Henri Estienne, 1575; N. Blancardus, Amsterdam, 1668; J. Gronovius, Leyden, 1704; G. Raphelius, Amsterdam, 1757; A. C. Borkeck, Lemgovia, 1792; F. Schmieder, Leipzig, 1798; Tauchnitz edition, Leipzig, 1818; J. O. Ellendt, Königsberg, 1832; C. W. Krüger, Berlin, 1835; F. Dübner, Paris, 1846; K. Abicht, Leipzig, 1871.

---

1 See *Photius* (codex 58); *Dio Cassius*, lxix. 15.

ARRIAN'S PREFACE.

I have admitted into my narrative as strictly authentic all the statements relating to Alexander and Philip which Ptolemy, son of Lagus,[1] and Aristobulus, son of Aristobulus,[2] agree in making; and from those statements which differ I have selected that which appears to me

[1] Ptolemaeus, surnamed Soter, the Preserver, but more commonly known as the Son of Lagus, a Macedonian of low birth. Ptolemy's mother, Arsinoe, had been a concubine of Philip of Macedon, for which reason it was generally believed that Ptolemy was the offspring of that king. Ptolemy was one of the earliest friends of Alexander before his accession to the throne, and accompanied him throughout his campaigns, being one of his most skilful generals and most intimate friends. On the division of the empire after Alexander's death, Ptolemy obtained the kingdom of Egypt, which he transmitted to his descendants. After a distinguished reign of thirty-eight years, he abdicated the throne to his youngest son, Ptolemy Philadelphus. He survived this event two years, and died B.C. 283. He was a liberal patron of literature and the arts, and wrote a history of the wars of Alexander, which is one of the chief authorities on which Arrian composed his narrative. For his beneficence, see Aelian (*Varia Historia*, xiii. 12). Not only Arrian, but Plutarch and Strabo, derived much information from Ptolemy's work, which is highly commended by Athenaeus.

[2] Aristobulus of Potidaea, a town in Macedonia, which was afterwards called Cassandrea, served under Alexander, and wrote a history of his wars, which, like that of Ptolemy, was sometimes more panegyrical than the facts warranted. Neither of these histories has survived, but they served Arrian as the groundwork for the composition of his own narrative. Lucian in his treatise, *Quomodo historia sit conscribenda*, ch. 12, accuses Aristobulus of inventing marvellous tales of Alexander's valour for the sake of flattery. Plutarch based his *Life of Alexander* chiefly on the work of this writer. We learn from Lucian (*Macrobioi*, c. 22), that Aristobulus wrote his history at the advanced age of eighty-four. He was employed by Alexander to superintend the restoration of Cyrus's tomb (*Arrian*, vi. 30).

the more credible and at the same time the more deserving of record. Different authors have given different accounts of Alexander's life; and there is no one about whom more have written, or more at variance with each other. But in my opinion the narratives of Ptolemy and Aristobulus are more worthy of credit than the rest; Aristobulus, because he served under king Alexander in his expedition, and Ptolemy, not only because he accompanied Alexander in his expedition, but also because he was himself a king afterwards, and falsification of facts would have been more disgraceful to him than to any other man. Moreover, they are both more worthy of credit, because they compiled their histories after Alexander's death, when neither compulsion was used nor reward offered them to write anything different from what really occurred. Some statements made by other writers I have incorporated in my narrative, because they seemed to me worthy of mention and not altogether improbable; but I have given them merely as reports of Alexander's proceedings. And if any man wonders why, after so many other men have written of Alexander, the compilation of this history came into my mind, after perusing[1] the narratives of all the rest, let him read this of mine, and then wonder (if he can).

---

[1] *ἀναλέγομαι* in the sense of *reading through* = *ἀναγιγνώσκειν*, is found only in the later writers, Arrian, Plutarch, Dion, Callimachus, etc.

THE ANABASIS OF ALEXANDER.

BOOK I.

CHAPTER I.

DEATH OF PHILIP AND ACCESSION OF ALEXANDER.—HIS WARS WITH THE THRACIANS.

It is said that Philip died[1] when Pythodemus was archon at Athens,[2] and that his son Alexander,[3] being then

[1] B.C. 336. He was murdered by a young noble named Pausanias, who stabbed him at the festival which he was holding to celebrate the marriage of his daughter with Alexander, king of Epirus. It was suspected that both Olympias and her son Alexander were implicated in the plot. At the time of his assassination Philip was just about to start on an expedition against Persia, which his son afterwards so successfully carried out. See Plutarch (*Alex.*, 10); *Diod.*, xix. 93, 94; Aristotle (*Polit.*, v. 8, 10).

[2] It was the custom of the Athenians to name the years from the president of the college of nine archons at Athens, who were elected annually. The Attic writers adopted this method of determining dates. See Smith's *Dictionary of Antiquities*.

[3] Alexander the Great was the son of Philip II. and Olympias, and was born at Pella B.C. 356. In his youth he was placed under the tuition of Aristotle, who acquired very great influence over his mind and character, and retained it until his pupil was spoiled by his unparalleled successes. See Aelian (*Varia Historia*, xii. 54). Such was his ability, that at the age of 16 he was entrusted with the government of Macedonia by his father, when he marched against Byzantium. At the age of 18 by his skill and courage he greatly assisted Philip in gaining the battle of Chaeronea. When Philip was murdered, Alexander ascended the throne, and after putting down rebellion at home, he advanced into Greece to secure the power which his father had acquired. See *Diod.*, xvi. 85; *Arrian*, vii. 9.

about twenty years of age, marched into Peloponnesus[1] as soon as he had secured the regal power. There he assembled all the Greeks who were within the limits of Peloponnesus,[2] and asked from them the supreme command of the expedition against the Persians, an office which they had already conferred upon Philip. He received the honour which he asked from all except the Lacedaemonians,[3] who replied that it was an hereditary custom of theirs, not to follow others but to lead them. The Athenians also attempted to bring about some political change; but they were so alarmed at the very approach of Alexander, that they conceded to him even more ample public honours than those which had been bestowed upon Philip.[4] He then returned into Macedonia and busied himself in preparing for the expedition into Asia.

However, at the approach of spring (B.C. 335), he marched towards Thrace, into the lands of the Triballians and Illyrians,[5] because he ascertained that these nations were meditating a change of policy; and at the same time, as they were lying on his frontier, he thought it inexpedient, when he was about to start on a campaign so far away from his own land, to leave them behind him

---

[1] See *Justin*, xi. 2.

[2] "Arrian speaks as if this request had been addressed only to the Greeks *within* Peloponnesus; moreover he mentions no assembly at Corinth, which is noticed, though with some confusion, by Diodorus, Justin, and Plutarch. Cities out of Peloponnesus, as well as within it, must have been included; unless we suppose that the resolution of the Amphictyonic assembly, which had been previously passed, was held to comprehend all the extra-Peloponnesian cities, which seems not probable."—*Grote.*

[3] Justin (ix. 5) says: "Soli Lacedaemonii et legem et regem contempserunt." The king here referred to was Philip.

[4] See *Justin*, xi. 3; Aeschines, *Contra Ctesiphontem*, p. 564.

[5] The Triballians were a tribe inhabiting the part of Servia bordering on Bulgaria. The Illyrians inhabited the eastern coast of the Adriatic Sea, the districts now called North Albania, Bosnia, Dalmatia and Croatia.

without being entirely subjugated. Setting out then from Amphipolis, he invaded the land of the people who were called independent Thracians,[1] keeping the city of Philippi and mount Orbelus on the left. Crossing the river Nessus,[2] they say he arrived at mount Haemus[3] on the tenth day. Here, along the defiles up the ascent to the mountain, he was met by many of the traders equipped with arms, as well as by the independent Thracians, who had made preparations to check the further advance of his expedition by seizing the summit of the Haemus, along which was the route for the passage of his army. They had collected their waggons, and placed them in front of them, not only using them as a rampart from which they might defend themselves, in case they should be forced back, but also intending to let them loose upon the phalanx of the Macedonians, where the mountain was most precipitous, if they tried to ascend. They had come to the conclusion[4] that the denser the phalanx was with which the waggons rushing down came into collision, the more easily would they scatter it by the violence of their fall upon it.

But Alexander formed a plan by which he might cross the mountain with the least danger possible; and since he was resolved to run all risks, knowing that there were no means of passing elsewhere, he ordered the heavy-armed soldiers, as soon as the waggons began to rush down the declivity, to open their ranks, and directed that those whom the road was sufficiently wide to permit

---

[1] We learn from *Thucydides*, ii. 96, that these people were called Dii.

[2] The Nessus, or Nestus, is now called Mesto by the Greeks, and Karasu by the Turks.

[3] Now known as the Balkan. The defiles mentioned by Arrian are probably what was afterwards called Porta Trajani. Cf. Vergil (*Georg.*, ii. 488); Horace (*Carm.*, i. 12, 6).

[4] *πεποίηντο*:—Arrian often forms the pluperfect tense without the augment. *διασκεδάσουσι*:—The Attic future of this verb is *διασκεδῶ*. Cf. Aristoph. (*Birds*, 1053).

to do so should stand apart, so that the waggons might roll through the gap; but that those who were hemmed in on all sides should either stoop down together or even fall flat on the ground, and lock their shields compactly together, so that the waggons rushing down upon them, and in all probability by their very impetus leaping over them, might pass on without injuring them. And it turned out just as Alexander had conjectured and exhorted. For some of the men made gaps in the phalanx, and others locked their shields together. The waggons rolled over the shields without doing much injury, not a single man being killed under them. Then the Macedonians regained their courage, inasmuch as the waggons, which they had excessively dreaded, had inflicted no damage upon them. With a loud cry they assaulted the Thracians. Alexander ordered his archers to march from the right wing in front of the rest of the phalanx, because there the passage was easier, and to shoot at the Thracians where they advanced. He himself took his own guard, the shield-bearing infantry and the Agrianians,[1] and led them to the left. Then the archers shot at the Thracians who sallied forward, and repulsed them; and the phalanx, coming to close fighting, easily drove away from their position men who were light-armed and badly equipped barbarians. The consequence was, they no longer waited to receive Alexander marching against them from the left, but casting away their arms they fled down the mountain as each man best could. About 1,500 of them were killed; but only a few were taken prisoners on account of their swiftness of foot and acquaintance with the country. However, all the women who were accompanying them were captured, as were also their children and all their booty.

---

[1] The Agrianes were a tribe of Eastern Paeonia who lived near the Triballians. They served in the Macedonian army chiefly as cavalry and light infantry.

CHAPTER II.

Battle with the Triballians.

Alexander sent the booty away southward to the cities on the seashore,[1] entrusting to Lysanias and Philotas[2] the duty of setting it up for sale. But he himself crossed the summit, and advancing through the Haemus into the land of the Triballians, he arrived at the river Lyginus.[3] This river is distant from the Ister[4] three days' march to one intending to go to the Haemus. Syrmus, king of the Triballians, hearing of Alexander's expedition long before, had sent the women and children of the nation on in advance to the Ister, ordering them to pass over into one of the islands in that river, the name of which was Peuce.[5] To this island also the Thracians, whose territories were conterminous with those of the Triballians, had fled together for refuge at the approach of Alexander. Syrmus himself likewise, accompanied by his train, had fled for refuge to the same place. But the main body of the Triballians fled back to the river, from which Alexander had started the day before.

When he heard of their starting, he wheeled round again, and, marching against them, surprised them just

---

1 Perhaps Neapolis and Eion, which were the harbours of Philippi and Amphipolis.

2 This officer was commander of the royal body-guard. His father was Parmenio, the most experienced of Alexander's generals.

3 Thucydides says (Bk. ii. 96): "On the side of the Triballians, who were also independent, the border tribes were the Trerians and the Tilatæans, who live to the north of mount Scombrus, and stretch towards the west as far as the river Oscius. This river flows from the same mountains as the Nestus and the Hebrus, an uninhabited and extensive range, joining on to Rhodope." The Oscius is now called Isker. It is uncertain which river is the Lyginus; but perhaps it was another name for the Oscius.

4 Also named *Danube*. Cf. Hesiod (*Theog.*, 339); Ovid (*Met.*, ii. 249); Pindar (*Olym.* iii. 24).

5 It is uncertain in what part of the Danube this island was. It cannot be the Peuce of Strabo (vii. 3). Cf. *Apollonius Rhodius* (iv. 309); *Martialis* (vii. 84); *Valerius Flaccus* (viii. 217).

as they were encamping. And those who were surprised drew themselves up in battle array in a woody glen along the bank of the river. Alexander drew out his phalanx into a deep column, and led it on in person. He also ordered the archers and slingers to run forward and discharge arrows and stones at the barbarians, hoping to provoke them by this to come out of the woody glen into the ground unencumbered with trees. When they were within reach of the missiles, and were struck by them, they rushed out against the archers, who were undefended by shields, with the purpose of fighting them hand-to-hand. But when Alexander had drawn them thus out of the woody glen, he ordered Philotas to take the cavalry which came from upper Macedonia, and to charge their right wing, where they had advanced furthest in their sally. He also commanded Heraclides and Sopolis[1] to lead on the cavalry which came from Bottiaea[2] and Amphipolis against the left wing; while he himself extended the phalanx of infantry and the rest of the horse in front of the phalanx and led them against the enemy's centre. And indeed as long as there was only skirmishing on both sides, the Triballians did not get the worst of it; but as soon as the phalanx in dense array attacked them with vigour, and the cavalry fell upon them in various quarters, no longer merely striking them with the javelin, but pushing them with their very horses, then at length they turned and fled through the woody glen to the river. Three thousand were slain in the flight; few of them were taken prisoners, both because there was a dense wood in front of the river, and the approach of night deprived the Macedonians of certainty in their pursuit. Ptolemy says, that of the Macedonians themselves eleven horsemen and about forty foot soldiers were killed.

---

[1] These two generals are mentioned (iii. 11 infra) as being present at the battle of Arbela. Sopolis is also mentioned (iv. 13 and 18 infra).

[2] Bottiaea was a district of Macedonia on the right bank of the Axius.

CHAPTER III.

Alexander at the Danube and in the Country of the Getae.

On the third day after the battle, Alexander reached the river Ister, which is the largest of all the rivers in Europe, traverses a very great tract of country, and separates very warlike nations. Most of these belong to the Celtic race,[1] in whose territory the sources of the river take their rise. Of these nations the remotest are the Quadi[2] and Marcomanni[3]; then the Iazygianns,[4] a branch of the Sauromatians[5]; then the Getae,[6] who hold

---

[1] The classical writers have three names to denote this race:—Celts, Galatians, and Gauls. These names were originally given to all the people of the North and West of Europe; and it was not till Caesar's time that the Romans made any distinction between Celts and Germans. The name of Celts was then confined to the people north of the Pyrenees and west of the Rhine. Cf. *Ammianus* (xv. 9); *Herodotus* (iv. 49); *Livy* (v. 33, 34); *Polybius* (iii. 39).

[2] Arrian is here speaking, not of Alexander's time, but of his own, the second century of the Christian era. The Quadi were a race dwelling in the south-east of Germany. They are generally mentioned with the Marcomanni, and were formidable enemies of the Romans, especially in the reign of Marcus Aurelius, when Arrian wrote. This nation disappears from history about the end of the fourth century.

[3] The Marcomanni, like the Quadi, were a powerful branch of the Suevic race, originally dwelling in the south-west of Germany; but in the reign of Tiberius they dispossessed the Boii of the country now called Bohemia. In conjunction with the Quadi, they were very formidable to the Romans until Commodus purchased peace from them. The name denotes "border men." Cf. Caesar (*Bel. Gal.*, i. 51).

[4] The Iazygians were a tribe of Sarmatians, who migrated from the coast of the Black Sea, between the Dnieper and the Sea of Azov, in the reign of Claudius, and settled in Dacia, near the Quadi, with whom they formed a close alliance. They were conquered by the Goths in the fifth century. Cf. Ovid (*Tristia*, ii. 191).

[5] Called also Sarmatians. Herodotus (iv. 21) says that these people lived east of the Don, and were allied to the Scythians. Subsequent writers understood by Sarmatia the east part of Poland, the south of Russia, and the country southward as far as the Danube.

[6] These people were called Dacians by the Romans. They were Thracians, and are said by Herodotus and Thucydides to have lived

the doctrine of immortality; then the main body of the Sauromatians; and, lastly, the Scythiaus,[1] whose land stretches as far as the outlets of the river, where through five mouths it discharges its water into the Euxine Sea.[2] Here Alexander found some ships of war which had come to him from Byzantium, through the Euxine Sea and up the river. Filling these with archers and heavy-armed troops, he sailed to the island to which the Triballians and Thracians had fled for refuge. He tried to force a landing; but the barbarians came to meet him at the brink of the river, where the ships were making the assault. But these were only few in number, and the army in them small. The shores of the island, also, were in most places too steep and precipitous for landing, and the current of the river alongside it, being, as it were, shut up into a narrow channel by the nearness of the banks, was rapid and exceedingly difficult to stem.

Alexander therefore led back his ships, and determined to cross the Ister and march against the Getae, who dwelt on the other side of that river; for he observed that many of them had collected on the bank of the river for the purpose of barring his way, if he should cross. There were of them about 4,000 cavalry and more than 10,000

---

south of the Danube, near its mouths. They subsequently migrated north of this river, and were driven further west by the Sarmatians. They were very formidable to the Romans in the reigns of Augustus and Domitian. Dacia was conquered by Trajan; but ultimately abandoned by Aurelian, who made the Danube the boundary of the Roman Empire. About the Getae holding the doctrine of immortality, see *Herodotus* (iv. 94). Cf. Horace (*Carm.*, iii. 6, 13; *Sat.*, ii. 6, 53).

[1] The Scythians are said by Herodotus to have inhabited the south of Russia. His supposition that they came from Asia is doubtless correct. He gives ample information about this race in the fourth book of his History.

[2] Herodotus (iv. 47) says the Danube had five mouths; but Strabo (vii. 3) says there were seven. At the present time it has only three mouths. The Greeks called the Black Sea *πόντος εὔξεινος*, *the sea kind to strangers*. Cf. Ovid (*Tristia*, iv. 4, 55):—"Frigida me cohibent Euxini litora Ponti, Dictus ab antiquis Axenus ille fuit."

infantry. At the same time a strong desire seized him to advance beyond the Ister. He therefore went on board the fleet himself. He also filled with hay the hides which served them as tent-coverings, and collected from the country around all the boats made from single trunks of trees. Of these there was a great abundance, because the people who dwell near the Ister use them for fishing in the river, sometimes also for journeying to each other for traffic up the river; and most of them carry on piracy with them. Having collected as many of these as he could, upon them he conveyed across as many of his soldiers as was possible in such a fashion. Those who crossed with Alexander amounted in number to 1,500 cavalry and 4,000 infantry.

CHAPTER IV.

Alexander Destroys the City of the Getae.—The Ambassadors of the Celts.

They crossed over by night to a spot where the corn stood high; and in this way they reached the bank more secretly. At the approach of dawn Alexander led his men through the field of standing corn, ordering the infantry to lean upon the corn with their pikes [1] held transversely, and thus to advance into the untilled ground. As long as the phalanx was advancing through the standing corn, the cavalry followed; but when they marched out of the tilled land, Alexander himself led the horse round to the right wing, and commanded Nicanor [2] to lead the phalanx in a square. The Getae did not even sustain the first charge of the cavalry; for Alexander's audacity

---

[1] The *sarissa*, or more correctly *sarisa*, was a spear peculiar to the Macedonians. It was from fourteen to sixteen feet long. See Grote's *Greece*, vol. xi. ch. 92, Appendix.

[2] Son of Parmenio and brother of Philotas.

seemed incredible to them, in having thus easily crossed the Ister, the largest of rivers, in a single night, without throwing a bridge over the stream. Terrible to them also was the closely-locked order of the phalanx, and violent the charge of the cavalry. At first they fled for refuge into their city, which was distant about a parasang[1] from the Ister; but when they saw that Alexander was leading his phalanx carefully along the river, to prevent his infantry being anywhere surrounded by the Getae lying in ambush; whereas he was leading his cavalry straight on, they again abandoned the city, because it was badly fortified. They carried off as many of their women and children as their horses could carry, and betook themselves into the steppes, in a direction which led as far as possible from the river. Alexander took the city and all the booty which the Getae left behind. This he gave to Meleager[2] and Philip[3] to carry off. After razing the city to the ground, he offered sacrifice upon the bank of the river, to Zeus the preserver, to Heracles,[4] and to Ister himself, because he had allowed him to cross; and while it was still day he brought all his men back safe to the camp.

There ambassadors came to him from Syrmus, king of the Triballians, and from the other independent nations dwelling near the Ister. Some even arrived from the

---

[1] The parasang was a Persian measure, containing thirty stades, nearly three and three-quarter English miles. It is still used by the Persians, who call it *ferseng*. See *Herodotus* (vi. 42) and Grote's *History of Greece*, vol. viii. p. 316.

[2] Son of Neoptolemus. After Alexander's death Meleager resisted the claim of Perdiccas to the regency, and was associated with him in the office. He was, however, soon afterwards put to death by the order of his rival.

[3] Son of Machatas, was an eminent general, slain in India. See vi. 27 infra.

[4] The Macedonian kings believed they were sprung from Hercules. See *Curtius*, iv. 7.

Celts who dwelt near the Ionian gulf.[1] These people are of great stature, and of a haughty disposition. All the envoys said that they had come to seek Alexander's friendship. To all of them he gave pledges of amity, and received pledges from them in return. He then asked the Celts what thing in the world caused them special alarm, expecting that his own great fame had reached the Celts and had penetrated still further, and that they would say that they feared him most of all things. But the answer of the Celts turned out quite contrary to his expectation; for, as they dwelt so far away from Alexander, inhabiting districts difficult of access, and as they saw he was about to set out in another direction, they said they were afraid that the sky would some time or other fall down upon them. These men also he sent back, calling them friends, and ranking them as allies, making the remark that the Celts were braggarts.[2]

CHAPTER V.

Revolt of Clitus and Glaucias.

He then advanced into the land of the Agrianians and Paeonians,[3] where messengers reached him, who reported that Clitus, son of Bardylis,[4] had revolted, and that

---

[1] The Adriatic Sea.

[2] Cf. Aelian (*Varia Historia*, xii. 23); *Strabo*, vii. p. 293; Aristotle (*Nicom. Ethics*, iii. 7; *Eudem. Eth.*, iii. 1):—*οἷον οἱ Κελτοὶ πρὸς τὰ κύματα ὅπλα ἀπαντῶσι λαβόντες*; *Ammianus*, xv. 12.

[3] The Paeonians were a powerful Thracian people, who in early times spread over a great part of Thrace and Macedonia. In historical times they inhabited the country on the northern border of Macedonia. They were long troublesome to Macedonia, but were subdued by Philip the father of Alexander, who, however, allowed them to retain their own chiefs. The Agrianians were the chief tribe of Paeonians, from whom Philip and Alexander formed a valuable body of light-armed troops.

[4] Bardylis was a chieftain of Illyria who carried on frequent wars with

Glaucias,[1] king of the Taulantians,[2] had gone over to him. They also reported that the Autariatians [3] intended to attack him on his way. He accordingly resolved to commence his march without delay. But Langarus, king of the Agrianians, who, in the lifetime of Philip, had been an open and avowed friend of Alexander, and had gone on an embassy to him in his private capacity, at that time also came to him with the finest and best armed of the shield-bearing troops, which he kept as a body-guard. When this man heard that Alexander was inquiring who the Autariatians were, and what was the number of their men, he said that he need take no account of them, since they were the least warlike of the tribes of that district; and that he would himself make an inroad into their land, so that they might have too much occupation about their own affairs to attack others. Accordingly, at Alexander's order, he made an attack upon them; and not only did he attack them, but he swept their land clean of captives and booty. Thus the Autariatians were indeed occupied with their own affairs. Langarus was rewarded by Alexander with the greatest honours, and received from him the gifts which were considered most valuable in the eyes of the king of the Macedonians. Alexander also promised to give him his sister Cyna [4] in

---

the Macedonians, but was at last defeated and slain by Philip, B.C. 359. Clitus had been subdued by Philip in 349 B.C.

[1] This Glaucias subsequently afforded asylum to the celebrated Pyrrhus, King of Epirus, when an infant of two years of age. He took the child into his own family and brought him up with his own children. He not only refused to surrender Pyrrhus to Cassander, but marched into Epirus and placed the boy, when twelve years of age, upon the throne, leaving him under the care of guardians, B.C. 307.

[2] The Taulantians were a people of Illyria in the neighbourhood of Epidamnus, now called Durazzo.

[3] These were an Illyrian people in the Dalmatian mountains.

[4] Cyna was the daughter of Philip, by Audata, an Illyrian woman. See *Athenæus*, p. 557 D. She was given in marriage to her cousin Amyntas, who had a preferable claim to the Macedonian throne as the

marriage when he arrived at Pella.[1] But Langarus fell ill and died on his return home.

After this, Alexander marched along the river Erigon,[2] and proceeded to the city of Pelium;[3] for Clitus had seized this city, as it was the strongest in the country. When Alexander arrived at this place, and had encamped near the river Eordaicus,[4] he resolved to make an assault upon the wall the next day. But Clitus held the mountains which encircled the city, and commanded it from their height; moreover, they were covered with dense thickets. His intention was to fall upon the Macedonians from all sides, if they assaulted the city. But Glaucias, king of the Taulantians, had not yet joined him. Alexander, however, led his forces towards the city; and the enemy, after sacrificing three boys, an equal number of girls, and three black rams, sallied forth for the purpose of receiving the Macedonians in a hand-to-hand conflict. But as soon as they came to close quarters, they left the positions which they had occupied, strong as they were,[5] in such haste that even their sacrificial victims were captured still lying on the ground.

On this day he shut them up in the city, and encamping near the wall, he resolved to intercept them by a circumvallation; but on the next day Glaucias, king of

---

son of Philip's elder brother, Perdiccas. This Amyntas was put to death by Alexander soon after his accession. Cyna was put to death by Alcetas, at the order of Perdiccas, the regent after Alexander's death. See *Diodorus*, xix. 52.

[1] The capital of Macedonia. On its site stands the modern village of Neokhori, or Yenikiuy. Philip and Alexander were born here.

[2] A tributary of the Axius, called Agrianus by Herodotus. It is now called Tscherna.

[3] This city was situated south of lake Lychnitis, on the west side of the chain of Scardus and Pindus. The locality is described in *Livy*, xxxi. 39, 40.

[4] Now called Devol.

[5] The use of *καίτοι* with a participle instead of the Attic *καίπερ* is frequent in Arrian and the later writers.

the Taulantians, arrived with a great force. Then, indeed, Alexander gave up the hope of capturing the city with his present force, since many warlike troops had fled for refuge into it, and Glaucias with his large army would be likely to follow him up closely if he assailed the wall. But he sent Philotas on a foraging expedition, with the beasts of burden from the camp and a sufficient body of cavalry to serve as a guard. When Glaucias heard of the expedition of Philotas he marched out to meet him, and seized the mountains which surrounded the plain, from which Philotas intended to procure forage. As soon as Alexander was informed that his cavalry and beasts of burden would be in danger if night overtook them, taking the shield-bearing troops,[1] the archers, the Agrianians, and about four hundred cavalry, he went with all speed to their aid. The rest of the army he left behind near the city, to prevent the citizens from hastening forth to form a junction with Glaucias (as they would have done), if all the Macedonian army had withdrawn. Directly Glaucias perceived that Alexander was advancing, he evacuated the mountains, and Philotas and his forces returned to the camp in safety. But Clitus and Glaucias still imagined that they had caught Alexander in a disadvantageous position; for they were occupying the mountains, which commanded the plain by their height, with a large body of cavalry, javelin-throwers, and slingers, besides a considerable number of heavy-armed infantry. Moreover, the men who had been

---

[1] The Hypaspists—shield-bearers, or guards—were a body of infantry organized by Philip, originally few in number, and employed as personal defenders of the king, but afterwards enlarged into several distinct brigades. They were hoplites intended for close combat, but more lightly armed and more fit for rapid evolutions than the phalanx. Like the Greeks, they fought with the one-handed pike and shield. They occupied an intermediate position between the heavy infantry of the phalanx, and the peltasts and other light troops. See Grote's *Greece*, vol. xi. ch. 92.

beleaguered in the city were expected to pursue the Macedonians closely if they made a retreat. The ground also through which Alexander had to march was evidently narrow and covered with wood; on one side it was hemmed in by a river, and on the other there was a very lofty and craggy mountain, so that there would not be room for the army to pass, even if only four shield-bearers marched abreast.

CHAPTER VI.

Defeat of Clitus and Glaucias.

Then Alexander drew up his army in such a way that the depth of the phalanx was 120 men; and stationing 200 cavalry on each wing, he ordered them to preserve silence, in order to receive the word of command quickly. Accordingly he gave the signal to the heavy-armed infantry in the first place to hold their spears erect, and then to couch them at the concerted sign; at one time to incline their spears to the right, closely locked together, and at another time towards the left. He then set the phalanx itself into quick motion forward, and marched it towards the wings, now to the right, and then to the left. After thus arranging and re-arranging his army many times very rapidly, he at last formed his phalanx into a sort of wedge, and led it towards the left against the enemy, who had long been in a state of amazement at seeing both the order and the rapidity of his evolutions. Consequently they did not sustain Alexander's attack, but quitted the first ridges of the mountain. Upon this, Alexander ordered the Macedonians to raise the battle cry and make a clatter with their spears upon their shields; and the Taulantians, being still more alarmed at the noise, led their army back to the city with all speed.

As Alexander saw only a few of the enemy still occupying a ridge, along which lay his route, he ordered his body-guards and personal companions to take their shields, mount their horses, and ride to the hill; and when they reached it, if those who had occupied the position awaited them, he said that half of them were to leap from their horses, and to fight as foot-soldiers, being mingled with the cavalry. But when the enemy saw Alexander's advance, they quitted the hill and retreated to the mountains in both directions. Then Alexander, with his companions,[1] seized the hill, and sent for the Agrianians and archers, who numbered 2,000. He also ordered the shield-bearing guards to cross the river, and after them the regiments of Macedonian infantry, with instructions that, as soon as they had succeeded in crossing, they should draw out in rank towards the left, so that the phalanx of men crossing might appear compact at once. He himself, in the vanguard, was all the time observing from the ridge the enemy's advance. They, seeing the force crossing the river, marched down the mountains to meet them, with the purpose of attacking Alexander's rear in its retreat. But, as they were just drawing near, Alexander rushed forth with his own division, and the phalanx raised the battle-cry, as if about to advance through the river. When the enemy saw all the Macedonians marching against them, they turned and fled. Upon this, Alexander led the Agrianians and archers at full speed towards the river, and succeeded in being himself the first man to cross it. But

---

[1] The heavy cavalry, wholly or chiefly composed of Macedonians by birth, was known by the honourable name of *ἑταῖροι*, Companions, or Brothers in Arms. It was divided, as it seems, into 15 *ἶλαι*, which were named after the States or districts from which they came. Their strength varied from 150 to 250 men. A separate one, the 16th Ilē, formed the so-called *agema*, or royal horse-guard, at the head of which Alexander himself generally charged. See *Arrian*, iii. 11, 13, 18.

when he saw the enemy pressing upon the men in the rear, he stationed his engines of war upon the bank, and ordered the engineers to shoot from them as far forward as possible all sorts of projectiles which are usually shot from military engines.[1] He directed the archers, who had also entered the water, to shoot their arrows from the middle of the river. But Glaucias durst not advance within range of the missiles; so that the Macedonians passed over in such safety, that not one of them lost his life in the retreat.

Three days after this, Alexander discovered that Clitus and Glaucias lay carelessly encamped; that neither were their sentinels on guard in military order, nor had they protected themselves with a rampart or ditch, as if they imagined he had withdrawn through fear; and that they had extended their line to a disadvantageous length. He therefore crossed the river again secretly, at the approach of night, leading with him the shield-bearing guards, the Agrianians, the archers, and the brigades of Perdiccas[2] and Coenus,[3] after having given orders for the

---

[1] In addition to his other military improvements, Philip had organized an effective siege-train with projectile and battering engines superior to anything of the kind existing before. This artillery was at once made use of by Alexander in this campaign against the Illyrians.

[2] Perdiccas, son of Orontes, a Macedonian, was one of Alexander's most distinguished generals. The king is said on his death-bed to have taken the royal signet from his finger and to have given it to Perdiccas. After Alexander's death he was appointed regent; but an alliance was formed against him by Antipater, Craterus, and Ptolemy. He marched into Egypt against Ptolemy. Being defeated in his attempts to force the passage of the Nile, his own troops mutinied against him and slew him (B.C. 321). See *Diodorus*, xviii. 36. For his personal valour see Aelian (*Varia Historia*, xii. 39).

[3] Coenus, son of Polemocrates, was a son-in-law of Parmenio, and one of Alexander's best generals. He violently accused his brother-in-law Philotas of treason, and personally superintended the torturing of that famous officer previous to his execution (*Curtius*, vi. 36, 42). He was put forward by the army to dissuade Alexander from advancing beyond the Hyphasis (*Arrian*, v. 27). Soon after this he died and was

rest of the army to follow. As soon as he saw a favourable opportunity for the attack, without waiting for all to be present, he despatched the archers and Agrianians against the foe. These, being arranged in phalanx, fell unawares with the most furious charge upon their flank, where they were likely to come into conflict with their weakest point, and slew some of them still in their beds, others being easily caught in their flight. Accordingly, many were there captured and killed, as were many also in the disorderly and panic-stricken retreat which ensued. Not a few, moreover, were taken prisoners. Alexander kept up the pursuit as far as the Taulantian mountains; and as many of them as escaped, preserved their lives by throwing away their arms. Clitus first fled for refuge into the city, which, however, he set on fire, and withdrew to Glaucias, in the land of the Taulantians.

CHAPTER VII.

Revolt of Thebes (*September*, B.C. 335).

While these events were occurring, some of the exiles who had been banished from Thebes, coming to the city by night, and being brought in by some of the citizens, in order to effect a change in the government, apprehended and slew outside the Cadmea,[1] Amyntas and Timolaus,[2] two of the men who held that fortress, having no suspicion that any hostile attempt was about to be made. Then entering the public assembly, they incited

---

buried with all possible magnificence near that river, B.C. 327 (*Arrian*, vi. 2).

[1] The Cadmea was the Acropolis of Thebes, an oval eminence of no great height, named after Cadmus, the leader of a Phoenician colony, who is said to have founded it. Since the battle of Chaeronea, this citadel had been held by a Macedonian garrison.

[2] Amyntas was a Macedonian officer, and Timolaus a leading Theban of the Macedonian faction.

the Thebans to revolt from Alexander, holding out to them as pretexts the ancient and glorious words, liberty and freedom of speech, and urging them now at last to rid themselves of the heavy yoke of the Macedonians. By stoutly maintaining that Alexander had been killed in Illyria they gained more power in persuading the multitude;[1] for this report was prevalent, and for many reasons it gained credit, both because he had been absent a long time, and because no news had arrived from him. Accordingly, as is usual in such cases, not knowing the facts, each man conjectured what was most pleasing to himself.

When Alexander heard what was being done at Thebes, he thought it was a movement not at all to be slighted, inasmuch as he had for a long time suspected the city of Athens and deemed the audacious action of the Thebans no trivial matter, if the Lacedaemonians, who had long been disaffected in their feelings to him, and the Aetolians and certain other States in the Peloponnese, who were not firm in their allegiance to him, should take part with the Thebans in their revolutionary effort. He therefore led his army through Eordaea and Elimiotis[2] and along the peaks of Stymphaea and Paravaea,[3] and on the seventh day arrived at Pelina[4] in Thessaly. Starting thence, he entered Boeotia on the sixth day; so that the Thebans did not learn that he had passed south of Thermopylae, until he was at Onchestus[5] with the whole of his army. Even then the authors of the revolt asserted that Antipater's army had arrived out of Macedonia, stoutly affirming that

[1] Cf. Aelian (*Varia Historia*, xii. 57).

[2] These were two provinces in the west of Macedonia.

[3] Two divisions of Epirus.

[4] A town on the Penēus in Hestiaeotis.

[5] A town in Boeotia, on the lake Copais, distant 50 stades north-west of Thebes.

Alexander himself was dead, and being very angry with those who announced that it was Alexander himself who was advancing.[1] For they said it must be another Alexander, the son of Aëropus, who was coming.[2] On the following day Alexander set out from Onchestus, and advanced towards the city along the territory consecrated to Iolaus;[3] where indeed he encamped, in order to give the Thebans further time to repent of their evil resolutions and to send an embassy to him. But so far were they from showing any sign of wishing to come to an accommodation, that their cavalry and a large body of light-armed infantry sallied forth from the city as far as the camp, and, skirmishing with the Macedonian outposts, slew a few of their men. Alexander hereupon sent forth a party of his light-armed infantry and archers to repel their sortie; and these men repelled them with ease, just as they were approaching the very camp. The next day he took the whole of his army and marched round towards the gate which led to Eleutherae and Attica. But not even then did he assault the wall itself, but encamped not far away from the Cadmea, in order that succour might be at hand to the Macedonians who were occupying that citadel. For the Thebans had blockaded the Cadmea with a double stockade and were guarding it, so that no one from without might be able to give succour to those who were beleagured, and that the garrison might not be able, by making a sally, to do them any injury, when they were attacking the enemy outside. But Alexander remained encamped near the

[1] It seems from Plutarch that Alexander was really wounded in the head by a stone, in a battle with the Illyrians.

[2] This Alexander was also called Lyncestes, from being a native of Lyncestis, a district of Macedonia. He was an accomplice in Philip's murder, but was pardoned by his successor. He accompanied Alexander the Great into Asia, but was put to death in B.C. 330, for having carried on a treasonable correspondence with Darius. See *Arrian*, i. 25.

[3] The friend and charioteer of Hercules.

Cadmea, for he still wished rather to come to friendly terms with the Thebans than to come to a contest with them.[1] Then those of the Thebans who knew what was for the best interest of the commonwealth were eager to go out to Alexander and obtain pardon for the commonalty of Thebes for their revolt; but the exiles and those who had summoned them home kept on inciting the populace to war by every means in their power, since they despaired of obtaining for themselves any indulgence from Alexander, especially as some of them were also Boeotarchs.[2] However not even for this did Alexander assault the city.

CHAPTER VIII.

Fall of Thebes.

But Ptolemy, son of Lagus, tells us that Perdiccas, who had been posted in the advanced guard of the camp with his own brigade, and was not far from the enemy's stockade, did not wait for the signal from Alexander to commence the battle; but of his own accord was the first to assault the stockade, and, having made a breach in it, fell upon the advanced guard of the Thebans.[3]

---

[1] He sent to demand the surrender of the anti-Macedonian leaders, Phoenix and Prothytes, but offering any other Thebans who came out to him the terms agreed upon in the preceding year. See Plutarch (*Life of Alexander*, 11); and *Diodorus*, xvii. 9.

[2] The Boeotarchs were the chief magistrates of the Boeotian confederacy, chosen annually by the different States. The number varied from ten to twelve. At the time of the battle of Delium, in the Peloponnesian war, they were eleven in number, two of them being Thebans. See Grote, *History of Greece*, vol. ii. p. 296.

[3] Arrian says that the attack of the Macedonians upon Thebes was made by Perdiccas, without orders from Alexander; and that the capture was effected in a short time and with no labour on the part of the captors (ch. ix.). But Diodorus says that Alexander ordered and arranged the assault, that the Thebans made a brave and desperate resistance for a

Amyntas,[1] son of Andromenes, followed Perdiccas, because he had been stationed with him. This general also of his own accord led on his brigade when he saw that Perdiccas had advanced within the stockade. When Alexander saw this, he led on the rest of his army, fearing that unsupported they might be intercepted by the Thebans and be in danger of destruction. He gave instructions to the archers and Agrianians to rush within the stockade, but he still retained the guards and shield-bearing troops outside. Then indeed Perdiccas, after forcing his way within the second stockade, fell there wounded with a dart, and was carried back grievously injured to the camp, where he was with difficulty cured of his wound. However the men of Perdiccas, in company with the archers sent by Alexander, fell upon the Thebans and shut them up in the hollow way leading to the temple of Heracles, and followed them in their retreat as far as the temple itself. The Thebans, having wheeled round, again advanced from that position with a shout, and put the Macedonians to flight. Eurybotas the Cretan, the captain of the archers, fell with about seventy of his men; but the rest fled to the Macedonian guard and the royal shield-bearing troops. Now, when Alexander saw that his own men were in flight, and that the Thebans had broken their ranks in pursuit, he attacked them with his phalanx drawn up in proper order, and drove them back within the gates. The Thebans fled in such a panic that being driven into the

---

long time, and that not only the Boeotian allies, but the Macedonians themselves committed great slaughter of the besieged (*Diod.* xvii. 11–14). It is probable that Ptolemy, who was Arrian's authority, wished to exonerate Alexander from the guilt of destroying Thebes.

[1] Amyntas was one of Alexander's leading officers. He and his brothers were accused of being accomplices in the plot of Philotas, but were acquitted. He was however soon afterwards killed in a skirmish (*Arrian*, iii. 27).

city through the gates they had not time to shut them; for the Macedonians, who were close behind the fugitives, rushed with them within the fortifications, inasmuch as the walls were destitute of defenders on account of the numerous pickets in front of them. When the Macedonians had entered the Cadmea, some of them marched out of it, in company with those who held the fortress, into the other part of the city opposite the temple of Amphion,[1] but others crossing along the walls, which were now in the possession of those who had rushed in together with the fugitives, advanced with a run into the market-place. Those of the Thebans who had been drawn up opposite the temple of Amphion stood their ground for a short time; but when the Macedonians under the command of Alexander were seen to be pressing hard upon them in various directions, their cavalry rushed through the city and sallied forth into the plain, and their infantry fled for safety as each man found it possible. Then indeed the Thebans, no longer defending themselves, were slain, not so much by the Macedonians as by the Phocians, Plataeans and other Boeotians,[2] who by indiscriminate slaughter vented their rage against them. Some were even attacked in the houses, having there turned to defend themselves from the enemy, and others were slain as they were supplicating the protection of the gods in the temples; not even the women and children being spared.[3]

---

[1] The mythical founder of the walls of Thebes. See *Pausanias* (ix. 17).

[2] The Thebans had incurred the enmity of the other Boeotians by treating them as subjects instead of allies. They had destroyed the restored Plataea, and had been the chief enemies of the Phocians in the Sacred War, which ended in the subjugation of that people by Philip. See Smith's *History of Greece*, pp. 467, 473, 506.

[3] More than 500 Macedonians were killed, while 6,000 Thebans were slain, and 30,000 sold into slavery. See Aelian (*Varia Historia*, xiii. 7); *Diodorus* (xvii. 14); *Pausanias* (viii. 30); Plutarch (*Life of Alexander*, 11).

CHAPTER IX.

Destruction of Thebes.

This was felt by the Greeks to be a general calamity for it struck the rest of the Greeks with no less consternation than it did those who had themselves taken part in the struggle, both on account of the magnitude of the captured city and the celerity of the action, the result of which was in the highest degree contrary to the expectation both of the sufferers and the perpetrators. For the disasters which befell the Athenians in relation to Sicily,[1] though in regard to the number of those who perished they brought no less misfortune to the city, yet, because their army was destroyed far away from their own land, being composed for the most part rather of auxiliary troops than of native Athenians, and because their city itself was left to them intact, so that afterwards they held their own in war even for a long time, though fighting against the Lacedaemonians and their allies, as well as the Great King; these disasters, I say, neither produced in the persons who were themselves involved in the calamity an equal sensation of the misfortune, nor did they cause the other Greeks a similar consternation at the catastrophe. Again, the defeat sustained by the Athenians at Aegospotami[2] was a naval one, and the city received no other humiliation than the demolition of the Long Walls, the surrender of most of her ships, and the loss of supremacy. However, they still retained their hereditary form of government, and not long after recovered their former power to such a degree as not only to build up the Long Walls but to recover the rule

---

The sale of the captives realized 440 talents, or about £107,000; and *Justin* (xi. 4) says that large sums were offered from feelings of hostility towards Thebes on the part of the bidders.

[1] B.C. 415–413. See Grote's *Greece*, vol. vii.

[2] B.C. 405. See *Thucydides* (ii. 13); Xenophon (*Hellenics*, ii. 2).

of the sea[1] and in their turn to preserve from extreme danger those very Lacedaemonians then so formidable to them, who had come and almost obliterated their city. Moreover, the defeat of the Lacedaemonians at Leuctra and Mantinea filled them with consternation rather by the unexpectedness of the disaster than because of the number of those who perished.[2] And the attack made by the Boeotians and Arcadians under Epaminondas upon the city of Sparta, even this terrified both the Lacedaemonians themselves and those who participated with them in the transactions at that time,[3] rather by the novelty of the sight than by the reality of the danger. The capture of the city of the Plataeans was not a great calamity, by reason of the small number of those who were taken in it; most of the citizens having long before escaped to Athens.[4] Again, the capture of Melus and Scione simply related to insular States, and rather brought disgrace to those who perpetrated the outrages than produced great surprise among the Grecian community as[5] a whole.

But the Thebans having effected their revolt suddenly and without any previous consideration, the capture of the city being brought about in so short a time and without difficulty on the part of the captors, the slaughter, being great, as was natural, from its being made by men of the same race who were glutting their revenge on them for ancient injuries, the complete enslavement of a city which excelled among those in Greece at that

---

[1] By Conon's victory at Cnidus, B.C. 394.

[2] At Leuctra they lost 400 Spartans and 1,000 other Lacedaemonians. See Xen. (*Hellen.*, vi. 4).

[3] The Achaeans, Eleans, Athenians, and some of the Arcadians, were allies of Sparta at this crisis, B.C. 369. See Xen. (*Hellen.*, vii. 5); *Diodorus* (xv. 85).

[4] B.C. 426. See *Thuc.*, iii. 52, etc.

[5] B.C. 416 and 421. See *Thuc.*, v. 32, 84, etc.

time both in power and warlike reputation, all this was attributed not without probability to the avenging wrath of the deity. It seemed as if the Thebans had after a long time suffered this punishment for their betrayal of the Greeks in the Median war,[1] for their seizure of the city of Plataeae during the truce, and for their complete enslavement of it, as well as for the un-Hellenic slaughter of the men who had surrendered to the Lacedaemonians, which had been committed at the instigation of the Thebans; and for the devastation of the territory in which the Greeks had stood in battle-array against the Medes and had repelled danger from Greece; lastly, because by their vote they had tried to ruin the Athenians when a motion was brought forward among the allies of the Lacedaemonians for the enslavement of Athens.[2] Moreover it was reported that before the disaster many portents were sent from the deity, which indeed at the time were treated with neglect, but afterwards when men called them to remembrance they were compelled to consider that the events which occurred had been long before prognosticated.[3]

The settlement of Theban affairs was entrusted by Alexander to the allies who had taken part in the action. They resolved to occupy the Cadmea with a garrison; to raze the city to the ground; to distribute among themselves all the territory, except what was dedicated to the gods; and to sell into slavery the women and children, and as many of the males as survived, except those who were priests or priestesses, and those who were bound to Philip or Alexander by the ties of hospitality or had been public agents of the Macedonians. It

---

[1] These persons must have forgotten that Alexander's predecessor and namesake had served in the army of Xerxes along with the Thebans. See *Herodotus* vii. 173.

[2] Plutarch (*Lysander*, 15) says that the Theban Erianthus moved that Athens should be destroyed.

[3] See Aelian (*Varia Historia*, xii. 57).

is said that Alexander preserved the house and the descendants of Pindar the poet, out of respect for his memory.[1] In addition to these things, the allies decreed that Orchomenus[2] and Plataeae should be rebuilt and fortified.

CHAPTER X.

Alexander's Dealings with Athens.

As soon as news of the calamity which had befallen the Thebans reached the other Greeks, the Arcadians, who had set out from their own land for the purpose of giving aid to the Thebans, passed sentence of death on those who had instigated them to render aid. The Eleans also received back their exiles from banishment, because they were Alexander's adherents; and the Aetolians, each tribe for itself, sent embassies to him, begging to receive pardon, because they also had attempted to effect a revolution, on the receipt of the report which had been spread by the Thebans. The Athenians also, who, at the time when some of the Thebans, escaping from the carnage, arrived at Athens, were engaged in celebrating the Great Mysteries,[3] abandoned the sacred rites in great consternation, and carried their goods and chattels from the rural districts into the city. The people came together in public assembly, and, on the motion of Demades, elected from all the citizens ten

[1] Plutarch (*Alexander*, 13) tells us that Alexander was afterwards sorry for his cruelty to the Thebans. He believed that he had incurred the wrath of Dionysus, the tutelary deity of Thebes, who incited him to kill his friend Clitus, and induced his soldiers to refuse to follow him into the interior of India.

[2] Orchomenus was destroyed by the Thebans B.C. 364. See *Diod.*, xv. 79; Demosthenes (*Contra Leptimem*, p. 489). It was restored by Philip, according to *Pausanias*, iv. 27.

[3] The Great Mysteries of Demeter were celebrated at Eleusis, from the 15th to the 23rd of the month Boedromion, our September.

ambassadors, men whom they knew to be Alexander's special adherents, and sent them to signify to him, though somewhat unseasonably, that the Athenian people rejoiced at his safe return from the land of the Illyrians and Triballians, and at the punishment which he had inflicted upon the Thebans for their rebellion. In regard to other matters he gave the embassy a courteous reply, but wrote a letter to the people demanding the surrender of Demosthenes and Lycurgus, as well as that of Hyperides, Polyeuctus, Chares, Charidemus, Ephialtes, Diotimus, and Moerocles;[1] alleging that these men were the cause of the disaster which befell the city at Chaeronea, and the authors of the subsequent offensive proceedings after Philip's death, both against himself and his father.[2] He also declared that they had instigated the Thebans to revolt no less than had those of the Thebans themselves who favoured a revolution. The Athenians, however, did not surrender the men, but sent another embassy to Alexander,[3] entreating him to remit his wrath against the persons whom he had demanded. The king did remit his wrath against them, either out of respect for the city of Athens, or from an earnest desire to start on the expedition into Asia, not wishing to leave behind him among the Greeks any cause for distrust. However, he ordered Charidemus alone of the men whom he had demanded as prisoners and who had not been given up, to go into banishment. Charidemus therefore went as an exile to King Darius in Asia.[4]

---

[1] All these nine men were orators except Chares, Charidemus, and Ephialtes, who were military men. Plutarch (*Life of Demosthenes*, 23) does not mention Chares, Diotimus, and Hyperides, but puts the names of Callisthenes and Damon in the list.

[2] See Aeschines (*Adversus Ctesiphontem*, pp. 469, 547, 551, 603, 633); Plutarch (*Demosthenes*, 22; *Phocion*, 16); *Diodorus*, xvii. 5.

[3] At the head of this embassy was Phocion.

[4] He was put to death by Darius shortly before the battle of Issus, for

CHAPTER XI.

Alexander Crosses the Hellespont and Visits Troy.

Having settled these affairs, he returned into Macedonia. He then offered to the Olympian Zeus the sacrifice which had been instituted by Archelaus,[1] and had been customary up to that time; and he celebrated the public contest of the Olympic games at Aegae.[2] It is said that he also held a public contest in honour of the Muses. At this time it was reported that the statue of Orpheus, son of Oeagrus the Thracian, which was in Pieris,[3] sweated incessantly.[4] Various were the explanations of this prodigy given by the soothsayers; but Aristander,[5] a man of Telmissus, a soothsayer, bade Alexander take courage; for he said it was evident from this that there would be much labour for the epic and lyric poets, and for the writers of odes, to compose and sing about Alexander and his achievements.

(B.C. 334.) At the beginning of the spring he marched towards the Hellespont, entrusting the affairs of Macedonia and Greece to Antipater. He led not much above

---

advising him not to rely on his Asiatic troops in the contest with Alexander, but to subsidize an army of Grecian mercenaries. See *Curtius*, iii. 5; *Diodorus*, xvii. 30.

1 Archelaus was king of Macedonia from B.C. 413–399. He improved the internal arrangements of his kingdom, and patronised art and literature. He induced the tragic poets, Euripides and Agathon, as well as the epic poet Choerilus, to visit him; and treated Euripides especially with favour. He also invited Socrates, who declined the invitation.

2 Aegae, or Edessa, was the earlier capital of Macedonia, and the burial place of its kings. Philip was murdered here, B.C. 336.

3 A narrow strip of land in Macedonia, between the mouths of the Haliacmon and Penēus, the reputed home of Orpheus and the Muses.

4 Cf. *Apollonius Rhodius*, iv. 1284; *Livy*, xxii. i.

5 This man was the most noted soothsayer of his time. Telmissus was a city of Caria, celebrated for the skill of its inhabitants in divination. Cf. Arrian (*Anab.* i. 25, ii. 18, iii. 2, iii. 7, iii. 15, iv. 4, iv. 15); *Herodotus*, i. 78; and Cicero (*De Divinatione*, i. 41)

30,000 infantry together with light-armed troops and archers, and more than 5,000 cavalry.[1] His march was past the lake Cercinitis,[2] towards Amphipolis and the mouths of the river Strymon. Having crossed this river he passed by the Pangaean mountain,[3] along the road leading to Abdera and Maronea, Grecian cities built on the coast. Thence he arrived at the river Hebrus,[4] and easily crossed it. Thence he proceeded through Paetica to the river Melas, having crossed which he arrived at Sestus, in twenty days altogether from the time of his starting from home. When he came to Elaeūs he offered sacrifice to Protesilaus upon the tomb of that hero, both for other reasons and because Protesilaus seemed to have been the first of the Greeks who took part with Agamemnon in the expedition to Ilium to disembark in Asia. The design of this sacrifice was, that his disembarking in Asia might be more fortunate than that of Protesilaus had been.[5] He then committed to Parmenio the duty of conveying the cavalry and the greater part of the infantry from Sestus to Abydus; and they were transported in 160 triremes, besides many trading vessels.[6] The prevailing account is, that Alexander started from Elaeus and put into the Port of Achaeans,[7] that with his own hand he steered the general's ship

---

[1] *Diodorus* (xvii. 17) says that there were 30,000 infantry and 4,500 cavalry. He gives the numbers in the different brigades as well as the names of the commanders. Plutarch (*Life of Alexander*, 15) says that the lowest numbers recorded were 30,000 infantry and 5,000 cavalry; and the highest, 34,000 infantry and 4,000 cavalry.

[2] This lake is near the mouth of the Strymon. It is called Prasias by *Herodotus* (v. 16). Its present name is Tak-hyno.

[3] This mountain is now called Pirnari. Xerxes took the same route when marching into Greece. See *Herodotus*, v. 16, vii. 112; Aeschylus (*Persae*, 494); Euripides (*Rhesus*, 922, 972).

[4] Now called Maritza. See *Theocritus*, vii. 110.

[5] Cf. Homer (*Iliad*, ii. 701); Ovid (*Epistolae Heroidum*, xiii. 93); *Herodotus* (ix. 116).

[6] The Athenians supplied twenty ships of war. See *Diodorus*, xvii. 22.

[7] A landing-place in the north-west of Troas, near Cape Sigaeum.

across, and that when he was about the middle of the channel of the Hellespont he sacrificed a bull to Poseidon and the Nereids, and poured forth a libation to them into the sea from a golden goblet. They say also that he was the first man to step out of the ship in full armour on the land of Asia,[1] and that he erected altars to Zeus, the protector of people landing, to Athena, and to Heracles, at the place in Europe whence he started, and at the place in Asia where he disembarked. It is also said that he went up to Ilium and offered sacrifice to the Trojan Athena; that he set up his own panoply in the temple as a votive offering, and in exchange for it took away some of the consecrated arms which had been preserved from the time of the Trojan war. These arms were said to have been carried in front of him into the battles by the shield-bearing guards. A report also prevails that he offered sacrifice to Priam upon the altar of Zeus the household god, deprecating the wrath of Priam against the progeny of Neoptolemus, from whom Alexander himself derived his origin.

CHAPTER XII.

Alexander at the Tomb of Achilles.—Memnon's Advice Rejected by the Persian Generals.

When he went up to Ilium, Menoetius the pilot crowned him with a golden crown; after him Chares the Athenian,[2] coming from Sigeum, as well as certain others, both Greeks and natives, did the same. Alexander then encircled the tomb of Achilles with a garland; and it is said that Hephaestion[3] decorated that of Patroclus in the

---

[1] Cf. *Diodorus*, xvii. 17; *Justin*, xi. 5.

[2] The celebrated general, mentioned already in chap. 10.

[3] Son of Amyntas, a Macedonian of Pella. He was the most intimate

same way. There is indeed a report that Alexander pronounced Achilles fortunate in getting Homer as the herald of his fame to posterity.[1] And in truth it was meet that Alexander should deem Achilles fortunate for this reason especially; for to Alexander himself this privilege was wanting, a thing which was not in accordance with the rest of his good fortune. His achievements have, therefore, not been related to mankind in a manner worthy of the hero. Neither in prose nor in verse has any one suitably honoured him; nor has he ever been sung of in a lyric poem, in which style of poetry Hiero, Gelo, Thero, and many others not at all comparable with Alexander, have been praised.[2] Consequently Alexander's deeds are far less known than the meanest achievements of antiquity. For instance, the march of the ten thousand with Cyrus up to Persia against King Artaxerxes, the tragic fate of Clearchus and those who were captured along with him,[3] and the march of the same men down to the sea, in which they were led by Xenophon, are events much better known to men through Xenophon's narrative than are Alexander and his achievements. And yet Alexander neither accompanied another man's expedition, nor did he in flight from the Great King overcome those who obstructed his march down to the sea. And, indeed, there is no other single individual among Greeks or barbarians who achieved exploits so great or important either in regard to number or magnitude as he did. This was the reason

---

friend of Alexander, with whom he had been brought up. Cf. Aelian (*Varia Historia*, xii. 7).

1 Plutarch (*Life of Alex.*, 15), says that Alexander also went through the ceremony, still customary in his own day, of anointing himself with oil and running up to the tomb naked. Cf. Aelian (*Varia Historia*, x. 4) Cicero (*Pro Archia*, ch. 10).

2 By Pindar and Bacchylides.

3 See Xenophon's *Anabasis*, Book ii.

which induced me to undertake this history, not thinking myself incompetent to make Alexander's deeds known to men. For whoever I may be, this I know about myself, that there is no need for me to assert my name, for it is not unknown to men; nor is it needful for me to say what my native land and family are, or if I have held any public office in my own country. But this I do assert, that this historical work is and has been from my youth up, in place of native land, family, and public offices to me; and for this reason I do not deem myself unworthy to rank among the first authors in the Greek language, if Alexander indeed is among the first in arms.

From Ilium Alexander came to Arisbe, where his entire force had encamped after crossing the Hellespont; and on the following day he came to Percote. On the next, passing by Lampsacus, he encamped near the river Practius, which flows from the Idaean mountains and discharges itself into the sea between the Hellespont and the Euxine Sea. Thence passing by the city of Colonae, he arrived at Hermotus. He now sent scouts before the army under the command of Amyntas, son of Arrhabaeus, who had the squadron of the Companion cavalry which came from Apollonia,[1] under the captain Socrates, son of Sathon, and four squadrons of what were called Prodromi (runners forward). In the march he despatched Panegorus, son of Lycagoras, one of the Companions, to take possession of the city of Priapus, which was surrendered by the inhabitants.

The Persian generals were Arsames, Rheomithres, Petines, Niphates, and with them Spithridates, viceroy of Lydia and Ionia, and Arsites, governor of the Phrygia near the Hellespont. These had encamped near the city

[1] A town in the Macedonia district of Mygdonia, south of Lake Bolbe. It is now called Polina.

of Zeleia with the Persian cavalry and the Grecian mercenaries. When they were holding a council about the state of affairs, it was reported to them that Alexander had crossed (the Hellespont). Memnon, the Rhodian,[1] advised them not to risk a conflict with the Macedonians, since they were far superior to them in infantry, and Alexander was there in person; whereas Darius was not with them. He advised them to advance and destroy the fodder, by trampling it down under their horses' hoofs, to burn the crops of the country, and not even to spare the very cities. "For then Alexander," said he, "will not be able to stay in the land from lack of provisions."[2] It is said that in the Persian conference Arsites asserted that he would not allow a single house belonging to the people placed under his rule to be burned, and that the other Persians agreed with Arsites, because they had a suspicion that Memnon was deliberately contriving to protract the war for the purpose of obtaining honour from the king.

CHAPTER XIII.

Battle of the Granicus (B.C. 334).

Meantime Alexander was advancing to the river Granicus,[3] with his army arranged for battle, having drawn up his

---

1 We find from *Diodorus* (xvii. 7), that the Persian king had subsidized this great general and 5,000 Greek mercenaries to protect his seaboard from the Macedonians. Before the arrival of Alexander, he had succeeded in checking the advance of Parmenio and Callas. If Memnon had lived and his advice been adopted by Darius, the fate of Persia might have been very different. Cf. Plutarch (*Life of Alex.*, 18).

2 *Diodorus* (xvii. 18) says that Memnon, while advising the Persian generals to lay waste the country, and to prevent the Macedonians from advancing through scarcity of provisions, also urged them to carry a large force into Greece and Macedonia, and thus transfer the war into Europe.

3 The Granicus rises in Mount Ida, and falls into the Propontis near Cyzicus. Ovid (*Metam.*, xi. 763) calls it *Granicus bicornis.*

heavy-armed troops in a double phalanx, leading the cavalry on the wings, and having ordered that the baggage should follow in the rear. And Hegelochus at the head of the cavalry, who were armed with the long pike,[1] and about 500 of the light-armed troops, was sent by him to reconnoitre the proceedings of the enemy. When Alexander was not far from the river Granicus, some of his scouts rode up to him at full speed and announced that the Persians had taken up their position on the other side of the Granicus, drawn up ready for battle. Thereupon Alexander arranged all his army with the intention of fighting. Then Parmenio approached him and spoke as follows: "I think, O king, that it is advisable for the present to pitch our camp on the bank of the river as we are. For I think that the enemy, being, as they are, much inferior to us in infantry, will not dare to pass the night near us, and therefore they will permit the army to cross the ford with ease at daybreak. For we shall then pass over before they can put themselves in order of battle;[2] whereas, I do not think that we can now attempt the operation without evident risk, because it is not possible to lead the army through the river with its front extended. Besides, it is clear that many parts of the stream are deep, and you see that these banks are steep and in some places abrupt. Therefore the enemy's cavalry, being formed into a dense square, will attack us as we emerge from the water in broken ranks and in column, in the place where we are weakest. At the present juncture the first repulse would be difficult to retrieve, as well as perilous for the issue of the whole war."

But to this Alexander replied: "I recognise the force

---

[1] This was a brigade of about 1,000 men. See *Livy*, xxxvii. 42.

[2] ὑποφθάσομεν. This future is used by the later writers for the Attic ὑποφθήσομαι. It is found however in Xenophon.

of these arguments, O Parmenio; but I should feel it a disgrace, if, after crossing the Hellespont so easily, this brook (for with such an appellation he made light of the Granicus) should bar our passage for a moment. I consider that this would be in accordance neither with the fame of the Macedonians nor with my own eagerness for encountering danger. Moreover, I think that the Persians will regain courage, as being a match in war for Macedonians, since up to the present time they have suffered no defeat from me to warrant the fear they entertain."

CHAPTER XIV.

Arrangement of the Hostile Armies.

Having spoken thus, he sent Parmenio to command upon the left wing, while he led in person on the right. And at the head of the right wing he placed the following officers:—Philotas, son of Parmenio, with the cavalry Companions, the archers, and the Agrianian javelin-men; and Amyntas, son of Arrhabaeus, with the cavalry carrying the long pike, the Paeonians, and the squadron of Socrates, was posted near Philotas. Close to these were posted the Companions who were shield-bearing infantry under the command of Nicanor, son of Parmenio. Next to these the brigade of Perdiccas, son of Orontes, then that of Coenus, son of Polemocrates; then that of Craterus,[1] son of Alexander, and that of Amyntas, son of Andromenes; finally, the men commanded by Philip, son of Amyntas. The first on the left wing were the Thes-

[1] Craterus was one of Alexander's best generals. On the death of the king he received the government of Macedonia and Greece in conjunction with Antipater, whose daughter he married. He fell in battle against Eumenes (B.C. 321).

salian cavalry, commanded by Calas, son of Harpalus;[1] next to these, the cavalry of the Grecian allies, commanded by Philip, son of Menelaus;[2] next to these the Thracians, commanded by Agatho.[3] Close to these were the infantry, the brigades of Craterus, Meleager, and Philip, reaching as far as the centre of the entire line.

The Persian cavalry were about 20,000 in number, and their infantry, consisting of Grecian mercenaries, fell a little short of the same number.[4] They had extended their horse along the bank of the river in a long phalanx, and had posted the infantry behind the cavalry, for the ground above the bank was steep and commanding. They also marshalled dense squadrons of cavalry upon that part of the bank where they observed Alexander himself advancing against their left wing; for he was conspicuous both by the brightness of his arms and by the respectful service of his attendants. Both armies stood a long time at the margin of the river, keeping quiet from dread of the result; and profound silence was observed on both sides. For the Persians were waiting till the Macedonians should step into the water, with the intention of attacking them as they emerged. Alexander leaped upon his steed, ordering those about him to follow, and exhorting them to show themselves valiant men. He then commanded Amyntas, son of Arrhabaeus, to make the first rush into the river at the

---

[1] Calas was appointed viceroy of Phrygia. He consequently took no further part in Alexander's campaigns after this.

[2] Alexander had three generals named Philip, two of whom are mentioned here as sons of Amyntas and Menelaus. The third was son of Machatas, and was left in India as viceroy.

[3] Son of Tyrimmas, was commander of the Odrysian cavalry. See iii. 12 infra.

[4] *Diodorus* (xvii. 19) says that the Persian cavalry numbered 10,000, and their infantry 100,000. Both these numbers are inaccurate. We know from *Arrian* (chaps. 12 and 13) that the Persian infantry was inferior in number to that of Alexander.

head of the skirmishing cavalry, the Paeonians, and one regiment of infantry; and in front of these he had placed Ptolemy, son of Philip, in command of the squadron of Socrates, which body of men indeed on that day happened to have the lead of all the cavalry force. He himself led the right wing with sounding of trumpets, and the men raising the war-cry to Enyalius.[1] He entered the ford, keeping his line always extended obliquely in the direction in which the stream flowed, in order that the Persians might not fall upon him on the flank as he was emerging from the water, but that he might, as far as practicable,[2] encounter them with his phalanx.

CHAPTER XV.

Description of the Battle of the Granicus.

The Persians began the contest by hurling missiles from above in the direction where the men of Amyntas and Socrates were the first to reach the bank; some of them casting javelins into the river from their commanding position on the bank, and others stepping down along the flatter parts of it to the very edge of the water. Then ensued a violent struggle on the part of the cavalry, on the one side to emerge from the river, and on the other to prevent the landing. From the Persians there was a terrible discharge of darts; but the Macedonians fought with spears. The Macedonians, being far inferior

---

[1] This is an Homeric name for Mars the war-god. In *Homer* Ares is the Trojan and Enyalius the Grecian war-god. Hence they are mentioned as different in Aristophanes (*Pax*, 457). See Paley's note on *Homer* (vii. 166). As to the practice of shouting the war-cry to Mars before battle, see Xenophon (*Anab.*, i. 8, 18; v. 2, 14). The Scholiast on *Thucydides* (i. 50) says that the Greeks used to sing two paeans, one to Mars before battle, another to Apollo after it.

[2] *ὡς ἀνυστόν = ὡς δυνατόν.* Cf. *Arrian*, iv. 12, 6; Xenophon (*Anab.*, i, 8, 11; *Res. Laced.*, i. 3).

in number, suffered severely at the first onset, because they were obliged to defend themselves in the river, where their footing was unsteady, and where they were below the level of their assailants; whereas the Persians were fighting from the top of the bank, which gave them an advantage, especially as the best of the Persian horse had been posted there. Memnon himself, as well as his sons, were running every risk with these; and the Macedonians who first came into conflict with the Persians, though they showed great valour, were cut down, except those who retreated to Alexander, who was now approaching. For the king was already near, leading with him the right wing. He made his first assault upon the Persians at the place where the whole mass of their horse and the leaders themselves were posted; and around him a desperate conflict raged,[1] during which one rank of the Macedonians after another easily kept on crossing the river. Though they fought on horseback, it seemed more like an infantry than a cavalry battle; for they struggled for the mastery, horses being jammed with horses and men with men, the Macedonians striving to drive the Persians entirely away from the bank and to force them into the plain, and the Persians striving to obstruct their landing and to push them back again into the river. At last Alexander's men began to gain the advantage, both through their superior strength and military discipline, and because they fought with spear-shafts made of cornel-wood, whereas the Persians used only darts.

Then indeed, Alexander's spear being broken to shivers in the conflict, he asked Aretis, one of the royal guards, whose duty it was to assist the king to mount his horse, for another spear. But this man's spear had also been

---

[1] ξυνειστήκει μάχη. This is a common expression with Arrian, copied from *Herodotus* (i. 74, *et passim*).

shivered whilst he was in the thickest of the struggle, and he was conspicuous fighting with the half of his broken spear. Showing this to Alexander, he bade him ask some one else for one. Then Demaratus, a man of Corinth, one of his personal Companions, gave him his own spear; which he had no sooner taken than seeing Mithridates, the son-in-law of Darius, riding far in front of the others, and leading with him a body of cavalry arranged like a wedge, he rode on in front of the others, and hitting at the face of Mithridates with his spear, struck him to the ground. But hereupon, Rhoesaces rode up to Alexander and hit him on the head with his scimitar, breaking off a piece of his helmet. But the helmet broke the force of the blow. This man also Alexander struck to the ground, hitting him in the chest through the breastplate with his lance. And now Spithridates from behind had already raised aloft his scimitar against the king, when Clitus, son of Dropidas, anticipated his blow, and hitting him on the arm, cut it off, scimitar and all.[1] Meantime the horsemen, as many as were able, kept on securing a landing all down the river, and were joining Alexander's forces.

CHAPTER XVI.

Defeat of the Persians.—Loss on Both Sides.

The Persians themselves, as well as their horses, were now being struck on their faces with the lances from all sides, and were being repulsed by the cavalry. They also received much damage from the light-armed troops who were mingled with the cavalry. They first began to give way where Alexander himself was braving danger in the front. When their centre had given way, the

---

[1] Plutarch (*Alex.*, 16); *Diodorus* (xvii. 20).

horse on both wings were also naturally broken through, and took to speedy flight. Of the Persian cavalry only about 1,000 were killed; for Alexander did not pursue them far, but turned aside to attack the Greek mercenaries, the main body of whom was still remaining where it was posted at first. This they did rather from amazement at the unexpected result of the struggle than from any steady resolution. Leading the phalanx against these, and ordering the cavalry to fall upon them from all sides in the midst, he soon cut them up, so that none of them escaped except such as might have concealed themselves among the dead bodies. About 2,000 were taken prisoners.[1] The following leaders of the Persians also fell in the battle: Niphates, Petines, Spithridates, viceroy of Lydia, Mithrobuzanes, governor of Cappadocia, Mithridates, the son-in-law of Darius, Arbupales, son of Darius the son of Artaxerxes, Pharnaces, brother of the wife of Darius,[2] and Onares, commander of the auxiliaries. Arsites fled from the battle into Phrygia, where he is reported to have committed suicide, because he was deemed by the Persians the cause of their defeat on that occasion.

Of the Macedonians, about twenty-five of the Companions were killed at the first onset; brazen statues of whom were erected at Dium,[3] executed by Lysippus,[4] at

---

[1] *Diodorus* (xvii. 21) says that more than 10,000 of the Persian infantry were killed, and 2,000 cavalry; and that more than 20,000 were made prisoners.

[2] Her name was Statira.

[3] An important city in Macedonia on the Thermaic gulf, named after a temple of Zeus.

[4] Lysippus of Sicyon was one of the most famous of Greek statuaries. None of his works remain, inasmuch as they were all executed in bronze. Alexander published an edict that no one should paint his portrait but Apelles, and that no one should make a statue of him but Lysippus. When Metellus conquered Macedonia, he removed this group of bronze statues to Rome, to decorate his own portico. See Pliny (*Nat. Hist.*, xxxiv. 19); *Velleius Paterculus* (i. 11).

Alexander's order. The same statuary also executed a statue of Alexander himself, being chosen by him for the work in preference to all other artists. Of the other cavalry over sixty were slain, and of the infantry about thirty.[1] These were buried by Alexander the next day, together with their arms and other decorations. To their parents and children he granted exemption from imposts on agricultural produce, and he relieved them from all personal services and taxes upon property. He also exhibited great solicitude in regard to the wounded, for he himself visited each man, looked at their wounds, and inquired how and in the performance of what duty they had received them, allowing them both to speak and brag of their own deeds. He also buried the Persian commanders and the Greek mercenaries who were killed fighting on the side of the enemy. But as many of them as he took prisoners he bound in fetters and sent them away to Macedonia to till the soil, because, though they were Greeks, they were fighting against Greece on behalf of the foreigners in opposition to the decrees which the Greeks had made in their federal council.[2] To Athens also he sent 300 suits of Persian armour to be hung up in the Acropolis[3] as a votive offering to Athena, and ordered this inscription to be fixed over them: "Alexander, son of Philip, and all the Greeks except the Lacedaemonians, present this offering from the spoils taken from the foreigners inhabiting Asia."

---

1 As most of the infantry on the Persian side were Grecian mercenaries, who, according to *Plutarch*, fought with desperate valour, and, according to *Arrian* himself, all the infantry were killed except 2,000, the number of Alexander's slain must have been larger than Arrian here states.

2 At Corinth, B.C. 336.

3 For the fact that the Acropolis of Athens was often called simply *polis*, see *Thucydides*, ii. 15; Xenophon (*Anab.* vii. 1, 27); *Antiphon* (146, 2); Aristophanes (*Equites*, 1093; *Lysistrata*, 758).

CHAPTER XVII.

Alexander in Sardis and Ephesus.

Having appointed Calas to the post of viceroy of the territory which had been under the rule of Arsites, and having commanded the inhabitants to pay to him the same tribute which they had paid to Darius, he ordered as many of the natives as came down from the mountains and surrendered to him to depart to their several abodes. He also acquitted the people of Zeleia [1] of blame, because he knew they had been compelled to assist the Persians in the war. He then despatched Parmenio to occupy Dascylium,[2] which he easily performed; for the garrison evacuated it. He himself advanced towards Sardis; and when he was about 70 stades [3] distant from that city, he was met by Mithrines, the commandant of the garrison in the Acropolis, accompanied by the most influential of the citizens of Sardis. The latter surrendered the city into his hands, and Mithrines the fortress and the money laid up in it. Alexander encamped near the river Hermus,[4] which is about twenty stades[5] distant from Sardis; but he sent Amyntas, son of Andromenes, to occupy the citadel of Sardis.[6] He took Mithrines with him, treating him with honour; and granted the Sardians and other Lydians the privilege of enjoying the ancient laws of Lydia, and permitted them to be free. He then ascended into the citadel, which was garrisoned by the Persians. And the position seemed to him a strong one; for it was very lofty, precipitous on every side, and fenced round by a triple wall. He therefore resolved to

---

[1] A city at the foot of Mount Ida.

[2] A city of Bithynia, on the Propontis.

[3] About eight miles.

[4] This river flows through Phrygia and Lydia, and falls into the gulf of Smyrna. Its present name is Kodus-Chai. See Vergil (*Georg.*, ii. 137); *Silius*, i. 159; Claudian (*Raptus Proserpinae*, ii. 67).

[5] Nearly two-and-a-half miles.

[6] For a description of this fortress, see *Herodotus*, i. 84.

build a temple to the Olympian Zeus on the hill, and to erect an altar in it; but while he was considering which part of the hill was the most suitable site, suddenly a winter storm arose, though it was the summer season, loud claps of thunder were heard, and rain fell on the spot where the palace of the kings of Lydia had stood. From this Alexander thought that the deity had revealed to him where the temple to Zeus ought to be built; and he gave orders accordingly. He left Pausanias, one of the Companions, to be superintendent of the citadel of Sardis, Nicias to supervise the collection of the tribute and taxes, and Asander, son of Philotas, to be superintendent of Lydia and the rest of the dominion of Spithridates, giving him as large a number of cavalry and light-armed infantry as seemed sufficient for present emergencies. He also sent Calas and Alexander, son of Aëropus, into the country of Memnon,[1] in command of the Peloponnesians and most of the other Grecian allies, except the Argives, who had been left behind to guard the citadel of Sardis.

Meantime, when the news of the cavalry battle was spread abroad, the Grecian mercenaries who formed the garrison of Ephesus, seized two of the Ephesian triremes and set off in flight. They were accompanied by Amyntas,[2] son of Antiochus, who had fled from Alexander out of Macedonia, not because he had received any injury from the king, but from ill-will to him, and thinking it not unlikely that he should suffer some ill-treatment from him (on account of his disloyalty). On the fourth day Alexander arrived at Ephesus, where he recalled from exile all the men who had been banished

---

[1] Memnon had succeeded his brother Mentor as governor for the Persian king of the territory near the Hellespont. See *Diodorus*, xvii. 7.

[2] This man took refuge with Darius, and distinguished himself at the battle of Issus. See Plutarch (*Alex.*, 20); *Curtius*, iii. 28. He met with his death soon after in Egypt. See *Arrian*, ii. 6 and 13; *Diod.*, xvii. 48.

from the city on account of their adherence to him; and having broken up the oligarchy, he established a democratical form of government there. He also ordered the Ephesians to contribute to Artemis[1] all the tribute which they were in the habit of paying to the Persians. When the people of Ephesus were relieved of their dread of the oligarchs, they rushed headlong to kill the men who had brought Memnon into the city, as also those who had pillaged the temple of Artemis, and those who had thrown down the statue of Philip which was in the temple, and those who had dug up and carried off from the tomb in the market place the bones of Heropythus, the liberator of their city. They also led Syrphax, and his son Pelagon, and the sons of Syrphax's brothers out of the temple and stoned them to death. But Alexander prevented them making any further quest of the rest of the oligarchs for the purpose of wreaking their vengeance upon them; for he knew that if the people were not checked, they would kill the innocent along with the guilty, some from hatred, and others for the sake of seizing their property. At this time Alexander gained great popularity both by his general course of action and especially by what he did at Ephesus.

CHAPTER XVIII.

Alexander Marches to Miletus and Occupies the Island of Lade.

Men now came to him both from Magnesia[2] and Tralles,

---

[1] The temple of Artemis at Ephesus had been burnt down by Herostratus in the night on which Alexander was born (Oct. 13–14, B.C. 356), and at this time was being restored by the joint efforts of the Ionian cities. See *Strabo*, xiv. 1. Heropythus and Syrphax are not mentioned by any other writers.

[2] This was the Carian Magnesia, situated on the Lethaeus, a tributary of the Maeander. Tralles was on the Eudon, another tributary of the Maeander. See *Juvenal*, iii. 70.

offering to surrender those cities; and to them he sent Parmenio, giving him 2,500 infantry from the Grecian auxiliaries, an equal number of Macedonians, and about 200 of the Cavalry Companions. He also sent Lysimachus, son of Agathocles,[1] with an equal force to the Aeolic cities,[2] and to as many of the Ionic cities[3] as were still under the Persians. He was ordered to break up the oligarchies everywhere, to set up the democratical form of government, to restore their own laws to each of the cities, and to remit the tribute which they were accustomed to pay to the foreigners. But Alexander himself remained behind at Ephesus, where he offered a sacrifice to Artemis and conducted a procession in her honour with the whole of his army fully armed and marshalled for battle.[4]

On the following day he took the rest of his infantry, the archers, the Agrianians, the Thracian cavalry, the royal squadron of the Companions, and three other squadrons in addition, and set out for Miletus. At his first assault he captured that which was called the outer city; for the garrison had evacuated it. There he encamped and resolved to blockade the inner city; for Hegesistratus, to whom the king Darius had entrusted the command of the garrison in Miletus, kept on sending

---

[1] Lysimachus was of mean origin, his father having been a serf in Sicily. He was one of Alexander's confidential body-guards, and on the death of the great king obtained Thrace as his portion of the dismembered empire. In conjunction with Seleucus he won the battle of Ipsus, by which he obtained a great part of Asia Minor. He ultimately acquired all the European dominions of Alexander in addition to Asia Minor; but in his eightieth year he was defeated and slain by Seleucus at the battle of Corus, B.C. 281. Sintenis was the first to substitute *Lysimachus* for *Antimachus*, the reading of the MSS. Cf. vi. 28 infra.

[2] Eleven in number. See *Herodotus*, i. 149–151.

[3] Thirteen in number, of which Miletus and Ephesus were the chief in importance.

[4] For the celebrated interview of Alexander with Apelles at Ephesus, see Aelian (*Varia Historia*, ii. 3).

letters before this to Alexander, offering to surrender Miletus to him. But then, having regained his courage from the fact that the Persian fleet was not far off, he made up his mind to preserve the city for Darius. But Nicanor, the commander of the Grecian fleet, anticipated the Persians by sailing into the port of Miletus three days before they approached; and with 160 ships he anchored at the island of Lade, which lies near Miletus.[1] The Persian ships arriving too late, and the admirals discovering that Nicanor had occupied the anchorage at Lade before them, they took moorings near Mount Mycale.[2] Alexander had forestalled them in seizing the island, not only by mooring his ships near it, but also by transporting into it the Thracians and about 4,000 of the other auxiliary troops. The ships of the foreigners were about 400 in number.

Notwithstanding the superiority of the Persian fleet, Parmenio advised Alexander to fight a sea-battle, expecting that the Greeks would be victorious with their fleet both for other reasons and especially because an omen from the deity made him confident of the result; for an eagle had been seen sitting upon the shore, opposite the sterns of Alexander's ships.[3] He also urged that if they won the battle, they would reap a great advantage from it in regard to their main object in the war; and if they were beaten, their defeat would not be of any great moment; for even as it was, the Persians held the sovereignty of the sea. He added that he was willing to go on board the fleet himself and to share the danger. However, Alexander replied that Parmenio was

---

[1] Cf. *Herodotus*, vi. 7. Here the Persians destroyed the Ionic fleet, B.C. 497.

[2] Famous for the victory won near it by Leotychides and Xanthippus over the Persians, B.C. 479.

[3] Cf. Vergil (*Aeneid*, vi. 3). *Obvertunt pelago proras.* See Conington's note.

mistaken in his judgment, and did not explain the sign according to probability. For it would be rash for him with a few ships to fight a battle against a fleet far more numerous than his own, and with his unpractised naval force to contend against the disciplined fleet of the Cyprians and Phoenicians. Besides, he did not wish to deliver over to the foreigners on so unstable an element the advantage which the Macedonians derived from their skill and courage; and if they were beaten in the sea-battle, their defeat would be no small hindrance to their final success in the war, both for other reasons, and especially because the Greeks, being animated with courage at the news of his naval defeat, would attempt to effect a revolution. Taking all these things into consideration, he declared that he did not think that it was a suitable time for fighting a sea-battle; and for his part, he expounded the divine omen in a different way. He admitted that the eagle was in his favour; but as it was seen sitting on the land, it seemed to him rather to be a sign that he should get the mastery over the Persian fleet by defeating their army on land.

CHAPTER XIX.

SIEGE AND CAPTURE OF MILETUS.

AT this time Glaucippus, one of the most notable men in Miletus, was sent out to Alexander by the people and the Grecian mercenaries, to whom rather than to the citizens the town had been entrusted, to tell him that the Milesians were willing to make their walls and harbours[1] free to him and the Persians in common; and on these terms to demand that he should raise the siege. But Alexander ordered Glaucippus to depart without delay into the city, and tell the citizens to prepare for

[1] *Strabo* (xiv. 1) says that Miletus had four harbours.

a battle at daybreak. He then stationed his military engines near the wall, and having in a short time partly broken and partly shaken down a large piece of it, he led his army near, that the men might enter wherever the wall had been thrown down or shaken. The Persians from Mycale were following close[1] upon them and could almost see their friends and allies being besieged. In the meantime, Nicanor, observing from Lade Alexander's commencement of the attack, began to sail into the harbour of Miletus, rowing along the shore; and mooring his triremes as close as possible together, with their prows facing the enemy, across the narrowest part of the mouth of the harbour, he shut off the Persian fleet from the port and made it impossible for the Persians to give succour to the Milesians. Then the Macedonians from all sides pressed close upon the citizens and the Grecian mercenaries, who took to flight; some of them, casting themselves into the sea, floated along upon their shields with the hollow upwards to an unnamed islet which lies near the city; others getting into their skiffs and hastening to get the start of the Macedonian triremes, were captured by them at the mouth of the harbour. But the majority of them were slain in the city itself. As soon as Alexander had got possession of the city, he sailed against those who had fled for refuge into the island; ordering the men to carry ladders upon the prows of the triremes, with the intention of effecting a landing along the cliffs of the island, as one would mount a wall. But when he saw that the men on the island were resolved to run every risk, he was moved with pity for them, because they appeared to him both brave and loyal; wherefore he made a truce with them on the condition that they would serve as his soldiers. These

---

[1] ἐφομαρτούντων. This word is rare in prose. See Homer (*Iliad*, viii. 191); *Apollonius Rhodius*, i. 201.

Grecian mercenaries were about 300 in number. He likewise pardoned all the citizens of Miletus who had escaped death in the capture of the city, and he granted them their freedom.

The foreigners used to start from Mycale every day and sail up to the Grecian fleet, hoping to induce them to accept the challenge and come forth to a battle; but during the night they used to moor their vessels near Mycale, which was an inconvenient station, because they were under the necessity of fetching water from the mouth of the river Maeander, a great way off.[1] Alexander guarded the harbour of Miletus with his ships, in order to prevent the foreigners from forcing an entrance; and at the same time he sent Philotas to Mycale in command of the cavalry and three regiments of infantry, with instructions to prevent the men in the ships from landing. Accordingly, they, being through the scarcity of fresh water and of the other necessaries of life as good as besieged in their ships, sailed away to Samos; where furnishing themselves with food, they sailed back again to Miletus. They then drew up most of their ships in front of the harbour on the deep sea, with the hope that they might in some way or other induce the Macedonians to come out into the open sea. Five of their ships sailed into the roadstead which lay between the island of Lade and the camp, expecting to surprise Alexander's ships while empty of their crews; for they had ascertained that the sailors for the most part were dispersed from the ships, some to gather fuel, others to collect provisions, and others being arranged in foraging parties.[2] And indeed it happened that a number of the sailors were absent; but as soon as Alexander observed the five Persian ships sailing towards him, he manned ten ships with the sailors

---

[1] Miletus lay nearly ten miles south of the mouth of the Maeander.

[2] A similar stratagem was used by Lysander at Aegospotami, B.C. 405. See Xenophon (*Hellenics*, ii. 1).

who happened to be at hand, and sent them with all speed against them with orders to attack prow to prow. No sooner did the men in the five Persian ships see the Macedonians bearing up against them, contrary to their expectation, than they immediately tacked about, though far off, and fled to the rest of their fleet. However, the ship of the Iassians,[1] not being a fast sailer, was captured in the flight, men and all; but the other four succeeded in escaping to their own triremes. After this the Persians sailed away from Miletus without effecting anything.

CHAPTER XX.

Siege of Halicarnassus.—Abortive Attack on Myndus.

Alexander now resolved to disband his fleet, partly from lack of money at the time, and partly because he saw that his own fleet was not a match in battle for that of the Persians. On this account he was unwilling to run the risk of losing even a part of his armament. Besides, he considered, that now he was occupying Asia with his land force, he would no longer be in need of a fleet; and that he would be able to break up that of the Persians, if he captured the maritime cities; since they would neither have any ports from which they could recruit their crews, nor any harbour in Asia to which they could bring their ships. Thus he explained the omen of the eagle to signify that he should get the mastery over the enemy's ships by his land force. After doing this, he set forth into Caria,[2] because it was reported

[1] Iassus was a city in Caria on the Iassian Gulf, founded by the Argives and further colonized by the Milesians.

[2] Caria formed the south-west angle of Asia Minor. The Greeks asserted that the Carians were emigrants from Crete. We learn from Thucydides and Herodotus that they entered the service of foreign rulers. They formed the body-guard of queen Athaliah, who had usurped the throne and stood in need of foreign mercenaries. The word translated

that a considerable force, both of foreigners and of Grecian auxiliaries, had collected in Halicarnassus.[1] Having taken all the cities between Miletus and Halicarnassus as soon as he approached them, he encamped near the latter city, at a distance from it of about five stades,[2] as if he expected a long siege. For the natural position of the place made it strong; and wherever there seemed to be any deficiency in security, it had been entirely supplied long before by Memnon, who was there in person, having now been proclaimed by Darius governor of lower Asia and commander of the entire fleet. Many Grecian mercenary soldiers had been left in the city, as well as many Persian troops; the triremes also were moored in the harbour, so that the sailors might render him valuable aid in the operations. On the first day of the siege, while Alexander was leading his men up to the wall in the direction of the gate leading towards Mylasa,[3] the men in the city made a sortie, and a skirmish took place; but Alexander's men making a rush upon them repulsed them with ease, and shut them up in the city. A few days after this, the king took the shield-bearing guards, the Cavalry Companions, the infantry regiments of Amyntas, Perdiccas and Meleager, and in addition to these the archers and Agrianians, and went round to the part of the city which is in the direction of Myndus, both for the purpose of inspecting the wall, to see if it happened to be more easy to be assaulted there than elsewhere; and at the same time to see if he could get hold of Myndus[4] by

---

in our Bible in 2 Kings xi. 4, 19 as *captains*, ought to be rendered *Carians*. See Fuerst's *Hebrew Lexicon, sub voce* כָּרִי.

[1] Now called Budrum. It was the birthplace of the historians Herodotus and Dionysius.

[2] Little more than half a mile.

[3] Now called Melasso, a city of Caria, about ten miles from the Gulf of Iassus.

[4] A colony of Troezen, on the western extremity of the same peninsula on which stood Halicarnassus.

a sudden and secret attack. For he thought that if Myndus were his own, it would be no small help in the siege of Halicarnassus; moreover, an offer to surrender had been made by the Myndians if he would approach the town secretly, under the cover of night. About midnight, therefore, he approached the wall, according to the plan agreed on; but as no sign of surrender was made by the men within, and though he had with him no military engines or ladders, inasmuch as he had not set out to besiege the town, but to receive it on surrender, he nevertheless led the Macedonian phalanx near and ordered them to undermine the wall. They threw down one of the towers, which, however, in its fall did not make a breach in the wall. But the men in the city stoutly defending themselves, and at the same time many from Halicarnassus having already come to their aid by sea, made it impossible for Alexander to capture Myndus by surprise or sudden assault. Wherefore he returned without accomplishing any of the plans for which he had set out, and devoted himself once more to the siege of Halicarnassus.

In the first place he filled up with earth the ditch which the enemy had dug in front of the city, about thirty cubits wide and fifteen deep; so that it might be easy to bring forward the towers, from which he intended to discharge missiles against the defenders of the wall; and that he might bring up the other engines with which he was planning to batter the wall down. He easily filled up the ditch, and the towers were then brought forward. But the men in Halicarnassus made a sally by night with the design of setting fire both to the towers and the other engines which had been brought up to the wall, or were nearly brought up to it. They were, however, easily repelled and shut up again within the walls by the Macedonians who were guarding the engines, and by others who were aroused by the noise of the struggle and who came to their aid. Neoptolemus, the brother of Arrhabaeus, son of Amyntas, one of those who had deserted to Darius, was killed, with about 170 others of the enemy. Of Alexander's soldiers sixteen were killed and 300 wounded; for the sally being made in the night, they were less able to guard themselves from being wounded.

CHAPTER XXI.

Siege of Halicarnassus.

A few days after this, two Macedonian hoplites of the brigade of Perdiccas, living in the same tent and being messmates, happened in the course of conversation each to be extolling himself and his own exploits. Hence a quarrel arose between them as to which of them was the braver, and, being somewhat inflamed with wine, they agreed to arm themselves, and of their own accord go and assault the wall facing the citadel, which for the most part was turned towards Mylasa. This they did rather to make a display of their own valour than to engage in a dangerous conflict with the enemy. Some of the men in the city, however, perceiving that there were only two of them, and that they were approaching the wall inconsiderately, rushed out upon them; but they slew those who came near, and hurled darts at those who stood at a distance. At last, however, they were overmatched both by the number of their assailants and the disadvantage of their own position; for the enemy made the attack upon them, and threw darts at them from a higher level.[1] Meanwhile some other men from the brigade of Perdiccas, and others from Halicarnassus, rushed out against each

---

[1] *Diodorus* (xvii. 25) says that this incident occurred in the night, which is scarcely probable. Compare the conduct of the two centurions Pulfio and Varenus in the country of the Nervii. Caesar (*Gallic Wur*, v. 44).

other; and a sharp contest ensued near the wall. Those who had made the sally from the city were driven back, and again shut up within the gates by the Macedonians. The city also narrowly escaped capture; for the walls at that time were not under strict guard, and two towers, with the whole intermediate space, having already fallen to the ground, would have offered an easy entrance within the wall to the army, if the whole of it had undertaken the task. The third tower, which had been thoroughly shaken, would likewise have been easily thrown down if it had been undermined; but the enemy easily succeeded in building inside a crescent-shaped brick wall to take the place of the one which had fallen. This they were able to do so quickly because of the multitude of hands at their disposal. On the following day Alexander brought his engines up to this wall also; and the men in the city made another sally to set them on fire. A part of the wicker-work shed near the wall and a piece of one of the wooden towers were burnt, but the rest were protected by Philotas and Hellanicus, to whom the charge of them had been committed. But as soon as those who were making the sally saw Alexander, the men who had come out to render aid by holding torches threw them away, and the majority of them cast away their arms and fled within the walls of the city. Then at first they had the advantage from the nature of their position, which was commanding on account of its height; for not only did they cast missiles right in front against the men who were guarding the engines, but also from the towers which alone had been left standing at each end of the battered-down wall, they were able to cast them against the sides, and almost against the backs, of those who were assaulting the wall which had just been built in place of the ruined one.[1]

---

[1] Compare the sieges of Avaricum, Gergovia, and Alesia by Caesar (*Gallic War*, lib. vii.); and that of Saguntum by Hannibal. See *Livy*, xxi. 7–15.

CHAPTER XXII.

SIEGE OF HALICARNASSUS.

A few days after this, when Alexander again brought his military engines up to the inner brick wall, and was himself superintending the work, a sortie in mass was made from the city, some advancing by the breach in the wall, where Alexander himself was posted, others by the triple gate, where the Macedonians did not at all expect them. The first party cast torches and other combustibles at the engines, in order to set them on fire and to defy the engineers excessively. But when the men around Alexander attacked them vigorously, hurling great stones with the engines from the towers, and launching darts at them, they were easily put to rout and fled into the city; and as a great number of them had sallied forth and great audacity had been exhibited in the fight, no small slaughter of them took place. For some of them were slain fighting hand-to-hand with the Macedonians, others were killed near the ruins of the wall,[1] because the breach was too narrow for such a multitude to pass through, and the fragments of the wall made it difficult for them to scale it. The second party, which sallied forth by the triple gate, was met by Ptolemy,[2] one of the royal body-guards, who had with him the regiments of Addaeus and Timander and some of the light-armed troops. These soldiers by themselves easily put the men of the city to rout; but as the latter in their retreat were fleeing over a narrow bridge which had been made over the ditch, they had the misfortune to break it down by the weight of their multitude. Many of them fell into the ditch, some of whom were

1 This use of ἀμφί with the Dative, is poetical. The Attic writers use περί with the Accusative. Cf. ii. 3, 8; iii. 30, 1.

2 There were at least four generals in Alexander's army of this name. The one here mentioned was probably not the famous son of Lagus.

trampled to death by their own comrades, and others were killed by the Macedonian weapons from above. A very great slaughter was also made at the very gates, because they were shut before the proper time in a state of panic. For the enemy, being afraid that the Macedonians, who were close upon the fugitives, would rush in with them, shut many of their friends out, who were slain by the Macedonians near the very walls. The city narrowly escaped capture; indeed it would have been taken, had not Alexander called back his army, to see if some friendly sign of surrender would be made by the Halicarnassians; for he was still desirous of saving their city. Of the men in the city about one thousand were slain; and of Alexander's men about forty, among whom were Ptolemy, one of the king's body-guards, Clearchus, a captain of the archers, Addaeus, who had the command of a thousand infantry, and other Macedonians of no mean position.[1]

CHAPTER XXIII.

Destruction of Halicarnassus.—Ada, Queen of Caria.

Then Orontobates and Memnon, the commanders of the Persians, met and decided from the state of affairs that they could not hold out long against the siege, seeing that part of the wall had already fallen down and part had been battered and weakened, and that many of their

---

[1] *Diodorus* (xvii. 25–27) gives a very different account of the last struggle of the besieged in Halicarnassus. When the leaders saw that they must eventually succumb, they made a last desperate effort to destroy Alexander's military engines. Ephialtes, the eminent Athenian exile, headed the sally, which was effected by troops simultaneously issuing from all the gates at daybreak. The advanced guard of the Macedonians, consisting of young troops, were put to rout; but the veterans of Philip restored the battle under a man named Atharrias. Ephialtes was slain, and his men driven back into the city.

soldiers had either perished in the sorties or been wounded and disabled. Taking these things into consideration, about the second watch of the night they set fire to the wooden tower which they had themselves built to resist the enemy's military engines, and to the magazines in which their weapons were stored. They also cast fire into the houses near the wall; and others were burned by the flames, which were carried with great fury from the magazines and the tower by the wind bearing in that direction. Some of the enemy then withdrew to the stronghold in the island (called Arconnesus), and others to another fortress called Salmacis. When this was reported to Alexander by some deserters from the incendiaries, and he himself could see the raging fire, though the occurrence took place about midnight, yet he led out the Macedonians and slew those who were still engaged in setting fire to the city. But he issued orders to preserve all the Halicarnassians who should be taken in their houses. As soon as the daylight appeared he could discern the strongholds which the Persians and the Grecian mercenaries had occupied; but he decided not to besiege them, considering that he would meet with no small delay beleaguering them, from the nature of their position, and moreover thinking that they would be of little importance to him now that he had captured the whole city.

Wherefore, burying the dead in the night, he ordered the men who had been placed in charge of the military engines to convey them to Tralles. He himself marched into Phrygia, after razing the city to the ground, and leaving 3,000 Grecian infantry and 200 cavalry as a guard both of this place and of the rest of Caria, under the command of Ptolemy. He appointed Ada to act as his viceroy of the whole of Caria.[1] This queen was

[1] Hecatomnus, king of Caria, left three sons, Mausolus, Hidrieus, and

daughter of Hecatomnus and wife of Hidrieus, who, though he was her brother, lived with her in wedlock, according to the custom of the Carians. When Hidrieus was dying, he confided the administration of affairs to her, for it had been a custom in Asia, ever since the time of Semiramis, even for women to rule men. But Pixodarus expelled her from the rule, and seized the administration of affairs himself. On the death of Pixodarus, his son-in-law Orontobates was sent by the king of the Persians to rule over the Carians. Ada retained Alinda alone, the strongest place in Caria; and when Alexander invaded Caria she went to meet him, offering to surrender Alinda to him, and adopting him as her son.[1] Alexander confided Alinda to her, and did not think the title of son unworthy of his acceptance; moreover, when he had captured Halicarnassus and become master of the rest of Caria, he granted her the privilege of ruling over the whole country.

CHAPTER XXIV.

ALEXANDER IN LYCIA AND PAMPHYLIA.

SOME of the Macedonians who served in Alexander's army had married just before he undertook the expedition. He thought that he ought not to treat these men with neglect, and therefore sent them back from Caria to spend the winter in Macedonia with their wives. He placed them under the command of Ptolemy, son of Seleucus, one of the royal body-guards, and of the two

---

Pixodarus; and two daughters, Artemisia and Ada. Artemisia married Mausolus, and Ada married Hidrieus. All these children succeeded their father in the sovereignty, Pixodarus being the last surviving son.

[1] Amyntas, king of Macedonia, grandfather of Alexander the Great, adopted the celebrated Athenian general Iphicrates, in gratitude to him as the preserver of Macedonia. See Aeschines (*De Falsa Legatione*, pp. 249, 250).

generals Coenus, son of Polemocrates, and Meleager, son of Neoptolemus, because they were also newly married. He gave these officers instructions to levy as many horse and foot soldiers as they could from the country, when they returned to him and brought back the men who had been sent away with them. By this act more than by any other Alexander acquired popularity among the Macedonians. He also sent Cleander, son of Polemocrates, to levy soldiers in Peloponnesus,[1] and Parmenio to Sardis, giving him the command of a regiment of the Cavalry Companions, the Thessalian cavalry, and the rest of the Grecian allies. He ordered him to take the wagons to Sardis aud to advance from that place into Phrygia.

He himself marched towards Lycia and Pamphylia, in order to gain command of the coast-land, and by that means render the enemy's fleet useless. The first place on his route was Hyparna, a strong position, having a garrison of Grecian mercenaries; but he took it at the first assault, and allowed the Greeks to depart from the citadel under a truce. Then he invaded Lycia and brought over the Telmissians by capitulation; and crossing the river Xanthus, the cities of Pinara, Xanthus, Patara, and about thirty other smaller towns were surrendered to him.[2] Having accomplished this, though it was now the very depth of winter, he invaded the land called Milyas,[3] which is a part of Great Phrygia, but at that time paid tribute to Lycia, according to an arrangement made by the Great King. Hither came envoys

---

[1] See *Arrian*, ii. 20 infra.

[2] The Marmarians alone defended their city with desperate valour. They finally set fire to it, and escaped through the Macedonian camp to the mountains. See *Diodorus* (xvii. 28). As to Xanthus the river, see Homer (*Iliad*, ii. 877; vi. 172); Horace (*Carm.*, iv. 6, 26).

[3] Lycia was originally called Milyas; but the name was afterwards applied to the high table in the north of Lycia, extending into Pisidia. See *Herodotus*, i. 173.

from the Phaselites,[1] to treat for his friendship, and to crown him with a golden crown; and the majority of the maritime Lycians also sent heralds to him as ambassadors to treat for the same object. He ordered the Phaselites and Lycians to surrender their cities to those who were despatched by him to receive them; and they were all surrendered. He soon afterwards arrived himself at Phaselis, and helped the men of that city to capture a strong fort which had been constructed by the Pisidians to overawe the country; and sallying forth from which those barbarians used to inflict much damage upon the Phaselites who tilled the land.[2]

CHAPTER XXV.

Treason of Alexander, Son of Aëropus.

While the king was still near Phaselis he received information that Alexander, son of Aëropus, who was not only one of the Companions, but also at that time commander of the Thessalian horse, was conspiring against him. This Alexander was brother of Heromenes and Arrhabaeus, who had taken part in the murder of Philip.[3] At that time King Alexander pardoned him, though he

---

[1] Phaselis was a seaport of Lycia on the Gulf of Pamphylia. It is now called Tekrova.

[2] He also crowned with garlands the statue of Theodectes the rhetorician, which the people of Phaselis, his native city, had erected to his memory. This man was a friend and pupil of Aristotle, the tutor of Alexander. See Plutarch (*Life of Alex.*, 17); Aristotle (*Nicom. Ethics*, vii. 7).

[3] Philip was murdered by Pausanias. Three only of his reputed accomplices are known by name, and they were Alexander, Heromenes, and Arrhabaeus, sons of Aëropus. The two latter were put to death; but the first named was not only spared, but advanced to high military command for being the first to salute Alexander as king. Compare *Curtius* (vii. 1); *Justin* (xi. 2). Alexander was accused by some of forgiving his father's murderers. Probably the reference was to his kind treatment of Olympias and this Alexander. See *Curtius*, vi. 43.

was accused of complicity with them, because after Philip's death he was among the first of his friends to come to him, and, helping him on with his breastplate, accompanied him to the palace. The king afterwards showed him honour at his court, sent him as general into Thrace; and when Calas the commander of the Thessalian horse was sent away to a viceroyalty[1] he was appointed to succeed that general. The details of the conspiracy were reported as follows: When Amyntas deserted to Darius,[2] he conveyed to him certain messages and a letter from this Alexander. Darius then sent Sisines, one of his own faithful Persian courtiers, down to the sea-coast, under pretence of going to Atizyes, viceroy of Phrygia, but really to communicate with this Alexander, and to give him pledges, that if he would kill king Alexander, Darius would appoint him king of Macedonia, and would give him 1,000 talents of gold[3] in addition to the kingdom. But Sisines, being captured by Parmenio, told him the real object of his mission. Parmenio sent him immediately under guard to the king, who obtained the same intelligence from him. The king then, having collected his friends, proposed to them as a subject for deliberation what decision he ought to make in regard to this Alexander. The Companions thought that formerly he had not resolved wisely in confiding the best part of his cavalry to a faithless man, and that now it was advisable to put him out of the way as speedily as possible, before he became even more popular among the Thessalians and should try to effect some revolutionary plan with their aid. Moreover they were terrified by a certain divine portent. For, while Alexander the king was still besieging Halicarnassus, it is said that he was

---

[1] That of the Hellespontine Phrygia. See chap. xvii. supra.

[2] See chap. xvii. supra.

[3] Nearly £250,000.

once taking rest at mid-day, when a swallow flew about over his head loudly twittering, and perched now on this side of his couch and now on that, chirping more noisily than usual. On account of his fatigue he could not be roused from sleep, but being disquieted by the sound he brushed her away gently with his hand. But though struck she was so far from trying to escape, that she perched upon the very head of the king, and did not desist until he was wide awake. Thinking the affair of the swallow of no trivial import, he communicated it to a soothsayer, Aristander the Telmissian,[1] who told him that it signified a plot formed by one of his friends. He said it also signified that the plot would be discovered, because the swallow was a bird fond of man's society and well disposed to him as well as more loquacious than any other bird. Therefore, comparing this with the depositions of the Persian, the king sent Amphoterus, son of Alexander and brother of Craterus to Parmenio; and with him he sent some Pergaeans to show him the way. Amphoterus, putting on a native dress, so that he should not be recognised on the road, reached Parmenio by stealth. He did not carry a letter from Alexander, because it did not appear to the king advisable to write openly about such a matter; but he reported the message entrusted to him by word of mouth. Consequently this Alexander was arrested and kept under guard.

CHAPTER XXVI.

Alexander in Pamphylia.—Capture of Aspendus and Side.

Alexander then, moving from Phaselis, sent part of his army to Perga through the mountains, where the

[1] See chap. xi. supra.

Thracians had levelled a road for him by a route which was otherwise difficult and long. But he himself led his own brigade by the beach along the sea, where there is no route, except when the north wind blows. But if the south wind prevails it is impossible to journey along the beach. At that time, after a strong south wind, the north winds blew, and rendered his passage easy and quick, not without the divine intervention, as both he and his men interpreted.[1] As he was advancing from Perga, he was met on the road by envoys from the Aspendians[2] with full powers, who offered to surrender their city, but begged him not lead a garrison into it. Having gained their request in regard to the garrison, they went back; but he ordered them to give him fifty talents[3] as pay for his army, as well as the horses which they were rearing as tribute to Darius. Having agreed with him about the money, and having likewise promised to hand over the horses, they departed.

Alexander then marched to Sidē,[4] the inhabitants of which were Cymaeans from Cyme, in Aeolis. These people give the following account of themselves, saying that their ancestors starting from Cyme, arrived in that country, and disembarked to found a settlement. They immediately forgot the Grecian language, and forthwith began to utter a foreign speech, not, indeed, that of the

---

[1] Compare Plutarch (*Alex.*, 17). Just as the historians of Alexander affirmed that the sea near Pamphylia providentially made way for him, so the people of Thapsacus, when they saw the army of Cyrus cross the Euphrates on foot, said that the river made way for him to come and take the sceptre (Xen., *Anab.*, i. 4). So also the inhabitants prostrated themselves before Lucullus when the same river subsided and allowed his army to cross (Plutarch, *Lucullus*, chap. xxiv.). There was the same omen in the reign of Tiberius, when Vitellius, with a Roman army, crossed the Euphrates to restore Tiridates to the throne of Parthia (Tacitus, *Annals*, vi. 37). Cf. *Strabo*, xiv. 3.

[2] Aspendus was on the Eurymedon.

[3] About £12,000.

[4] Sidē was on the coast of Pamphylia, a little west of the river Melas.

neighbouring barbarians, but a speech peculiar to themselves, which had never before existed. From that time the Sidetans used to speak a foreign language unlike that of the neighbouring nations. Having left a garrison in Side, Alexander advanced to Syllium,[1] a strong place, containing a garrison of Grecian mercenaries as well as of native barbarians themselves. But he was unable to take Syllium offhand by a sudden assault, for he was informed on his march that the Aspendians refused to perform any of their agreements, and would neither deliver the horses to those who were sent to receive them, nor pay the money; but that they had collected their property out of the fields into the city, shut their gates against his men, and were repairing their walls where they had become dilapidated. Hearing this, he marched off to Aspendus.

CHAPTER XXVII.

Alexander in Phrygia and Pisidia.

The greater part of Aspendus had been built upon a strong and precipitous rock, at the very foot of which flows the river Eurymedon[2]; but round the rock, on the low ground, were many of the citizens' houses, surrounded by a small wall. As soon as they ascertained that Alexander was approaching, the inhabitants deserted the wall and the houses situated on the low ground, which they thought they were unable to protect; and they fled in a body to the rock. When he arrived with his forces, he passed within the deserted wall and

[1] Syllium was about five miles from the coast, between Aspendus and Side.

[2] This river is celebrated for the double victory of Cimon the Athenian over the Persians, in B.C. 466. See Smith's *Greece*, p. 252; *Grote*, vol. v. p. 163.

took up his quarters in the houses which had been abandoned by the Aspendians. When these saw that Alexander himself had come, contrary to their expectation, and that his camp was encircling them on all sides, they sent envoys to him, entreating him to form an agreement with them on the former terms. Alexander, considering the strength of the place, and how unprepared he was to undertake a long siege, entered into an agreement with them, though not on the same terms as before. For he ordered them to give him their most influential men as hostages, to hand over the horses which they had formerly agreed to give him, to pay 100 talents instead of fifty, to obey the viceroy appointed by him, and to pay an annual tribute to the Macedonians. Moreover he directed an inquiry to be held about the land which they were accused of holding by force, though it belonged of right to their neighbours.

When all these concessions had been made to him, he marched away to Perga, and thence set out for Phrygia, his route leading him past the city of Termessus. The people of this city are foreigners, of the Pisidian race, inhabiting a very lofty place, precipitous on every side; so that the road to the city is a difficult one. For a mountain stretches from the city as far as the road, where it suddenly stops short; and over against it rises another mountain, no less precipitous. These mountains form gates, as it were, upon the road; and it is possible for those who occupy these eminences even with a small guard to render the passage impracticable. On this occasion the Termissians had come out in a body, and were occupying both the mountains; seeing which, Alexander ordered the Macedonians to encamp there, armed as they were, imagining that the Termissians would not remain in a body when they saw them bivouacking, but that most of them would withdraw into their city, which was near, leaving upon the mountains only sufficient men to form a guard. And it turned out just as he conjectured; for most of them retired, and only a guard remained. He forthwith took the archers, the regiments of javelin-throwers, and the lighter hoplites, and led them against those who were guarding the pass. When these were attacked with missiles, they did not stand their ground, but abandoned the position. Alexander then passed through the defile, and encamped near the city.

CHAPTER XXVIII.

Operations in Pisidia.

While he was there, ambassadors came to him from the Selgians, who are also Pisidian barbarians, inhabiting a large city, and being warlike. Because they happened to be inveterate enemies to the Termessians they had despatched this embassy to Alexander, to treat for his friendship. He made a treaty with them, and from this time found them faithful allies in all his proceedings. Despairing of being able to capture Termessus without a great loss of time, he marched on to Sagalassus. This was also a large city, inhabited likewise by Pisidians; and though all the Pisidians are warlike, the men of this city were deemed the most so. On this occasion they had occupied the hill in front of the city, because it was no less strong than the walls, from which to attack the enemy; and there they were awaiting him. But Alexander drew up the phalanx of Macedonians in the following way: on the right wing, where he had himself taken up his position, he held the shield-bearing guards, and next to these he extended the foot Companions as far as the left wing, in the order that each of the generals had precedence in the array that day. On the left wing he stationed Amyntas, son of Arrhabaeus, as commander.

In front of the right wing were posted the archers and Agrianians, and in front of the left wing the Thracian javelin-throwers under the command of Sitalces. But the cavalry were no use to him in a place so rough and unfavourable. The Termessians also had come to the aid of the Pisidians, and arrayed themselves with them. Alexander had already made an attack upon the mountain which the Pisidians were occupying, advancing up the most abrupt part of the ascent, when the barbarians from an ambuscade attacked him on both wings, in a place where it was very easy for themselves to advance, but where the route was very difficult for their enemy. The archers, who were the first to approach, were put to rout, inasmuch as they were insufficiently armed; but the Agrianians stood their ground, for the Macedonian phalanx was already drawing near, at the head of which Alexander himself was seen. When the battle became a hand-to-hand one, though the barbarians were destitute of armour, they rushed against the Macedonian hoplites, and fell wounded on all sides. Then, indeed, they gave way, after about 500 of them had been killed. As they were nimble and well-acquainted with the locality, they effected their retreat without difficulty; whereas the Macedonians, on account of the heaviness of their arms and their ignorance of the roads, durst not pursue them vigorously. Alexander therefore held off from the fugitives, and took their city by storm. Of those with him, Cleander, the general of the archers, and about twenty others were slain. Alexander then marched against the rest of the Pisidians, and took some of their strongholds by storm; others he won over to him by granting them terms of capitulation.

CHAPTER XXIX.

ALEXANDER IN PHRYGIA.

THENCE he went into Phrygia, passing by the lake called Ascania,[1] in which salt is naturally concreted. The natives use this salt, and do not need the sea at all for this article. On the fifth day of his march, he arrived at Celaenae,[2] in which city there was a fortified rock, precipitous on all sides. This citadel was occupied by the viceroy of Phrygia with a garrison of 1,000 Carians and 100 Grecian mercenaries. These men despatched ambassadors to Alexander, promising to surrender the place to him, if succour did not reach them by a day which had been agreed upon with them, naming the day.[3] This arrangement seemed to Alexander more advantageous than to besiege the fortified rock, which was inaccessible on all sides to attack. At Celaenae he left a garrison of 1,500 soldiers. Remaining here ten days, he appointed Antigonus, son of Philip,[4] viceroy of Phrygia, placed Balacrus, son of Amyntas[5] as general over the Grecian allies in place of Antigonus, and then directed his march to Gordium.[6] He sent an order to Parmenio to meet

---

[1] This lake is mentioned by *Herodotus* (vii. 30), as being near the city of Anava. It is now called Burdur.

[2] Here Cyrus the Younger reviewed his Grecian forces and found them to be 11,000 hoplites and 2,000 peltasts. Here that prince had a palace and park, in which rose the river Maeander, close to the source of the Marsyas. See Xenophon (*Anab.*, i. 2); compare *Curtius* (iii. 1).

[3] *Curtius* (iii. 1) says they made a truce with Alexander for sixty days.

[4] Antigonus, called the One-eyed, was father of Demetrius Poliorcetes. On the division of Alexander's empire he received Phrygia, Lycia, and Pamphylia. He eventually acquired the whole of Asia Minor; but was defeated and slain at the battle of Ipsus by the allied forces of Cassander, Lysimachus, Ptolemy, and Seleucus (B.C. 301). When he was slain he was in his eighty-first year.

[5] Balacrus was left by Alexander to command in Egypt. See *Arrian* (iii. 5).

[6] The capital of the old Phrygian kings. It was rebuilt in the time of Augustus, and called Juliopolis.

him there with the forces under his command; an order which that general obeyed. The newly-married men also, who had been despatched to Macedonia, now arrived at Gordium, and with them another army which had been levied, and put under the command of Ptolemy, son of Seleucus,[1] Coenus, son of Polemocrates, and Meleager, son of Neoptolemus. This army consisted of 3,000 Macedonian foot-soldiers and 300 horse-soldiers, 200 Thessalian cavalry, and 150 Eleans under the command of Alcias the Elean.

Gordium is in the Phrygia which lies near the Hellespont, and is situated upon the river Sangarius, which takes its rise in Phrygia, but, flowing through the land of the Bithynian Thracians, falls into the Euxine Sea. Here an embassy reached Alexander from the Athenians, beseeching him to release to them the Athenian prisoners who had been captured at the river Granicus, fighting for the Persians, and were then in Macedonia serving in chains with the two thousand others captured in that battle. The envoys departed without obtaining their request on behalf of the prisoners for the present. For Alexander did not think it safe, whilst the war against the Persian was still going on, to relax in the slightest degree the terror with which he inspired the Greeks, who did not deem it unbecoming for them to serve as soldiers on behalf of the foreigners against Greece. However, he replied that whenever his present enterprise had been successfully achieved, they might then come as ambassadors to treat on behalf of the same persons.[2]

---

[1] This Ptolemy was killed at the battle of Issus (*Arrian*, ii. 110).

[2] We learn from *Curtius* (iv. 34) that Alexander released these prisoners at the request of ambassadors from Athens, who met him in Syria after his return from Egypt.

BOOK II.

CHAPTER I.

Capture of Mitylene by the Persians.—Death of Memnon.

Soon after this, Memnon, whom King Darius had appointed commander of the whole fleet and of the entire sea-coast, with the design of moving the seat of war into Macedonia and Greece, acquired possession of Chios, which was surrendered to him by treachery. Thence he sailed to Lesbos and brought over to his side all the cities of the island,[1] except Mitylene, the inhabitants of which did not submit to him. When he had gained these cities over, he turned his attention to Mitylene; and walling off the city from the rest of the island by constructing a double stockade from sea to sea, he easily got the mastery on the land side by building five camps. A part of his fleet guarded their harbour, and, intercepting the ships passing by, he kept the rest of his fleet as a guard off Sigrium,[2] the headland of Lesbos, where is the best landing-place for trading vessels from Chios, Geraestus,[3] and Malea.[4] By this means he deprived the Mitylenaeans of all hope of succour by sea. But mean-

[1] The other cities of Lesbos were Methymna, Antissa, Eresus, and Pyrrha.

[2] Now called Cape Sigri, the west point of the island.

[3] The southern point of Euboea, now called Cape Mandili. Cf. Homer (*Odyss.*, iii. 177).

[4] The south-eastern point of Laconia, now called Cape Malia di St. Angelo. It was dreaded by ancient mariners: see Homer (*Odyssey*, ix. 80); Ovid (*Amores*, ii. 16, 24); Vergil (*Aeneid*, v. 193). There was a saying:—Μαλέας δὲ κάμψας ἐπιλάθου τῶν οἴκαδε (*Strabo*, viii. p. 250).

time he himself fell ill and died, and his death at that crisis was exceedingly injurious to the king's interests. Nevertheless Autophradates, and Pharnabazus, son of Artabazus, prosecuted the siege with vigour. To the latter indeed, Memnon, when dying, had entrusted his command, as he was his sister's son, till Darius should come to some decision on the matter. The Mitylenaeans, therefore, being excluded from the land, and being blockaded on the sea by many ships lying at anchor, sent to Pharnabazus and came to the following agreement:—That the auxiliary troops which had come to their aid from Alexander should depart, that the citizens should demolish the pillars on which the treaty made by them with Alexander was inscribed,[1] that they should become allies of Darius on the terms of the peace which was made with King Darius in the time of Antalcidas,[2] and that their exiles should return from banishment on condition of receiving back half the property which they possessed when they were banished. Upon these terms the compact was made between the Mitylenaeans and the Persians. But as soon as Pharnabazus and Autophradates once got within the city, they introduced a garrison with Lycomedes, a Rhodian, as its commandant. They also appointed Diogenes, one of the exiles, to be despot of the city, and exacted money from the Mitylenaeans, taking part of it by violence for themselves from the wealthy citizens, and laying the rest as a tax upon the community.

---

[1] In accordance with the convention of Corinth. Compare next chapter. For the pillars compare *Herodotus* (ii. 102, 106); *Thucydides* v. 18, 47, 56); Aristophanes (*Acharnians*, 727; *Lysistrata*, 513).

[2] This treaty was concluded by the Spartans with the king of Persia, B.C. 387. It was designed to break up the Athenian supremacy. It stipulated that all the Grecian colonies in Asia were to be given to the Persian king; the Athenians were to retain only Imbros, Lesbos, and Scyros; and all the other Grecian cities were to be autonomous. See Xenophon (*Hellenics*, iv. 8; v. 1).

CHAPTER II.

The Persians Capture Tenedus.—They are Defeated at Sea.

After accomplishing this, Pharnabazus sailed to Lycia, taking with him the Grecian mercenaries; but Autophradates sailed to the other islands. Meantime Darius sent Thymondas, son of Mentor,[1] down to the maritime districts, to take over the Grecian auxiliaries from Pharnabazus and to lead them up to him; and to tell Pharnabazus that he was to be the ruler of all that Memnon had ruled. So Pharnabazus handed over to him the Grecian auxiliaries and then sailed to join Autophradates and the fleet. When they met, they despatched Datames, a Persian, with ten ships to the islands called Cyclades,[2] whilst they with 100 sailed to Tenedus.[3] Having sailed into the harbour of Tenedus which is called Borēus, they sent a message to the inhabitants, commanding them to demolish the pillars on which the treaty made by them with Alexander and the Greeks was inscribed, and to observe in regard to Darius the terms of the peace which they had ratified with the king of Persia in the time of Antalcidas. The Tenedians preferred to be on terms of amity with Alexander and the Greeks; but in the present crisis it seemed impossible to save themselves except by yielding to the Persians, since Hegelochus, who had been commissioned by Alexander to collect another naval force, had not yet gathered so large a fleet as to warrant them in expecting any speedy succour from him. Accordingly Pharnabazus made the Tenedians comply with his demands rather from fear than good-will.

---

[1] Cf. ii. 13 infra.

[2] "Cyclades ideo sic appellatae, quod omnes ambiunt Delon partu deorum insignem."—*Ammianus*, xxii. 8, 2. Cf. Horace (*Carm.*, i. 14, 19; iii. 28, 14).

[3] Cf. Vergil (*Aeneid*, ii. 21).

Meantime Proteas, son of Andronicus, by command of Antipater,[1] succeeded in collecting ships of war from Euboea and the Peloponnese, so that there might be some protection both for the islands and for Greece itself, if the foreigners attacked them by sea, as it was reported they intended to do. Learning that Datames with ten ships was moored near Siphnus,[2] Proteas set out by night with fifteen from Chalcis on the Euripus,[3] and approaching the island of Cythnus[4] at dawn, he spent the day there in order to get more certain information of the movements of the ten ships, resolving at the same time to fall upon the Phoenicians by night, when he would be likely to strike them with greater terror. Having discovered with certainty that Datames was moored with his ships at Siphnus, he sailed thither while it was still dark, and just at the very dawn fell upon them when they least expected it, and captured eight of the ships, men and all. But Datames, with the other two triremes, escaped by stealth at the beginning of the attack made by the ships with Proteas, and reached the rest of the Persian fleet in safety.

---

[1] The regent of Macedonia and Greece during Alexander's absence.

[2] One of the Cyclades, a little to the north-east of Melos. It was noted for the low morality of its inhabitants. See Aristophanes (*Fragment*, 558; on the authority of Suidas).

[3] Euripus properly means any narrow sea, where the ebb and flow of the tide is violent. The name was especially applied to the strait between Boeotia and Euboea, where the ancients asserted the sea ebbed and flowed seven times in the day (*Strabo*, ix. 1). Modern observers have noticed these extraordinary tides. The present name of the island, Negropont, is the Italian name formed from Egripo, the modern corruption of Euripus. Cf. Cicero, *pro Muraena*, xvii. :—Quod fretum, quem Euripum tot motus, tantas, tam varias habere putatis agitationes fluctuum, quantas perturbationes et quantos aestus habet ratio comitiorum. Aristotle, *Ethica Nicomachea*, ix. 6 :—*τῶν τοιούτων γὰρ μένει τὰ βουλήματα, καὶ οὐ μεταῤῥεῖ ὥσπερ* Εὔριπος.

[4] One of the Cyclades, about half-way between Attica and Siphnus.

CHAPTER III.

Alexander at Gordium.

When Alexander arrived at Gordium, he was seized with an ardent desire to go up into the citadel, which contained the palace of Gordius and his son Midas. He was also desirous of seeing the wagon of Gordius and the cord which bound the yoke to the wagon. There was a great deal of talk about this wagon among the neighbouring population. It was said that Gordius was a poor man among the ancient Phrygians, who had a small piece of land to till, and two yoke of oxen. He used one of these in ploughing and the other to draw the wagon. On one occasion, while he was ploughing, an eagle settled upon the yoke,[1] and remained sitting there until the time came for unyoking the oxen. Being alarmed at the sight, he went to the Telmissian soothsayers to consult them about the sign from the deity; for the Telmissians were skilful in interpreting the meaning of Divine manifestations, and the power of divination has been bestowed not only upon the men, but also upon their wives and children from generation to generation. When Gordius was driving his wagon near a certain village of the Telmissians, he met a maiden fetching water from the spring, and to her he related how the sign of the eagle had appeared to him. As she herself was of the prophetic race, she instructed him to return to the very spot and offer sacrifice to Zeus the king. Gordius requested her to accompany him and direct him how to perform the sacrifice. He offered the sacrifice in the way the girl suggested, and afterwards married her. A son was born to them named Midas, who, when he arrived at the age of maturity, was both handsome and valiant. At this time the Phrygians were harassed by

[1] *ἐπιπτῆναι*, a poetical form for *ἐπιπτέσθαι*.

civil discord, and consulting the oracle, they were told that a wagon would bring them a king, who would put an end to their discord.[1] While they were still deliberating about this very matter, Midas arrived with his father and mother, and stopped near the assembly with the very wagon in question. They, interpreting the oracular response to refer to him, decided that this was the person whom the god told them the wagon would bring. They therefore appointed Midas king; and he, putting an end to their discord, dedicated his father's wagon in the citadel as a thank-offering to Zeus the king for sending the eagle. In addition to this the following report was current concerning the wagon, that whosoever could loosen the cord with which the yoke of the wagon was tied, was destined to be the ruler of Asia. The cord was made of cornel bark, and neither end nor beginning to it could be seen. It is said by some that when Alexander could find out no way to loosen the cord and yet was unwilling to allow it to remain unloosened, lest it should exercise some disturbing influence upon the multitude, he struck the cord with his sword and cut it through, saying that it had been untied by him. But Aristobulus says that he pulled out the pin of the wagon-pole, which was a wooden peg driven right through it, holding the cord together. Having done this, he drew out the yoke from the wagon-pole. How Alexander performed the feat in connection with this cord, I cannot affirm with confidence. At any rate both he and his troops departed from the wagon as if the oracular prediction concerning the untying of the cord had been fulfilled. Moreover, that very night, the thunder and lightning were signs from heaven of its fulfilment; and for this reason Alexander offered sacrifice on the following day to the gods who had revealed the signs and

[1] Cf. *Justin*, xi. 7.

assured him that the cord had been untied in a proper way.[1]

CHAPTER IV.

Conquest of Cappadocia.—Alexander's Illness at Tarsus.

The next day he sent out to Ancyra[2] in Galatia, where he was met by an embassy from the Paphlagonians, offering to surrender their nation to him and to enter into an alliance with him; but they requested him not to invade their land with his forces. He therefore commanded them to submit to the authority of Calas, the viceroy of Phrygia. Marching thence into Cappadocia, he subjugated all that part of it which lies on this side of the river Halys,[3] and much of that which lies beyond it. Having appointed Sabictas viceroy of Cappadocia, he advanced to the Gates of Cilicia,[4] and when he arrived at the Camp of Cyrus, who (went) with Xenophon,[5] and saw that the Gates were occupied by strong guards, he left Parmenio there with the regiments of infantry which were more heavily armed; and about the first watch, taking the shield-bearing guards, the archers, and the Agrianians, he advanced by night to the Gates, in order to fall upon the guards when they least expected it. However, his advance was not unobserved; but his

[1] Cf. *Curtius*, iii. 2 (Zumpt's edition); Plutarch (*Alexander*, 18).

[2] Now called Angora. In the time of Alexander the country was named Great Phrygia, the term Galatia being afterwards applied to it, from the fact that it was conquered by the Gauls in the 3rd century B.C.

[3] Now called Kizil-Irmak, *i.e.* the Red River. It is the largest river in Asia Minor, and separated the empires of Persia and Lydia, until the conquest of the latter by Cyrus.

[4] The chief pass over the Taurus between Cappadocia and Cilicia. It is more than 3,600 feet above the sea-level. Its modern name is Golek-Boghaz. Cf. *Curtius*, iii. 9–11. It is called Tauri Pylae by Cicero (*Epistolae ad Atticum*, v. 20, 2).

[5] See Xenophon (*Anabasis*, i. 2, 20, 21).

boldness served him equally well, for the guards, perceiving that Alexander was advancing in person, deserted their post and set off in flight. At dawn next day he passed through the Gates with all his forces and descended into Cilicia.[1] Here he was informed that Arsames had previously intended to preserve Tarsus for the Persians; but when he heard that Alexander had already passed through the Gates, he resolved to abandon the city; and that the Tarsians were therefore afraid he would turn to plunder their city and afterwards evacuate it. Hearing this, Alexander led his cavalry and the lightest of his light infantry to Tarsus with a forced march; consequently Arsames, hearing of his start, fled with speed from Tarsus to King Darius without inflicting any injury upon the city.

Alexander now fell ill from the toils he had undergone, according to the account of Aristobulus; but other authors say that while he was very hot and in profuse perspiration he leaped into the river Cydnus[2] and swam, being eager to bathe in its water. This river flows through the midst of the city; and as its source is in mount Taurus and it flows through a clean district, it is cold and its water is clear. Alexander therefore was seized with convulsions, accompanied with high fever and continuous sleeplessness. None of the physicians thought he was likely to survive,[3] except Philip, an

---

[1] *Curtius* (iii. 11) says, that Alexander wondered at his own good fortune, when he observed how easily Arsames might have blocked up the pass. Cyrus the Younger was equally fortunate in finding this impregnable pass abandoned by Syennesis, king of Cilicia. See Xenophon (*Anabasis*, i. 2, 21).

[2] Now called Tersoos-Chai. See *Curtius*, iii. 12; *Justin*, xi. 8; and Lucian (*De Domo*, i.). At Tarsus the emperor Julian was buried. See *Ammianus*, xxv. 10, 5.

[3] Probably none of the physicians would venture to prescribe, for fear of being held responsible for his death, which seemed likely to ensue. Nine years after, when Hephaestion died of fever at Ecbatana, Alexander

Acarnanian, a physician in attendance on the king, and very much trusted by him in medical matters, who also enjoyed a great reputation in the army in general affairs. This man wished to administer a purgative draught to Alexander, and the king ordered him to administer it. While Philip was preparing the cup, a letter was given to the king from Parmenio, warning him to beware of Philip; for he heard that the physician had been bribed by Darius to poison Alexander with medicine. But he, having read the letter, and still holding it in his hand, took the cup which contained the medicine and gave Philip the letter to read. While Philip was reading the news from Parmenio, Alexander drank the potion. It was at once evident to the king that the physician was acting honourably in giving the medicine, for he was not alarmed at the letter, but only so much the more exhorted the king to obey all the other prescriptions which he might give, promising that his life would be saved if he obeyed his instructions. Alexander was purged by the draught, and his illness then took a favourable turn. He afterwards proved to Philip that he was a faithful friend to him; and to the rest of those about he proved that he had perfect confidence in his friends by refusing to entertain any suspicion of their fidelity; and at the same time he showed that he could meet death with dauntless courage.[1]

---

caused the physician who had attended him to be crucified. See *Arrian*, vii. 14; Plutarch (*Alexander*, 72).

[1] Cf. *Curtius*, iii. 14–16; *Diodorus*, xvii. 31; *Justin*, xi. 8; Plutarch (*Alex.*, 19). The barbarous conduct of Alexander towards Philotas four years after, when contrasted with his noble confidence in Philip, shows the bad effect of his unparalleled success, upon his moral character.

CHAPTER V.

Alexander at the Tomb of Sardanapalus.—Proceedings in Cilicia.

After this he sent Parmenio to the other Gates which separate the land of the Cilicians from that of the Assyrians, in order to capture them before the enemy could do so, and to guard the pass.[1] He gave him the allied infantry, the Grecian mercenaries, the Thracians who were under the command of Sitalces, and the Thessalian cavalry. He afterwards marched from Tarsus, and on the first day arrived at the city of Anchialus.[2] According to report, this city was founded by Sardanapalus the Assyrian;[3] and both from the circumference and from the foundations of the walls it is evident that a large city had been founded and that it had reached a great pitch of power. Also near the wall of Anchialus was the monument of Sardanapalus, upon the top of which stood the statue of that king with the hands joined to each other just as they are joined for clapping.[4] An inscription had been placed upon it in Assyrian characters,[5] which the Assyrians asserted to be in metre. The meaning which the words expressed was this:—"Sardanapalus, son of Anacyndaraxas, built Anchialus and Tarsus in one day; but do thou, O stranger, eat, drink, and

---

1 This pass was called the *Syrian Gates*, lying between the shore of the Gulf of Issus and Mount Amanus. Cyrus the Younger was six days marching from Tarsus through this pass. See Xenophon (*Anab.*, i. 4). The Greeks often gave the name of Assyria to the country usually called by them Syria. The Hebrew name for it is Aram (high-land). Cf. Cicero (*ad Diversos*, xv. 4, 4); *Diod.*, xiv. 21.

2 A city of Cilicia on the coast, a little west of the mouth of the Cydnus.

3 Said to have been the last of the Assyrian kings.

4 Cf. *Strabo* (xiv. 5) for a description of this statue.

5 This was, doubtless, the arrow-headed writing which has been deciphered by Sir Henry Rawlinson. Cf. *Herodotus*, iv. 87; *Thucydides*, iv. 50.

play, since all other human things are not worth this!" referring, as in a riddle, to the empty sound which the hands make in clapping. It was also said that the word translated *play* had been expressed by a more lewd one in the Assyrian language.

From Anchialus Alexander went to Soli,[1] into which city he introduced a garrison, and imposed upon the inhabitants a fine of 200 talents of silver,[2] because they were more inclined to favour the Persians than himself. Then, having taken three regiments of Macedonian infantry, all the archers, and the Agrianians, he marched away thence against the Cilicians, who were holding the mountains; and in seven days in all, having expelled some by force, and having brought the rest over by composition, he marched back to Soli. Here he ascertained that Ptolemy and Asander[3] had gained the mastery over Orontobates the Persian who was guarding the citadel of Halicarnassus, and was also holding Myndus, Caunus, Thera, and Callipolis.[4] Cos and Triopium[5] also had been brought into subjection. They wrote to inform him that Orontobates had been worsted in a great battle; that about 700 of his infantry and 50 of his cavalry had been killed, and not less than 1,000 taken prisoners. In Soli Alexander offered sacrifice to Asclepius,[6] conducting

---

[1] Now called Mezetlu. It was a Rhodian colony on the coast of Cilicia, between the rivers Cydnus and Lamus. It was afterwards re-named Pompeiopolis. The birthplace of Philemon, Aratus, and Chrysippus.

[2] About £49,000.

[3] Asander was a nephew of Parmenio. He afterwards brought a reinforcement to Alexander from Greece (*Arrian*, iv. 7). After the king's death he obtained the rule of Caria, but joining the party of Ptolemy and Cassander, he was defeated by Antigonus, B.C. 313.

[4] These were Carian cities.

[5] Cos, the birthplace of Apelles and Hippocrates, is one of the group of islands called Sporades, off the coast of Caria. Triopium is the promontory terminating the peninsula of Cnidus, the south-west headland of Asia Minor. Cf. *Tibullus*, ii. 3, 57; *Propertius*, i. 2, 1; ii. 1, 5; *Herodotus*, i. 174.

[6] Called by the Romans, Aesculapius. He was the god of the medical

a procession of the entire army, celebrating a torch race, and superintending a gymnastic and musical contest. He granted the Solians the privilege of a democratical constitution; and then marched away to Tarsus, despatching the cavalry under Philotas to march through the Aleian plain to the river Pyramus.[1] But he himself with the infantry and the royal squadron of cavalry came to Magarsus, where he offered sacrifice to the Magarsian Athena. Thence he marched to Mallus, where he rendered to Amphilochus the sacrificial honours due to a hero.[2] He also arrested those who were creating a sedition among the citizens, and thus put a stop to it. He remitted the tribute which they were paying to King Darius, because the Malliotes were a colony of the Argives, and he himself claimed to have sprung from Argos, being a descendant of Heracles.

CHAPTER VI.

Alexander Advances to Myriandrus.—Darius Marches against him.

While he was still at Mallus, he was informed that Darius was encamped with all his forces at Sochi, a place in the land of Assyria, distant about two days' march from the Assyrian Gates.[3] Then indeed he collected the Companions and told them what was reported about Darius

---

art, and no doubt Alexander sacrificed to him, and celebrated the games, in gratitude for his recovery from the fever he had had at Tarsus.

[1] This plain is mentioned in *Homer*, vi. 201; *Herodotus*, vi. 95. The large river Pyramus, now called Jihan, falls into the sea near Mallus.

[2] Mallus was said to have been founded by Amphilochus after the fall of Troy. This hero was the son of Amphiaraus, the great prophet of Argos, whom Zeus is said to have made immortal. Magarsus, of Megarsa, was the port of Mallus. The difference of meaning between θύειν and ἐναγίζειν is seen from *Herodotus*, ii. 44; Plutarch (*Moralia*, ii. p. 857 D).

[3] Usually called the Syrian Gates. See chap. v. note [1] supra.

and his army. They urged him to lead them on as they were, without delay. At that time be commended them, and broke up the conference; but next day he led them forward against Darius and the Persians. On the second day he passed through the Gates and encamped near the city of Myriandrus;[1] but in the night a heavy tempest and a violent storm of wind and rain occurred which detained him in his camp. Darius, on the other hand, had been spending a long time with his army, having chosen a plain in the land of Assyria which stretches out in every direction, suitable for the immense size of his army and convenient for the evolutions of cavalry. Amyntas, son of Antiochus, the deserter from Alexander, advised him not to abandon this position, because there was plenty of room for the great multitude of the Persians and for the vast quantity of their baggage. So Darius remained. But as Alexander made a long stay at Tarsus on account of his illness, and not a short one at Soli, where he offered sacrifice and conducted his army in procession, and moreover spent some time in marching against the Cilician mountaineers, Darius was induced to swerve from his resolution. He was also not unwilling to be led to form whatever decision was most agreeable to his own wishes; and being influenced by those who gave him the advice which they thought would be pleasant to him, without consideration of its utility (for kings will always have associates to give them bad advice),[2] he came to the conclusion that Alexander was no longer desirous of advancing further, but was shrinking from an encounter on learning that Darius himself was marching against him. On all sides they were urging him on, asserting that he would trample down the army of the Macedonians

---

[1] A city on the Gulf of Issus, being a settlement of the Phoenicians. *Herodotus* (iv. 38) calls the gulf the Myriandric Gulf. Cf. Xenophon (*Anab.*, i. 4).

[2] Cf. *Arrian*, vii. 29; *Curtius*, viii. 17.

with his cavalry.[1] Nevertheless, Amyntas, at any rate, confidently affirmed that Alexander would certainly come to any place where he heard Darius might be; and he exhorted him by all means to stay where he was. But the worse advice, because at the immediate time it was more pleasant to hear, prevailed; moreover he was led by some divine influence into that locality where he derived little advantage from his cavalry and from the sheer number of his men, javelins and bows, and where he could not even exhibit the mere magnificence of his army, but surrendered to Alexander and his troops an easy victory. For it was already decreed by fate that the Persians should be deprived of the rule of Asia by the Macedonians, just as the Medes had been deprived of it by the Persians, and still earlier the Assyrians by the Medes.

CHAPTER VII.

Darius at Issus.—Alexander's Speech to his Army.

Darius crossed the mountain range by what are called the Amanic Gates, and advancing towards Issus, came without being noticed to the rear of Alexander.[2] Having reached Issus, he captured as many of the Macedonians as had

[1] Aeschines tells us in his speech against Ctesiphon (p. 552), that the anti-Macedonian statesmen at Athens at this time received letters from their friends, stating that Alexander was caught and pinned up in Cilicia. He says Demosthenes went about showing these letters and boasting of the news. Josephus (*Antiquities of the Jews*, xi. 7, 3) says that "not only Sanballat at Samaria but all those that were in Asia also were persuaded that the Macedonians would not so much as come to a battle with the Persians, on account of their multitude."

[2] There are two passes by which the eastern countries are entered from Cilicia; one on the south, near the sea, leads into Syria. The other pass lies more to the north, and leads to the country near the Euphrates. The latter was called the Amanic, and the former the Syrian gate. Alexander had just passed through the Syrian gate in order to march against Darius, at the very time that Darius was descending into

been left behind there on account of illness. These he cruelly mutilated and slew. Next day he proceeded to the river Pinarus. As soon as Alexander heard that Darius was in his rear, because the news did not seem to him trustworthy, he embarked some of the Companions in a ship with thirty oars, and sent them back to Issus, to observe whether the report was true. The men who sailed in the thirty-oared ship discovered the Persians encamped there more easily, because the sea in this part takes the form of a bay. They therefore brought back word to Alexander that Darius was at hand. Alexander then called together the generals, the commanders of cavalry, and the leaders of the Grecian allies, and exhorted them to take courage from the dangers which they had already surmounted, asserting that the struggle would be between themselves who had been previously victorious and a foe who had already been beaten; and that the deity was acting the part of general on their behalf better than himself, by putting it into the mind of Darius to move his forces from the spacions plain and shut them up in a narrow place, where there was sufficient room for them to deepen their phalanx by marching from front to rear, but where their vast multitude would be useless to their enemy in battle. He added that their foes were similar to them neither in strength nor in courage; for the Macedonians, who had long been practised in warlike toils accompanied with danger, were coming into close conflict with Persians and Medes, men who had become enervated by a long course of luxurious ease; and, to crown all, they, being freemen, were about to engage in battle with men who were slaves. He said, moreover, that the Greeks who were in the two armies would not be fighting for the

---

Cilicia by the Amanic gate, and occupying Issus with his advanced guard. Alexander, who had reached Myriandrus in Syria, made a countermarch to meet Darius. Plutarch (*Alex.*, 20) says that they missed each other in the night, which is quite a mistake.

same objects; for those with Darius were braving danger for pay, and that pay not high; whereas, those on their side were voluntarily defending the interests of Greece. Again, of foreigners, the Thracians, Paeonians, Illyrians, and Agrianians, who were the most robust and warlike of men in Europe, were about to be arrayed against the most sluggish and effeminate races of Asia. In addition to all this, Alexander was commanding in the field against Darius. These things he enumerated as evidences of their superiority in the struggle; and then he began to point out the great rewards they would win from the danger to be incurred. For he told them that on that occasion they would overcome, not merely the viceroys of Darius, nor the cavalry drawn up at the Granicus, nor the 20,000 Grecian mercenaries, but would overcome all the available forces of the Persians and Medes, as well as all the other races subject to them dwelling in Asia, and the Great King present in person. After this conflict nothing would be left for them to do, except to take possession of all Asia, and to put an end to their many labours. In addition to this, he reminded them of their brilliant achievements in their collective capacity in days gone by; and if any man had individually performed any distinguished feat of valour from love of glory, he mentioned him by name in commendation of the deed.[1] He then recapitulated as modestly as possible his own daring deeds in the various battles. He is also said to have reminded them of Xenophon and the ten thousand men who accompanied him, asserting that the latter were in no way comparable with them either in number or in general excellence. Besides, they had had with them neither Thessalian, Boeotian, Peloponnesian, Macedonian, or Thracian horsemen, nor any of the other cavalry which was in the Macedonian army; nor had they any archers

---

[1] Cf. Sallust (*Catilina*, 59); Caesar (*Bell. Gall.*, ii. 25).

or slingers except a few Cretans and Rhodians, and even these were got ready by Xenophon on the spur of the moment in the very crisis of danger.[1] And yet even these put the king and all his forces to rout close to Babylon[2] itself, and succeeded in reaching the Euxine Sea after defeating all the races which lay in their way as they were marching down thither. He also adduced whatever other arguments were suitable for a great commander to use in order to encourage brave men in such a critical moment before the perils of battle. They urged him to lead them against the foe without delay, coming from all sides to grasp the king's right hand, and encouraging him by their promises.

CHAPTER VIII.

Arrangement of the Hostile Armies.

Alexander then ordered his soldiers to take their dinner, and having sent a few of his horsemen and archers forward to the Gates to reconnoitre the road in the rear, he took the whole of his army and marched in the night to occupy the pass again. When about midnight he had again got possession of it, he caused the army to rest the remainder of the night there upon the rocks, havin posted vigilant sentries. At the approach of dawn he began to descend from the pass along the road; and as long as the space was narrow everywhere, he led his army in column, but when the mountains parted so as to leave a plain between them, he kept on opening out the column into the phalanx, marching one line of heavy

---

[1] See Xenophon (*Anab.*, iii. 3).

[2] At Cunaxa. *Xenophon* (ii. 2, 6) does not mention the name of the place where the battle was fought, but says that he was informed it was only 360 stadia (about 40 miles) from Babylon. We get the name Cunaxa from Plutarch (*Life of Artaxerxes*, c. 8), who says it was 500 stadia (about 58 miles) from Babylon.

armed infantry after another up into line towards the mountain on the right and towards the sea on the left. Up to this time his cavalry had been ranged behind the infantry; but when they advanced into the open country, he began to draw up his army in order of battle. First, upon the right wing near the mountain he placed his infantry guard and the shield-bearers, under the command of Nicanor, son of Parmenio; next to these the regiment of Coenus, and close to them that of Perdiccas. These troops were posted as far as the middle of the heavy-armed infantry to one beginning from the right. On the left wing first stood the regiment of Amyntas, then that of Ptolemy, and close to this that of Meleager. The infantry on the left had been placed under the command of Craterus; but Parmenio held the chief direction of the whole left wing. This general had been ordered not to abandon the sea, so that they might not be surrounded by the foreigners, who were likely to outflank them on all sides by their superior numbers.[1]

But as soon as Darius was certified of Alexander's approach for battle, he conveyed about 30,000 of his cavalry and with them 20,000 of his light-armed infantry across the river Pinarus, in order that he might be able to draw up the rest of his forces with ease. Of the heavy armed infantry, he placed first the 30,000 Greek mercenaries to oppose the phalanx of the Macedonians, and on both sides of these he placed 60,000 of the men called Cardaces,[2] who were also heavy-armed infantry.[3] For

---

[1] Callisthenes the historian, who accompanied Alexander into Asia, states that the breadth of the plain between the mountain and the sea was not more than fourteen stadia, or a little more than one English mile and a half. See *Polybius*, xii. 17.

[2] These seem to have been foreign mercenaries. See *Polybius*, v. 79, 82; *Strabo*, xv. 3. Hesychius says that they were not a nation, but foreigners serving for pay.

[3] Callisthenes—as quoted in *Polybius*, xii. 18—reckoned the Grecian mercenaries of Darius at 30,000, and the cavalry at 30,000. Arrian

the place where they were posted was able to contain only this number in a single phalanx.[1] He also posted 20,000 men near the mountain on their left and facing Alexander's right. Some of these troops were also in the rear of Alexander's army; for the mountain near which they were posted in one part sloped a great way back and formed a sort of bay, like a bay in the sea, and afterwards bending forwards caused the men who had been posted at the foot of it to be behind Alexander's right wing. The remaining multitude of Darius's light-armed and heavy-armed infantry was marshalled by nations to an unserviceable depth and placed behind the Grecian mercenaries and the Persian army arranged in phalanx. The whole of the army with Darius was said to number about 600,000 fighting men.[2]

As Alexander advanced, he found that the ground spread out a little in breadth, and he accordingly brought up his horsemen, both those called Companions, and the Thessalians as well as the Macedonians, and posted them with himself on the right wing. The Peloponnesians and the rest of the allied force of Greeks he sent to

---

enumerates 90,000 heavy-armed, not inclnding the cavalry. Yet Polybius tries to prove that there was not room even for the 60,000 troops mentioned by Callisthenes,

[1] "The depth of this single phalanx is not given, nor do we know the exact width of the ground which it occupied. Assuming a depth of sixteen, and one pace in breadth to each soldier, 4,000 men would stand in the breadth of a stadium of 250 paces; and therefore 80,000 men in a breadth of twenty stadia. Assuming a depth of twenty-six, 6,500 men would stand in the breadth of the stadium, and therefore 90,000 in a total breadth of 14 stadia, which is that given by Kallisthenes. Mr. Kinneir states that the breadth between Mount Amanus and the sea varies between one and a half mile and three miles."—*Grote.*

[2] *Diodorus* (xvii. 31), and Plutarch (*Alex.*, 18), give the same number; but *Justin* (xi. 9) says the Persians numbered 400,000 infantry and 100,000 cavalry. It took five days for them to cross the Euphrates, over bridges of boats (*Curtius*, iii. 17). The money alone of the king required 600 mules and 300 camels to convey it (*Curtius*, iii. 8).

Parmenio on the left. When Darius had marshalled his phalanx, by a pre-concerted signal he recalled the cavalry which he had posted in front of the river for the express purpose of rendering the arranging of his army easy. Most of these he placed on the right wing near the sea facing Parmenio; because here the ground was more suitable for the evolutions of cavalry. A certain part of them also he led up to the mountain towards the left. But when they were seen to be useless there on account of the narrowness of the ground, he ordered most of these also to ride round to the right wing and join their comrades there. Darius himself occupied the centre of the whole army, inasmuch as it was the custom for the kings of Persia to take up that position, the reason of which arrangement has been recorded by Xenophon, son of Gryllus.[1]

CHAPTER IX.

Alexander Changes the Disposition of his Forces.

Meantime when Alexander perceived that nearly all the Persian cavalry had changed their ground and gone to his left towards the sea, and that on his side only the Peloponnesians and the rest of the Grecian cavalry were posted there, he sent the Thessalian cavalry thither with speed, ordering them not to ride along before the front of the whole array, lest they should be seen by the enemy to be shifting their ground, but to proceed by stealth in the rear of the phalanx.[2] In front of the cavalry on the right, he posted the lancers under the command of Protomachus, and the Paeonians under that of Aristo; and of the infantry, the archers under the direction of Antiochus, and the Agrianians under that of

[1] Cf. *Arrian*, iii. 11; and Xenophon (*Anab.*, i. 8, 21, 22).

[2] See Donaldson's *New Cratylus*, sect. 178.

Attalus. Some of the cavalry and archers also he drew up so as to form an angle with the centre[1] towards the mountain which was in the rear; so on the right his phalanx had been drawn up separated into two wings, the one fronting Darius and the main body of Persians beyond the river, and the other facing those who had been posted at the mountain in their rear. On the left wing the infantry consisting of the Cretan archers and the Thracians under command of Sitalces were posted in front; and before these the cavalry towards the left. The Grecian mercenaries were drawn up as a reserve for all of them. When he perceived that the phalanx towards the right was too thin, and it seemed likely that the Persians would outflank him here considerably, he ordered two squadrons of the Companion cavalry, viz. the Anthemusian,[2] of which Peroedas, son of Menestheus, was captain, and that which was called Leugaean, under the command of Pantordanus, son of Cleander, to proceed from the centre to the right without being seen. Having also marched the archers, part of the Agrianians and of the Grecian mercenaries up along his right in the front, he extended his phalanx beyond the wing of the Persians. But when those who had been posted upon the mountain did not descend, a charge was made by a few of the Agrianians and archers at Alexander's order, by which they were easily put to the rout from the foot of the mountain. As they fled to the summit he decided that he could make use of the men who had been drawn up to keep these in check, to fill up the ranks of his phalanx.

---

1 Cf. Xenophon (*Cyropaedia*, vii. 1, 6).

2 In describing the battle of Arbela, Arrian mentions eight distinct squadrons of Macedonian heavy cavalry, which was known by the name of the Companions. Among the squadrons several, if not all, were named after particular towns or districts of Macedonia, as here, Anthemus, and Leuge. We also find mention of the squadrons of Bottiaea, Amphipolis, and Apollonia. See also *Arrian*, i. 2; i. 12; iii. 11.

He thought it quite sufficient to post 300 horsemen to watch the meu on the mountain.

CHAPTER X.

Battle of Issus.

Having thus marshalled his men, he caused them to rest for some time, and then led them forward, as he thought the enemy's approach was very slow. For Darius was no longer leading the foreigners against him, as he had arranged them at first, but he remained in his position, upon the bank of the river, which was in many parts steep and precipitous; and in certain places, where it seemed more easy to ascend, he extended a stockade along it. By this it was at once evident to Alexander's men that Darius had become cowed in spirit.[1] But when the armies at length met in conflict, Alexander rode about in every direction to exhort his troops to show their valour; mentioning with befitting epithets the names, not only of the generals, but also those of the captains of cavalry and infantry, and of the Grecian mercenaries as many as were more distinguished either by rank or merit. From all sides arose a shout not to delay but to attack the enemy. At first he still led them on in close array with measured step, although he had the forces of Darius already in full view, lest by a more hasty march any part of the phalanx should fluctuate from the line[2] and get separated from the rest. But when they came within range of darts, Alexander himself and those around him being posted on the right wing, advanced first into the river with a run,

---

[1] *τῇ γνώμῃ δεδουλωμένος.* An expression imitated from *Thucydides*, iv. 34; compare *Arrian*, iii. 11; v. 19; vi. 16, where the same words are used of Porus and the Indians.

[2] *κυμῆναι τῆς φάλαγγος.* An expression imitated from Xenophon (*Anab.*, i. 8, 18). It is praised by Demetrius (*De Elocutione*, 84). Krüger reads *ἐκκυμῆναι.* Cf. Plutarch (*Pompey*, 69).

in order to alarm the Persians by the rapidity of their onset, and by coming sooner to close conflict to receive little damage from the archers. And it turned out just as Alexander had conjectured; for as soon as the battle became a hand-to-hand one, the part of the Persian army stationed on the left wing was put to rout; and here Alexander and his men won a brilliant victory. But the Grecian mercenaries serving under Darius attacked the Macedonians at the point where they saw their phalanx especially disordered. For the Macedonian phalanx had been broken and disjoined towards the right wing; because Alexander had charged into the river with eagerness, and engaging in a hand-to-hand conflict was already driving back the Persians posted there; but the Macedonians in the centre did not execute their task with equal speed; and finding many parts of the bank steep and precipitous, they were unable to preserve the front of the phalanx in the same line. Here then the struggle was desperate; the aim of the Grecian mercenaries of Darius being to push the Macedonians back into the river, and regain the victory, though their own forces were already flying; the aim of the Macedonians being not to fall short of Alexander's good-fortune, which was already manifest, and not to tarnish the glory of the phalanx, which up to that time had been commonly asserted to be invincible. Moreover the feeling of rivalry which existed between the Grecian and Macedonian races inspired each side in the conflict. Here fell Ptolemy, son of Seleucus, after proving himself a valiant man, besides about one hundred and twenty other Macedonians of no mean repute.[1]

---

[1] *Curtius* (iii. 29) says that on Alexander's side 504 were wounded, and 182 killed. *Diodorus* (xvii. 36) says, that 450 Macedonians were killed. *Justin* (xi. 9) states that 280 were slain.

CHAPTER XI.

Defeat and Flight of Darius.

Hereupon the regiments on the right wing, perceiving that the Persians opposed to them had already been put to rout, wheeled round towards the Grecian mercenaries of Darius and their own hard-pressed detachment. Having driven the Greeks away from the river, they extended their phalanx beyond the Persian army on the side which had been broken; and attacking the Greeks on the flank, were already beginning to cut them up. However the Persian cavalry which had been posted opposite the Thessalians did not remain on the other side of the river during the struggle, but came through the water and made a vigorous attack upon the Thessalian squadrons.[1] In this place a fierce cavalry battle ensued; for the Persians did not give way until they perceived that Darius had fled and the Grecian mercenaries had been cut up by the phalanx and severed from them. Then at last the flight of all the Persians was plainly visible. Their horses suffered much injury in the retreat, because the riders[2] were heavily armed; and the horsemen themselves, being so many in number and retreating in panic terror without any regard to order along narrow roads, were trampled on and injured no less by each other than by the pursuing enemy. The Thessalians also followed them up with vigour, so that no fewer of the cavalry than of the infantry[3] were slaughtered in the flight.

But as soon as the left wing of Darius was terrified and

---

1 Polybius, who lived nearly three centuries before Arrian, censures Callisthenes for asserting that the Persian cavalry crossed the river Pinarus and attacked the Thessalians. No doubt Arrian received this information from the lost works of Ptolemy and Aristobulus (*Poly.*, xii. 18).

2 ἀμβάτης is the poetical form of ἀναβάτης, the word used by Xenophon, Plato, and other Attic writers. The latter is found only once in Arrian (III. xiii. 5).

3 ἢ τῶν πεζῶν is Martin's emendation for ἢ ὡς πεζῶν.

routed by Alexander, and the Persian king perceived that this part of his army was severed from the rest, without any further delay he began to flee in his chariot along with the first, just as he was.[1] He was conveyed safely in the chariot as long as he met with level ground in his flight; but when he lighted upon ravines and other rough ground, he left the chariot there, divesting himself of his shield and Median mantle. He even left his bow in the chariot; and mounting a horse continued his flight. The night, which came on soon after, alone rescued him from being captured by Alexander;[2] for as long as there was daylight the latter kept up the pursuit at full speed. But when it began to grow dark and the ground before the feet became invisible, he turned back again to the camp, after capturing the chariot of Darius with the shield, the Median mantle, and the bow in it.[3] For his pursuit had

---

[1] *Curtius* (iii. 27) and *Diodorus* (xvii. 34) give a graphic description of a direct charge made by Alexander upon Darius, and a sanguinary conflict between Alexander's body-guard and the Persian nobles, in which the Great King's horses were wounded and became unmanageable, whereupon Darius got out, mounted a horse, and fled. We learn from Plutarch (*Alex.*, 20) that Chares affirmed Alexander came into hand-to-hand conflict with Darius, and that he received a wound in the thigh from that king's sword. Plutarch says that Alexander wrote to Antipater that he had been wounded in the thigh with a dagger, but did not say by whom. He also wrote that nothing serious had resulted from the wound. The account of Arrian is far the most trustworthy. Callisthenes stated that Alexander made a direct attack upon Darius (*Polybius*, xii. 22). We know from Xenophon that the Persian kings were in the habit of occupying the centre, and that Cyrus directed Clearchus to make the attack against the person of his brother Artaxerxes at the battle of Cunaxa. Polybius seems to have been ignorant of this custom of the Persian kings when he wrote his criticism on the statement of Callisthenes.

[2] ἀφείλετο. On this word see Donaldson (*New Cratylus*, sect. 315). Cf. Aeschylus (*Persae*, 428); *Thucydides* (iv. 134); Xenophon (*Hellenics*, i. 2, 16).

[3] The victories of the Greeks and Macedonians over the Persians were materially aided by the pusillanimity of Xerxes and Darius. Compare the conduct of Xerxes at Salamis (*Herodotus*, viii. 97; Aeschylus, *Persae*, 465–470, with Mr. Paley's note) and that of Darius at Arbela (*Arrian*, iii. 14).

been too slow for him to overtake Darius, because, though he wheeled round at the first breaking asunder of the phalanx, yet he did not turn to pursue him until he observed that the Grecian mercenaries and the Persian cavalry had been driven away from the river.

Of the Persians were killed Arsames, Rheomithres, and Atizyes who had commanded the cavalry at the Granicus. Sabaces, viceroy of Egypt, and Bubaces, one of the Persian dignitaries, were also killed, besides about 100,000 of the private soldiers, among them being more than 10,000 cavalry.[1] So great was the slaughter that Ptolemy, son of Lagus, who then accompanied Alexander, says that the men who were with them pursuing Darius, coming in the pursuit to a ravine, filled it up with the corpses and so passed over it. The camp of Darius was taken forthwith at the first assault, containing his mother, his wife,—who was also his sister,—and his infant son.[2] His two daughters, and a few other women, wives of Persian peers,[3] who were in attendance upon them, were likewise captured. For the other Persians happened to have despatched their women along with the rest of their property to Damascus;[4] because Darius had sent to that city the greater part of his money and all the other things which the Great King was in the habit of taking with him as necessary for his luxurious mode of living, even though

---

1 *Diodorus* (xvii. 36) and *Curtius* (iii. 29) agree with Arrian as to the number of slain in the army of Darius. Plutarch (*Alex.*, 20) gives the number as 110,000.

2 *Justin* (xi. 9) agrees with Arrian, that the wife of Darius was also his sister. Grote speaks of the mother, wife, and sister of Darius being captured, which is an error. *Diodorus* (xvii. 38) and *Curtius* (iii. 29) say that the son was about six years of age.

3 Cf. Xenophon (*Cyropaedia*, ii. 1, 3; vii. 5, 85).

4 Damascus,—the Hebrew name of which is Dammesek,—a very ancient city in Syria, at the foot of the Antilibanus, at an elevation of 220 feet above the sea, in a spacious and fertile plain about 30 miles in diameter, which is watered by three rivers, two of which are called in the Bible Abana and Pharpar. It has still a population of 150,000. The emperor Julian, in one of his letters, calls it "the Eye of all the East."

he was going on a military expedition. The consequence was, that in the camp no more than 3,000 talents[1] were captured; and soon after, the money in Damascus was, also seized by Parmenio, who was despatched thither for that very purpose. Such was the result of this famous battle (which was fought) in the month Maimacterion, when Nicostratus was archon of the Athenians.[2]

CHAPTER XII.

Kind Treatment of Darius's Family.

The next day, Alexander, though suffering from a wound which he had received in the thigh from a sword, visited the wounded, and having collected the bodies of the slain, he gave them a splendid burial with all his forces most brilliantly marshalled in order of battle. He also spoke with eulogy to those whom he himself had recognised performing any gallant deed in the battle, and also to those whose exploits he had learnt by report fully corroborated. He likewise honoured each of them individually with a gift of money in proportion to his desert.[3] He then appointed Balacrus, son of Nicanor, one of the royal body-guards, viceroy of Cilicia; and in his place among the body-guards he chose Menes, son of Dionysius. In the room of Ptolemy, son of Seleucus, who had been killed in the battle, he appointed Polysperchon, son of Simmias, to the command of a brigade. He remitted to the Solians the fifty talents[4] which were still due of the money imposed on them as a fine, and he gave them back their hostages.

---

[1] About £730,000.

[2] B.C. 333; end of October or beginning of November.

[3] Alexander erected three altars on the bank of the Pinarus, to Zeus, Heracles, and Athena (*Curtius*, iii. 33). Cicero, who was proconsul of Cilicia, speaks of "the altars of Alexander at the foot of Amanus," and says that he encamped there four days (*Epistolae ad Diversos*, xv. 4).

[4] About £12,000.

Nor did he treat the mother, wife, and children of Darius with neglect; for some of those who have written Alexander's history say that on the very night in which he returned from the pursuit of Darius, entering the Persian king's tent, which had been selected for his use, he heard the lamentation of women and other noise of a similar kind not far from the tent. Inquiring therefore who the women were, and why they were in a tent so near, he was answered by some one as follows:—"O king, the mother, wife, and children of Darius are lamenting for him as slain, since they have been informed that thou hast his bow and his royal mantle, and that his shield has been brought back." When Alexander heard this, he sent Leonnatus,[1] one of his Companions, to them, with injunctions to tell them:—"Darius is still alive; in his flight he left his arms and mantle in the chariot; and these are the only things of his that Alexander has." Leonnatus entered the tent and told them the news about Darius, saying, moreover, that Alexander would allow them to retain the state and retinue befitting their royal rank, as well as the title of queens; for he had not undertaken the war against Darius from a feeling of hatred, but he had conducted it in a legitimate manner for the empire of Asia. Such are the statements of Ptolemy and Aristobulus.[2] But there is another report, to the effect that on the following day Alexander himself went into the tent, accompanied alone by Hephaestion one of his Companions. The mother of Darius,[3] being in doubt which

---

[1] This distinguished general saved Alexander's life in India, in the assault on the city of the Mallians. After the king's death, he received the rule of the lesser or Hellespontine Phrygia. He was defeated and slain by the Athenians under Antiphilus, against whom he was fighting in alliance with Antipater, B.C. 323. See *Diodorus*, xviii. 14, 15; Plutarch (*Phocion*, 25).

[2] Compare *Diodorus*, xvii. 37, 38; *Curtius*, iii. 29–32.

[3] Named Sisygambis.

of them was the king (for they had both arrayed themselves in the same style of dress), went up to Hephaestion, because he appeared to her the taller of the two, and prostrated herself before him. But when he drew back, and one of her attendants pointed out Alexander, saying he was the king, she was ashamed of her mistake, and was going to retire. But the king told her she had made no mistake, for Hephaestion was also an Alexander. This I record neither being sure of its truth nor thinking it altogether unreliable. If it really occurred, I commend Alexander for his compassionate treatment of the women, and the confidence he felt in his companion, and the honour bestowed on him; but if it merely seems probable to historians that Alexander would have acted and spoken thus, even for this reason I think him worthy of commendation.[1]

CHAPTER XIII.

FLIGHT OF MACEDONIAN DESERTERS INTO EGYPT.—PROCEEDINGS OF AGIS, KING OF SPARTA.—ALEXANDER OCCUPIES PHOENICIA.

DARIUS fled through the night with a few attendants; but in the daytime, picking up as he went along the Persians and Grecian mercenaries who had come safely out of the battle, he had in all 4,000 men under his command.

[1] In a letter written by Alexander to Parmenio, an extract from which is preserved by Plutarch (*Alex.*, 22), he says that he never saw nor entertained the desire of seeing the wife of Darius, who was said to be the most beautiful woman in Asia; and that he would not allow himself to listen to those who spoke about her beauty. Cf. *Ammianus* (xxiv. 4, 27), speaking of Julian: "Ex virginibus autem, quae speciosae sunt captae, ut in Perside, ubi feminarum pulchritudo excellit, nec contrectare aliquam voluit, nec videre: Alexandrum imitatus et Africanum, qui haec declinabant, ne frangeretur cupiditate, qui se invictos a laboribus ubique praestiterunt."

He then made a forced march towards the city of Thapsacus[1] and the river Euphrates,[2] in order to put that river as soon as possible between himself and Alexander. But Amyntas son of Antiochus, Thymondas son of Mentor, Aristomedes the Pheraean, and Bianor the Acarnanian, all being deserters, fled without delay from the posts assigned them in the battle, with about 8,000 soldiers under their command, and passing through the mountains, they arrived at Tripolis in Phoenicia.[3] There

---

[1] Thapsacus is understood to be identical with the city called Tiphsach (passage) in 1 Kings iv. 24; which is there said to have been the eastern boundary of Solomon's empire. It is generally supposed that the modern Deir occupies the site of the ancient Thapsacus; but it has been discovered that the only ford in this part of the river is at Suriyeh, 165 miles above Deir. This was probably the site of Thapsacus. From the time of Seleucus Nicator the city was called Amphipolis (*Pliny*, v. 21). See *Stephanus* of Byzantium, *sub voce* Amphipolis. Cf. Xenophon (*Anabasis*, i. 4, 11).

[2] The Euphrates is the largest river of western Asia, and rises in the mountains of Armenia. It unites with the Tigris, and after a course of 1,780 miles flows into the Persian Gulf. It is navigable by boats for 1,200 miles. The annual inundation, caused by the melting of the snow in the mountains of Armenia, takes place in the month of May. The Euphrates, Tigris, and Eulaeus had formerly three separate outlets into the Persian Gulf; but the three now unite in a single stream, which is called Shat-el-Arab. The Hebrew name for the river which the Greeks called Euphrates, was Pĕrath (rapid stream). It is called in the Bible, the *Great River*, and *the River* (Gen. xv. 18; Exod. xxiii. 31; *et passim*). In Jeremiah xiii. 4–7, the word *Pĕrath* stands for Ephrath, another name for Bethlehem; in our Bible it is mis-translated. See Fürst's *Hebrew Lexicon.*

[3] The term *Cĕnaan* was applied to the lowland plain from Aradus to Gaza. The northern portion, from Aradus to Carmel, is known to us under its Grecian name of Phoenicia, which is probably derived from the Greek *phoinix* (a palm-tree), which grew abundantly in the country, and was the emblem of some of its towns. Others derive it from another Greek word *phoinix* (red dye), which formed one of its most important manufactures. The Phoenicians applied the term Cenaan to their land in contrast to the highlands to the west, which they called *Aram* (highland), the Hebrew name for Syria. The country of Phoenicia was 120 miles long and with an average breadth of 12 miles, never exceeding 20 miles. The chief cities of Phoenicia were Tyre, Sidon, Aradus, Byblus,

they seized the ships which had been hauled up on shore in which they had previously been transported from Lesbos; they launched as many of these vessel as they thought sufficient to convey them, and the rest they burnt there in the docks, in order not to supply their enemy with the means of quickly pursuing them. They fled

---

Berytus, Tripolis, and Accho or Ptolemais. Its central position between the eastern and western countries, early developed its commercial power, and its intercourse with foreign nations at an early period produced an advanced state of civilization and refinement. The Phoenicians were a Semitic nation like the Israelites; and their language bears a remarkable affinity with the Hebrew, as is seen by fragments of the Carthaginian language preserved in Plautus. In an inscription discovered at Marseilles in 1845, out of 94 words 74 were found in the Hebrew Bible. The Phoenicians were asserted by the Greeks to have communicated to them the knowledge of letters; and this statement is corroborated by the similarity of the Hebrew and ancient Greek letters. Their colonies spread from Cyprus to Crete and the Cyclades, thence to Euboea, Greece, and Thrace. The coasts of Asia Minor and Bithynia were dotted with their settlements, and they carried their commerce into the Black Sea. They also had colonies in Sicily, Sardinia, Ivica, and Spain, where they founded Cadiz. The northern coast of Africa was lined with their colonies, the most flourishing of which was Carthage, which rose to be one of the great powers of the world. Strabo says that they had 300 colonies on the western coast of Africa. They visited the coasts of England for tin; and thus, to quote the words of Humboldt, "the Tyrian flag waved at the same time in Britain and the India Ocean." *Herodotus* (iv. 42, 43) says that under the patronage of Necho, king of Egypt, they circumnavigated Africa; but he states that he does not believe it was a fact. The reason which he assigns for his disbelief is, that the navigators alleged that the sun was on their right hand, which is the strongest argument in favour of the truth of their statement. In Isaiah xxiii. 11, Phoenicia is called Cĕnaan, where the English Bible has erroneously, *the merchant city*. In the Bible the word *Cĕnaanim* is frequently used for *merchants*, because the Phoenicians were the principal commercial people of antiquity (Job xli. 6; Prov. xxxi. 24; Isaiah xxiii. 8; Hos. xii. 7; Zeph. i. 2; Zech. xiv. 21). Tripolis consisted of three distinct cities, 600 feet apart, each having its own walls, but all united in a common constitution with one place of assembly. These cities were colonies respectively of Sidon, Tyre, and Aradus. Tripolis was a flourishing port on a headland which is a spur of Lebanon. It is now called Tripoli, and is still a large town. See Dr. Smith's *Dictionary of Classical Geography*.

first to Cyprus,[1] thence to Egypt; where Amyntas shortly after, meddling in political disputes, was killed by the natives.

Meantime Pharnabazus and Autophradates were staying near Chios; then having established a garrison in this island they despatched some of their ships to Cos and Halicarnassus, and with 100 of their best sailing vessels they put to sea themselves and landed at Siphnus. And Agis, king of the Lacedaemonians,[2] came to them with one trireme, both to ask for money to carry on the war, and also to urge them to send with him into the Peloponnese as large a force both naval and military as they could. At that very time news reached them of the battle which had been fought at Issus; and being alarmed at the report, Pharnabazus started off to Chios with twelve triremes and 1,500 Grecian mercenaries, for fear that the Chians might attempt to effect a revolution when they received the news of the Persian defeat. Agis, having received from Autophradates thirty talents of silver[3] and ten triremes, despatched Hippias to lead these

---

[1] The oldest towns in Cyprus,—Citium, Amathus, and Paphus,—were Phoenician colonies. These were afterwards eclipsed by the Greek colonies, Salamis, Soli, and New Paphus. In Hebrew the island is called *Ceth*, and the inhabitants *Cittim*. Gesenius says, that upon a Sidonian coin *Ceth* in Cyprus, which the Greeks called Citium, is described as a Sidonian colony. *Diodorus* (xvi. 42) says there were nine kings in Cyprus. It is probable that the kings of the Hittites mentioned in 1 Kings x. 29, were from Cyprus. Also the Hittite women whom Solomon married were probably Cyprians (1 Kings xi. 1). The kings of the Hittites of whom the Syrians were afraid were also Cypriotes (2 Kings vii. 6); and the *land of the Hittites* mentioned in Judges i. 26, probably means Cyprus. Josephus, Eusebius, and Jerome understand these passages to refer to Cyprus. In Isaiah xxiii. 1, the *land of Cittim* refers to Cyprus, which belonged to Tyre, the revolt of which the prophet announced. This revolt is confirmed by Menander (*Josephus*, ix. 14, 9).

[2] Agis III. was ultimately defeated and slain by Antipater, B.C. 330. See *Curtius*, vi. 1 and 2; Grote's *Greece*, vol. xii. pp. 102–106.

[3] About £7,300.

ships to his brother Agesilaus at Taenarum,[1] ordering him also to instruct Agesilaus to give full pay to the sailors and then to sail as quickly as possible to Crete,[2] in order to set things in order there. For a time he himself remained there among the islands, but afterwards joined Autophradates at Halicarnassus.[3]

Alexander appointed Menon, son of Cerdimmas, viceroy of Coele-Syria,[4] giving him the cavalry of the Grecian

---

[1] Now Cape Matapan. Cf. *Propertius*, iii. 2, 11; *Tibullus*, iii. 3, 13; Homer (*Hymn to Apollo*, 411).

[2] The Cretans were very early civilized and powerful, for we read in Homer of their 100 cities. Before the Trojan war lived the famous king Minos, who is said to have given laws to Crete, and to have been the first potentate who possessed a navy, with which he suppressed piracy in the Aegean Sea. The Cretans gradually degenerated, so that we find in the New Testament St. Paul quoting from their own poet, Epimenides: "Always liars and beasts are the Cretans, and inwardly sluggish" (Titus i. 12). The lying propensity of the Cretans is proved from the fact that the verb *to Cretize*, was used in Greek with the meaning "to speak falsely." In Hebrew, Crete is called *Caphtor* (cypress). It is mentioned in Jer. xlvii. 4. It was the native land of a tribe of Philistines called Caphtorim (Gen. x. 14; Deut. ii. 23; 1 Chron. i. 12). The fact that the Philistines came partly from Crete is also affirmed in Amos ix. 7. Another branch of the Philistines came from Casloach in Egypt. The Caphtorim emigrated originally from Egypt to Crete, from which island they were probably driven by the Greeks. Tacitus asserts that the inhabitants of Palestine came from Crete (*Historiae*, v. 2); and the early name of Gaza was Minoa, after the famous king of Crete. Another Hebrew name for Crete is Cĕrēth, whence the inhabitants were called *Cĕrēthim*. They are mentioned in Ezek. xxv. 16, and Zeph. ii. 5; where the Septuagint and the Syriac have *Cretans*. We find the Philistines, who were partly emigrants from Crete, called Cerethim in 1 Sam. xxx. 14. From among these Cerethim and Philistines David chose his body-guard, which was composed of men skilled in shooting and slinging (2 Sam. viii. 18, xv. 18, xx. 7, 23; 1 Kings i. 38, 44; 1 Chron. xviii. 17).

[3] From *Diodorus* (xvii. 48) it appears that Agis went personally to Crete, and compelled most of the cities to join the Persian side. We also learn that the deputies of the Greeks assembled at the Isthmian games at Corinth sent an embassy to Alexander to congratulate him on his victory at Issus, and to present him with a golden wreath. (See also *Curtius*, iv. 22.)

[4] Coele-Syria, or Hollow Syria, is, in its more limited sense, the country

allies to guard the country. He then went in person towards Phoenicia; and on the march he was met by Strato, son of Gerostratus, king of the Aradians and of the people living near Aradus.[1] But Gerostratus himself was serving in the fleet with Autophradates, as were also the other kings both of the Phoenicians and the Cyprians. When Strato fell in with Alexander, he placed a golden crown upon his head, promising to surrender to him both the island of Aradus and the great and prosperous city of Marathus, situated on the mainland right opposite Aradus; also Sigon, the city of Mariamme, and all the other places under his own dominion and that of his father.

CHAPTER XIV.

Darius's Letter, and Alexander's Reply.

While Alexander was still in Marathus, ambassadors came bringing a letter from Darius, entreating him to give up to their king his mother, wife, and children. They were also instructed to support this petition by word of mouth. The letter pointed out to him that

---

between the ranges of Libanus and Anti-Libanus, in which Damascus and Baalbek are situated; in its wider meaning, it comprises the whole of Northern Syria, in opposition to the countries of Phoenicia and Palestine.

[1] Aradus is an island lying two or three miles from the mainland of Phoenicia. According to Strabo, a State was founded in it by refugees from Sidon. For a long time the island was independent, under its own kings; and even after it fell under the sway of the Macedonian kings of Syria, and subsequently under that of the Romans, it retained a great deal of its commercial prosperity. Aradus appears in Hebrew under the form *Arvad.* It is evident from Ezek. xxvii. 8, 11, that its inhabitants were skilful sailors and brave warriors. They sent out colonies to Aradus south of Carmel, the island of Aradus near Crete, and the islands in the Persian gulf. The present name of this island is Ruad. The Aradians inhabited the mainland opposite the island, as well as the island itself.

friendship and alliance had subsisted between Philip and Artaxerxes;[1] and that when Arses, son of Artaxerxes, ascended the throne, Philip was the first to practise injustice towards him, though he had suffered no injury from the Persians. Alexander also, from the time when Darius began to reign over the Persians, had not sent any one to him to confirm the friendship and alliance which had so long existed, but had crossed over into Asia with his army and had inflicted much injury upon the Persians. For this reason he had come down in person, to defend his country and to preserve the empire of his fathers. As to the battle, it had been decided as seemed good to some one of the gods. And now he, a king, begged his captured wife, mother, and children from a king; and he wished to form a friendship with him and become his ally. For this purpose he requested Alexander to send men to him with Meniscus and Arsimas, the messengers who came from the Persians, to receive pledges of fidelity from him and to give them on behalf of Alexander.

To this Alexander wrote a reply, and sent Thersippus with the men who had come from Darius, with instructions to give the letter to Darius, but not to converse about anything. Alexander's letter ran thus: "Your ancestors came into Macedonia and the rest of Greece and treated us ill, without any previous injury from us. I, having been appointed commander-in-chief of the Greeks, and wishing to take revenge on the Persians, crossed over into Asia, hostilities being begun by you. For you sent aid to the Perinthians,[2] who were dealing unjustly with my father; and Ochus sent forces into Thrace, which was under our rule. My father was killed by

[1] Artaxerxes Ochus reigned B.C. 359–338.

[2] Perinthus was a Samian colony on the Propontis. For the siege by Philip, see *Diodorus*, xvi. 74–76.

conspirators whom you instigated, as you have yourself boasted to all in your letters;[1] and after slaying Arses, as well as Bagoas, and unjustly seizing the throne contrary to the law of the Persians,[2] and ruling your subjects unjustly, you sent unfriendly letters about me to the Greeks, urging them to wage war with me. You have also despatched money to the Lacedaemonians, and certain other Greeks; but none of the States received it, except the Lacedaemonians.[3] As your agents destroyed my friends, and were striving to dissolve the league which I had formed among the Greeks, I took the field against you, because you were the party who commenced the hostility. Since I have vanquished your generals and viceroys in the previous battle, and now yourself and your forces in like manner, I am, by the gift of the gods, in possession of your land. As many of the men who fought in your army as were not killed in the battle, but fled to me for refuge, I am protecting; and they are with me, not against their own will, but they are serving in my army as volunteers. Come to me therefore, since I am lord of

---

[1] Impartial historians deny that Philip's murderers were bribed; they committed the murder from private resentment.

[2] Ochus was poisoned about B.C. 338, by the eunuch Bagoas, who placed upon the throne Arses, one of the king's sons, killing all the rest. Cf. Aelian (*Varia Historia*, vi. 8). Two years afterwards, Bagoas put Arses and all his children to death; thus leaving no direct heir of the regal family alive. He then placed upon the throne one of his adherents, named Darius Codomannus, a descendant of one of the brothers of Artaxerxes Mnemon. Bagoas soon afterwards tried to poison this Darius; but the latter, discovering his treachery, forced him to drink the deadly draught himself (*Diod.*, xvii. 5; *Justin.*, x. 3). From *Arrian*, iii. 19, we learn that Bistanes, a son of Ochus, was alive after the battle of Arbela.

[3] Aeschines, in his speech against Ctesiphon (p. 634), asserts that Darius sent 300 talents to Athens, that the Athenians refused them, and that Demosthenes took them, reserving 70 talents for his own private use. Deinarchus repeats this statement in his speech against Demosthenes. (pp. 9–14). If Demosthenes had really acted thus, it is strange Alexander knew nothing about it.

all Asia; but if you are afraid you may suffer any harsh treatment from me in case you come to me, send some of your friends to receive pledges of safety from me. Come to me then, and ask for your mother, wife, and children, and anything else you wish. For whatever you ask for you will receive; and nothing shall be denied you. But for the future, whenever you send to me, send to me as the king of Asia, and do not address to me your wishes as to an equal; but if you are in need of anything, speak to me as to the man who is lord of all your territories. If you act otherwise, I shall deliberate concerning you as an evil-doer; and if you dispute my right to the kingdom, stay and fight another battle for it; but do not run away. For wherever you may be, I intend to march against you." This is the letter which he sent to Darius.

CHAPTER XV.

Alexander's Treatment of the Captured Greek Ambassadors.—Submission of Byblus and Sidon.

When Alexander ascertained that all the money which Darius had sent off to Damascus with Cophen, son of Artabazus, was captured, and also that the Persians who had been left in charge of it, as well as the rest of the royal property, were taken prisoners, he ordered Parmenio to take the treasure back to Damascus, and there guard it.[1] When he also ascertained that the Grecian ambassadors who had reached Darius before the battle had likewise been captured, he ordered them to be sent to him.[2] They were Euthycles, a Spartan; Thessaliscus,

[1] This statement of Arrian is confirmed by *Curtius* (iii. 34), who says that Parmenio captured the treasure, not in the city, but from fugitives who were conveying it away.

[2] In giving the names of the captured Grecian envoys, *Curtius* (iii. 35) seems to have confounded this with a future occasion, mentioned in *Arrian* (iii. 24).

son of Ismenias, and Dionysodorus, a victor in the Olympic games, Thebans; and Iphicrates, son of Iphicrates the general, an Athenian.[1] When these men came to Alexander, he immediately released Thessaliscus and Dionysodorus, though they were Thebans, partly out of compassion for Thebes, and partly because they seemed to have acted in a pardonable manner. For their native city had been reduced to slavery by the Macedonians, and they were trying to find whatever succour they could for themselves and perhaps also for their native city from Darius and the Persians. Thinking thus compassionately about both of them, he released them, saying that he dismissed Thessaliscus individually out of respect for his pedigree, for he belonged to the ranks of the distinguished men of Thebes. Dionysodorus also he released because he had been conqueror at the Olympic games; and he kept Iphricrates in attendance on himself as long as he lived, treating him with special honour both from friendship to the city of Athens and from recollection of his father's glory. When he died soon after from sickness, he sent his bones back to his relations at Athens. But Euthycles at first he kept in custody, though without fetters, both because he was a Lacedaemonian of a city at that time openly and eminently hostile to him, and because in the man as an individual he could find nothing to warrant his pardon. Afterwards, when he met with great success, he released even this man also.

He set out from Marathus and took possession of Byblus[2] on terms of capitulation, as he did also of

---

[1] The great Iphicrates had been adopted by Alexander's grandfather, as is stated in a note on Book I. chap. 23.

[2] Byblus is said by *Strabo* (xvi. 2) to have been situated on a height not far from the sea. It was reported to be the oldest city in the world. It possessed a considerable extent of territory, including Berytus, and was an independent State for a long period, the last king being deposed by Pompey. On a Byblus coin of Alexander's time appears the name

Sidon,[1] the inhabitants of which spontaneously invited him from hatred of the Persians and Darius.[2] Thence he advanced towards Tyre;[3] ambassadors from which city,

---

Einel, which is the king Enylus mentioned by *Arrian* (ii. 20). Byblus was the chief seat of the worship of Adonis, or Thammuz, who was supposed to have been born there. In the Bible it appears under its Hebrew name *Gebal* (mountain-district). The inhabitants of Gebal are said in Ezek. xxvii. 9 to have been skilled in building ships. In Josh. xiii. 5 the northern boundary of the Holy Land is said to reach as far as the land of the Giblite, or inhabitant of Gebal. In 1 Kings v. 18 the word translated in our Bible *stone-squarers* ought to be rendered *Giblites*. The Arabs still call the place Jebail. Cf. Milton (*Paradise Lost*, viii. 18).

[1] Sidon, or in Hebrew *Tsidon* (fortress), is called in Gen. x. 15, 19 the firstborn son of Canaan, *i.e.* it was the first city founded by the Canaanites or Phoenicians. It lay about twenty miles south of Tyre, on a small promontory two miles south of the river Bostremus. We read in *Homer* that it was famous for its embroidered robes and metal utensils, and from other ancient writers we find that it manufactured glass and linen and also prepared dyes. Before the time of David it fell under the rule of Tyre; but when Shalmanesser, king of Assyria, invaded Phoenicia, it revolted from Tyre and submitted to the invader. It was governed by its own kings under the Babylonian and Persian empires; and under the latter power it reached its highest prosperity, surpassing Tyre in wealth and importance. In the expedition of Xerxes against Greece, the Sidonians furnished the best ships in the whole fleet, and their king obtained the highest place under Xerxes in the council. But they revolted against Ochus, king of Persia, and being betrayed to him by their own king Tennes, they burnt their city and ships. It is said that 40,000 persons perished in the fire and by the sword, B.C. 351. (*Diodorus*, xvi. 43–45). No doubt this barbarous treatment of Ochus induced the Sidonians to take the side of Alexander. The city was already built and again flourishing when that king appeared on the scene. Near the site of the ancient city is the present town of Saida, with a population of about 5,000. Cf. Homer (*Iliad*, vi. 289; xxiii. 741); *Lucan*, iii. 217.

[2] At Sidon, Alexander deposed the reigning king Strato, a friend of the Persians; and a poor man, named Abdalonymus, distantly related to the regal family, was put into his place (*Curtius*, iv. 3, 4). *Diodorus* (xvii. 47) tells the same story, but applies it to Tyre, probably by mistake.

[3] The Hebrew name for Tyre is *Tsor* (rock). In Isa. xxiii. 4 it is called the fortress of the sea; and in ver. 8, "Tsor, the crowning one," because Tyre gave rulers to the Phoenician cities and colonies. Valuable information about the power, trade, and customs of Tyre is derived from Ezek. xxvi–xxviii.; and we learn the fact that she employed mercenaries like her colony Carthage (Ezek. xxvii. 10, 11). In the classical writers

despatched by the commonwealth, met him on the march, announcing that the Tyrians had decided to do whatever he might command.[1] He commended both the city and its ambassadors, and ordered them to return and tell the Tyrians that he wished to enter their city and offer sacrifice to Heracles. The son of the king of the Tyrians was one of the ambassadors, and the others were conspicuous men in Tyre; but the king Azemilcus[2] himself was sailing with Autophradates.

CHAPTER XVI.

The Worship of Hercules in Tyre.—The Tyrians Refuse to Admit Alexander.

The reason of this demand was, that in Tyre there existed a temple of Heracles,[3] the most ancient of all those which are mentioned in history. It was not dedicated to the Argive Heracles, the son of Alcmena; for this Heracles was honoured in Tyre many generations before Cadmus set out from Phoenicia and occupied Thebes, and before Semele, the daughter of Cadmus, was born, from whom Dionysus, the son of Zeus, was born. This Dionysus

---

the name is corrupted into *Tyrus*, and sometimes into *Sarra*. Tyre was unsuccessfully besieged for five years by Shalmaneser. It was also besieged for thirteen years by Nebuchadnezzar, and in the end an alliance was formed, by which the Tyrians retained their own king as a vassal of the king of Babylon. This arrangement was continued under the kings of Persia.

[1] *Curtius* (iv. 7) tells us that the envoys also brought to Alexander a golden wreath, together with abundant supplies for his army.

[2] This king must have brought home his ships for the defence of Tyre, for he was in the city when it was captured. See chap. 24.

[3] The Phoenician god *Melkarth* (lord of the city), whom the Syrians called *Baal* (lord), was supposed to be identical with the Grecian Heracles, or Hercules, who was the mythical ancestor of the Macedonian kings. *Curtius* (iv. 7) tells us that Alexander affirmed he had been ordered by an oracle to sacrifice in Tyre to Heracles. Gesenius informs us that a Maltese inscription identifies the Tyrian Melkarth with Heracles.

would be third from Cadmus, being a contemporary of Labdacus, son of Polydorus, the son of Cadmus; and the Argive Heracles lived about the time of Oedipus, son of Laius.[1] The Egyptians also worshipped another Heracles, not the one which either the Tyrians or Greeks worship. But Herodotus says that the Egyptians considered Heracles to be one of the twelve gods,[2] just as the Athenians worshipped a different Dionysus, who was the son of Zeus and Core; and the mystic chant called Iacchus was sung to this Dionysus, not to the Theban. So also I think that the Heracles honoured in Tartessus[3] by the Iberians, where are certain pillars named after Heracles, is the Tyrian Heracles; for Tartessus was a colony of the Phœnicians, and the temple to Heracles there was built and the sacrifices offered after the usage of the Phoenicians. Hecataeus the historian[4] says Geryones, against whom the Argive Heracles was despatched by Eurystheus to drive his oxen away and bring them to Mycenae, had nothing to do with the land of the Iberians;[5] nor was Heracles despatched to any island

---

[1] Who was the son of Labdacus.

[2] See *Herodotus*, ii. 43, 44.

[3] The district comprising all the south-west of Spain outside the pillars of Heracles, or Straits of Gibraltar, was called Tartessis, of which the chief city was Tartessus. Here the Phoenicians planted colonies, one of which still remains under the name of Cadiz. The Romans called the district Baetica, from the principal river, the Baetis or Guadalquivir. The Hebrew name for this region is *Tarshish*, of which Tartessus is the Greek form. Tarshish was the station for the Phoenician trade with the West, which extended as far as Cornwall. The Tyrians fetched from this locality silver, iron, lead, tin, and gold (Isa. xxiii. 1, 6, 10, lxvi. 19; Jer. x. 9; Ezek. xxvii. 12, xxxviii. 13). Martial, Seneca, and Avienus, the first two of whom were Spaniards, understood Tartessus to stand for the south-west of Spain and Portugal. The word Tarshish probably means *sea-coast*, from the Sanscrit *tarischa*, the sea. Ovid (*Met.*, xiv. 416); *Martial*, viii. 28; *Silius*, xiii. 673.

[4] Of Miletus. Herodotus knew his writings well, but they have not come down to us. See *Herod.* (ii. 143; v. 36 and 125).

[5] The Iberians were originally called Tibarenes, or Tibari. They dwelt

called Erythia[1] outside the Great Sea; but that Geryones was king of the mainland (Epirus) around Ambracia[2] and the Amphilochians, that Heracles drove the oxen from this Epirus, and that this was deemed no mean task. I know that to the present time this part of the mainland is rich in pasture land and rears a very fine breed of oxen; and I do not think it beyond the bounds of probability that the fame of the oxen from Epirus, and the name of the king of Epirus, Geryones, had reached Eurystheus. But I do not think that Eurystheus would know the name of the king of the Iberians, who were the remotest nation in Europe, or whether a fine breed of oxen grazed in their land, unless some one, by introducing Hera into the account, as herself giving these commands to Heracles through Eurystheus, wished, by means of the fable, to disguise the incredibility of the tale.

To this Tyrian Heracles, Alexander said he wished to offer sacrifice. But when this message was brought to Tyre by the ambassadors, the people passed a decree to obey any other command of Alexander, but not to admit into the city any Persian or Macedonian; thinking that under the existing circumstances, this was the most specious answer, and that it would be the safest course for them to pursue in reference to the issue of the war, which was still uncertain.[3] When the answer from Tyre

---

on the east of the Black Sea, and west of Colchis, whence they emigrated to Spain. This nation is called *Tubal* in the Hebrew Bible; in Isa. lxvi. 19 the Iberians of western Europe are referred to.

[1] An island near Cadiz, now called Leon. Cf. Hesiod (*Theogonia*, 287–294); *Herodotus*, iv. 8.

[2] Now called Arta.

[3] Arrian omits to mention that the Tyrians pointed out to him that his wish to sacrifice to Hercules might be gratified without entering their city, since at Palaetyrus, on the mainland, separated from Tyre only by a narrow strait, was a temple of that deity more ancient than that in Tyre. See *Curtius*, iv. 7; *Justin*, xi. 10. We learn from *Arrian*, i. 18, that when Alexander offered sacrifice to the Ephesian Diana he marched to the temple with his whole army in battle array. No doubt it was

was brought to Alexander, he sent the ambassadors back in a rage. He then summoned a council of his Companions and the leaders of his army, together with the captains of infantry and cavalry, and spoke as follows :—

CHAPTER XVII.

Speech of Alexander to his Officers.

"Friends and allies, I see that an expedition to Egypt will not be safe for us, so long as the Persians retain the sovereignty of the sea; nor is it a safe course, both for other reasons, and especially looking at the state of matters in Greece, for us to pursue Darius, leaving in our rear the city of Tyre itself in doubtful allegiance, and Egypt and Cyprus in the occupation of the Persians. I am apprehensive lest while we advance with our forces towards Babylon and in pursuit of Darius, the Persians should again forsooth conquer the maritime districts, and transfer the war into Greece with a larger army, considering that the Lacedaemonians are now waging war against us without disguise, and the city of Athens is restrained for the present rather by fear than by any good-will towards us. But if Tyre were captured, the whole of Phoenicia would be in our possession, and the fleet of the Phoenicians, which is the most numerous and the best in the Persian navy, would in all probability come over to us. For the Phoenician sailors and marines will not put to sea in order to incur danger on behalf of others, when their own cities are occupied by us. After this, Cyprus will either yield to us without delay, or will be captured with ease at the mere arrival of a naval force; and then navigating the sea with the ships from Macedonia in conjunction with those of the Phoenicians,

---

this kind of thing the Tyrians objected to. Alexander actually did the same at Tyre after its capture. (See chapter 24.)

Cyprus at the same time coming over to us, we shall acquire the absolute sovereignty of the sea, and at the same time an expedition into Egypt will become an easy matter for us. After we have brought Egypt into subjection, no anxiety about Greece and our own land will any longer remain, and we shall be able to undertake the expedition to Babylon with safety in regard to affairs at home, and at the same time with greater reputation, in consequence of having cut off from the Persian empire all the maritime provinces and all the land this side of the Euphrates."

CHAPTER XVIII.

Siege of Tyre.—Construction of a Mole from the Mainland to the Island.

By this speech he easily persuaded his officers to make an attempt upon Tyre. Moreover he was encouraged by a divine admonition, for that very night in his sleep[1] he seemed to be approaching the Tyrian walls, and Heracles seemed to take him by the right hand and lead him up into the city. This was interpreted by Aristander[2] to mean that Tyre would be taken with labour, because the deeds of Heracles were accomplished with labour. Certainly, the siege of Tyre appeared to be a great enterprise; for the city was an island[3] and fortified all round with lofty walls. Moreover naval operations seemed at that time more favourable to the Tyrians, both because the Persians still possessed the sovereignty of the sea and many ships were still remaining with the citizens themselves. However, as these arguments of his had

---

1 For this use of ἐνύπνιον, cf. Homer (*Iliad*, ii. 56); Aristophanes (*Wasps*, 1218).

2 Cf. *Arrian*, i. 11 and 25 supra.

3 The island was about half a mile from the mainland, and about a mile in length.

prevailed, he resolved to construct a mole from the mainland to the city.[1] The place is a narrow strait full of pools; and the part of it near the mainland is shallow water and muddy, but the part near the city itself, where was the deepest part of the channel, was the depth of about three fathoms. But there was an abundant supply of stones and wood, which they put on the top of the stones.[2] Stakes were easily fixed down firmly in the mud, which itself served as a cement to the stones to hold them firm. The zeal of the Macedonians in the work was great, and it was increased by the presence of Alexander himself, who took the lead[3] in everything, now rousing the men to exertion by speech, and now by presents of money, lightening the labour of those who were toiling more than their fellows from the desire of gaining praise for their exertions. As long as the mole was being constructed near the mainland, the work made easy and rapid progress, as the material was poured into a small depth of water, and there was no one to hinder them; but when they began to approach the deeper water, and at the same time came near the city itself, they suffered severely, being assailed with missiles from the walls, which were lofty, inasmuch as they had been expressly equipped for work rather than for fighting. Moreover, as the Tyrians still retained command of the sea, they kept on sailing with their triremes to various parts of the mole, and made it impossible in many places for the Macedonians to pour in the material. But the latter erected two towers upon the mole, which they had now projected over a long stretch of sea, and upon these towers they placed engines of war. Skins and prepared hides served

[1] We learn from *Diodorus* (xvii. 40) that the breadth of this mole was about 200 feet.

[2] *Curtius* (iv. 10) says that the timber was procured from Lebanon, and the stones from Old Tyre on the mainland.

[3] Cf. *Polyaenus* (iv. 3).

as coverings in front of them, to prevent them being struck by fire-bearing missiles from the wall, and at the same time to be a screen against arrows to those who were working. It was likewise intended that the Tyrians who might sail near to injure the men engaged in the construction of the mole should not retire easily, being assailed by missiles from the towers.

CHAPTER XIX.

The Siege of Tyre.

But to counteract this the Tyrians adopted the following contrivance. They filled a vessel, which had been used for transporting horses, with dry twigs and other combustible wood, fixed two masts on the prow, and fenced it round in the form of a circle as large as possible, so that the enclosure might contain as much chaff and as many torches as possible. Moreover they placed upon this vessel quantities of pitch, brimstone, and whatever else was calculated to foment a great flame.[1] They also stretched out a double yard-arm upon each mast; and from these they hung caldrons into which they had poured or cast materials likely to kindle flame which would extend to a great distance. They then put ballast into the stern, in order to raise the prow aloft, the vessel being weighed down abaft.[2] Then watching for a wind bearing towards the mole, they fastened the vessel to some triremes which towed it before the breeze. As soon as they approached the mole and the towers, they threw fire among the wood, and at the same time ran the vessel, with the triremes, aground as violently as possible, dashing against the end of the mole. The men

---

[1] Cf. Cæsar (*Bell. Gall.*, vii. 24)—reliquasque res, quibus ignis excitari potest, fundebant. Krüger has unnecessarily altered *ἐπὶ ταύτῃ* into *ἐπ' αὐτήν* (*i.e.* *πρῷραν*).

[2] *Curtius* (iv. 12) says that the stern was loaded with stones and sand.

in the vessel easily swam away, as soon as it was set on fire. A great flame soon caught the towers; and the yard-arms being twisted round poured out into the fire the materials that had been prepared for kindling the flame. The men also in the triremes tarrying near the mole kept on shooting arrows into the towers, so that it was not safe for men to approach in order to bring materials to quench the fire. Upon this, when the towers had already caught fire, many men hastened from the city, and embarking in light vessels, and striking against various parts of the mole, easily tore down the stockade which had been placed in front of it for protection, and burnt up all the engines of war which the fire from the vessel did not reach.[1] But Alexander began to construct a wider mole from the mainland, capable of containing more towers; and he ordered the engine-makers to prepare fresh engines. While this was being performed, he took the shield-bearing guards and the Agrianians and set out to Sidon, to collect there all the triremes he could; since it was evident that the successful conclusion of the siege would be much more difficult to attain, so long as the Tyrians retained the superiority at sea.[2]

CHAPTER XX.

Tyre Besieged by Sea as well as Land.

About this time Gerostratus, King of Aradus, and Enylus, King of Byblus, ascertaining that their cities were in the possession of Alexander, deserted Autophradates and the fleet under his command, and came to Alexander

---

[1] *Diodorus* (xvii. 42) and *Curtius* (iv. 12) say that a great tempest helped to demolish the palisade.

[2] We learn from Josephus (*Antiquities of the Jews*, ix. 14), on the authority of Menander, that when Shalmaneser, king of Assyria, four centuries before Alexander's time, besieged Tyre, the other Phoenicians supplied him with ships in like manner.

with their naval force, accompanied by the Sidonian triremes; so that about eighty Phoenician ships joined him. About the same time triremes also came to him from Rhodes, both the one called *Peripolus*,[1] and with it nine others. From Soli and Mallus also came three, and from Lycia ten; from Macedonia also a ship with fifty oars, in which sailed Proteas, son of Andronicus.[2] Not long after, too, the kings of Cyprus put into Sidon with about one hundred and twenty ships, when they heard of the defeat of Darius at Issus, and were terrified, because the whole of Phoenicia was already in the possession of Alexander. To all of these Alexander granted indemnity for their previous conduct, because they seemed to have joined the Persian fleet rather by necessity than by their own choice. While the engines of war were being constructed for him, and the ships were being fitted up for a naval attack on the city and for the trial of a sea-battle, he took some squadrons of cavalry, the Agrianians and archers, and made an expedition into the range of mountains called Anti-Libanus.[3] Having subdued some of the mountaineers by force, and drawn others over to him by terms of capitulation, he returned to Sidon in ten days.[4] Here he found Cleander, son of Polemocrates, just arrived from Peloponnesus, having 4,000 Grecian mercenaries with him.[5]

---

[1] This was a state vessel, or guardship, similar to the *Paralus* and *Salaminia* at Athens. See *Alciphron*, Bk. I. Epistle 11, with Bergler's note.

[2] See *Arrian*, ii. 2 supra.

[3] *Curtius* (iv. 11) says that about thirty of the Macedonians collecting timber in Lebanon were killed by a party of wild Arabs, and that a few were also captured by them. *Lebanon* is a Hebrew word meaning *white*, like *Alpes*. It was so called on account of its white cliffs, just as Britain is called by Aristotle, *Albion*, the Celtic for white.

[4] Plutarch (*Life of Alexander*, 24) gives us, on the authority of Chares, some details of daring valour on the part of Alexander in this expedition.

[5] Cleander was put to death by Alexander for oppression in exercising his duties as governor of Media. See *Arrian*, vi. 27 infra.

When his fleet had been arranged in due order, he embarked upon the decks as many of his shield-bearing guards as seemed sufficient for his enterprise, unless a sea-battle were to be fought rather by breaking the enemy's line[1] than by a close conflict. He then started from Sidon and sailed towards Tyre with his ships arranged in proper order, himself being on the right wing which stretched out seaward; and with him were the kings of the Cyprians, and all those of the Phoenicians except Pnytagoras, who with Craterus was commanding the left wing of the whole line. The Tyrians had previously resolved to fight a sea-battle, if Alexander should sail against them by sea. But then with surprise they beheld the vast multitude of his ships; for they had not yet learnt that Alexander had all the ships of the Cyprians and Phoenicians. At the same time they were surprised to see that he was sailing against them with his fleet arranged in due order; for Alexander's fleet a little before it came near the city, tarried for a while out in the open sea, with the view of provoking the Tyrians to come out to a battle; but afterwards, as the enemy did not put out to sea against them, though they were thus arranged in line, they advanced to the attack with a great dashing of oars. Seeing this, the Tyrians decided not to fight a battle at sea, but closely blocked up the passage for ships with as many triremes as the mouths of their harbour would contain, and guarded it, so that the enemy's fleet might not find an anchorage in any of the harbours.

As the Tyrians did not put out to sea against him, Alexander sailed near the city, but resolved not to try to force an entrance into the harbour towards Sidon on account of the narrowness of its mouth; and at the same

---

[1] In regard to this manœuvre, see *Herodotus*, vi. 12; *Thucydides*, i. 49, with Arnold's note.

time because he saw that the entrance had been blocked up with many triremes having their prows turned towards him. But the Phoenicians fell upon the three triremes moored furthest out at the mouth of the harbour, and attacking them prow to prow, succeeded in sinking them. However, the men in the ships easily swam off to the land which was friendly to them. Then, indeed, Alexander moored his ships along the shore not far from the mole which had been made, where there appeared to be shelter from the winds; and on the following day he ordered the Cyprians with their ships and their admiral Andromachus to moor near the city opposite the harbour which faces towards Sidon, and the Phoenicians opposite the harbour which looks towards Egypt, situated on the other side of the mole, where also was his own tent.

CHAPTER XXI.

Siege of Tyre.

He had now collected many engineers both from Cyprus and the whole of Phoenicia, and many engines of war had been constructed,[1] some upon the mole, others upon vessels used for transporting horses, which he brought with him from Sidon, and others upon the triremes which were not fast sailers. When all the preparations had been completed they brought up the engines of war along the mole that had been made and also began to shoot from ships moored near various parts of the wall and making trial of its strength. The Tyrians erected wooden towers on their battlements opposite the mole, from which they might annoy the enemy; and if the engines of war were brought near any other part, they defended themselves with missiles and shot at

[1] συμπεπηγμέναι:—"In the best authors πέπηγα is used as the perf. pass. of πήγνυμι" (*Liddell & Scott*). Cf. v. 12, 4; 24, 4, infra.

the very ships with fire-bearing arrows, so that they deterred the Macedonians from approaching the wall. Their walls opposite the mole were about one hundred and fifty feet high, with a breadth in proportion, and constructed with large stones imbedded in gypsum. It was not easy for the horse-transports and the triremes of the Macedonians, which were conveying the engines of war up to the wall, to approach the city, because a great quantity of stones hurled forward into the sea prevented their near assault. These stones Alexander determined to drag out of the sea; but this was a work accomplished with great difficulty, since it was performed from ships and not from the firm earth; especially as the Tyrians, covering their ships with mail, brought them alongside the anchors of the triremes, and cutting the cables of the anchors underneath, made anchoring impossible for the enemy's ships. But Alexander covered many thirty-oared vessels with mail in the same way, and placed them athwart in front of the anchors, so that the assault of the ships was repelled by them. But, notwithstanding this, divers under the sea secretly cut their cables. The Macedonians then used chains to their anchors instead of cables, and let them down so that the divers could do no more harm. Then, fastening slip-knots to the stones, they dragged them out of the sea from the mole; and having raised them aloft with cranes, they discharged them into deep water, where they were no longer likely to do injury by being hurled forward. The ships now easily approached the part of the wall where it had been made clear of the stones which had been hurled forward. The Tyrians being now reduced to great straits on all sides, resolved to make an attack on the Cyprian ships, which were moored opposite the harbour turned towards Sidon. For a long time they spread sails across the mouth of the harbour, in order that the filling of the triremes might not be discernible;

and about the middle of the day, when the sailors were scattered in quest of necessaries, and when Alexander usually retired from the fleet to his tent on the other side of the city, they filled three quinqueremes, an equal number of quadriremes and seven triremes with the most expert complement of rowers possible, and with the best-armed men adapted for fighting from the decks, together with the men most daring in naval contests. At first they rowed out slowly and quietly in single file, moving forward the handles of their oars without any signal from the men who give the time to the rowers [1]; but when they were already tacking against the Cyprians, and were near enough to be seen, then indeed with a loud shout and encouragement to each other, and at the same time with impetuous rowing, they commenced the attack.

CHAPTER XXII.

Siege of Tyre.—Naval Defeat of the Tyrians.

It happened on that day that Alexander went away to his tent, but after a short time returned to his ships, not tarrying according to his usual custom. The Tyrians fell all of a sudden upon the ships lying at their moorings, finding some entirely empty and others being filled with difficulty from the men who happened to be present at the very time of the noise and attack. At the first onset they at once sank the quinquereme of the king Pnytagoras, that of Androcles the Amathusian [2] and that of Pasicrates the Curian; [3] and they shattered the other ships by pushing them ashore. But when Alexander

---

[1] Cf. Plautus (*Mercator*, iv. 2, 5), *hortator remigum.*

[2] Amathus was a town on the south coast of Cyprus. It is now called Limasol. Cf. *Herodotus*, v. 104–115; Tacitus (*Ann.*, iii. 62); Vergil (*Aeneid*, x. 51).

[3] Curium was also a town on the south coast of Cyprus.

perceived the sailing out of the Tyrian triremes, he ordered most of the ships under his command to be manned and to take position at the mouth of the harbour, so that the rest of the Tyrian ships might not sail out. He then took the quinqueremes which he had and about five of the triremes, which were manned by him in haste before the rest were ready, and sailed round the city against the Tyrians who had sailed out of the harbour. The men on the wall, perceiving the enemy's attack and observing that Alexander himself was in the fleet, began to shout to those in their own ships, urging them to return; but as their shouts were not audible, on account of the noise of those who were engaged in the action, they exhorted them to retreat by various kinds of signals. At last after a long time, perceiving the impending attack of Alexander's fleet, they tacked about and began to flee into the harbour; and a few of their ships succeeded in escaping, but Alexander's vessels assaulted the greater number, and rendered some of them unfit for sailing; and a quinquereme and a quadrireme were captured at the very mouth of the harbour. But the slaughter of the marines was not great; for when they perceived that their ships were in possession of the enemy, they swam off without difficulty into the harbour. As the Tyrians could no longer derive any aid from their ships, the Macedonians now brought up their military engines to the wall itself. Those which were brought near the city along the mole, did no damage worth mentioning on account of the strength of the wall there. Others brought up some of the ships conveying military engines opposite the part of the city turned towards Sidon. But when even there they met with no success, Alexander passed round to the wall projecting towards the south wind and towards Egypt, and tested the strength of the works everywhere. Here first a large piece of the wall was thoroughly shaken, and a part of it was even broken and thrown down. Then indeed for a short time he tried to make an assault to the extent of throwing a bridge upon the part of the wall where a breach had been made. But the Tyrians without much difficulty beat the Macedonians back.

CHAPTER XXIII.

SIEGE OF TYRE.

THE third day after this, having waited for a calm sea, after encouraging the leaders of the regiments for the action, he led the ships containing the military engines up to the city. In the first place he shook down a large piece of the wall; and when the breach appeared to be sufficiently wide, he ordered the vessels conveying the military engines to retire, and brought up two others, which carried his bridges, which he intended to throw upon the breach in the wall. The shield-bearing guards occupied one of these vessels, which he had put under the command of Admetus; and the other was occupied by the regiment of Coenus, called the foot Companions. Alexander himself, with the shield-bearing guards, intended to scale the wall where it might be practicable. He ordered some of his triremes to sail against both of the harbours, to see if by any means they could force an entrance when the Tyrians had turned themselves to oppose him. He also ordered those of his triremes which contained the missiles to be hurled from engines, or which were carrying archers upon deck, to sail right round the wall and to put in where it was practicable, and to take up position within shooting range, until it became impossible to put in, so that the Tyrians, being shot at from all quarters, might become distracted, and not know whither to turn in their distress. When Alexander's ships drew close to the city and the bridges were thrown from them upon the wall, the shield-bearing guards mounted valiantly along these upon the wall; for their captain, Admetus, proved himself brave on that occasion, and Alexander accompanied them, both as a courageous participant in the action itself, and as a witness of brilliant and dangerous feats of valour performed by others. The first part of the wall that was captured was where Alexander had posted himself; the Tyrians being easily beaten back from it, as soon as the Macedonians found firm footing, and at the same time a way of entrance not abrupt on every side. Admetus was the first to mount the wall; but while cheering on his men to mount, he was struck with a spear and died on the spot.

After him, Alexander with the Companions got possession of the wall[1]; and when some of the towers and the parts of the wall between them were in his hands, he advanced through the battlements to the royal palace, because the descent into the city that way seemed the easiest.

CHAPTER XXIV.

Capture of Tyre.

To return to the fleet, the Phoenicians posted opposite the harbour looking towards Egypt, facing which they happened to be moored, forcing their way and bursting the bars asunder, shattered the ships in the harbour, attacking some of them in deep water and driving others ashore. The Cyprians also sailed into the other harbour looking towards Sidon, which had no bar across it, and made a speedy capture of the city on that side. The main body of the Tyrians deserted the wall when they

---

[1] *Diodorus* (xvii. 45) says, that after Admetus was killed, Alexander recalled his men from the assault that night, but renewed it next day.

saw it in the enemy's possession; and rallying opposite what was called the chapel of Agenor,[1] they there turned round to resist the Macedonians. Against these Alexander advanced with his shield-bearing guards, destroyed the men who fought there, and pursued those who fled. Great was the slaughter also made both by those who were now occupying the city from the harbour and by the regiment of Coenus, which had also entered it. For the Macedonians were now for the most part advancing full of rage, being angry both at the length of the siege and also because the Tyrians, having captured some of their men sailing from Sidon, had conveyed them to the top of their wall, so that the deed might be visible from the camp, and after slaughtering them, had cast their bodies into the sea. About 8,000 of the Tyrians were killed; and of the Macedonians, besides Admetus, who had proved himself a valiant man, being the first to scale the wall, twenty of the shield-bearing guards were killed in the assault on that occasion. In the whole siege about 400 Macedonians were slain. Alexander gave an amnesty to all those who fled for refuge into the temple of Heracles; among them being most of the Tyrian magistrates, including the king Azemilcus, as well as certain envoys from the Carthaginians, who had come to their mother-city to attend the sacrifice in honour of Heracles, according to an ancient custom.[2] The rest of the prisoners were reduced to slavery; all the Tyrians and mercenary troops, to the number of about 30,000, who had been captured,

---

[1] Agenor, the father of Cadmus, was the reputed founder of Tyre and Sidon. See *Curtius*, iv. 19.

[2] The Tyrians had been encouraged in their resistance by the promise of aid from their colony Carthage. But the Carthaginians excused themselves on the ground of their own difficulties in contending with the Greeks. The Tyrians however despatched their women, children, and old men to Carthage for safety. See *Diodorus*, xvii. 40, 41; *Curtius*, iv. 8 and 15. We learn from *Diod.*, xx. 14, that the Carthaginians were in the habit of sending to the Tyrian Hercules the tenth of their revenues.

being sold.[1] Alexander then offered sacrifice to Heracles, and conducted a procession in honour of that deity with all his soldiers fully armed. The ships also took part in this religious procession in honour of Heracles. He moreover held a gymnastic contest in the temple, and celebrated a torch race. The military engine, also, with which the wall had been battered down, was brought into the temple and dedicated as a thank-offering; and the Tyrian ship sacred to Heracles, which had been captured in the naval attack, was likewise dedicated to the god. An inscription was placed on it, either composed by Alexander himself or by some one else; but as it is not worthy of recollection, I have not deemed it worth while to describe it. Thus then was Tyre captured in the month Hecatombaion, when Anicetus was archon at Athens.[2]

CHAPTER XXV.

The Offers of Darius Rejected.—Batis, Governor of Gaza, Refuses to Submit.

While Alexander was still occupied by the siege of Tyre, ambassadors came to him from Darius, announcing that he would give him ten thousand talents [3] in exchange for his mother, wife, and children; that all the territory west of the river Euphrates, as far as the Grecian Sea, should be Alexander's; and proposing that he should marry the daughter of Darius, and become his friend and

---

[1] *Diodorus* (xvii. 46) and *Curtius* (iv. 19) state that 2,000 Tyrians who had escaped the massacre were hanged on the sea-shore by Alexander's order.

[2] The end of July and beginning of August B.C. 332. *Diodorus* (xvii. 46) tells us that the siege lasted seven months. See also *Curtius* (iv. 20) and Plutarch (*Life of Alexander*, 24). We find from *Strabo* (xvi. 2) that Tyre again became a flourishing city.

[3] About £2,440,000.

ally.[1] When these proposals were announced in a conference of the Companions, Parmenio is said to have told Alexander, that if he were Alexander he should be delighted to put an end to the war on these terms, and incur no further hazard of success. Alexander is said to have replied, So would he also do, if he were Parmenio, but as he was Alexander he replied to Darius as he did. For he said that he was neither in want of money from Darius, nor would he receive a part of his territory instead of the whole; for that all his money and territory were his; and that if he wished to marry the daughter of Darius, he would marry her, even though Darius refused her to him. He commanded Darius to come to him if he wished to experience any generous treatment from him. When Darius heard this answer, he despaired of coming to terms with Alexander, and began to make fresh preparations for war.

Alexander now resolved to make an expedition into Egypt. All the other parts of what was called Palestine Syria[2] had already yielded to him; but a certain eunuch, named Batis, who was in possession of the city of Gaza, paid no heed to him; but procuring Arabian mercenaries, and having been long employed in laying up sufficient food for a long siege, he resolved not to admit Alexander into the city, feeling confident that the place could never be taken by storm.

---

[1] *Diodorus* (xvii. 54) puts the arrival of this embassy after Alexander's conquest of Egypt. *Curtius* (iv. 21) says that the name of the daughter whom Darius offered to Alexander was Statira.

[2] The term Palestine is derived from *Pĕlesheth*, the name given in Hebrew to the coast district in the south-west of Palestine, the inhabitants of which were called *Pĕlishtim*, or Philistines. As this tract of country lay directly between Phoenicia and Egypt, it became known to the Greeks sooner than the rest of the Holy Land, and they called it Syria Palaestinē. The name was gradually extended until it became the usual one for all the Holy Land among Greek and Latin writers. An interesting account of Alexander's visit to Jerusalem and his dealings with the Jews is found in Josephus (*Antiquities*, xi. 8).

CHAPTER XXVI.

Siege of Gaza.

Gaza is about twenty stades from the sea;[1] the approach to it is sandy and over heavy soil, and the sea near the city everywhere shallow. The city of Gaza[2] was large, and had been built upon a lofty mound, around which a strong wall had been carried. It is the last city the traveller meets with going from Phoenicia to Egypt, being situated on the edge of the desert. When Alexander arrived near the city, on the first day he encamped at the spot where the wall seemed to him most easy to assail, and ordered his military engines to be constructed. But the engineers expressed the opinion that it was not possible to capture the wall by force, on account of the height of the mound. However, the more impracticable it seemed to be, the more resolutely Alexander determined that it must be captured. For he said that the action would strike the enemy with great alarm from its being contrary to their expectation; whereas his failure to capture the place would redound to his disgrace when mentioned either to the Greeks or to Darius. He therefore resolved to construct a mound right round the city, so as to be able to bring his military engines up to the walls from the artificial mound which had been raised to the same level with them. The mound was constructed especially over against the southern wall of the city, where it appeared easiest to make an assault. When he

---

[1] Nearly two miles and a half. *Strabo* (xvi. 2) says that the city was only seven stades from the sea.

[2] Gaza is the Greek form of the Hebrew name *Azzah* (fortress). Its position on the border of Egypt and Palestine has given it importance from the earliest times. It was one of the five cities of the Philistines; and retained its own king till a late period, as we learn from Zechariah ix. 5. It was the scene of a battle between Richard I. and the Saracens. It is now called Guzzeh, with a population of 15,000.

thought that the mound had been raised to the proper level with the walls, the Macedonians placed their military engines upon it, and brought them close to the wall of Gaza. At this time while Alexander was offering sacrifice, and, crowned with a garland, was about to commence the first sacred rite according to custom, a certain carnivorous bird, flying over the altar, let a stone which it was carrying with its claws fall upon his head. Alexander asked Aristander, the soothsayer,[1] what this omen meant. He replied: "O king, thou wilt indeed capture the city, but thou must take care of thyself on this day."

CHAPTER XXVII.

Capture of Gaza.

When Alexander heard this, he kept himself for a time near the military engines, out of the reach of missiles. But when a vigorous sortie was made from the city, and the Arabs were carrying torches to set fire to the military engines, and from their commanding position above hurling missiles at the Macedonians, who were defending themselves from lower ground, were driving them down from the mound which they had made, then Alexander either wilfully disobeyed the soothsayer, or forgot the prophecy from excitement in the heat of action. Taking the shield-bearing guards, he hastened to the rescue where the Macedonians were especially hard pressed, and prevented them from being driven down from the mound in disgraceful flight. But he was himself wounded by a bolt from a catapult, right through the shield and breastplate into the shoulder. When he perceived that Aristander had spoken the truth about the wound, he

---

[1] Compare *Arrian*, i. 11 and 25; ii. 18. Plutarch (*Alex.*, 25) says that the bird was entangled and caught among the nets and cords. See also *Curtius*, iv. 26.

rejoiced, because he thought he should also capture the city by the aid of the soothsayer. And yet indeed he was not easily cured of the wound. In the meantime the military engines with which he had captured Tyre arrived, having been sent for by sea; and he ordered the mound to be constructed quite round the city on all sides, two stades[1] in breadth and 250 feet in height. When his engines had been prepared, and brought up along the mound, they shook down a large extent of wall; and mines being dug in various places, and the earth being drawn out by stealth, the wall fell down in many parts, subsiding into the emptied space.[2] The Macedonians then commanded a large extent of ground with their missiles, driving back the men who were defending the city, from the towers. Nevertheless, the men of the city sustained three assaults, though many of their number were killed or wounded; but at the fourth attack, Alexander led up the phalanx of the Macedonians from all sides, threw down the part of the wall which was undermined, and shook down another large portion of it by battering it with his engines, so that he rendered the assault an easy matter through the breaches with his scaling ladders. Accordingly the ladders were brought up to the wall; and then there arose a great emulation among those of the Macedonians who laid any claim to valour, to see who should be the first to scale the wall. The first to do so was Neoptolemus, one of the Companions, of the family of the Aeacidae; and after him mounted one, rank after another with their officers. When once some of the Macedonians got within the wall, they split open in succession the gates which each party happened to light upon, and thus admitted the whole army into the city. But though their city was now in

---

[1] A stadium equalled 606¾ feet.

[2] Cf. *Thucydides*, ii. 76 (description of the siege of Plataeae).

the hands of the enemy, the Gazaeans nevertheless stood together and fought; so that they were all slain fighting there, as each man had been stationed. Alexander sold their wives and children into slavery; and having peopled the city again from the neighbouring settlers, he made use of it as a fortified post for the war.[1]

---

[1] *Diodorus* (xvii. 48) says that the siege of Gaza lasted two months. *Polybius* (xvi. 40) speaks of the resolution and valour of the Gazaeans. We learn from *Curtius* (iv. 28) and from *Dionysius* of Halicarnassus (*De Compositione Verborum*, pp. 123–125) that Alexander treated the brave Batis with horrible cruelty. He ordered his feet to be bored and brazen rings to be put through them, after which the naked body was tied to the back of a chariot which was driven by Alexander himself round the city, in imitation of the treatment of Hector by Achilles at Troy. Cf. *Arrian*, vii. 14. Dionysius quotes from Hegesias of Magnesia, who wrote a history of Alexander, not now extant. Curtius says that nearly 10,000 of the Persians and Arabs were slain at Gaza. *Strabo* (xvi. 2) says that in his time (*i.e.* in the reign of Augustus) the city still remained desolate, as it was left by Alexander.

BOOK III.

CHAPTER I.

Conquest of Egypt.—Foundation of Alexandria.

Alexander now led an expedition into Egypt, whither he had set out at first (from Tyre); and marching from Gaza, on the seventh day he arrived at Pelusium[1] in Egypt. His fleet had also set sail from Phoenicia to Egypt; and he found the ships already moored at Pelusium.[2] When Mazaces the Persian, whom Darius had appointed viceroy of Egypt,[3] ascertained how the battle at Issus had resulted, that Darius had fled in disgraceful flight, and that Phoenicia, Syria, and most of Arabia were already in Alexander's possession, as he had no Persian force with which he could offer resistance, he admitted Alexander into the cities and the country in a friendly

---

[1] Pelusium is identical with the Hebrew *Sin* (a marsh) the most easterly city of Egypt, which is called in Ezekiel xxx. 15, the *strength of Egypt*, because it was the key to that country from its frontier position. Cf. *Herodotus*, iii. 5. *Strabo* (xvii. 1) says it was situated near marshes. It stood east of the Pelusiac branch of the Nile, about 2½ miles from the sea. This mouth of the river was choked up with sand as early as the first century of the Christian era (*Lucan*, viii. 465). Sennacherib advanced as far as this city, and here Cambyses defeated the Egyptians, B.C. 525. Iphicrates the Athenian advanced to Pelusium with the satrap Pharnabazus, B.C. 373. Cf. Vergil (*Georgic*, i. 228); *Martial*, xiii. 9; *Silius*, iii. 375.

[2] *Curtius* (iv. 22) says that this fleet was under the command of Hephaestion.

[3] His predecessor, Sabaces, was slain at Issus. See *Arrian*, ii. 11 supra.

way.[1] Alexander introduced a garrison into Pelusium, and ordering the men in the ships to sail up the river as far as the city of Memphis,[2] he went in person towards Heliopolis,[3] having the river Nile[4] on his right. He reached that city through the desert, after getting possession of all the places on the march through the voluntary surrender of the inhabitants. Thence he

---

[1] *Curtius* (iv. 29) says that Mazaces surrendered to Alexander treasure to the amount of 800 talents, nearly £200,000.

[2] Memphis, the capital of Egypt, is called in the Hebrew Bible, *Noph*. In Hosea ix. 6 it is called *Moph*. The Egyptian name was *Mĕnoph*, of which both Moph and Noph are contractions. The name signifies *place of Ftah*, the Egyptian name for Vulcan. Memphis stood on the west bank of the Nile, and is said by *Herodotus* (ii. 99) to have been founded by Menes. It had a circumference of fifteen miles. Its numerous temples were famous and are mentioned in the poems of Martial, Ovid, and Tibullus. It never recovered the devastation committed by Cambyses, who was exasperated by its resistance. The rise of Alexandria as the capital under the Ptolemies, hastened the decline of Memphis. At Gizeh, near Memphis, are the three great pyramids, being of the height respectively of 460, 446, and 203 feet. Not far off are six smaller ones. Near the second pyramid is the Sphinx, cut out of the solid rock, which was probably an object of worship. Cf. *Apollodorus*, ii. 4.

[3] Heliopolis is known in Hebrew as *On*, which is an Egyptian word meaning *Sun*. It is mentioned in Gen. xli. 45, 50; xlvi. 20. In Ezek. xxx. 17, it is called *Aven*, which is the same word in Hebrew as On, with a variation of the vowels. In Jer. xliii. 13 it is called *Beith-Shemesh*, which in Hebrew means *House of the Sun*, a translation of the Egyptian name. The Greeks called it Heliopolis, *City of the Sun*. The great temple of the Sun and its priesthood are described by Herodotus and Strabo. There are still remaining a beautiful obelisk of red granite nearly 70 feet high, and the brick wall of the temple 3,750 feet long by 2,370 feet broad. Cf. *Apollodorus*, ii. 4.

[4] The word Nile never occurs in the Hebrew Bible; but that river is called *Yeor* (river). In Amos viii. 8 it is called *Yeor Mitsraim*, the river of Egypt; but it is usually called simply *Yeor*, the river. In Isa. xxiii. 3 the corn of Egypt is called *the harvest of Yeor*, or the Nile. In like manner Avon, Ganges, Rhine, mean *river*. The Greek name *Neilos*, or Nile, means a *bed with a stream*, and was originally applied to the land of Egypt, as the valley of the Nile. It rises in the lake Victoria Nyanza, and has a course of 3,300 miles. In Isa. xxiii. 3 and Jer. ii. 18 the Nile is called *Shichor* (turbid). In Homer (*Odys.*, iv. 477, etc.) the river is called Egypt as well as the country. Cf. *Ammianus*, xxii. 15.

crossed the stream and came to Memphis; where he offered sacrifice to Apis[1] and the other gods, and celebrated a gymnastic and musical contest, the most distinguished artists in these matters coming to him from Greece. From Memphis he sailed down the river towards the sea, embarking the shield-bearing guards, the archers, the Agrianians, and of the cavalry the royal squadron of the Companions. Coming to Canobus,[2] he sailed round the Marian lake,[3] and disembarked where now is situated the city of Alexandria, which takes its name from him. The position seemed to him a very fine one in which to found a city, and he foresaw that it would become a prosperous one.[4] Therefore he was seized by an ardent desire to undertake the enterprise, and himself marked out the boundaries of the city, pointing out the place where the agora was to be constructed, where the temples were to be built, stating how many there were to be, and to what Grecian gods they were to be dedicated, and specially marking a spot for a temple to the Egyptian Isis.[5] He also pointed out where the wall was to be carried round it. In regard to these matters he offered sacrifice, and the victims appeared favourable.

CHAPTER II.

Foundation of Alexandria.—Events in the Aegean.

The following story is told, which seems to me not un-

---

[1] The Bull of Memphis, sacred to *Ftah*, the god of fire. See *Herodotus*, iii. 27, 28; *Strabo*, xvii. 1; *Ammianus*, xxii. 14; Ovid (*Met.*, ix. 690).

[2] Now Aboukir, about 13 miles north-east of Alexandria, near the westernmost mouth of the Nile. Cf. Aeschylus (*Supp.*, 311; *Prom.*, 846); *Strabo*, xvii. 1, 17; Tacitus (*Ann.*, ii. 60).

[3] Usually called Lake Mareotis, now Mariût. Cf. Vergil (*Georgic*, ii. 91).

[4] We learn, from *Curtius* (iv. 33), that Alexander at first resolved to build the city on the island of Pharos, but finding it too small, built it on the mainland.

[5] A goddess representing the moon, and wife of Osiris the sun-god.

worthy of belief[1]:—that Alexander himself wished to leave behind for the builders the marks for the boundaries of the fortification, but that there was nothing at hand with which to make a furrow in the ground. One of the builders[2] hit upon the plan of collecting in vessels the barley which the soldiers were carrying, and throwing it upon the ground where the king led the way; and thus the circle of the fortification which he was making[3] for the city was completely marked out. The soothsayers, and especially Aristander the Telmissian, who was said already to have given many other true predictions, pondering this, told Alexander that the city would become prosperous in every respect, but especially in regard to the fruits of the earth.

At this time Hegelochus[4] sailed to Egypt and informed Alexander that the Tenedians had revolted from the Persians and attached themselves to him; because they had gone over to the Persians against their own wish. He also said that the democracy of Chios were introducing Alexander's adherents in spite of those who held the city, being established in it by Autophradates and Pharnabazus. The latter commander had been caught there and kept as a prisoner, as was also the despot Aristonicus, a Methymnaean,[5] who sailed into the harbour of Chios with five piratical vessels, fitted with one and a half banks of oars, not knowing that the harbour was in the hands of Alexander's adherents, but being misled by those who kept the bars of the harbour, because forsooth the fleet of Pharnabazus was moored in it. All

---

[1] Cf. *Strabo* (xvii. 1); Plutarch (*Alex.*, 26); *Diodorus* (xvii. 52); *Curtius* (iv. 33); *Ammianus* (xxii. 16).

[2] We find from *Valerius Maximus* (i. 4) and *Ammianus*, l.c., that his name was Dinocrates.

[3] Krüger substitutes ἐπενόει for ἐποίει, comparing iv. 1, 3, and 4, 1 infra.

[4] See *Arrian*, ii. 2 supra.

[5] Methymna was, next to Mitylene, the most important city in Lesbos.

the pirates were there massacred by the Chians; and Hegelochus brought to Alexander, as prisoners Aristonicus, Apollonides the Chian, Phisinus, Megareus, and all the others who had taken part in the revolt of Chios to the Persians, and who at that time were holding the government of the island by force. He also announced that he had deprived Chares[1] of the possession of Mitylene, that he had brought over the other cities in Lesbos by a voluntary agreement, and that he had sent Amphoterus to Cos with sixty ships, for the Coans themselves invited him to their island. He said that he himself had sailed to Cos and found it already in the hands of Amphoterus. Hegelochus brought all the prisoners with him except Pharnabazus, who had eluded his guards at Cos and got away by stealth. Alexander sent the despots who had been brought from the cities back to their fellow-citizens, to be treated as they pleased; but Apollonides and his Chian partisans he sent under a strict guard to Elephantinē, an Egyptian city.[2]

CHAPTER III.

Alexander Visits the Temple of Ammon.

After these transactions, Alexander was seized by an ardent desire to visit Ammon[3] in Libya, partly in order

---

[1] Chares was an Athenian who had been one of the generals at the fatal battle of Chaeronea. *Curtius* (iv. 24) says that he consented to evacuate Mitylene with his force of 2,000 men on condition of a free departure.

[2] On an island in the Nile, of the same name, opposite Syene. It served as the southern frontier garrison station.

[3] The temple of Jupiter Ammon was in the oasis of Siwah, to the west of Egypt. Its ruins were discovered by Browne in 1792. This oasis is about 6 miles long and 3 broad. The people called Libyans occupied the whole of North Africa excluding Egypt. In Hebrew they are called *Lubim* (sunburnt). See 2 Chron. xii. 3; xvi. 8; Dan. xi. 43; Nah. iii. 9. Cf. *Herodotus*, ii. 32; iv. 168–199.

to consult the god, because the oracle of Ammon was said to be exact in its information, and Perseus and Heracles were said to have consulted it, the former when he was despatched by Polydectes [1] against the Gorgons, and the latter, when he visited Antaeus [2] in Libya and Busiris [3] in Egypt. Alexander was also partly urged by a desire of emulating Perseus and Heracles, from both of whom he traced his descent.[4] He also deduced his pedigree from Ammon, just as the legends traced that of Heracles and Perseus to Zeus. Accordingly he made the expedition to Ammon with the design of learning his own origin more certainly, or at least that he might be able to say that he had learned it. According to Aristobulus, he advanced along the sea-shore to Paraetonium through a country which was a desert, but not destitute of water, a distance of about 1,600 stades.[5] Thence he turned into the interior, where the oracle of Ammon was located. The route is desert, and most of it is sand and destitute of water. But there was a copious supply of rain for Alexander, a thing which was attributed to the influence of the deity; as was also the following occurrence. Whenever a south wind blows in that district, it heaps up the sand upon the route far and wide, rendering the tracks of the road invisible, so that it is impossible to discover where one ought to direct one's course in the sand, just as if one were at sea; for there are no landmarks along the road, neither mountain anywhere, nor tree, nor permanent hill standing erect, by which travellers might be able to form a conjecture of the right course, as

---

[1] King of the island Seriphus. Cf. *Herodotus*, ii. 91.

[2] The gigantic son of Poseidon and Ge.

[3] King of Egypt, who was said to have sacrificed all foreigners that visited the land.

[4] Perseus was the grandfather of Alcmena, the mother of Hercules.

[5] About 183 miles. This city lay at the extreme west of Egypt, in Marmarica.

sailors do by the stars.[1] Consequently, Alexander's army lost the way, and even the guides were in doubt about the course to take. Ptolemy, son of Lagus, says that two serpents went in front of the army, uttering a voice, and Alexander ordered the guides to follow them, trusting in the divine portent. He says too that they showed the way to the oracle and back again. But Aristobulus, whose account is generally admitted as correct, says that two ravens flew in front of the army, and that these acted as Alexander's guides. I am able to assert with confidence that some divine assistance was afforded him, for probability also coincides with the supposition; but the discrepancies in the details of the various narratives have deprived the story of certainty.[2]

---

[1] "For some distance onward the engineers had erected a line of telegraph poles to guide us, but after they ceased the desert was absolutely trackless. Onr guides were the stars—had the night been overcast the enterprise would have been impossible—and we were steered by a naval officer, Lieutenant Rawson, who had doubtless studied on previous nights the relation of these celestial beacons to the course of our march. The centre of the line was the point of direction; therefore he rode between the centre battalions (75th and 79th) of the Highland Brigade. Frequently in the course of the night, after duly ascertaining what dark figure I was addressing, I represented to him that his particular star was clouded over; but he always replied that he had another in view, a second string to his bow, which he showed me, and that he was convinced he had not deviated in the least from the proper direction. And he was right, his guidance was marvellously correct; for his reward, poor fellow, he was shot down in the assault, mortally wounded. Here we were adrift, but for the stars, in a region where no token existed on the surface by which to mark the course—any more than on the ocean without a compass—and the distance to be traversed was many miles."—Sir Edward Hamley: "The Second Division at Tel-el-Kebir," *Nineteenth Century*, December, 1882.

[2] *Strabo* (xvii. 1) quotes from Callisthenes, whose work on Alexander is lost. He agrees with Aristobulus about the two ravens. Callisthenes is also quoted by Plutarch (*Alex.*, 27) in regard to this prodigy. *Curtius* (iv. 30) says that there were *several ravens;* and *Diodorus* (xvii. 49) speaks of *ravens.*

CHAPTER IV.

THE OASIS OF AMMON.

THE place where the temple of Ammon is located is entirely surrounded by a desert of far-stretching sand, which is destitute of water. The fertile spot in the midst of this desert, is not extensive; for where it stretches into its greater expanse, it is only about forty stades broad.[1] It is full of cultivated trees, olives and palms; and it is the only place in those parts which is refreshed with dew. A spring also rises from it, quite unlike all the other springs which issue from the earth.[2] For at mid-day the water is cold to the taste, and still more so to the touch, as cold as cold can be. But when the sun has sunk into the west, it gets warmer, and from the evening it keeps on growing warmer until midnight, when it reaches the warmest point. After midnight it goes on getting gradually colder: at day-break it is already cold; but at midday it reaches the coldest point. Every day it undergoes these alternate changes in regular succession. In this place also natural salt is procured by digging, and certain of the priests of Ammon convey quantities of it into Egypt. For whenever they set out for Egypt they put it into little boxes plaited out of palm, and carry it as a present to the king, or some other great man. The grains of this salt are large, some of them being even longer than three fingers' breadth; and it is clear like crystal.[3] The Egyptians and others who are respectful to the deity, use this salt in their sacrifices, as it is

---

[1] Nearly five miles. Cf. *Lucan*, ix. 511–543.

[2] This *Fountain of the Sun*, as it is called, is 30 paces long and 20 broad; 6 fathoms deep, with bubbles constantly rising from the surface. Cf. *Herodotus*, iv. 181; *Lucretius*, vi. 849–878; *Ptolemy*, iv. 5, 37.

[3] This is what we call sal ammoniac, known to chemists as hydrochlorate of ammonia. The *dactylos* was the smallest Greek measure of length, about $\frac{7}{10}$ of an inch.

clearer than that which is procured from the sea. Alexander then was struck with wonder at the place, and consulted the oracle of the god. Having heard what was agreeable to his wishes, as he himself said, he set out on the journey back to Egypt by the same route, according to the statement of Aristobulus; but according to that of Ptolemy, son of Lagus, he took another road, leading straight to Memphis.[1]

CHAPTER V.

Settlement of the Affairs of Egypt.

At Memphis, many embassies from Greece reached him; and he sent away no one disappointed by the rejection of his suit. From Antipater also arrived an army of 400 Grecian mercenaries under the command of Menidas, son of Hegesander: likewise from Thrace 500 cavalry, under the direction of Asclepiodorus, son of Eunicus. Here he offered sacrifice to Zeus the King, led his soldiers fully armed in solemn procession, and celebrated a gymnastic and musical contest. He then settled the affairs of Egypt, by appointing two Egyptians, Doloaspis and Petisis, governors of the country, dividing between them the whole land; but as Petisis declined his province, Doloaspis received the whole. He appointed two of the Companions to be commandants of garrisons: Pantaleon the Pydnaean in Memphis, and Polemo, son of Megacles, a Pellaean, in Pelusium. He also gave the command of the Grecian auxiliaries to Lycidas, an Aetolian, and ap-

---

[1] We learn from *Strabo* (xvii. 1), on the authority of Callisthenes, that the declaration of the oracle of Ammon was confirmed by those of Apollo at Branchidae near Miletus, and of Athena at Erythrae in Ionia. Plutarch (*Alex.*, 28) and *Arrian* (vii. 29) assert that Alexander set afloat the declaration that he was the son of Zeus to overawe the foreigners over whom he was extending his rule.

pointed Eugnostus, son of Xenophantes, one of the Companions, to be secretary over the same troops. As their overseers he placed Aeschylus and Ephippus the Chalcidean. The government of the neighbouring country of Libya he granted to Apollonius, son of Charinus; and the part of Arabia near Heroöpolis[1] he put under Cleomenes, a man of Naucratis.[2] This last was ordered to allow the governors to rule their respective districts according to the ancient custom; but to collect from them the tribute due to him. The native governors were also ordered to pay it to Cleomenes. He appointed Peucestas, son of Macartatus, and Balacrus, son of Amyntas, generals of the army which he left behind in Egypt; and he placed Polemo, son of Theramenes, over the fleet as admiral. He made Leonnatus, son of Anteas, one of his body-guards instead of Arrhybas, who had died of disease. Antiochus, the commander of the archers, also died; and in his stead Ombrion the Cretan was appointed. When Balacrus was left behind in Egypt, the allied Grecian infantry, which had been under his command, was put under that of Calanus. Alexander was said to have divided the government of Egypt among so many men, because he was surprised at the natural strength of the country, and he thought it unsafe to entrust the rule of the whole to a single person. The Romans also seem to me to have learned a lesson from him, and therefore keep Egypt under strong guard; for they do not send any of the senators thither as proconsul for the same reason, but only men who have the rank among them of Equites (Knights).[3]

---

[1] Ewald and others think that Heroöpolis was identical with the Raamses of the Bible. Raamses, or Rameses, is a Coptic word meaning "the son of the sun."

[2] A city founded by the Milesians on the Canopic branch of the Nile. It remained a purely Greek city, being the only place where Greeks were allowed to settle and trade in Egypt. Cf. *Herodotus*, ii. 97, 135, 178, 179.

[3] Cf. Tacitus (*Historiae*, i. 11).

CHAPTER VI.

MARCH INTO SYRIA.—ALEXANDER'S KINDNESS TO HARPALUS AND HIS OTHER EARLY ADHERENTS.

As soon as spring began to appear, he went from Memphis to Phoenicia, bridging the stream of the Nile near Memphis, as well as the canals issuing from it. When he arrived at Tyre, he found his fleet already there.[1] In this city he again offered sacrifice to Heracles, and celebrated both a gymnastic and musical contest. While there, the state vessel called the *Paralus* came to him from Athens, bringing Diophantus and Achilleus as envoys to him; and all the crew of the *Paralus* were joined with them in the embassy.[2] These men obtained all the requests which they were despatched to make, and the king gave up to the Athenians all their fellow-citizens who had been captured at the Granicus.[3] Being informed that revolutionary plans had been carried out in the Peloponnese, he sent Amphoterus thither to assist those of the Peloponnesians who were firm in their support of his war against Persia, and were not under the control of the Lacedaemonians. He also commanded the Phoenicians and Cyprians to despatch to the Peloponnese 100 other ships in addition to those which he was sending with Amphoterus. He now started up into the interior

---

[1] We learn, from *Curtius* (iv. 34), that Alexander went to Samaria to chastise the inhabitants, who had burnt his deputy, Andromachus, to death.

[2] From early times the Athenians kept two sacred vessels for state purposes, the one called the *Paralus* and the other *Salaminia*. In the earliest times the former was used for coasting purposes, and the latter for the journey to Salamis. Hence their respective names. See Dr. Smith's *Dict. of Antiquities*. Aeschines, in his oration against Ctesiphon (p. 550), asserts that he was informed by the seamen of the *Paralus* that Demosthenes on this occasion sent a letter to Alexander soliciting pardon and favour.

[3] Cf. Aelian, *Varia Historia*, i. 25; *Curtius*, iv. 34.

towards Thapsacus and the river Euphrates, after placing Coeranus, a Beroean [1] over the levy of tribute in Phoenicia, and Philoxenus to collect it in Asia as far as the Taurus. In the place of these men he entrusted the custody of the money which he had with him to Harpalus, son of Machatas, who had just returned from exile. For this man at first had been banished, while Philip was still king, because he was an adherent of Alexander; as also was Ptolemy, son of Lagus, for the same reason; likewise Nearchus, son of Androtimus, Erigyius, son of Larichus, and his brother Laomedon. For Alexander fell under Philip's suspicion when the latter married Eurydice [2] and treated Alexander's mother Olympias with dishonour. But after Philip's death those who had been banished on Alexander's account returned from exile and were received into favour. He made Ptolemy one of his confidential body-guards; he placed Harpalus over the money, because his bodily strength was unequal to the fatigues of war. Erigyius was made commander of the allied Grecian cavalry; and his brother Laomedon, because he could speak both the Greek and Persian languages and could read Persian writings, was put in charge of the foreign prisoners. Nearchus also was appointed viceroy of Lycia and of the land adjacent to it as far as mount Taurus. But shortly before the battle which was fought at Issus, Harpalus fell under the influence of Tauriscus, an evil man, and fled in his company. The

---

[1] Beroea was a city of Macedonia, on the Astraeus, a tributary of the Haliacmon, about 20 miles from the sea.

[2] Other historians call this queen Cleopatra. She was the daughter of a Macedonian named Attalus. Plutarch (*Alex.*, 9 and 10) says that she was cruelly put to death by Olympias during Alexander's absence. *Justin* (ix. 7; xi. 2) states that Olympias first slew her daughter on her mother's bosom and then had Cleopatra hanged; while Alexander put to death Caranus, the infant son of Philip and Cleopatra. *Pausanias* (viii. 7) says that Olympias caused Cleopatra and her infant son to be roasted on a brazen vessel. Cf. Aelian (*Varia Historia*, xiii. 35).

latter started off to Alexander the Epirote[1] in Italy, where he soon after died. But Harpalus found a refuge in Megaris, whence however Alexander persuaded him to return, giving him a pledge that he should be none the worse on account of his desertion. When he came back, he not only received no punishment, but was even reinstated in the office of treasurer. Menander, one of the Companions, was sent away into Lydia as viceroy; and Clearchus was put in command of the Grecian auxiliaries who had been under Menander. Asclepiodorus, son of Eunicus, was also appointed viceroy of Syria instead of Arimmas, because the latter seemed to have been remiss in collecting the supplies which he had been ordered to collect for the army which the king was about to lead into the interior.

CHAPTER VII.

Passage of the Euphrates and Tigris.

Alexander arrived at Thapsacus in the month Hecatombaion,[2] in the archonship of Aristophanes at Athens; and he found that two bridges of boats had been constructed over the stream. But Mazaeus, to whom Darius had committed the duty of guarding the river, with about 3,000 cavalry, 2,000 of which were Grecian mercenaries, was up to that time keeping guard there at the river. For this reason the Macedonians had not constructed the complete bridge as far as the opposite bank, being afraid that Mazaeus might make an assault upon the bridge where it ended. But when he heard that Alexander was approaching, he went off in flight with all his army.

---

[1] This king was brother of Alexander's mother Olympias, and husband of Cleopatra the daughter of Philip and Olympias. He crossed over into Italy to aid the Tarentines against the Lucanians and Bruttians, but was eventually defeated and slain near Pandosia, B.C. 326.

[2] June–July, B.C. 331.

As soon as he had fled, the bridges were completed as far as the further bank, and Alexander crossed upon them with his army.[1] Thence he marched up into the interior through the land called Mesopotamia, having the river Euphrates and the mountains of Armenia on his left. When he started from the Euphrates he did not march to Babylon by the direct road; because by going the other route he found all things easier for the march of his army, and it was also easier to obtain fodder for the horses and provisions for the men from the country. Besides this, the heat was not so scorching on the indirect route. Some of the men from Darius's army, who were dispersed for the purpose of scouting, were taken prisoners; and they reported that Darius was encamped near the river Tigris, having resolved to prevent Alexander from crossing that stream. They also said that he had a much larger army than that with which he had fought in Cilicia. Hearing this, Alexander went with all speed towards the Tigris; but when he reached it he found neither Darius himself nor any guard which he had left. However he experienced great difficulty in crossing the stream, on account of the swiftness of the current,[2] though no one tried to stop him. There he made his army rest, and while so doing, an eclipse of the moon nearly total occurred.[3] Alexander thereupon

---

[1] We learn, from *Curtius* (iv. 37), that Alexander took eleven days to march from Phoenicia to the Euphrates.

[2] *Curtius* (iv. 37) says that Tigris is the Persian word for *arrow;* and that the river was so named on account of the swiftness of its current. The Hebrew name is Chiddekel, which means *arrow*. See Gen. ii. 14; and Dan. x. 4, where it is called *the great river*. The name Tigris is derived from the Zend *Tighra*, which comes from the Sanscrit *Tig*, to sharpen. It is now called Dijleh. It joins the Euphrates 90 miles from the sea, and the united stream is called Shat-el-Arab. Its entire length is 1,146 miles. In ancient times the two rivers had distinct mouths. So the Rhon formerly had several mouths. See *Livy*, xxi. 26. *Strabo* (iv. 1, 8) says that Timaeus gave it five mouths; Polybius gives it two; others give seven.

[3] This eclipse occurred September 20th, B.C. 331.

offered sacrifice to the moon, the sun and the earth, whose deed this was, according to common report. Aristander thought that this eclipse of the moon was a portent favourable to Alexander and the Macedonians; that there would be a battle that very month, and that victory for Alexander was signified by the sacrificial victims. Having therefore decamped from the Tigris, he went through the land of Aturia,[1] having the mountains of the Gordyaeans [2] on the left and the Tigris itself on the right; and on the fourth day after the passage of the river, his scouts brought word to him that the enemy's cavalry were visible there along the plain, but how many of them there were they could not guess. Accordingly he drew his army up in order and advanced prepared for battle. Other scouts again riding forward and taking more accurate observations, told him that the cavalry did not seem to them to be more than 1,000 in number.

CHAPTER VIII.

Description of Darius's Army at Arbela.

Alexander therefore took the royal squadron of cavalry, and one squadron of the Companions, together with the Paeonian scouts, and marched with all speed; having ordered the rest of his army to follow at leisure. The Persian cavalry, seeing Alexander advancing quickly, began to flee with all their might. Though he pressed close upon them in pursuit, most of them escaped; but a few, whose horses were fatigued by the flight, were slain, others were taken prisoners, horses and all. From these they ascertained that Darius with a large force was

---

[1] The part of Assyria lying between the Upper Tigris and the Lycus was called Aturia.

[2] Called Carduchi by Xenophon. These mountains separate Assyria and Mesopotamia from Media and Armenia

not far off. For the Indians who were conterminous with the Bactrians, as also the Bactrians themselves and the Sogdianians had come to the aid of Darius, all being under the command of Bessus, the viceroy of the land of Bactria. They were accompanied by the Sacians, a Scythian tribe belonging to the Scythians who dwell in Asia.[1] These were not subject to Bessus, but were in alliance with Darius. They were commanded by Mavaces, and were horse-bowmen. Barsaentes, the viceroy of Arachotia, led the Arachotians[2] and the men who were called mountaineer Indians. Satibarzanes, the viceroy of Areia, led the Areians,[3] as did Phrataphernes the Parthians, Hyrcanians, and Tapurians,[4] all of whom were horsemen. Atropates commanded the Medes, with whom were arrayed the Cadusians, Albanians, and Sacesinians.[5] The men who dwelt near the Red Sea[6] were marshalled by Ocondobates, Ariobarzanes, and Otanes. The Uxians and Susianians[7] acknowledged Oxathres son of Aboulites as their leader, and the Babylonians were commanded by Boupares. The Carians who had

---

[1] Cf. Aelian (*Varia Historia*, xii. 38).

[2] Arachosia comprised what is now the south-east part of Afghanistan and the north-east part of Beloochistan.

[3] Aria comprised the west and north-west part of Afghanistan and the east part of Khorasan.

[4] Parthia is the modern Khorasan. Hyrcania was the country south and south-east of the Caspian Sea. The Tapurians dwelt in the north of Media, on the borders of Parthia between the Caspian passes. Cf. *Ammianus*, xxiii. 6.

[5] The Cadusians lived south-west of the Caspian, the Albanians on the west of the same sea, in the south-east part of Georgia, and the Sacesinians in the north-east of Armenia, on the river Kur.

[6] The Red Sea was the name originally given to the whole expanse of sea to the west of India as far as Africa. The name was subsequently given to the Arabian Gulf exclusively. In Hebrew it is called *Yam-Suph* (Sea of Sedge, or a seaweed resembling wool). The Egyptians called it the Sea of Weeds.

[7] The Uxians occupied the north-west of Persis, and Susiana was the country to the north and west of Persis.

been deported into central Asia, and the Sitacenians[1] had been placed in the same ranks as the Babylonians. The Armenians were commanded by Orontes and Mithraustes, and the Cappadocians by Ariaces. The Syrians from the vale between Lebanon and Anti-Lebanon (*i.e.* Coele-Syria) and the men of Syria which lies between the rivers[2] were led by Mazaeus. The whole army of Darius was said to contain 40,000 cavalry, 1,000,000 infantry, and 200 scythe-bearing chariots.[3] There were only a few elephants, about fifteen in number, belonging to the Indians who live this side of the Indus.[4] With these forces Darïus had encamped at Gaugamela, near the river Bumodus, about 600 stades distant from the city of Arbela, in a district everywhere level;[5] for whatever ground thereabouts was unlevel and unfit for the evolutions of cavalry, had long before been levelled by the Persians, and made fit for the easy rolling of chariots and for the galloping of horses. For there were some who persuaded Darius that he had forsooth got the

---

[1] The Sitacenians lived in the south of Assyria. ἐτετάχατο is the Ionic form for τεταγμένοι ἦσαν.

[2] The Greeks called this country Mesopotamia because it lies between the rivers Euphrates and Tigris. In the Bible it is called Paddan-Aram (the plain of *Aram*, which is the Hebrew name of Syria). In Gen. xlviii. 7 it is called merely *Paddan*, the plain. In Hos. xii. 12, it is called the *field of Aram*, or, as our Bible has it, the *country of Syria*. Elsewhere in the Bible it is called *Aram-naharaim*, Aram of the two rivers, which the Greeks translated Mesopotamia. It is called "*the Island*," by Arabian geographers.

[3] *Curtius* (iv. 35 and 45) states that Darius had 200,000 infantry, 45,000 cavalry, and 200 scythed chariots; *Diodorus* (xvii. 53) says, 800,000 infantry, 200,000 cavalry, and 200 scythed chariots; *Justin* (xi. 12) gives 400,000 foot and 100,000 horse; and Plutarch (*Alex.*, 31) speaks of a million of men. For the chariots cf. Xenophon (*Anab.*, i. 8, 10); *Livy*, xxxvii. 41.

[4] This is the first instance on record of the employment of elephants in battle.

[5] This river is now called Ghasir, a tributary of the Great Zab. The village Gaugamela was in the district of Assyria called Aturia, about 69 miles from the city of Arbela, now called Erbil.

worst of it in the battle fought at Issus, from the narrowness of the battle-field; and this he was easily induced to believe.

CHAPTER IX.

ALEXANDER'S TACTICS.—HIS SPEECH TO THE OFFICERS.

WHEN Alexander had received all this information from the Persian scouts who had been captured, he remained four days in the place where he had received the news; and gave his army rest after the march. He meanwhile fortified his camp with a ditch and stockade, as he intended to leave behind the baggage and all the soldiers who were unfit for fighting, and to go into the contest accompanied by his warriors carrying with them nothing except their weapons. Accordingly he took his forces by night, and began the march about the second watch, in order to come into collision with the foreigners at break of day. As soon as Darius was informed of Alexander's approach, he at once drew out his army for battle; and Alexander led on his men drawn up in like manner. Though the armies were only sixty stades [1] from each other, yet they were not in sight of each other, for between the hostile forces some hills intervened. But when Alexander was only thirty stades distant from the enemy, and his army was already marching down from the hills just mentioned, catching sight of the foreigners, he caused his phalanx to halt there. Calling a council of the Companions, generals, cavalry officers, and leaders of the Grecian allies and mercenaries, he deliberated with them, whether he should at once lead on the phalanx without delay, as most of them urged him to do; or, whether, as Parmenio thought preferable, to pitch their tents there for the present, to reconnoitre all the ground, in order to

[1] About 7 miles.

see if there was anything there to excite suspicion or to impede their progress, or if there were ditches or stakes firmly fixed in the earth out of sight, as well as to make a more accurate survey of the enemy's tactical arrangements. Parmenio's opinion prevailed, so they encamped there, drawn up in the order in which they intended to enter the battle. But Alexander took the light infantry and the cavalry Companions and went all round, reconnoitring the whole country where he was about to fight the battle. Having returned, he again called together the same leaders, and said that they did not require to be encouraged by him to enter the contest; for they had been long before encouraged by their own valour, and by the gallant deeds which they had already so often achieved. He thought it expedient that each of them individually should stir up his own men separately; the infantry captain the men of his company, the cavalry captain his own squadron, the brigadiers their various brigades, and each of the leaders of the infantry the phalanx entrusted to him. He assured them that in this battle they were going to fight, not as before, either for Coele-Syria, Phoenicia, or Egypt, but for the whole of Asia. For he said this battle would decide who were to be the rulers of that continent. It was not necessary for him to stir them up to gallant deeds by many words, since they had this valour by nature; but they should see that each man took care, so far as in him lay, to preserve discipline in the critical moment of action, and to keep perfect silence when it was expedient to advance in silence. On the other hand, they should see that each man uttered a sonorous shout, where it would be advantageous to shout, and to raise as terrible a battle-cry as possible, when a suitable opportunity occurred of raising the battle-cry. He told them to take care to obey his orders as quickly as possible, and to transmit the orders they had received to the ranks with all rapidity; each man remembering that both as an individual and in the aggregate he was increasing the general danger if he was remiss in the discharge of his duty, and that he was assisting to gain a victory if he zealously put forth his utmost exertions.

CHAPTER X.

Rejection of Parmenio's Advice.

With these words and others like them he briefly exhorted his officers, and in return was exhorted by them to feel confidence in their valour. He then ordered the soldiers to take dinner and to rest themselves. It is said that Parmenio came to him in his tent, and urged him to make a night attack on the Persians; saying that thus he would fall upon them unprepared and in a state of confusion, and at the same time more liable to a panic in the dark.[1] But the reply which he made, as others were listening to their conversation, was, that it would be mean to steal a victory, and that Alexander ought to conquer in open daylight, and without any artifice. This vaunting did not appear any arrogance on his part, but rather to indicate self-confidence amid dangers. To me at any rate, he seems to have used correct reasoning in such a matter. For in the night many accidents have occurred unexpectedly to those who were sufficiently prepared for battle as well as to those who were deficiently prepared, which have caused the superior party to fail in their plans, and have handed the victory over to the inferior party, contrary to the expectations of both sides. Though Alexander was generally fond of encountering danger in battle, the night appeared to him perilous; and, besides, if Darius were again defeated,

---

[1] Xenophon (*Anab.*, iii. 4, 35) explains why this was so.

a furtive and nocturnal attack on the part of the Macedonians would relieve him of the necessity of confessing that he was an inferior general and commanded inferior troops. Moreover, if any unexpected defeat befell his army, the circumjacent country was friendly to the enemy, and they were acquainted with the locality, whereas the Macedonians[1] were unacquainted with it, and surrounded by nothing but foes, of whom there were a great number prisoners. These would be a great source of anxiety, as they would be likely to assist in attacking them in the night, not only if they should meet with defeat, but even if they did not appear to be gaining a decisive victory. For this way of reasoning I commend Alexander; and I think him no less worthy of admiration for his excessive desire to fight in open daylight.

CHAPTER XI.

Tactics of the Opposing Generals.

Darius and his army remained drawn up during the night in the same order as that in which they had first arrayed themselves; because they had not surrounded themselves with a completely entrenched camp, and, moreover, they were afraid that the enemy would attack them in the night. The success of the Persians, on this occasion, was impeded especially by this long standing on watch with their arms, and by the fear which usually springs up before great dangers; which, however, was not then suddenly aroused by a momentary panic, but had been experienced for a long time, and had thoroughly cowed their spirits.[2] The army of Darius was drawn up in the following manner: for, according to the statement of Aristobulus, the written scheme of arrangement drawn

[1] σφεῖς here stands for αὐτοί.

[2] See note 1 to ii. 10 supra.

up by Darius was afterwards captured. His left wing was held by the Bactrian cavalry, in conjunction with the Daans[1] and Arachotians; near these had been posted the Persians, horse and foot mixed together; next to these the Susians, and then the Cadusians. This was the arrangement of the left wing as far as the middle of the whole phalanx. On the right had been posted the men from Coele-Syria and Mesopotamia. On the right again were the Medes; next to them the Parthians and Sacians; then the Tapurians and Hyrcanians, and last the Albanians and Sacesinians, extending as far as the middle of the whole phalanx. In the centre where King Darius was, had been posted the king's kinsmen,[2] the Persian guards carrying spears with golden apples at the butt end,[3] the Indians, the Carians who had been forcibly removed to Central Asia, and the Mardian archers.[4] The Uxians, the Babylonians, the men who dwell near the Red Sea, and the Sitacenians had also been drawn up in deep column. On the left, opposite Alexander's right, had been posted the Scythian cavalry, about 1,000 Bactrians and 100 scythe-bearing chariots. In front of Darius's royal squadron of cavalry stood the elephants and 50 chariots. In front of the right wing the Armenian and Cappadocian cavalry with 50 scythe-bearing chariots had been posted. The Greek mercenaries, as alone capable of coping with the Macedonians, were stationed right opposite their phalanx, in

---

[1] These people were a Scythian tribe leading a nomadic life east of the Caspian. They are called Daoi by *Herodotus*, i. 125; Dahae by *Ammianus*, xxii. 8, 21; *Livy*, xxxv. 48; xxxvii. 38; Vergil (*Aeneid*, viii. 728); *Pliny*, vi. 19; *Strabo*, xi. 7. They are mentioned in Ezra iv. 9 as subjects of Persia. The district is now called Daikh. See Fürst's *Hebrew Lexicon*, sub voce דֶּה.

[2] A title of honour. Curtius says that they numbered 15,000.

[3] Cf. *Herodotus*, vii. 41.

[4] This people lived to the south of the Caspian.

two divisions close beside Darius himself and his Persian attendants, one division on each side.[1]

Alexander's army was marshalled as follows: The right wing was held by the cavalry Companions, in front of whom had been posted the royal squadron, commanded by Clitus, son of Dropidas. Near this was the squadron of Glaucias, next to it that of Aristo, then that of Sopolis, son of Hermodorus, then that of Heraclides, son of Antiochus. Near this was that of Demetrius, son of Althaemenes, then that of Meleager, and last one of the royal squadrons commanded by Hegelochus, son of Hippostratus. All the cavalry Companions were under the supreme command of Philotas, son of Parmenio. Of the phalanx of Macedonian infantry, nearest to the cavalry had been posted first the select corps of shield-bearing guards, and then the rest of the shield-bearing-guards, under the command of Nicanor, son of Parmenio. Next to these was the brigade of Coenus, son of Polemocrates; after these that of Perdiccas, son of Orontes, then that of Meleager, son of Neoptolemus, then that of Polysperchon,[2] son of Simmias, and last that of Amyntas, son of Andromenes, under the command of Simmias, because Amyntas had been despatched to Macedonia to levy au army. The brigade of Craterus, son of Alexander, held the left end of the Macedonian phalanx, and this general commanded the left wing of the infantry.[3] Next to him was the allied Grecian

---

[1] "Several names of various contingents stated to have been present in the field are not placed in the official return—thus the Sogdiani, the Arians, and the Indian mountaineers are mentioned by *Arrian* as having joined Darius (iii. 8); the Kossaeans by *Diodorus* (xvii. 59); the Sogdiani, Massagatae, Belitae, Kossaeans, Gortyae, Phrygians, and Kataonians, by *Curtius* (iv. 12)."—*Grote.*

[2] This distinguished general succeeded Antipater as regent of Macedonia, but was overcome by Cassander, the son of the former, and became subordinate to him.

[3] There were thus six taxeis, or brigades of foot Companions, as they

cavalry, under the command of Erigyius, son of Larichus. Next to these, towards the left wing of the army, were the Thessalian cavalry, under the command of Philip, son of Menelaüs. But the whole left wing was led by Parmenio, son of Philotas, round whose person were ranged the Pharsalian horsemen, who were both the best and most numerous squadron of the Thessalian cavalry.

CHAPTER XII.

Alexander's Tactics.

In this way had Alexander marshalled his army in front; but he also posted a second array, so that his phalanx might be a double one.[1] Directions had been given to the commanders of these men posted in reserve, to wheel round and receive the attack of the foreigners, if they should see their own comrades surrounded by the Persian army. Next to the royal squadron on the right wing, half of the Agrianians, under the command of Attalus, in conjunction with the Macedonian archers under Briso's command, were posted angular-wise (*i.e.* in such a way that the wings were thrown forward at an angle with the centre, so as to take the enemy in flank) in case they should be seized anyhow by the necessity of folding back the phalanx or of closing it up (*i.e.* of deepening it by countermarching from front to rear). Next to the archers were the men called the veteran mercenaries, whose commander was Cleander. In front of the Agrianians and archers were posted the light cavalry used for skirmishing, and the Paeonians, under

were called, in the phalanx of infantry at the battle of Arbela. Arrian's description of the battle at the Granicus (i. 14) seems to be erroneous in some of the words of the text; yet it may be gathered from it that there were also six taxeis in Alexander's phalanx on that occasion also.

[1] See Arrian's *Tactics*, 29.

the command of Aretes and Aristo. In front of all had been posted the Grecian mercenary cavalry under the direction of Menidas; and in front of the royal squadron of cavalry and the other Companions had been posted half of the Agrianians and archers, and the javelin-men of Balacrus who had been ranged opposite the scythe-bearing chariots. Instructions had been given to Menidas and the troops under him to wheel round and attack the enemy in flank, if they should ride round their wing. Thus had Alexander arranged matters on the right wing. On the left the Thracians under the command of Sitalces had been posted angular-wise, and near them the cavalry of the Grecian allies, under the direction of Coeranus. Next stood the Odrysian cavalry, under the command of Agatho, son of Tyrimmas. In this part, in front of all, were posted the auxiliary cavalry of the Grecian mercenaries, under the direction of Andromachus, son of Hiero. Near the baggage the infantry from Thrace were posted as a guard. The whole of Alexander's army numbered 7,000 cavalry and about 40,000 infantry.

CHAPTER XIII.

The Battle of Arbela.

When the armies drew near each other, Darius and the men around him were observed; viz. the apple-bearing Persians, the Indians, the Albanians, the Carians who had been forcibly transported into Central Asia, the Mardian archers ranged opposite Alexander himself and his royal squadron of cavalry. Alexander led his own army more towards the right, and the Persians marched along parallel with him, far outflanking him upon their left.[1] Then the Scythian cavalry rode along the line,

---

[1] Cf. *Diodorus* (xvii. 57).

and came into conflict with the front men of Alexander's array; but he nevertheless still oontinued to march towards the right, and almost entirely got beyond the ground which had been cleared and levelled by the Persians.[1] Then Darius, fearing that his chariots would become useless, if the Macedonians advanced into uneven ground, ordered the front ranks of his left wing to ride round the right wing of the Macedonians, where Alexander was commanding, to prevent him from marching his wing any further. This being done, Alexander ordered the cavalry of the Grecian mercenaries under the command of Menidas to attack them. But the Scythian cavalry and the Bactrians, who had been drawn up with them sallied forth against them, and being much more numerous they put the small body of Greeks to rout. Alexander then ordered Aristo at the head of the Paeonians and Grecian auxiliaries to attack the Scythians; and the barbarians gave way. But the rest of the Bactrians drawing near to the Paeonians and Grecian auxiliaries, caused their own comrades who were already in flight to turn and renew the battle; and thus they brought about a general cavalry engagement, in which many of Alexander's men fell, not only being overwhelmed by the multitude of the barbarians, but also because the Scythians themselves and their horses were much more completely protected with armour for guarding their bodies.[2] Notwithstanding this, the Macedonians sustained their assaults, and assailing them violently squadron by squadron, they succeeded in pushing them out of rank. Meantime the foreigners launched their scythe-bearing chariots against Alexander himself, for the purpose of throwing his phalanx into

---

[1] See Donaldson's *New Cratylus*, sect. 178.

[2] Cf. *Curtius*, iv. 35. "Equitibus equisque tegumenta erant ex ferreis laminis seris inter se connexis."

confusion; but in this they were grievously deceived. For as soon as some of them approached, the Agrianians and the javelin-men with Balacrus, who had been posted in front of the Companion cavalry, hurled their javelins at them; others they seized by the reins and pulled the drivers off, and standing round the horses killed them. Yet some rolled right through the ranks; for the men stood apart and opened their ranks, as they had been instructed, in the places where the chariots assaulted them. In this way it generally happened that the chariots passed through safely, and the men by whom they were driven were uninjured. But these also were afterwards overpowered by the grooms of Alexander's army and by the royal shield-bearing guards.[1]

CHAPTER XIV.

Battle of Arbela.—Flight of Darius.

As soon as Darius began to set his whole phalanx in motion, Alexander ordered Aretes to attack those who were riding completely round his right wing; and up to that time he was himself leading his men in column. But when the Persians had made a break in the front line of their army, in consequence of the cavalry sallying forth to assist those who were surrounding the right wing, Alexander wheeled round towards the gap, and forming a wedge as it were of the Companion cavalry and of the part of the phalanx which was posted here, he led them with a quick charge and loud battle-cry straight towards Darius himself. For a short time there ensued a hand-to-hand fight; but when the Macedonian cavalry, commanded by Alexander himself, pressed on

[1] Compare the uselessness of the Persian scythed chariots at the battle of Cunaxa. See Xenophon (*Anabasis*, i. 8). So also at the battle of Magnesia between Scipio and Antiochus. See *Livy*, xxxvii. 41.

vigorously, thrusting themselves against the Persians and striking their faces with their spears, and when the Macedonian phalanx in dense array and bristling[1] with long pikes had also made an attack upon them, all things at once appeared full of terror to Darius, who had already long been in a state of fear, so that he was the first to turn and flee.[2] The Persians also who were riding round the wing were seized with alarm when Aretes made a vigorous attack upon them. In this quarter indeed the Persians took to speedy flight; and the Macedonians followed up the fugitives and slaughtered them.[3] Simmias and his brigade were not yet able to start with Alexander in pursuit, but causing the phalanx to halt there, he took part in the struggle, because the left wing of the Macedonians was reported to be hard pressed. In this part of the field, their line being broken, some of the Indians and of the Persian cavalry burst through the gap towards the baggage of the Macedonians; and there the action became desperate. For the Persians fell boldly on the men, who were most of them unarmed, and never expected that any men would cut through the double phalanx and break through upon them.[4] When the Persians made this attack, the

---

[1] πεφρικυῖα, imitated from Homer (*Iliad*, iv. 282). Cf. Vergil (*Aeneid*, x. 178, *horrentibus hastis*); *Livy*, xliv. 41 (*horrendis hastis*).

[2] *Curtius* (iv. 58, 59) and *Diodorus* (xvii. 60) describe quite an Homeric battle, Darius hurling a spear at Alexander, and Alexander hurling his at Darius and killing his charioteer. They say that the Persians mistook the fall of the charioteer for that of the king, and fled, carrying Darius with them.

[3] *Curtius* (iv. 59) and *Diodorus* (xvii. 60) say that so thick a cloud of dust was raised by the mighty mass of fugitives, that nothiog could be clearly distinguished, and that thus the Macedonians lost the track of Darius. The noise of the shouting and the cracking of whips served as guides to the pursuers.

[4] Sisygambis, the mother of Darius, whom these Persians were especially anxious to liberate from the custody of the Macedonians, refused to go with them. See *Diodorus* and *Curtius*.

foreign prisoners also assisted them by falling upon the Macedonians in the midst of the action. But the commanders of the men who had been posted as a reserve to the first phalanx, learning what was taking place, quickly moved from the position which they had been ordered to take, and coming upon the Persians in the rear, killed many of them there collected round the baggage. But the rest of them gave way and fled. The Persians on the right wing, who had not yet become aware of the flight of Darius, rode round Alexander's left wing and attacked Parmenio in flank.[1]

CHAPTER XV.

Defeat of the Persians and Pursuit of Darius.

At this juncture, while the Macedonians were doubtful as to the result of the battle, Parmenio sent a messenger to Alexander in haste, to tell him that their side was in a critical position and that he must send him aid.[2] When this news was brought to Alexander, he immediately turned back again from the pursuit, and wheeling round with the Companion cavalry, led them with great speed against the right wing of the foreigners. In the first place he assaulted the fleeing cavalry of the enemy, the Parthians, some of the Indians, and the most numerous and the bravest division of the Persians. Then ensued the most obstinately contested cavalry fight in the whole engagement. For being drawn up by squadrons as it were, the foreigners wheeled round and falling on Alexander's men face to face, they no longer relied

[1] Arrian does not say much about this vigorous charge of Mazaeus, the commander of the Persian right wing. See *Curtius* (iv. 60); *Diodorus* (xvii. 60).

[2] We learn from *Diodorus* and *Curtius* that Parmenio had driven Mazaeus back before Alexander's arrival.

on the hurling of javelins or the dexterous deploying of horses, as is the common practice in cavalry battles, but every one on his own account strove eagerly to break through what stood in his way, as if this were their only means of safety. They struck and were struck without quarter, as if they were no longer struggling to secure the victory for another, but were contending for their own personal safety. Here about sixty of Alexander's Companions fell; and Hephaestion himself, as well as Coenus and Menidas, was wounded. But even these troops were overcome by Alexander; and as many of them as could force their way through his ranks fled with all their might. And now Alexander had nearly come into conflict with the enemy's right wing, but in the meantime the Thessalian cavalry in a splendid struggle, had not fallen short of Alexander's success in the engagement. For the foreigners on the right wing were already beginning to fly when he came on the scene of conflict; so that he wheeled round again and started off in pursuit of Darius once more, keeping up the chase as long as there was daylight. Parmenio's brigade also followed in pursuit of those who were opposed to them. But Alexander crossed the river Lycus[1] and pitched his camp there, to give his men and horses a little rest; while Parmenio seized the Persian camp with their baggage, elephants, and camels. After giving his horsemen rest until midnight, Alexander again advanced by a forced march towards Arbela, with the hope of seizing Darius there, together with his money and the rest of his royal property. He reached Arbela the next day, having pursued altogether about 600 stades from the battle-field.[2] But as Darius went on fleeing

[1] The Lycus, now called the Great Zab, is a tributary of the Tigris. Xenophon calls it Zabatus (*Anab.*, ii. 5). The Greek *Lycus* is a translation of the Syrian *Zaba* (wolf).

[2] About sixty-nine miles. Cf. *Strabo* (xvi. 1, 3).

without taking any rest,[1] he did not find him at Arbela. However the money and all the other property were captured, as was also the chariot of Darius. His spear and bow were likewise taken, as had been the case after the battle of Issus.[2] Of Alexander's men about 100 were killed, and more than 1,000 of his horses were lost either from wounds or from fatigue in the pursuit, nearly half of them belonging to the Companion cavalry. Of the foreigners there were said to have been about 300,000 slain, and far more were taken prisoners than were killed.[3] The elephants and all the chariots which had not been destroyed in the battle were also captured. Such was the result of this battle, which was fought in the archonship of Aristophanes at Athens, in the month Pyanepsion;[4] and thus Aristander's prediction was accomplished, that Alexander would both fight a battle and gain a victory in the same month in which the moon was seen to be eclipsed.[5]

CHAPTER XVI.

Escape of Darius into Media.—March of Alexander to Babylon and Susa.

Immediately after the battle, Darius marched through the mountains of Armenia towards Media, accompanied in his flight by the Bactrian cavalry, as they had then been posted with him in the battle; also by those Persians who were called the king's kinsmen, and by

---

[1] ἐλινύσας. This is an Ionic word used by *Herodotus* (viii. 71, etc.), and rarely in Attic poets and later prose writers.

[2] See *Arrian*, ii. 11 supra.

[3] *Curtius* (iv. 63) says that 40,000 of the Persians were slain, and that less than 300 Macedonians were killed. *Diodorus* (xvii. 61) states that more than 90,000 Persians and 500 Macedonians were slain.

[4] September 331 B.C. Cf. Plutarch (*Alex.*, 31).

[5] For this prediction, see iii. 7 supra.

a few of the men called apple-bearers.[1] About 2,000 of his Grecian mercenaries also accompanied him in his flight, under the command of Paron the Phocian, and Glaucus the Aetolian. He fled towards Media for this reason, because he thought Alexander would take the road to Susa and Babylon immediately after the battle, inasmuch as the whole of that country was inhabited and the road was not difficult for the transit of baggage; and besides Babylon and Susa appeared to be the prizes of the war; whereas the road towards Media was by no means easy for the march of a large army. In this conjecture Darius was mistaken; for when Alexander started from Arbela, he advanced straight towards Babylon; and when he was now not far from that city, he drew up his army in order of battle and marched forward. The Babylonians came out to meet him in mass, with their priests and rulers, each of whom individually brought gifts, and offered to surrender their city, citadel, and money.[2] Entering the city, he commanded the Babylonians to rebuild all the temples which Xerxes had destroyed, and especially that of Belus, whom the Babylonians venerate more than any other god.[3] He then appointed Mazaeus viceroy of the Babylonians, Apollodorus the Amphipolitan general of the soldiers who were left behind with Mazaeus, and Asclepiodorus, son of Philo, collector of the revenue. He also sent Mithrines, who had surrendered to him the citadel of Sardis, down into Armenia to be viceroy there.[4] Here

---

[1] As to the kinsmen and apple-bearers, see iii. 11 supra.

[2] *Diodorus* (xvii. 63) and *Curtius* (v. 6) state that from the treasure captured in Babylon, Alexander distributed to each Macedonian horseman about £24, to each of the Grecian horsemen £20, to each of the Macedonian infantry £8, and to the allied infantry two months' pay.

[3] Belus, or Bel, the supreme deity of the Babylonians, was identical with the Syrian Baal. The signification of the name is *mighty*. Cf. *Herodotus* (i. 181); *Diodorus* (ii. 9); *Strabo* (xvi. 1).

[4] See i. 17 supra.

also he met with the Chaldaeans; and whatever they directed in regard to the religious rites of Babylon he performed, and in particular he offered sacrifice to Belus according to their instructions.[1] He then marched away to Susa [2]; and on the way he was met by the son of the viceroy of the Susians, [3] and a man bearing a letter from Philoxenus, whom he had despatched to Susa directly after the battle. In the letter Philoxenus had written that the Susians had surrendered their city to him, and that all the money was safe for Alexander. In twenty days the king arrived at Susa from Babylon; and entering the city he took possession of the money, which amounted to 50,000 talents, as well as the rest of the royal property.[4] Many other things were also captured

---

[1] The Chaldees appear in Hebrew under the name of *Casdim*, who seem to have originally dwelt in Carduchia, the northern part of Assyria. The Assyrians transported these rude mountaineers to the plains of Babylonia (Isa. xxiii. 13). The name of Casdim, or Chaldees, was applied to the inhabitants of Mesopotamia (Gen. xi. 28); the inhabitants of the Arabian desert in the vicinity of Edom (Job i. 17); those who dwelt near the river Chaboras (Ezek. i. 3; xi. 24); and the priestly caste who had settled at a very early period in Babylon, as we are informed by Diodorus and Eusebius. Herodotus says that these priests were dedicated to Belus. It is proved by inscriptions that the ancient language was retained as a learned and religious literature. This is probably what is meant in Daniel i. 4 by "the book and tongue of the Casdim." Cf. *Diodorus* (ii. 29–31); *Ptolemy* (v. 20, 3); and Cicero (*De Divinatione*, i. 1). See Fürst's *Hebrew Lexicon*, sub voce כֶּשֶׂד.

[2] In the Bible this city is called Shushan. Near it was the fortress of Shushan, called in our Bible *the Palace* (Neh. i. 2; Esth. ii. 8). Susa was situated on the Choaspes, a river remarkable for the excellence of its water, a fact referred to by *Tibullus* (iv. 1, 140) and by Milton (*Paradise Reg.*, iii. 288). The name Shushan is derived from the Persian word for lily, which grew abundantly in the vicinity. The ruins of the palace mentioned in Esther i. have recently been explored, and were found to consist of an immense hall, the roof of which was supported by a central group of thirty-six pillars arranged in the form of a square. This was flanked by three porticoes, each containing two rows of six pillars. Cf. *Strabo* (xv. 7, 28).

[3] The name of the viceroy was Abulites (*Curtius*, v. 8).

[4] If these were Attic talents, the amount would be equivalent to

there, which Xerxes brought with him from Greece, especially the brazen statues of Harmodius and Aristogeiton.[1] These Alexander sent back to the Athenians, and they are now standing at Athens in the Ceramicus, where we go up into the Acropolis,[2] right opposite the temple of Rhea, the mother of the gods, not far from the altar of the Eudanemi. Whoever has been initiated in the mysteries of the two goddesses[3] at Eleusis, knows the altar of Eudanemus which is upon the plain. At Susa Alexander offered sacrifice after the custom of his fathers, and celebrated a torch race and a gymnastic contest; and then, leaving Abulites, a Persian, as viceroy of Susiana, Mazarus, one of his Companions, as commander of the garrison in the citadel of Susa, and Archelaüs, son of Theodorus, as general, he advanced towards the land of the Persians. He also sent Menes down to the sea, as governor of Syria, Phœnicia, and Cilicia, giving him 3,000 talents of silver[4] to convey to the sea, with orders to despatch as many of them to Antipater as he might need to carry on the war against the Lacedaemonians.[5] There also Amyntas, son of Andromenes, reached him with the forces which he was leading from

---

£11,600,000; but if they were Babylonian or Aeginetan talents, they were equal to £19,000,000. Cf. Plutarch (*Alex.*, 36, 37); *Justin* (xi. 14); and *Curtius* (v. 8). *Diodorus* (xvii. 66) tells us that 40,000 talents were of uncoined gold and silver, and 9,000 talents of gold bearing the effigy of Darius.

[1] Cf. *Arrian* (vii. 19); *Pausanias* (i. 8, 5); Pliny (*Nat. Hist.*, xxxiv. 9); *Valerius Maximus* (ii. 10, 1). For Harmodius and Aristogeiton see *Thucydides*, vi. 56–58.

[2] *Polis* meant in early times a particular part of Athens, viz. the citadel, usually called the Acropolis. Cf. Aristophanes (*Lysistrata*, 245 et passim).

[3] Demeter and Persephone.

[4] About £730,000.

[5] Antipater had been left by Alexander regent of Macedonia. Agis III., king of Sparta, refused to acknowledge Alexander's hegemony, and after a hard struggle was defeated and slain by Antipater at Megalopolis, B.C. 330. See *Diodorus*, xvii. 63; *Curtius*, vi. 1 and 2.

Macedonia[1]; of whom Alexander placed the horsemen in the ranks of the Companion cavalry, and the foot he added to the various regiments of infantry, arranging each according to nationalities. He also established two companies in each squadron of cavalry, whereas before this time companies did not exist in the cavalry; and over them he set as captains those of the Companions who were pre-eminent for merit.

CHAPTER XVII.

Subjugation of the Uxians.

He now set out from Susa, and, crossing the river Pasitigris,[2] invaded the country of the Uxians. Some of these people who inhabit the plains were under the rule of the viceroy of the Persians, and on this occasion surrendered to Alexander; but those who are called the mountaineers were not in subjection to the Persians, and at this time sent word to Alexander that they would not permit him to march with his forces into Persis, unless they received from him as much as they were in the habit of receiving from the king of the Persians for the passage through their mountains.[3] He sent the messengers back with instructions to come to the defiles, the possession of which made them think that the passage into Persis was in their power, promising them that they should there receive from him the prescribed toll. He then took the royal body-guards, the shield-bearing infantry, and 8,000 men from the rest of his army, and, under the guidance of the Susians, marched by night along a different road from the frequented one. Advancing by a route rough

---

1. According to *Curtius* (v. 6) these forces amounted to nearly 15,000 men. Amyntas also brought with him fifty sons of the chief men in Macedonia, who wished to serve as royal pages. Cf. *Diodorus*, xvii. 64.

2. A river flowing through Susiana, formed by the junction of the Eulaeus and Coprates.

3. Cf. *Strabo*, xv. 3.

and difficult, on the same day he fell upon the villages of the Uxians, where he captured much booty and killed many of the people while still in their beds; but others escaped into the mountains. He then made a forced march to the defiles, where the Uxians resolved to meet him in mass in order to receive the prescribed toll. But he had already previously despatched Craterus to seize the heights, to which he thought the Uxians would retire if they were repelled by force; and he himself went with great celerity, and got possession of the pass before their arrival. He then drew up his men in battle array, and led them from the higher and more commanding position against the barbarians. They, being alarmed at Alexander's celerity, and finding themselves deprived by stratagem [1] of the position in which they had especially confided, took to flight without ever coming to close combat. Some of them were killed by Alexander's men in their flight, and many lost their lives by falling over the precipices along the road; but most of them fled up into the mountains for refuge, and falling in with Craterus, were destroyed by his men. Having received these gifts of honour [2] from Alexander, they with difficulty, after much entreaty, procured from him the privilege of retaining possession of their own land on condition of paying him an annual tribute. Ptolemy, son of Lagus, says that the mother of Darius,[3] on their behalf, entreated Alexander to grant them the privilege of inhabiting the land. The tribute agreed upon was a hundred horses, five hundred oxen, and 30,000 sheep a year; for the Uxians had no money, nor was their country fit for tillage; but most of them were shepherds and herdsmen.

---

1 πλεονεκτούμενοι, with dative, defrauded of. Cf. *Demosthenes*, 1035, 26.

2 γέρα. An Homeric expression.

3 Named Sisygambis (*Curtius*, v. 11).

CHAPTER XVIII.

Defeat of Ariobarzanes and Capture of Persepolis.

After this, Alexander despatched Parmenio with the baggage, the Thessalian cavalry, the Grecian allies, the mercenary auxiliaries, and the rest of the more heavily armed soldiers, to march into Persis along the carriage road leading into that country. He himself took the Macedonian infantry, the Companion cavalry, the light cavalry used for skirmishing, the Agrianians, and the archers, and made a forced march through the mountains. But when he arrived at the Persian Gates, he found that Ariobarzanes, the viceroy of Persis, with 40,000 infantry and 700 cavalry, had built a wall across the pass, and had pitched his camp there near the wall to block Alexander's passage. Then indeed he pitched his camp there; but next day he marshalled his army, and led it up to the wall. When it was evident that it would be difficult to capture it on account of the rugged nature of the ground, and as many of his men were being wounded, the enemy assailing them with missiles from engines of war placed upon higher ground, which gave them an advantage over their assailants, he retreated to his camp. He was informed by the prisoners that they could lead him round by another route, so that he might get to the other end of the pass; but when he ascertained that this road was rough and narrow, he left Craterus there at the camp with his own brigade and that of Meleager, as well as a few archers and 500 cavalry, with orders that when he perceived he had got right round and was approaching the camp of the Persians (which he could easily perceive, because the trumpets would give him the signal), he should then assault the wall. Alexander advanced by night, and travelling about 100 stades, he took the shield-bearing guards, the brigade of Perdiccas, the lightest armed of the archers, the Agrianians, the royal squadron of cavalry Companions, and one regiment of cavalry besides these, containing four companies; and wheeling round with these troops, he marched towards the pass in the direction the prisoners led him. He ordered Amyntas, Philotas, and Coenus to lead the rest of the army towards the plain, and to make a bridge over the river[1] which one must cross to go into Persis. He himself went by a route difficult and rough, along which he nevertheless marched for the most part at full speed. Falling upon the first guard of the barbarians before daylight,[2] he destroyed them, and so he did most of the second; but the majority of the third guard escaped, not indeed by fleeing into the camp of Ariobarzanes, but into the mountains as they were, being seized with a sudden panic. Consequently he fell upon the enemy's camp at the approach of dawn without being observed. At the very time he began to assault the trench, the trumpets gave the signal to Craterus, who at once attacked the advanced fortification. The enemy then, being in a state of confusion from being attacked on all sides, fled without coming to close conflict; but they were hemmed in on all hands, Alexander pressing upon them in one direction and the men of Craterus running up in another. Therefore most of them were compelled to wheel round and flee into the fortifications, which were already in the hands of the Macedonians. For Alexander, expecting the very thing which really occurred, had left Ptolemy there with three thousand infantry; so that most of the barbarians were cut to pieces by the Macedonians at close quarters. Others perished in the terrible flight which ensued, hurling themselves over the precipices; but Ariobarzanes him-

---

[1] This was the Araxes. See *Strabo*, xv. 3.

[2] Notice the use of the adverb πρὶν with the genitive, instead of the preposition πρό. Cf. Pindar (*Pythia*, iv. 76) πρὶν ὥρας.

self, with a few horsemen, escaped into the mountains.[1]

Alexander now marched back with all speed to the river, and finding the bridge already constructed over it, he easily crossed with his army.[2] Thence he again continued his march to Persepolis, so that he arrived before the guards of the city could pillage the treasury.[3] He also captured the money which was at Pasargadae[4] in the treasury of the first Cyrus, and appointed Phrasaortes, son of Rheomithres, viceroy over the Persians. He burnt down the Persian palace, though Parmenio advised him to preserve it, for many reasons, and especially because it was not well to destroy what was now his own property, and because the men of Asia would not by this course of action be induced to come over to him, thinking that he himself had decided not to retain the rule of Asia, but only to conquer it and depart. But Alexander said that he wished to take vengeance on the Persians, in retaliation for their deeds in the invasion of Greece, when they razed Athens to the ground and burnt down the temples. He also desired to punish the Persians for

---

[1] *Curtius* (v. 16) says that Ariobarzanes after a bloody contest got away through the Macedonian lines, with about 40 horsemen and 5,000 foot, and made for Persepolis. Being shut out of that fortress, he was overtaken and slain with all his companions. Cf. *Diodorus* (xvii. 68).

[2] *Diodorus* (xvii. 69) and *Justin* (xi. 14) state that on approaching Persepolis, Alexander met 800 Grecian captives, mutilated by loss of arms, legs, eyes, ears, or other members. *Curtius* (v. 17–19) says there were 4,000 of them. Alexander offered to send these men home, with means of future support; but they preferred to remain in Persis. The king gave them money, clothing, cattle, and land.

[3] *Diodorus* (xvii. 71) and *Curtius* (v. 20) both state that the amount of treasure captured at Persepolis was 120,000 talents, or £27,600,000. In his own letter Alexander stated that there was sufficient treasure and valuable property to load 10,000 mule carts and 5,000 camels (Plutarch, *Alex.*, 37). Curtius tells us that 6,000 talents were captured at Pasargadae.

[4] Pasargadae was the old capital of Persia, founded by Cyrus; but its place was afterwards taken by Persepolis.

all the other injuries they had done the Greeks. But Alexander does not seem to me to have acted on this occasion with prudence; nor do I think that this was any retributive penalty at all on the ancient Persians.[1]

CHAPTER XIX.

Darius Pursued into Media and Parthia.

After bringing these matters to a successful issue, he advanced towards Media; for he ascertained that Darius was there. Now Darius had formed the resolution, if Alexander remained at Susa or Babylon, to stay there among the Medes, in order to see if any change of policy were made by Alexander. But if the latter marched against him, he resolved to proceed into the interior towards Parthia and Hyrcania, as far as Bactria, laying waste all the land and making it impossible for Alexander to advance any further. He therefore sent the women and the rest of the property which he still retained, together with the covered carriages, to what were called the Caspian Gates[2]; but he himself stayed at Ecbatana,[3]

---

[1] *Diodorus* (xvii. 70, 71) and *Curtius* (v. 20, 22) say that Alexander delivered Persepolis to his soldiers to pillage, and that he ordered a general massacre of the inhabitants. These authors agree with Plutarch (*Alex.*, 38) in asserting that in a drunken revel he was instigated by the courtesan Thais to set fire to the palace, and accompanied her to commence the act of destruction. See *Dryden's* famous ode. But Arrian's account establishes the fact that the fire was the result of a deliberate plan. As regards the massacre, *Plutarch* (37) expressly states that Alexander wrote home that he ordered it from motives of policy.

[2] This was the principal pass through the Elburz mountains from Media into Hyrcania and Parthia.

[3] This was the capital of Media, called in Chaldee *Achmetha* (Ezra vi. 2). The present city of Hamadan is on the same site. It is situated at the foot of Mount Orontes, and was used by the Persian and Parthian kings as their summer residence. It was surrounded by seven walls, each overtopping the one before it, from the outer to the inner, crowned with battlements of different colours. Its citadel was used as a royal

with the forces which had been collected from those who were at hand. Hearing this, Alexander advanced towards Media, and invading the land of the Paraetacae,[1] he subdued it, and appointed Oxathres, son of Abulites, the former viceroy of Susa, to rule as viceroy. Being informed on the march that Darius had determined to meet him for battle, and to try the fortune of war again (for the Scythians and Cadusians had come to him as allies), he ordered that the beasts of burden, with their guards and the rest of the baggage, should follow; and taking the rest of his army, he led it in order of battle, and on the twelfth day arrived in Media. There he ascertained that the forces of Darius were not fit for battle, and that his allies, the Cadusians and Scythians, had not arrived; but that he had resolved to flee. He therefore marched on with still greater speed; and when he was only three days' journey from Ecbatana, he was met by Bistanes, son of Ochus, who reigned over the Persians before Darius. This man announced that Darius had fled five days before, taking with him 7,000 talents of money[2] from the Medes, and an army of 3,000 cavalry and 6,000 infantry.

When Alexander reached Ecbatana, he sent the Thessalian cavalry and the other Grecian allies back to the sea, paying them the full hire which had been stipulated, and making them an additional donation from himself of 2,000 talents. He issued an order that if any man of his own accord wished still to continue to serve for hire with him, he should enlist; and those who enlisted in his service were not a few. He then ordered Epocillus,

treasury. Below it stood a splendid palace, with silver tiles, and adorned with wainscotings, capitals, and entablatures of gold and silver. These treasures, to the value of 4,000 talents, were coined into money by Antiochus the Great of Syria. See *Herodotus*, i. 98; *Polybius*, x. 27.

[1] This tribe lived in the mountains between Media and Persis.

[2] £1,700,000.

son of Polyeides, to conduct the rest down to the sea, taking other cavalry as a guard for them, since the Thessalians sold their horses there. He also sent word to Menes to take upon himself the duty of seeing that they were conveyed in triremes to Euboea, when they arrived at the sea.[1] He instructed Parmenio to deposit the money which was being conveyed from Persis in the citadel at Ecbatana, and to hand it over to the charge of Harpalus;[2] for he had left this man over the money with a guard of 6,000 Macedonians and a few horsemen and light-armed infantry to take care of it. He told Parmenio himself to take the Grecian mercenaries, the Thracians, and all the other horsemen except the Companion cavalry, and march by the land of the Cadusians into Hyrcania. He also sent word to Clitus, the commander of the royal squadron of cavalry, who had been left behind at Susa ill, that when he arrived at Ecbatana from Susa he should take the Macedonians who had been left there in charge of the money, and go in the direction of Parthia, where also he himself intended soon to arrive.

CHAPTER XX.

March through the Caspian Gates.

Then taking the Companion cavalry, the light cavalry used for skirmishing, the Greek mercenary cavalry, under the command of Erigyius, the Macedonian phalanx, except the men who had been placed in charge of the money, the archers, and the Agrianians, he marched against Darius. In the forced march which he made, many of his soldiers were left behind, worn out with

---

[1] *Curtius* (v. 23) says that 6,000 Grecian mercenaries under Plato the Athenian met Alexander in Media, having marched up from Cilicia.

[2] *Diodorus* (xvii. 80) says that the amount of treasure deposited at Ecbatana was 180,000 talents or £41,400,000.

fatigue, and many of the horses died. He nevertheless pressed on, and on the eleventh day arrived at Rhagae.[1] This place is distant from the Caspian Gates one day's journey to one marching as Alexander did. But Darius had already passed through this defile before Alexander came up, though many of those who were his companions in flight deserted him on the way and retired to their own abodes. Many also surrendered to Alexander. The latter now gave up the hope of capturing Darius by close pursuit, and remained there five days to give his troops repose. He appointed Oxodates a Persian, who had the ill fortune to be arrested by Darius and shut up at Susa, to the office of viceroy of Media; for this treatment was an inducement to Alexander to rely on his fidelity. He then marched towards Parthia; and on the first day encamped near the Caspian Gates, which he passed through on the second day as far as the country was inhabited.[2] Hearing that the country further on was desert, he resolved to procure a stock of provisions from the place where he was encamped, and accordingly sent Coenus out on a foraging expedition with the cavalry and a small body of infantry.

CHAPTER XXI.

Darius is Assassinated by Bessus.

At this time Bagistanes, one of the Babylonian nobles, came to him from the camp of Darius, accompanied by Antibelus, one of the sons of Mazaeus. These men informed him that Nabarzanes, the commander of the cavalry which accompanied Darius in his flight, Bessus,

---

[1] A large city in the extreme north of Media, mentioned in the Book of Tobit. It was famous in the Middle Ages under the name of Rai. The ruins of Rai lie south-east of Teheran.

[2] *ἔστε* generally means *until*. In its present use cf. ii. 11 supra, *ἔστε μὲν φάος ἦν*.

viceroy of Bactria, and Barsaentes, viceroy of the Arachotians and Drangians,[1] had jointly arrested the king. When Alexander heard this, he marched with still greater speed than ever, taking with him only the Companions and the skirmishing cavalry, as well as some of the foot-soldiers selected as the strongest and lightest men. He did not even wait for Coenus to return from the foraging expedition; but placed Craterus over the men left behind, with instructions to follow in short marches. His own men took with them nothing but their arms and provisions for two days. After marching the whole night and till noon of the next day, he gave his army a short rest, then went on again all night, and when day began to break reached the camp from which Bagistanes had set out to meet him; but he did not catch the enemy. However, in regard to Darius, he ascertained that he had been arrested and was being conveyed in a covered carriage[2]; that Bessus possessed the command instead of Darius, and had been nominated leader by the Bactrian cavalry and all the other barbarians who were companions of Darius in his flight, except Artabazus and his sons, together with the Grecian mercenaries, who still remained faithful to Darius; but they, not being able to prevent what was being done, had turned aside their march from the public thoroughfare and were marching towards the mountains by themselves, refusing to take part with Bessus and his adherents in their enterprise. He also learnt that those who had arrested Darius had come to the decision to

---

[1] The Drangians lived in a part of Ariana west of Arachosia.

[2] *Justin* (xi. 15) and *Curtius* (v. 34) state that Darius was bound in chains of gold. The former says that the name of the place was Thara in Parthia, where the king was arrested. Probably these chains were those worn by the king or his nobles, according to the Persian custom. This is the only sentence in Arrian where *περὶ* suffers anastrophe, coming after the noun.

surrender him to Alexander, and to procure some advantage for themselves, if they should find that Alexander was pursuing them; but if they should learn that he had gone back again, they had resolved to collect as large an army as they could and to preserve the rule for the commonwealth. He also ascertained that for the present Bessus held the supreme command, both on account of his relationship to Darius and because the war was being carried on in his viceregal province. Hearing this, Alexander thought it was advisable to pursue with all his might; and though his men and horses were already quite fatigued by the incessant severity of their labours, he nevertheless proceeded, and, travelling a long way all through the night and the next day till noon, arrived at a certain village, where those who were leading Darius had encamped the day before. Hearing there that the barbarians had decided to continue their march by night, he inquired of the natives if they knew any shorter road to the fugitives. They said they did know one, but that it ran through a country which was desert through lack of water. He nevertheless ordered them to show him this way, and perceiving that the infantry could not keep up with him if he marched at full speed, he caused 500 of the cavalry to dismount from their horses; and selecting the officers of the infantry and the best of the other foot-soldiers, he ordered them to mount the horses armed just as they were. He also directed Nicanor, the commander of the shield-bearing guards, and Attalus, commander of the Agrianians, to lead their men who were left behind, by the same route which Bessus had taken, having equipped them as lightly as possible; and he ordered that the rest of the infantry should follow in regular marching order. He himself began to march in the afternoon, and led the way with great rapidity.[1]

---

[1] Plutarch (*Alex.*, 42) says that Alexander rode 3,300 stades, or about

Having travelled 400 stades in the night, he came upon the barbarians just before daybreak, going along without any order and unarmed; so that few of them rushed to defend themselves, but most of them, as soon as they saw Alexander himself, took to flight without even coming to blows. A few of those who turned to resist being killed, the rest of these also took to flight. Up to this time Bessus and his adherents were still conveying Darius with them in a covered carriage; but when Alexander was already close upon their heels Nabarzanes and Barsaëntes wounded him and left him there, and with 600 horsemen took to flight. Darius died from his wounds soon after, before Alexander had seen him.[1]

CHAPTER XXII.

Reflections on the Fate of Darius.

Alexander sent the body of Darius into Persis, with orders that it should be buried in the royal sepulchre, in the same way as the other Persian kings before him had been buried.[2] He then proclaimed Amminaspes, a Parthian, viceroy over the Parthians and Hyrcanians. This man was one of those who with Mazaces had surrendered Egypt to Alexander. He also appointed Tlepolemus, son of Pythophanes, one of the Companions, to guard his interests in Parthia and Hyrcania. Such was the end of Darius, in the archonship of Aristophon at Athens, in the month Hecatombaion.[3] This king was

---

400 miles, in eleven days. In the next chapter he says that only sixty of his men were able to keep up with him in the pursuit.

[1] *Curtius* (v. 24–38) gives very ample details of what occurred during the last days of Darius. Cf. *Diodorus* (xvii. 73); *Justin* (xi. 15).

[2] The Persian kings were buried at Persepolis. See *Diodorus*, xvii. 71. Plutarch (*Alex.*, 43) says that Alexander sent the corpse of Darius to his mother.

[3] In the year B.C. 330, the first of Hecatombaion fell on the first of July.

a man pre-eminently effeminate and lacking in self-reliance in military enterprises; but as to civil matters he never exhibited any disposition to indulge in arbitrary conduct; nor indeed was it in his power to exhibit it. For it happened that he was involved in a war with the Macedonians and Greeks at the very time he succeeded to the regal power[1]; and consequently it was no longer possible for him to act the tyrant towards his subjects, even if he had been so inclined, standing as he did in greater danger than they. As long as he lived, one misfortune after another was accumulated upon him; nor did he experience any cessation of calamity from the time when he first succeeded to the rule. At the beginning of his reign the cavalry defeat was sustained by his viceroys at the Granicus, and forthwith Ionia Aeolis, both the Phrygias, Lydia, and all Caria[2] except Halicarnassus were occupied by his foe; soon after, Halicarnassus also was captured, as well as all the littoral as far as Cilicia. Then came his own discomfiture at Issus, where he saw his mother, wife, and children taken prisoners. Upon this Phoenicia and the whole of Egypt were lost; and then at Arbela he himself fled disgracefully among the first, and lost a very vast army composed of all the nations of his empire. After this, wandering as an exile from his own dominions, he died after being

---

[1] Darius came to the throne B.C. 336.

[2] In 2 Kings xi. 4, 19 the word translated *captains* in our Bible is *Carim*, the Carians. These men formed the body-guard of the usurper Athaliah, who stood in need of foreign mercenaries. David had a body-guard of Philistines and Cretans. The Carians served as mercenaries throughout the ancient world, as we learn from *Thucydides*, i. 8; *Herodotus*, i. 171; ii. 152; v. 111; *Strabo*, xiv. 2. The Lydians appear in the Bible under the name of *Lud* (Isa. lxvi. 19). *Herodotus* (i. 94) gives an account of the colonization of Umbria by the Lydians, from which sprung the state of the Etruscans. Hence Vergil (*Aeneid*, ii. 782) speaks of the "*Lydius Tybris.*" See also *Aeneid*, viii. 479; Horace (*Satires*, i. 6, 1); Tacitus (*Annals*, iv. 55); Dionysius (*Archaeologia Romana*, i. 28).

betrayed by his personal attendants to the worst treatment possible, being at the same time king and a prisoner ignominiously led in chains; and at last he perished through a conspiracy formed of those most intimately acquainted with him. Such were the misfortunes that befell Darius in his life-time; but after his death he received a royal burial; his children received from Alexander a princely rearing and education, just as if their father had still been king; and Alexander himself became his son-in-law.[1] When he died he was about fifty years of age.

CHAPTER XXIII.

Expedition into Hyrcania.

Alexander now took the soldiers who had been left behind in his pursuit and advanced into Hyrcania,[2] which is the country lying on the left of the road leading to Bactra.[3] On one side it is bounded by lofty mountains densely covered with wood, and on the other it is a plain stretching as far as the Great Sea[4] in this part of the world. He led his army by this route, because he ascertained that the Grecian mercenaries serving under Darius had succeeded in escaping by it into the mountains of Tapuria; at the same time he resolved to subdue the Tapurians themselves. Having divided his army into three parts, he himself led the way by the shortest and most difficult route, at the head of the most numerous and at the same time the lightest division of his

---

[1] He married Barsine, eldest daughter of Darius (*Arrian*, vii. 4 infra). She was also called Arsinoe and Stateira.

[2] According to *Curtius* (vi. 6–10) the soldiers were very desirous of returning home; but Alexander made an harangue and induced them to advance into Hyrcania.

[3] The modern Balkh.

[4] The Caspian.

forces. He despatched Craterus at the head of his own brigade and that of Amyntas, some of the archers, and a few of the cavalry against the Tapurians; and he ordered Erigyius to take the Grecian mercenaries and the rest of the cavalry, and lead the way by the public thoroughfare, though it was longer, conducting the waggons, the baggage, and the crowd of camp-followers. After crossing the first mountains, and encamping there, he took the shield-bearing guards together with the lightest men in the Macedonian phalanx and some of the archers, and went along a road difficult and hard to travel upon, leaving guards for the roads wherever he thought there was any peril, so that the barbarians who held the mountains might not at those points fall upon the men who were following. Having passed through the defiles with his archers, he encamped in the plain near a small river[1]; and while he was here, Nabarzanes, the commander of Darius's cavalry, Phrataphernes, the viceroy of Hyrcania and Parthia, and the other most distinguished of the Persians in attendance on Darius, arrived and surrendered themselves. After waiting four days in the camp, he took up those who had been left behind on the march, all of them advancing in safety except the Agrianians, who, while guarding the rear, were attacked by the barbarian mountaineers. But these soon drew off when they got the worst of it in the skirmish. Starting from this place, he advanced into Hyrcania as far as Zadracarta, the capital of the Hyrcanians. In this place[2] he was rejoined by Craterus, who had not succeeded in falling in with the Grecian mercenaries of Darius; but he had thoroughly traversed the whole country, gaining over part of it by force and the other part by the voluntary capitulation of the inhabit-

[1] *Diodorus* (xvii. 75) calls this river Stiboetis; *Curtius* (vi. 10) calls it Ziobetis.

[2] *Krüger* has ἐνταῦθα instead of ἐν τούτῳ.

ants. Erigyius also arrived here with the baggage and waggons; and soon after Artabazus[1] came to Alexander with three of his sons, Cophen, Ariobarzanes, and Arsames, accompanied by Autophradates, viceroy of Tapuria, and envoys from the Grecian mercenaries in the service of Darius. To Autophradates he restored his viceregal office; but Artabazus and his sons he kept near himself in a position of honour, both on account of their fidelity to Darius and because they were among the first nobles of Persia. To the envoys from the Greeks, begging him to make a truce with them on behalf of the whole mercenary force, he replied that he would not make any agreement with them; because they were acting with great guilt in serving as soldiers on the side of the barbarians against Greece, in contravention of the resolution of the Greeks. He commanded them to come in a body and surrender, leaving it to him to treat them as he pleased, or to preserve themselves as best they could. The envoys said that they yielded both themselves and their comrades to Alexander, and urged him to send some one with them to act as their leader, so that they might be conducted to him with safety. They said they were 1,500 in number. Accordingly he sent Andronicus, son of Agerrhus, and Artabazus to them.

CHAPTER XXIV.

Expedition against the Mardians.

He then marched forward against the Mardians[2] taking with him the shield-bearing guards, the archers, the

---

[1] *Curtius* (vi. 14) says Artabazus had nine sons, one of whom, Pharnabazus, was the admiral of the Persian fleet. See *Arrian* (ii. 1; ii. 2; iii. 2 supra).

[2] Cf. *Curtius*, vi. 16.

Agrianians, the brigades of Coenus and Amyntas, half of the Companion cavalry, and the horse-lancers; for he had now a troop of horse-lancers. Traversing the greater part of the land of the Mardians, he killed many of them in their flight, some indeed having turned to defend themselves; and many were taken prisoners. No one for a long time had invaded their land in a hostile manner, not only on account of its ruggedness, but also because the people were poor, and besides being poor were warlike. Therefore they never feared that Alexander would attack them, especially as he had already advanced further than their country. For this reason they were caught more easily off their guard. Many of them, however, escaped into the mountains, which in their land are very lofty and craggy, thinking that Alexander would not penetrate to these at any rate. But when he was approaching them even here, they sent envoys to surrender both the people and their land to him. He pardoned them, and appointed Autophradates, whom he had also recently placed over the Tapurians, viceroy over them. Returning to the camp, from which he had started to invade the country of the Mardians, he found that the Grecian mercenaries of Darius had arrived, accompanied by the envoys from the Lacedaemonians who were on an embassy to king Darius. The names of these men were, Callicratidas, Pausippus, Monimus, Onomas, and Dropides, a man from Athens. These were arrested and kept under guard; but he released the envoys from the Sinopeans,[1] because these people had no share in the commonwealth of the Greeks; and as they were in subjection to the Persians, they did not seem to be doing anything unreasonable in going on an embassy to their own king. He also released the rest of

---

[1] Sinope was a prosperous colony of Miletus on the Euxine. It is still called Sinoub. It was the birthplace of Diogenes.

the Greeks who were serving for pay with the Persians before the peace and alliance which had been made by the Greeks with the Macedonians. He likewise released Heraclides, the ambassador from the Chalcedonians[1] to Darius. The rest he ordered to serve in his army for the same pay as they had received from the Persian king, putting them under the command of Andronicus, who had led them, and had evidently been taking prudent measures to save the lives of the men.

CHAPTER XXV.

March to Bactra.—Bessus Aided by Satibarzanes.

Having settled these affairs, he marched to Zadracarta, the largest city of Hyrcania, where also was the seat of the Hyrcanian government. Tarrying here fifteen days, he offered sacrifice to the gods according to his custom, and celebrated a gymnastic contest, after which he began his march towards Parthia; thence to the confines of Areia[2] and to Susia, a city in that province, where Satibarzanes, the viceroy of the Areians, came to meet him. To this man he restored his viceregal dignity, and with him sent Anaxippus, one of the Companions, to whom he gave forty horse-lancers so that he might be able to station them as guards of the localities, in order that the Areians might not be injured by the army in its march through their land. At this time came to him some Persians, who informed him that Bessus had assumed the erect tiara[3] and was wearing the Persian

---

[1] Chalcedon was a colony of Megara, situated on the Propontis at the entrance of the Bosporus, nearly opposite Byzantium.

[2] Areia occupied what is now the east part of Khorasan, and the west and north-west of Afghanistan. Susia is the modern Tus.

[3] Compare the words of Tissaphernes to Clearchus (Xenophon, *Anabasis*, ii. 5): "Though the king is the only man who can wear the tiara

dress,[1] calling himself Artaxerxes instead of Bessus, and asserting that he was king of Asia. They said he had in attendance upon him the Persians who had escaped into Bactra and many of the Bactrians themselves; and that he was expecting the Scythians also to come to him as allies. Alexander, having now all his forces together, went towards Bactra, where Philip son of Menelaüs came to him out of Media with the Greek mercenary cavalry which were under his own command, those of the Thessalians who had volunteered to remain, and the men of Andromachus. Nicanor, the son of Parmenio, the commander of the shield-bearing guards, had already died of disease. While Alexander was on his way to Bactra, he was informed that Satibarzanes, viceroy of Areia, had killed Anaxippus and the horse-lancers who were with him, had armed the Areians and collected them in the city of Artacoana, which was the capital of that nation. It was also said that he had resolved, as soon as he ascertained that Alexander had advanced, to leave that place and go with his forces to Bessus, with the intention of joining that prince in an attack upon the Macedonians, wherever a chance might occur. When he received this news, he stopped the march towards Bactra, and taking with him the Companion cavalry, the horse-lancers, the archers, the Agrianians and the regiments of Amyntas and Coenus, and leaving the rest of

---

erect upon his head, I shall be able to wear mine erect upon my heart in full confidence, when you are in my service." Cf. *Curtius* (iii. 8); Aristophanes (*Birds*, 487). The cap of the ordinary Persians was low, loose, and clinging about the head in folds; whereas that of the king was high and erect above the head. From Xenophon (*Cyropaedia*, viii. 3, 13) we learn that the Persian king's vest was of a purple colour, half mixed with white, and that no one else was allowed to wear this mixture of white. He had loose trousers of a scarlet colour, and a robe entirely purple. Cf. also *Strabo* (xv. 3), where the tiara is said to be in the shape of a tower; and Seneca (*De Beneficiis*, vi. 31); *Ammianus*, xviii. 8, 5.

[1] See Xenophon (*Anab.*, i. 2, 27; *Cyropaedia*, viii. 3); *Curtius* (iii. 8).

his forces there under the command of Craterus, he made a forced march against Satibarzanes and the Areians; and having travelled 600 stades in two days came near Artacoana. Satibarzanes, however, no sooner perceived that Alexander was near, than being struck with terror at the quickness of his arrival, he took to flight with a few Areian horsemen. For he was deserted by the majority of his soldiers in his flight, when they also learned that Alexander was at hand. The latter made rapid marches in pursuit of the enemy, killed some of the men whom he discovered to be guilty of the revolt and who at that time had left their villages, fleeing, some one way, some another; and others of them he sold into slavery. He then proclaimed Arsames, a Persian, viceroy over the Areians. Being now joined by the men who had been left behind with Craterus, he marched into the land of the Zarangaeans,[1] and reached the place where their seat of government was. But Barsaentes, who at that time had possession of the land, being one of those who had fallen upon Darius in his flight, learning that Alexander was approaching, fled to the Indians who live this side of the river Indus. But they arrested him and sent him back to Alexander, by whom he was put to death on account of his guilty conduct towards Darius.

CHAPTER XXVI.

Philotas and Parmenio put to Death.

Here also Alexander discovered the conspiracy of Philōtas, son of Parmenio. Ptolemy and Aristobūlus say that it had already been reported to him before in Egypt[2]; but that it did not appear to him credible, both

---

[1] These people are also called Drangians. They lived west of Arachosia in Drangiana.

[2] According to Plutarch (*Alex.*, 48, 49) Alexander suborned Antigonē, the mistress of Philotas, to reveal his secret conversation.

on account of the long-existing friendship between them, the honour which he publicly conferred upon his father Parmenio, and the confidence he reposed in Philotas himself. Ptolemy, son of Lagus, says that Philotas was brought before the Macedonians,[1] that Alexander vehemently accused him, and that he defended himself from the charges. He says also that the divulgers[2] of the plot came forward and convicted him and his accomplices both by other clear proofs and especially because Philotas himself confessed that he had heard of a certain conspiracy which was being formed against Alexander. He was convicted of having said nothing to the king about this plot, though he visited the royal tent twice a day.[3] He and all the others who had taken part with him in the conspiracy were killed by the Macedonians with their javelins;[4] and Polydamas, one of the Companions, was despatched to Parmenio, carrying letters from Alexander to the generals in Media, Cleander, Sitalces, and Menidas, who had been placed over the army commanded by Parmenio. By these men Parmenio was put to death, perhaps because Alexander deemed it incredible that Philotas should conspire against him and Parmenio not participate in his son's plan; or perhaps, he thought that even if he had no share in it, he would now be a dangerous man if he survived, after the king had violently made away with his son. Moreover he was held in very great respect both by Alexander himself and by all the army, having great influence not only among the Macedonian troops but also among the

---

1 Cf. *Curtius*, vi. 32.

2 The word ἐπιμηνυτὴς is found nowhere else in any Greek author.

3 Full details of the conspiracy and trial of Philotas are given by *Curtius* (vi. 25–44).

4 Arrian says nothing about Philotas being put to the torture; but this fact is asserted with ample details by Plutarch (*Alex.*, 49); *Diodorus* (xvii. 80); *Curtius* (vi. 42, 43); and *Justin* (xii. 5).

Grecian auxiliaries, whom he often used to command according to Alexander's order, both in his own turn and out of his turn, with his sovereign's approbation and satisfaction.[1]

CHAPTER XXVII.

TREATMENT OF AMYNTAS.—THE ARIASPIANS.

THEY also say that about the same time Amyntas, son of Andromenes, was brought to trial, together with his brothers Polemo, Attalus, and Simmias, on the charge of being accessory to the conspiracy against Alexander, on account of their trust in Philotas and their intimate friendship with him. The belief in their participation in the plot was strengthened among the mass of men by the fact that when Philotas was arrested, Polemo, one of the brothers of Amyntas, fled to the enemy. But Amyntas with his other two brothers stayed to await the trial, and defended himself so vigorously among the Macedonians that he was declared innocent of the charge. As soon as he was acquitted in the assembly, he demanded that permission should be given him to go to his brother and bring him back to Alexander. To this the Macedonians acceded; so he went away and on the same day brought Polemo back. On this account he now seemed free from guilt much more than before. But soon after, as he was besieging a certain village, he was shot with an arrow and died of the wound; so that he derived no other advantage from his acquittal except that of dying with an unsullied reputation.[2]

Alexander appointed two commanders over the Companion cavalry, Hephaestion, son of Amyntor, and Clitus,

---

[1] Full particulars of the murder of Parmenio are given by *Curtius* (vii. 7–9).

[2] For the trial of Amyntas, cf. *Curtius*, vii. 2–6.

son of Dropidas, dividing the brigade of the Companions into two parts, because he did not wish any one of his friends to have the sole command of so many horsemen, especially as they were the best of all his cavalry, both in public estimation and in martial discipline.[1] He now arrived in the land of the people formerly called Ariaspians, but afterwards named Euergetae, because they assisted Cyrus, son of Cambyses, in his invasion of Scythia.[2] Alexander treated these people, whose ancestors had been serviceable to Cyrus, with honour; and when he ascertained that the men not only enjoyed a form of government unlike that of the other barbarians in that part of the world, but laid claim to justice equally with the best of the Greeks, he set them free, and gave them besides as much of the adjacent country as they asked for themselves; but they did not ask for much. Here he offered sacrifice to Apollo, and arrested Demetrius, one of his confidential body-guards, on suspicion of having been implicated with Philotas in the conspiracy. Ptolemy, son of Lagus, was appointed to the post vacated by Demetrius.

CHAPTER XXVIII.

Alexander Crosses the Hindu-Koosh.

After the transaction of this business, he advanced against Bactra and Bessus, reducing the Drangians and Gadrosians[3] to subjection on his march. He also re-

---

1 Alexander also formed a separate cohort of the men who were pronounced sympathisers with Parmenio, and this cohort afterwards greatly distinguished itself. See *Diodorus*, xvii. 80; *Curtius*, vii. 10; *Justin*, xii. 5.

2 The Ariaspians inhabited the south part of Drangiana on the borders of Gadrosia. The river Etymander, now known as the Hilmend, flowed through their territories. Cf. *Curtius*, vii. 11; *Diodorus*, xvii. 81.

3 Gadrosia was the furthest province of the Persian empire on the south-east It comprised the south-east part of Beloochistan.

duced the Arachotians to subjection and appointed Menon viceroy over them. He then reached the Indians, who inhabit the land bordering on that of the Arachotians. All these nations he reached marching through deep snow and his soldiers experiencing scarcity of provisions and severe hardship. Learning that the Areians had again revolted, in consequence of Satibarzanes invading their land with 2,000 cavalry, which he had received from Bessus, he despatched against them Artabazus the Persian with Erigyius and Caranus two of the Companions, also ordering Phrataphernes, viceroy of the Parthians, to assist them in attacking the Areians. An obstinately contested battle then took place between the troops of Erigyius and Caranus and those of Satibarzanes; nor did the barbarians give way until Satibarzanes, encountering Erigyius, was struck in the face with a spear and killed. Then the barbarians gave way and fled with headlong speed.

Meantime Alexander was leading his army towards Mount Caucasus,[1] where he founded a city and named it Alexandreia.[2] Having offered sacrifice here to the gods to whom it was his custom to sacrifice, he crossed Mount Caucasus, after appointing Proëxes, a Persian, viceroy over the land, and leaving Neiloxenus son of Satyrus, one of the Companions, with an army as superintendent. According to the account of Aristobulus, Mount Caucasus is as lofty as any in Asia, and most of it is bare, at any rate in that part where Alexander crossed it. This range of mountains stretches out so far that they say even that Mount Taurus, which forms the boundary of Cilicia and Pamphylia, springs from it, as do other great

---

[1] This was not the range usually so called, but what was known as the Indian Caucasus, the proper name being Paropanisus. It is now called Hindu-Koosh.

[2] This city was probably on the site of Beghram, twenty-five miles north-east of Cabul. See Grote's *Greece*, vol. xii. ch. 94.

ranges which have been distinguished from the Caucasus by various names according to the position of each. Aristobulus says that in this part of the Caucasus nothing grew except terebinth trees and silphium;[1] notwithstanding which, it was inhabited by many people, and many sheep and oxen graze there; because sheep are very fond of silphium. For if a sheep smells it even from a distance, it runs to it and feeds upon the flower. They also dig up the root, which is devoured by the sheep. For this reason in Cyrene,[2] some drive their flocks as far as possible away from the places where their silphium is growing; others even enclose the place with a fence, so that even if the sheep should approach it they would not be able to get within the enclosure. For the silphium is very valuable to the Cyrenaeans.

Bessus, accompanied by the Persians who had taken part with him in the seizure of Darius, and by 7,000 of the Bactrians themselves and the Daans who dwelt on this side the Tanais,[3] was laying waste the country at the foot of Mount Caucasus, in order to prevent Alexander from marching any further, both by the desolation of the land between the enemy and himself and by the lack of provisions. But none the less did Alexander keep up the march, though with difficulty, both on account of the deep snow and from the want of necessaries; but yet he persevered in his journey. When Bessus was informed that Alexander was now not far off, he crossed

---

[1] There are two kinds of silphium or laserpitium, the Cyrenaio, and the Persian. The latter is usually called asafœtida. See *Herodotus* (iv. 169); Pliny (*Historia Naturalis*, xix. 15; xxiii. 48); Aelian (*Varia Historia*, xii. 37); Aristophanes (*Plutus*, 925); Plautus (*Rud.*, iii. 2, 16); *Catullus* (vii. laserpitiferis Cyrenis).

[2] Cyrene was a colony founded by Battus from Thera, an island colonized by the Spartans. The territory of Cyrenaica is now a part of Tripoli. Cf. Pindar (*Pyth.*, iv. 457); *Herodotus* (iv. 159–205)

[3] This Tanais was usually called Jaxartes, now Sir, flowing into the sea of Aral.

the river Oxus,[1] and having burnt the boats upon which he had crossed, he withdrew to Nautaca[2] in the land of Sogdiana. He was followed by Spitamenes and Oxyartes, with the cavalry from Sogdiana, as well as by the Daans from the Tanais. But the Bactrian cavalry, perceiving that Bessus had resolved to take to flight, all dispersed in various directions to their own abodes.

CHAPTER XXIX.

Conquest of Bactria, and Pursuit of Bessus across the Oxus.

Alexander now arrived at Drapsaca, and having there given his army a rest, he marched to Aornus and Bactra, which are the largest cities in the land of the Bactrians. These he took at the first assault; and left a garrison in the citadel of Aornus, over which he placed Archelaüs son of Androcles, one of the Companions. He appointed Artabazus the Persian, viceroy over the rest of the Bactrians, who were easily reduced to submission. Then he marched towards the river Oxus, which flows from mount Caucasus, and is the largest of all the rivers in Asia which Alexander and his army reached, except the Indian rivers; but the Indian rivers are the largest in the world. The Oxus discharges its water into the great sea which is near Hyrcania. When he attempted to cross the river it appeared altogether impassable; for its breadth was about six stades, and its depth was much greater than the proportion of its breadth. The bed of the river was sandy, and the stream so rapid, that stakes fixed deep into the bottom were easily rooted up from

---

[1] The Oxus, now called Jihoun or Amou, flows into the sea of Aral, but formerly flowed into the Caspian.

[2] Some think this town stood where Naksheh now is, and others think it was at Kesch.

the earth by the mere force of the current, inasmuch as they could not be securely fixed in the sand. Besides this, there was a scarcity of timber in the locality, and he thought it would take a long time and cause great delay, if they brought from a distance the materials needful for making a bridge over the river. Therefore he collected the skins which the soldiers used for tent-coverings, and ordered them to be filled with chaff as dry as possible, and tied and stitched tightly together, so that the water might not penetrate into them.[1] When these were filled and stitched together, they were sufficient to convey the army across in five days. But before he crossed the river, he selected the oldest of the Macedonians, who were now unfit for military service, and such of the Thessalians as had volunteered to remain in the army, and sent them back home. He then dispatched Stasanor, one of the Companions, into the land of the Areians, with instructions to arrest Arsames, the viceroy of that people, because he thought him disaffected, and to assume the office of viceroy of Areia himself.

After passing over the river Oxus, he made a forced march to the place where he heard that Bessus was with his forces; but at this time messengers reached him from Spitamenes and Dataphernes, to announce that they would arrest Bessus and hand him over to Alexander if he would send to them a small army and a commander for it; since even at that very time they were holding him under guard, though they had not bound him with fetters. When Alexander heard this, he gave his army rest, and marched more slowly than before. But he despatched Ptolemy, son of Lagus, at the head of three troops of the Companion cavalry and all the horse-lancers, and of the infantry, the brigade of Philotas, one regiment

---

[1] Cf. Xenophon, *Anab.*, i. 5, 10.

of 1,000 shield-bearing guards, all the Agrianians, and half the archers, with orders to make a forced march to Spitamenes and Dataphernes. Ptolemy went according to his instructions, and completing ten days' march in four days, arrived at the camp where on the preceding day the barbarians under Spitamenes had bivouacked.

CHAPTER XXX.

Capture of Bessus.—Exploits in Sogdiana.

Here Ptolemy learned that Spitamenes and Dataphernes were not firmly resolved about the betrayal of Bessus. He therefore left the infantry behind with orders to follow him in regular order, and advanced with the cavalry till he arrived at a certain village, where Bessus was with a few soldiers; for Spitamenes and his party had already retired from thence, being ashamed to betray Bessus themselves. Ptolemy posted his cavalry right round the village, which was enclosed by a wall supplied with gates. He then issued a proclamation to the barbarians in the village, that they would be allowed to depart uninjured if they surrendered Bessus to him. They accordingly admitted Ptolemy and his men into the village. He then seized Bessus and departed; but sent a messenger on before to ask Alexander how he was to conduct Bessus into his presence. Alexander ordered him to bind the prisoner naked in a wooden collar, and thus to lead him and place him on the right-hand side of the road along which he was about to march with the army. Thus did Ptolemy. When Alexander saw Bessus, he caused his chariot to stop, and asked him, for what reason he had in the first place arrested Darius, his own king, who was also his kinsman and benefactor, and then led him as a prisoner in chains, and at last killed him? Bessus said that he was not the only person who had decided to do this, but that it was the joint act of those who were at the time in attendance upon Darius, with the view of procuring safety for themselves from Alexander. For this Alexander ordered that he should be scourged, and that the herald should repeat the very same reproaches which he had himself made to Bessus in his inquiry. After being thus disgracefully tortured, he was sent away to Bactra to be put to death. Such is the account given by Ptolemy in relation to Bessus; but Aristobulus says that Spitamenes and Dataphernes brought Bessus to Ptolemy, and having bound him naked in a wooden collar betrayed him to Alexander.[1]

Alexander supplied his cavalry with horses from that district, for many of his own horses had perished in the passage of the Caucasus and in the march to and from the Oxus. He then led his army to Maracanda,[2] which is the capital of the land of the Sogdianians. Thence he advanced to the river Tanais. This river, which Aristobulus says the neighbouring barbarians call by a different name, Jaxartes, has its source, like the Oxus, in mount Caucasus, and also discharges itself into the Hyrcanian Sea.[3] It must be a different Tanais from that of which Herodotus the historian speaks, saying that it is the eighth of the Scythian rivers, that it flows out of a great lake in which it originates, and discharges itself into a still larger lake, called the Maeotis.[4] There are some who make this Tanais the boundary of Europe

---

[1] *Curtius* (vii. 24) follows the account of Aristobulus, and so does *Diodorus* (xvii. 83) in the main. Cf. Aelian (*Varia Historia*, xii. 37).

[2] The modern Samarcand.

[3] Arrian and Strabo are wrong in stating that the Jáxartes rises in the Caucasus, or Hindu-Koosh. It springs from the Comedae Montes, now called Moussour. It does not flow into the Hyrcanian, or Caspian Sea, but into the Sea of Aral. It is about 900 miles long.

[4] The river Tanais, of which Herodotus speaks (iv. 45, 57), is the Don; and the Lake Maeotis, is the Sea of Azov. Cf. *Strabo* (vii. cc. 3 and 4).

and Asia, saying that the Palus Maeotis, issuing from the furthest recess of the Euxine[1] Sea, and this river Tanais, which discharges itself into the Maeotis, separate Asia and Europe,[2] just in the same way as the sea near Gadeira and the Nomad Libyans opposite Gadeira separates Libya and Europe.[3] Libya also is said by these men to be divided from the rest of Asia by the river Nile. In this place (viz. at the river Tanais), some of the Macedonians, being engaged in foraging, were cut to pieces by the barbarians. The perpetrators of this deed escaped to a mountain, which was very rugged and precipitous on all sides. In number they were about 30,000. Alexander took the lightest men in his army and marched against these. Then the Macedonians made many ineffectual assaults upon the mountain. At first they were beaten back by the missiles of the barbarians, and many of them were wounded, including Alexander himself, who was shot right through the leg with an arrow, and the fibula of his leg was broken. Notwithstanding this, he captured the place, and some of the barbarians were cut to pieces there by the Mace-

---

[1] *Euxeinos* (kind to strangers); called before the Greeks settled upon it *Axenos* (inhospitable). See Ovid (*Tristia*, iv. 4). Cf. *Ammianus* (xxii. 8, 33): "A contrario per cavillationem Pontus Euxinus adpellatur, et euethen Graeci dicimus stultum, et noctem euphronen et furias Eumenidas."

[2] So *Curtius* (vi. 6) makes the Don the boundary of Europe and Asia. "Tanais Europam et Asiam medius interfuit." Ammianus says: "Tanais inter Caucasias oriens rupes, per sinuosos labitur circumflexus, Asiamque disterminans ab Europa, in stagnis Maeoticis delitescit." The Rha, or Volga, is first mentioned by Ptolemy in the second century of the Christian era.

[3] Gadeira is now called Cadiz. The Greeks called the continent of Africa by the name of Libya. So *Polybius* (iii. 37) says that the Don is the boundary of Europe, and that Libya is separated from Asia and Europe respectively by the Nile and the Straits of Gibraltar, or, as he calls the latter, "the mouth at the pillars of Hercules." Arrian here, like many ancient authors, considers Libya a part of Asia. Cf. *Juvenal*, x. i.

donians, while many also cast themselves down from the rocks and perished; so that out of 30,000 not more than 8,000 were preserved.[1]

---

[1] *Curtius* (vii. 23) gives an account of the massacre by Alexander of the descendants of the Branchidae, who had surrendered to Xerxes the treasures of the temple of Apollo near Miletus, and who, to escape the vengeance of the Greeks, had accompanied Xerxes into the interior. They had been settled in Sogdiana, and their descendants had preserved themselves distinct from the barbarians for 150 years, till the arrival of Alexander. We learn from the table of contents of the 17th book of *Diodorus*, that that historian also gave an account of this atrocity of Alexander in the part of his history, now lost, which came after the 83rd chapter. Cf. *Herodotus* (i. 92, 157; v. 36); *Strabo* (xi. 11; xiv. 1).

BOOK IV.

CHAPTER I.

Rebellion of the Sogdianians.

A few days after this, envoys reached Alexander from the people called Abian Scythians, whom Homer commended in his poem, calling them the justest of men.[1] This nation dwells in Asia and is independent, chiefly by reason of its poverty and love of justice. Envoys also came from the Scythians of Europe, who are the largest nation dwelling in that continent.[2] Alexander sent some of the Companions with them, under the pretext indeed that they were to conclude a friendly alliance by the embassy; but the real object of the mission was rather to spy into the natural features of the Scythian land, the number of the inhabitants and their customs, as well as the armaments which they possessed for making military expeditions.[3] He formed a plan of founding a city near the river Tanais, which was to be named after himself; for the site seemed to him suitable and likely to cause the city to grow to large dimensions. He also thought it would be built in a place which would serve as a favourable basis of operations for an invasion of Scythia, if such an event should ever occur; and not

---

[1] See Homer's *Iliad*, xiii. 6. Cf. *Curtius*, vii. 26; *Ammianus*, xxiii. 6.

[2] Cf. *Thucydides*, ii. 97.

[3] *Curtius* (vii. 26) says, he sent one of his friends named Berdes on this mission.

only so, but it would also be a bulwark to secure the land against the incursions of the barbarians dwelling on the further side of the river. Moreover he thought that the city would become great, both by reason of the multitude of those who would join in colonizing it, and on account of the celebrity of the name conferred upon it.[1] Meantime the barbarians dwelling near the river seized upon the Macedonian soldiers who were garrisoning their cities and killed them; after which they began to strengthen the cities for their greater security. Most of the Sogdianians joined them in this revolt, being urged on to it by the men who had arrested Bessus. These men were so energetic that they even induced some of the Bactrians to join in the rebellion, either because they were afraid of Alexander, or because their seducers assigned as a reason for their revolt, that he had sent instructions to the rulers of that land to assemble for a conference at Zariaspa, the chief city; which conference, they said, would be for no good purpose.[2]

CHAPTER II.

Capture of Five Cities in Two Days.

When Alexander was informed of this, he gave instructions to the infantry, company by company, to prepare the ladders which were assigned to each company. He then started from the camp and advanced to the nearest city, the name of which was Gaza; for the barbarians of the land were said to have fled for refuge into seven cities. He sent Craterus to the one called Cyropolis,

---

[1] This was called Alexandria Ultima, on the Jaxartes, probably the modern Khojend.

[2] Cf. *Curtius* (vii. 26). Zariaspa was another name for Bactra. See *Pliny* (vi. 18) and *Strabo* (xi. 11).

the largest of them all, into which most of the barbarians had gathered.[1] The orders of Craterus were to encamp near the city, to dig a trench round it, to surround it with a stockade, and to fix together the military engines which were required for use, so that the men in this city, having had their attention drawn to his forces, might be unable to render aid to the other cities. As soon as Alexander arrived at Gaza, without any delay he gave the signal to his men to place the ladders against the wall all round and to take it by assault at once, as it was made merely of earth and was not at all high. Simultaneously with the assault of the infantry, his slingers, archers, and javelin-throwers assailed the defenders on the wall, and missiles were hurled from the military engines, so that the wall was quickly cleared of its defenders by the multitude of the missiles. Then the fixing of the ladders against the wall and the mounting of the Macedonians were matters soon effected. They killed all the men, according to Alexander's injunctions; but the women, the children, and the rest of the booty they carried off as plunder. Thence he immediately marched to the city situated next to that one; and this he took in the same way and on the same day, treating the captives in the same manner. Then he marched against the third city, and took it on the next day at the first assault. While he was thus occupied by these matters with the infantry, he sent out his cavalry to the two neighbouring cities, with orders to guard the men within them closely, so that when they heard of the capture of the neighbouring cities, and at the same time of his own near approach, they should not betake themselves to flight and render it impossible for him to pursue them. It turned out just as he had conjectured; and

---

[1] This city was also called Cyreschata, because it was the furthest city founded by Cyrus, and the extreme city of the Persian empire.

his despatch of the cavalry was made just at the nick of time. For when the barbarians who occupied the two cities still uncaptured, saw the smoke rising from the city in front of them which was then on fire, (and some men, escaping even from the midst of the calamity itself, became the reporters of the capture which they had themselves witnessed,) they began to flee in crowds out of the cities as fast as each man could; but falling in with the dense body of cavalry drawn up in array of battle, most of them were cut to pieces.

CHAPTER III.

Storming of Cyropolis.—Revolt of the Scythians.

Having thus captured the five cities and reduced them to slavery in two days,[1] he went to Cyropolis, the largest city in the country. It was fortified with a wall higher than those of the others, as it had been founded by Cyrus. The majority of the barbarians of this district, and at the same time the most warlike of them, had fled for refuge thither, and consequently it was not possible for the Macedonians to capture it so easily at the first assault. Wherefore Alexander brought his military engines up to the wall with the determination of battering it down in this way, and of making assaults wherever breaches might be made in it. When he observed that the channel of the river, which flows through the city when it is swollen by the winter rains, was at that time nearly dry and did not reach up to the wall, and would thus afford his soldiers a passage by which to penetrate into the city, he took the body-guards, the shield-bearing guards, the archers, and Agrianians, and made his way secretly into

---

[1] δυοῖν was not used in Attic Greek, or but seldom. It became common after the time of Alexander.

the city along the channel, at first with a few men, while the barbarians had turned their attention towards the military engines and those who were assailing them in that quarter. Having from within broken open the gates which were opposite this position, he gave an easy admittance to the rest of his soldiers. Then the barbarians, though they perceived that their city was already in the hands of the enemy, nevertheless turned against Alexander and his men and made a desperate assault upon them, in which Alexander himself received a violent blow on the head and neck with a stone, and Craterus was wounded with an arrow, as were also many other officers. Notwithstanding this, however, they drove the barbarians out of the market-place. Meantime, those who had made the assault upon the wall, took it, as it was now void of defenders. In the first capture of the city about 8,000 of the enemy were killed. The rest fled for refuge into the citadel; for 15,000 warriors in all had gathered together in the city. Alexander encamped around these and besieged them for one day,[1] and then they surrendered through lack of water. The seventh city he took at the first assault. Ptolemy says that the men in it surrendered; but Aristobulus asserts that this city was also taken by storm, and that he slew all who were captured therein. Ptolemy also says that he distributed the men among the army and ordered that they should be kept guarded in chains until he should depart from the country, so that none of those who had effected the revolt should be left behind. Meantime an army of the Asiatic Scythians arrived at the bank of the river Tanais, because most of them had heard that some of the barbarians on the opposite side of the river had revolted from Alexander. They intended to attack the Macedonians, if any revolutionary movement worthy of consideration were effected. News

---

[1] Instead of *ἡμέρᾳ μιᾷ*, Sintenis reads *ἡμέραν μίαν*.

was also brought that Spitamenes was besieging the men who had been left in the citadel at Maracanda. Against him Alexander then despatched Andromachus, Menedemus, and Caranus with sixty of the Companion cavalry, 800 of the mercenary cavalry under the command of Caranus, and 1,500 mercenary infantry. Over them he placed Pharnuches the interpreter, who, though by birth a Lycian, was skilled in the language of the barbarians of this country, and in other respects appeared clever in dealing with them.

CHAPTER IV.

Defeat of the Scythians beyond the Tanais.

In twenty days he fortified the city which he was projecting, and settled in it some of the Grecian mercenaries and those of the neighbouring barbarians who volunteered to take part in the settlement, as well as the Macedonians from his army who were now unfit for military service.[1] He then offered sacrifice to the gods in his customary manner and celebrated an equestrian and gymnastic contest. When he saw that the Scythians were not retiring from the river's bank, but were seen to be shooting arrows into the river, which was not wide here, and were uttering audacious words in their barbaric tongue to insult Alexander, to the effect that he durst not touch Scythians, or if he did, he would learn what was the difference between them and the Asiatic barbarians, he was irritated by these remarks, and having resolved to cross over against them, he began to prepare the skins for the passage of the river.[2] But when he offered sacrifice with a view to crossing, the victims proved to be unfavourable; and though he was vexed at this, he nevertheless con-

---

[1] This city was called by the Greeks, Alexandria on the Tanais. See *Curtius*, vii. 28.

[2] Cf. *Livy*, xxi. 27:—Hispani sine ulla mole in utres vestimentis conjectis ipsi caetris superpositis incubantes flumen tranavere.

trolled himself and remained where he was. But as the Scythians did not desist from their insults, he again offered sacrifice with a view to crossing; and Aristander told him that the omens still portended danger to himself. But Alexander said that it was better for him to come into extreme danger than that, after having subdued almost the whole of Asia, he should be a laughing-stock to the Scythians, as Darius, the father of Xerxes, had been in days of yore.[1] Aristander refused to explain the will of the gods contrary to the revelations made by the deity simply because Alexander wished to hear the contrary. When the skins had been prepared for the passage, and the army, fully equipped, had been posted near the river, the military engines, at the signal preconcerted, began to shoot at the Scythians riding along the river's bank. Some of them were wounded by the missiles, and one was struck right through the wicker-shield and breastplate and fell from his horse. The others, being alarmed at the discharge of missiles from so great a distance, and at the death of their champion, retreated a little from the bank. But Alexander, seeing them thrown into confusion by the effect of his missiles, began to cross the river with trumpets sounding, himself leading the way; and the rest of the army followed him. Having first got the archers and slingers across, he ordered them to sling and shoot at the Scythians, to prevent them approaching the phalanx of infantry stepping out of the water, until all his cavalry had passed over. When they were upon the bank in dense mass, he first of all launched against the Scythians one regiment of the Grecian auxiliary cavalry and four squadrons of pike-men. These the Scythians received, and in great numbers riding round them in circles, wounded them, as they were few in number, themselves escaping with ease. But Alexander mixed the archers,

[1] See *Herodotus*, iv. 122–142.

the Agrianians, and other light troops under the command of Balacrus, with the cavalry, and then led them against the enemy. As soon as they came to close quarters, he ordered three regiments of the cavalry Companions and all the horse-lancers to charge them. The rest of the cavalry he himself led, and made a rapid attack with his squadrons in column. Accordingly the enemy were no longer able as before to wheel their cavalry force round in circles, for at one and the same time the cavalry and the light-armed infantry mixed with the horsemen pressed upon them, and did not permit them to wheel about in safety. Then the flight of the Scythians was already apparent. 1,000 of them fell, including Satraces, one of their chiefs; and 150 were captured. But as the pursuit was keen and fatiguing on account of the excessive heat, the entire army was seized with thirst; and Alexander himself while riding drank of such water as was procurable in that country. He was seized with an incessant diarrhœa; for the water was bad; and for this reason he could not pursue all the Scythians. Otherwise I think all of them would have perished in the flight, if Alexander had not fallen ill. He was carried back to the camp, having fallen into extreme danger; and thus Aristander's prophecy was fulfilled.

CHAPTER V.

Spitamenes Destroys a Macedonian Detachment.

Soon after this, arrived envoys from the king of the Scythians, who were sent to apologize for what had been done, and to state that it was not the act of the Scythian State, but of certain men who set out for plunder after the manner of freebooters. They also assured him that their king was willing to obey the commands laid upon him. Alexander sent to him a courteous reply, because it did not seem honourable for him to abstain from marching against him if he distrusted him, and at that time there was not an convenient opportunity to do so. The Macedonians who were garrisoning the citadel at Maracanda, when an assault was made upon it by Spitamenes and his adherents, sallied forth, and killing some of the enemy and repulsing all the rest, retreated into the citadel without any loss. But when Spitamenes was informed that the men despatched by Alexander to Maracanda were now drawing near, he raised the siege of the citadel, and retired to the capital of Sogdiana.[1] Pharnuches and the generals with him, being eager to drive him out altogether, followed him up as he was retreating towards the frontiers of Sogdiana, and without due consideration made a joint attack upon the Nomad Scythians. Then Spitamenes, having received a reinforcement of 600 Scythian horsemen, was further emboldened by the Scythian alliance to wait and receive the Macedonians who were advancing upon him. Posting his men in a level place near the Scythian desert, he was not willing either to wait for the enemy or to attack them himself; but rode round and discharged arrows at the phalanx of infantry. When the forces of Pharnuches made a charge upon them, they easily escaped, since at that time their horses were swifter and more vigorous, while the horse of Andromachus had been damaged by the incessant marching, as well as by lack of fodder; and the Scythians pressed upon them with all their might whether they halted or retreated. Many of them then were wounded by the arrows, and some were killed. They therefore arranged the soldiers into the form of a square and proceeded to the river Polytimetus,[2] because there was a woody glen near it, and it would consequently no longer be easy for

---

[1] This was Maracanda, according to iii. 30 supra. There is an error in the text; Abicht proposes to read *ἐπὶ τὰ ὅρια*, instead of *ἐς τὰ βασίλεια*.

[2] This river is now called Sogd, or Kohik. The Greek name signifies "very precious," a translation of the native name. Cf. *Strabo*, p. 518.

the barbarians to shoot arrows at them, and their infantry would be more useful to them. But Caranus, the commander of the cavalry, without communicating with Andromachus, attempted to cross the river in order to put the cavalry in a place of safety on the other side. The infantry followed him without any word of command; their descent into the river being made in a panic and without any discipline down the precipitous banks. When the barbarians perceived the error of the Macedonians, they sprang into the ford here and there, horses and all. Some of them seized and held tight those who had already crossed and were departing; others being posted right in front of those who were crossing, rolled them over into the river; others shot arrows at them from the flanks; while others pressed upon the men who were just entering the water. The Macedonians being thus encompassed with difficulty on all sides, fled for refuge into one of the small islands in the river, where they were entirely surrounded by the Scythians and the cavalry of Spitamenes, and all killed with arrows, except a few of them, whom they reduced to slavery. All of these were afterwards killed.

CHAPTER VI.

Spitamenes Driven into the Desert.

But Aristobulus says the greater part of this army was destroyed by an ambuscade, the Scythians having hidden themselves in a park and fallen upon the Macedonians from their place of concealment, when Pharnuches was in the very act of retiring from the command in favour of the Macedonians who had been sent with him, on the ground of his not being skilled in military affairs, and of his having been sent by Alexander rather to win the favour of the barbarians than to take the supreme command in battles. He also alleged that the Macedonian officers present were the king's Companions. But Andromachus, Menedemus, and Caranus declined to accept the chief command, partly because it did not seem right to make any alteration on their own responsibility contrary to Alexander's instructions to them, and partly because in the very crisis of danger, they were unwilling, if they met with any defeat, not only individually to take a share of the blame, but also collectively to exercise the command unsuccessfully. In this confusion and disorder the barbarians fell upon them, and cut them all off, so that not more than forty horsemen and 300 foot preserved their lives.[1] When the report of this reached Alexander, he was chagrined at the loss of his soldiers, and resolved to march with all speed against Spitamenes and his barbarian adherents. He therefore took half of the Companion cavalry, all the shield-bearing guards, the archers, the Agrianians, and the lightest men of the phalanx, and went towards Maracanda, where he ascertained Spitamenes had returned and was again besieging the men in the citadel. Having travelled 1,500 stades in three days, at the approach of dawn on the fourth day he came near the city;[2] but when Spitamenes was informed of Alexander's approach, he did not remain, but abandoned the city and fled. Alexander pursued him closely; and coming to the place where the battle was fought, he buried his soldiers as well as the circumstances permitted, and then followed the fugitives as far as the desert. Returning thence, he laid the land waste, and slew the barbarians who had fled for refuge into the fortified places, because they were reported to have taken part in the attack upon the Macedonians.[3] He traversed the whole country which the

---

[1] *Curtius* (vii. 32) says that Spitamenes laid an ambush for the Macedonians, and slew 300 cavalry and 2,000 infantry.

[2] About 170 miles.

[3] *Curtius* (vii. 40) says that Alexander founded six cities in Bactria and Sogdiana. *Justin* (xii. 5) says there were twelve.

river Polytimetus waters in its course; but the country beyond the place where the water of this river disappears is desert; for though it has abundance of water, it disappears into the sand.[1] Other large and perennial rivers in that region disappear in a similar way:—the Epardus, which flows through the land of the Mardians; the Areius, after which the country of the Areians is named; and the Etymander, which flows through the territory of the Euergetae.[2] All of these are rivers of such a size that none of them is smaller than the Thessalian river Peneius, which flows through Tempē and discharges itself into the sea. The Polytimetus is much too large to be compared with the river Peneius.[3]

CHAPTER VII.

Treatment of Bessus.

When he had accomplished this, he came to Zariaspa; where he remained until the depth of winter arrived.[4] At this time came to him Phrataphernes the viceroy of Parthia, and Stasanor, who had been sent into the land of the Areians to arrest Arsames.[5] Him they brought with them in chains, as also Barzanes, whom Bessus had appointed viceroy of the land of the Parthians, and some others of those who at that time had joined Bessus in revolt. At the same time arrived from the sea, Epocillus,[6] Melamnidas and Ptolemy, the general of the Thracians, who had convoyed down to the sea the Grecian allies and

---

1 This is a mistake; for it ends in a lake Dengiz near Karakoul.

2 The Areius is now called Heri-rud. The Etymander is the modern Hilmend. Nothing is known of the Epardus.

3 The Peneius is now called Salambria. It forces its way through the vale of Tempe, between mounts Olympus and Ossa, into the sea. Cf. Ovid (*Met.*, i. 568–576).

4 On the analogy of πρὶν the later prose-writers use ἔστε with the infinitive. Cf. *Arrian*, ii. 1, 3; v. 16, 1.

5 See Bk. iii. ch. 29 supra.

6 See Bk. iii. ch. 19 supra.

the money sent with Menes.[1] At this time also arrived Asander and Nearchus at the head of an army of Grecian mercenaries.[2] Asclepiodorus, viceroy of Syria, and Menes the deputy also arrived from the sea, at the head of another army. Then Alexander gathered a conference of those who were then at hand, and led Bessus in before them. Having accused him of the betrayal of Darius, he ordered his nose and ears to be cut off, and that he should be taken to Ecbatana to be put to death there in the council of the Medes and Persians.[3] I do not commend this excessive punishment; on the contrary, I consider that the mutilation of the prominent features of the body is a barbaric[4] custom, and I agree with those who say that Alexander was induced to indulge his desire of emulating the Median and Persian wealth and to treat his subjects as inferior beings according to the custom of the foreign kings. Nor do I by any means commend him for changing the Macedonian style of dress which his fathers had adopted, for the Median one,[5] being as he was a descendant of Heracles.[6] Besides, he was not

---

1 See Bk. iii. ch. 16 supra.

2 *Curtius* (vii. 40) says that the reinforcement was 19,000 men.

3 Cf. Plutarch (*Alex.*, 43); *Diodorus* (xvii. 83).

4 *I.e.* non-Hellenic.

5 Cf. *Diodorus*, xvii. 77; *Justin.*, xii. 3. We learn from Plutarch (*Alex.*, 45), that he did not assume the tiara of the Persian kings. Cf. *Arrian*, vii. 9; vii. 29 infra. The Medic robe was a long silken garment reaching to the feet, and falling round the body in many deep folds.

6 Caranus, a descendant of Temenus, king of Argos, is said to have settled in Macedonia, and to have become the founder of the dynasty of Macedonian kings. Temenus was a descendant of Heracles. Cf. ii. 5; iv. 10. One of the chief causes of disgust which the Greeks felt at the conduct of Pausanias, the conqueror at Plataea, was, that he adopted the Persian attire. "This pedigree from Temenus and Hercules may be suspicious; yet it was allowed, after a strict inquiry by the judges of the Olympic games (*Herodotus*, v. 22), at a time when the Macedonian kings were obscure and unpopular in Greece. When the Achaean league declared against Philip, it was thought decent that the deputies of Argos should retire (*T. Liv.*, xxxii. 22)."—*Gibbon.* Cf. *Herodotus*, viii. 137; *Thucydides*, ii. 99, 100; v. 80.

ashamed to exchange the head-dress which he the conqueror had so long worn, for that of the conquered Persians. None of these things do I commend; but I consider Alexander's great achievements prove, if anything can, that supposing a man to have a vigorous bodily constitution, to be illustrious in descent, and to be even more successful in war than Alexander himself; even supposing he could sail right round Libya as well as Asia, and hold them both in subjection as Alexander indeed designed; even if he could add the possession of Europe to that of Asia and Libya; all these things would be no furtherance to such a man's happiness, unless at the same time he possess the power of self-control, though he has performed the great deeds which have been supposed.

CHAPTER VIII.

The Murder of Clitus.

Here also I shall give an account of the tragic fate of Clitus, son of Dropidas, and of Alexander's mishap in regard to it. Though it occurred a little while after this, it will not be out place here. The Macedonians kept a day sacred to Dionysus, and on that day Alexander used to offer sacrifice to him every year. But they say that on this occasion he was neglectful of Dionysus,[1] and sacrificed to the Dioscūri[2] instead; for he had resolved to offer sacrifice to those deities for some reason or other. When the drinking-party on this occasion had already gone on too long (for Alexander had now made innovations even in regard to drinking, by imitating the custom of foreigners), and in the midst of the carouse a discussion had arisen about the Dioscuri, how their procreation

---

[1] Cf. *Curtius*, viii. 6.

[2] The sons of Jove, Castor and Pollux. *ἐπιφρασθέντα* is a word borrowed from Homer and Herodotus.

had been taken away from Tyndareus and ascribed to Zeus, some of those present, in order to flatter Alexander, maintained that Polydeuces and Castor were in no way worthy to compare with him who had performed so many exploits. Such men have always corrupted the character of kings and will never cease to ruin the interests of those who happen to be reigning.[1] In their carousal they did not even abstain from (comparing him with) Heracles; saying that envy prevented the living from receiving the honours due to them from their associates. It was well known that Clitus had long been vexed at Alexander for the change in his style of living in imitation of foreign kings, and at those who flattered him with their speech. At that time also, being heated with wine, he would not permit them either to insult the deity or, by depreciating the deeds of the ancient heroes, to confer upon Alexander a gratification which deserved no thanks. He affirmed Alexander's deeds were neither in fact so great or marvellous as they represented in their laudation; nor had he achieved them by himself, but for the most part they were the deeds of the Macedonians. The delivery of this speech annoyed Alexander; and I do not commend it, for I think, in such a drunken bout, it would have been sufficient if, so far as he was personally concerned, he had kept silence, and not committed the error of indulging in the same flattery as the others. But when some even mentioned Philip's actions without exercising a just judgment, declaring that he had performed nothing great or marvellous, they gratified Alexander; but Clitus being then no longer able to contain himself, began to put Philip's achievements in the first rank, and to depreciate Alexander and his performances.[2] Clitus

---

[1] Cf. *Curtius*, viii. 17: "Non deerat talia concupiscenti perniciosa adulatio perpetuum malum regum, quorum opes saepius assentatio quam hostis evertit."

[2] *Curtius* (viii. 3 and 4) says that it was Alexander himself that spoke

being now quite intoxicated, made other insolent remarks and even greatly reviled him, because forsooth he had saved his life, when the cavalry battle had been fought with the Persians at the Granicus. Then indeed, arrogantly stretching out his right hand, he said:—"This hand, O Alexander, preserved thee on that occasion." Alexander could now no longer endure the drunken insolence of Clitus; but jumped up against him in a great rage. He was however restrained by his boon-companions. As Clitus did not desist from his insulting remarks, Alexander shouted out a summons for his shield-bearing guards to attend him; but when no one obeyed him, he said that he was reduced to the same position as Darius, when he was led about under arrest by Bessus and his adherents, and that he now possessed the mere name of king. Then his companions were no longer able to restrain him; for according to some he leaped up and snatched a javelin from one of his confidential body-guards; according to others, a long pike from one of his ordinary guards, with which he struck Clitus and killed him.[1] Aristobulus does not say whence the drunken quarrel originated, but asserts that the fault was entirely on the side of Clitus, who, when Alexander had got so enraged with him as to jump up against him with the intention of making an end of him, was led away by Ptolemy, son of Lagus, the confidential body-guard, through the gateway, beyond the wall and ditch of the citadel where the quarrel occurred. He adds that Clitus could not control himself, but went back again, and falling in with Alexander who was calling out for Clitus, he exclaimed:—"Alexander, here is Clitus!" Thereupon he was struck with a long pike and killed.

---

depreciatingly of Philip, and that Clitus even dared to defend the murdered Parmenio.

[1] Instead of the usual reading from *καὶ ταύτῃ* to *καὶ ταύτην*, Sintenis reads *οἱ δὲ σάρισαν παρὰ τῶν φυλάκων τινὸς καὶ ταύτῃ παίσαντα τὸν* Κλεῖτον *ἀποκτεῖναι.*

CHAPTER IX.

Alexander's Grief for Clitus.

I think Clitus deserving of severe censure for his insolent behaviour to his king, while at the same time I pity Alexander for his mishap, because on that occasion he showed himself the slave of two vices, anger and drunkenness, by neither of which is it seemly for a prudent man to be enslaved. But then on the other hand I think his subsequent behaviour worthy of praise, because directly after he had done the deed he recognised that it was a horrible one. Some of his biographers even say that he propped the pike against the wall with the intention of falling upon it himself, thinking that it was not proper for him to live who had killed his friend when under the influence of wine. Most historians do not mention this, but say that he went off to bed and lay there lamenting, calling Clitus himself by name, and his sister Lanice, daughter of Dropidas, who had been his nurse. He exclaimed that having reached man's estate he had forsooth bestowed on her a noble reward for her care in rearing him, as she lived to see her own sons die fighting on his behalf, and the king slaying her brother with his own hand.[1] He did not cease calling himself the murderer of his friends; and for three days rigidly abstained from food and drink, and paid no attention whatever to his personal appearance. Some of the soothsayers revealed that the avenging wrath of Dionysus had been the cause of his conduct, because he had omitted the sacrifice to that deity.[2] At last with great difficulty he was induced by his companions to touch food and to pay

---

[1] Cf. *Curtius* (viii. 3 and 6), who calls the sister of Clitus, Hellanice.

[2] From Plutarch (*Alex.*, 13) we learn that Alexander imagined he had incurred the avenging wrath of Bacchus by destroying Thebes, the birthplace of that deity, on which account it was supposed to be under his tutelary care.

proper attention to his person.[1] He then paid to Dionysus the sacrifice due to him, since he was not at all unwilling to attribute the fatality rather to the avenging wrath of the deity than to his own depravity. I think Alexander deserves great praise for this, that he did not obstinately persevere in evil, or still worse become a defender and advocate of the wrong which had been done, but confessed that he had committed a crime, being a man and not a god. There are some who say that Anaxarchus the Sophist[2] was summoned into Alexander's presence to give him consolation. Finding him lying down and groaning, he laughed at him, and said that he did not know that the wise men of old for this reason made Justice an assessor of Zeus, because whatever was done by him was justly done[3]; and therefore also that which was done by the Great King ought to be deemed just, in the first place by the king himself, and then by the rest of men. They say that Alexander was then greatly consoled by these remarks.[4] But I assert that Anaxarchus did Alexander a great injury and one still greater than that by which he was then oppressed, if he really thought this to be the opinion of a wise man, that forsooth it is proper for a king to come to hasty conclusions and act unjustly, and that whatever is done by a king must be deemed just, no

---

[1] *Curtius* (viii. 6) says, that in order to console the king, the Macedonian army passed a vote that Clitus had been justly slain, and that his corpse should not be buried. But the king ordered its burial.

[2] A philosopher of Abdera, and pupil of Democritus. After Alexander's death, Anaxarchus was thrown by shipwreck into the hands of Nicocreon, king of Cyprus, to whom he had given offence, and who had him pounded to death in a mortar.

[3] Cf. Sophocles (*Oedipus Col.*, 1382; *Antigone*, 451); Hesiod (*Opera et Dies*, 254–257); Pindar (*Olympia*, viii. 28); Demosthenes (*Advers. Aristogiton*, p. 772); *Herodotus*, iii. 31.

[4] Plutarch (*Alex.*, 52) tells us that Callisthenes the philosopher was also summoned with Anaxarchus to administer consolation, but he adopted such a different tone that Alexander was displeased with him.

matter how it is done. There is also a current report that Alexander wished men to prostrate themselves before him as to a god, entertaining the notion that Ammon was his father, rather than Philip; and that he now showed his admiration of the customs of the Persians and Medes by changing the style of his dress, and by the alteration he made in the general etiquette of his court. There were not wanting those who in regard to these matters gave way to his wishes with the design of flattering him; among others being Anaxarchus, one of the philosophers attending his court, and Agis, an Argive who was an epic poet.[1]

CHAPTER X.

Dispute between Callisthenes and Anaxarchus.

But it is said that Callisthenes the Olynthian, who had studied philosophy under Aristotle, and was somewhat brusque in his manner, did not approve of this conduct; and so far as this is concerned I quite agree with him. But the following remark of his, if indeed it has been correctly recorded, I do not think at all proper, when he declared that Alexander and his exploits were dependent upon him and his history, and that he had not come to him to acquire reputation from him, but to make him renowned in the eyes of men;[2] consequently that Alexander's participation in divinity did not depend on the false assertion of Olympias in regard to the author of his birth, but on

[1] *Curtius* (viii. 17) says that Agis was the composer of very poor poems.

[2] *Justin* (xii. 6) says that Callisthenes was a fellow-student with Alexander under Aristotle. He composed three historical works: I. *Hellenica*, from B.C. 387 to 337; II. *The History of the Sacred War*, from B.C. 357 to 346; III. *The History of Alexander*. Cf. *Diodorus*, xiv. 117. According to *Polybius* (xii. 23), he was accused by Timaeus of having flattered Alexander in his History.

what he might report to mankind in his history of the king. There are some writers also who have said that on one occasion Philotas forsooth asked him, what man he thought to be held in especial honour by the people of Athens; and that he replied:—"Harmodius and Aristogeiton; because they slew one of the two despots, and put an end to the despotism."[1] Philotas again asked:—"If it happened now that a man should kill a despot, to which of the Grecian States would you wish him to flee for preservation?" Callisthenes again replied:—"If not among others, at any rate among the Athenians an exile would find preservation; for they waged war on behalf of the sons of Heracles against Eurystheus, who at that time was ruling as a despot over Greece."[2] How he resisted Alexander in regard to the ceremony of prostration, the following is the most received account.[3] An arrangement was made between Alexander and the Sophists in conjunction with the most illustrious of the Persians and Medes who were in attendance upon him, that this topic should be mentioned at a wine-party. Anaxarchus commenced the discussion[4] by saying that he considered Alexander much more worthy of being deemed a god than either Dionysus or Heracles, not only on account of the very numerous and mighty exploits

---

[1] Hipparchus was slain B.C. 514, and Hippias was expelled from Athens B.C. 510. See *Thucydides*, vi. 53–59.

[2] Eurystheus was king over Argos and Mycenae alone.

[3] When Conon the famous Athenian visited Babylon, he would not see Artaxerxes, from repugnance to the ceremony of prostration, which was required from all who approached the Great King. We are also informed by Plutarch (*Artaxerxes*, 22), that Pelopidas declined to perform this ceremony, so degrading in the eyes of the Greeks. His colleague, Ismenias, however, dropped his ring in front of the king, and then stooped to pick it up, thus going through the act of prostration. Cf. Aelian (*Varia Historia*, i. 21). Xenophon said to his soldiers:—*οὐδένα γὰρ ἄνθρωπον δεσπότην ἀλλὰ τοὺς θεοὺς προσκυνεῖτε.* (*Anab.*, iii. 13).

[4] *Curtius* (viii. 18) says that the speech proposing to honour Alexander as a god was made by Cleon, a Sicilian Greek.

which he had performed, but also because Dionysus was only a Theban, in no way related to Macedonians; and Heracles was an Argive, not at all related to them, except that Alexander deduced his descent from him. He added that the Macedonians might with greater justice gratify their king with divine honours, for there was no doubt about this, that when he departed from men they would honour him as a god. How much more just then would it be to worship him while alive, than after his death, when it would be no advantage to him to be honoured.

CHAPTER XI.

Callisthenes Opposes the Proposal to Honour Alexander by Prostration.

When Anaxarchus had uttered these remarks and others of a similar kind, those who were privy to the plan applauded his speech, and wished at once to begin the ceremony of prostration. Most of the Macedonians, however, were vexed[1] at the speech and kept silence. But Callisthenes interposed and said:—"O Anaxarchus, I openly declare that there is no honour which Alexander is unworthy to receive, provided that it is consistent with his being human; but men have made distinctions between those honours which are due to men, and those due to gods, in many different ways, as for instance by the building of temples and by the erection of statues. Moreover for the gods sacred enclosures are selected, to them sacrifice is offered, and to them libations are made. Hymns also are composed in honour of the gods, and eulogies for men. But the greatest distinction is made by the custom of prostration. For it is the practice that men should be kissed by those who salute them[2]; but

[1] ἀχθομένους. The usual reading is μαχομένους.

[2] Cf. Xenophon (*Cyrop.*, i. 4, 27):—λέγεται τοὺς συγγενεῖς φιλοῦντας ἀποπέμπεσθαι αὐτὸν νόμῳ Περσικῷ.

because the deity is located somewhere above, it is not lawful even to touch him, and this is the reason no doubt why he is honoured by prostration. Bands of choral dancers are also appointed for the gods, and paeans are sung in their honour. And this is not at all wonderful, seeing that certain honours are specially assigned to some of the gods and certain others to other gods, and, by Zeus, quite different ones again are assigned to heroes, which are very distinct from those paid to the deities.[1] It is not therefore reasonable to confound all these distinctions without discrimination, exalting men to a rank above their condition by extravagant accumulation of honours, and debasing the gods, as far as lies in human power, to an unseemly level, by paying them honours only equal to those paid to men." He said that Alexander would not endure the affront, if some private individual were to be thrust into his royal honours by an unjust vote, either by show of hand or by ballot. Much more justly then would the gods be indignant at those mortals who usurp divine honours or suffer themselves to be thrust into them by others. "Alexander not only seems to be, but is in reality beyond any competition the bravest of brave men, of kings the most kingly, and of generals the most worthy to command an army. O Anaxarchus, it was thy duty, rather than any other man's, to become the special advocate of these arguments now adduced by me, and the opponent of those contrary to them, seeing that thou associatest with him for the purpose of imparting philosophy and instruction. Therefore it was unseemly to begin this discussion, when thou oughtest to have remembered that thou art not associating with and giving advice to Cambyses or Xerxes, but to the son of Philip, who derives his origin from Heracles and Aeacus,[2] whose

[1] *πρόσκεινται.* Cf. *Herodotus*, i. 118:—*τοῖσι θεῶν τιμὴ αὕτη προσκέεται.*

[2] Alexander's mother Olympias was daughter of Neoptolemus, king of Epirus, who traced his descent from Neoptolemus, son of Achilles, the grandson of Aeacus.

ancestors came into Macedonia from Argos, and have continued to rule the Macedonians, not by force, but by law. Not even to Heracles himself while still alive were divine honours paid by the Greeks; and even after his death they were withheld until a decree had been published by the oracle of the god at Delphi that men should honour Heracles as a god. But if, because the discussion is held [1] in the land of foreigners, we ought to adopt the sentiments of foreigners, I demand, O Alexander, that thou shouldst bethink thyself of Greece, for whose sake the whole of this expedition was undertaken by thee, that thou mightest join Asia to Greece. Therefore make up thy mind whether thou wilt return thither and compel the Greeks, who are men most devoted to freedom, to pay thee the honour of prostration, or whether thou wilt keep aloof from Greece, and inflict this honour on the Macedonians alone, or thirdly whether thou wilt thyself make a difference in every respect as to the honours to be paid thee, so as to be honoured by the Greeks and Macedonians as a human being and after the manner of the Greeks, and by foreigners alone after the foreign fashion of prostration. But if it is said that Cyrus, son of Cambyses, was the first man to whom the honour of prostration was paid, and that afterwards this degrading ceremony continued in vogue among the Persians and Medes, we ought to bear in mind that the Scythians, men poor but independent, chastised that Cyrus; [2] that other Scythians again chastised Darius, as the Athenians and Lacedaemonians did Xerxes, as Clearchus and Xenophon with their 10,000 followers did Artaxerxes; and finally, that Alexander, though not honoured with prostration, has conquered this Darius."

---

[1] *οἱ λόγοι γίγνονται.* There is another reading, *ὀλίγοι γίγνωνται.*

[2] Cf. *Herodotus*, i. 214, with Dean Blakesley's note.

CHAPTER XII.

Callisthenes Refuses to Prostrate Himself.

By making these and other remarks of a similar kind, Callisthenes greatly annoyed Alexander, but spoke the exact sentiments of the Macedonians. When the king perceived this, he sent to prevent the Macedonians from making any further mention of the ceremony of prostration. But after the discussion silence ensued; and then the most honourable of the Persians arose in due order and prostrated their bodies before him. But when one of the Persians seemed to have performed the ceremony in an awkward way, Leonnatus, one of the Companions, laughed at his posture as mean. Alexander at the time was angry with him for this, but was afterwards reconciled to him.[1] The following account has also been given :—Alexander drank from a golden goblet the health of the circle of guests, and handed it first to those with whom he had concerted the ceremony of prostration. The first who drank from the goblet rose up and performed the act of prostration, and received a kiss from him. This ceremony proceeded from one to another in due order. But when the pledging of health came to the turn of Callisthenes, he rose up and drank from the goblet, and drew near, wishing to kiss the king without performing the act of prostration. Alexander happened then to be conversing with Hephaestion, and consequently did not observe whether Callisthenes performed the ceremony properly or not. But when Callisthenes was approaching to kiss him, Demetrius, son of Pythonax, one of the Companions, said that he was doing so without having prostrated himself. So the king would not permit him to kiss him; whereupon the philosopher said :—"I

[1] *Curtius* (viii. 20) says, that it was Polysperchon who made sport of the Persian, and incurred the king's wrath.

am going away only with the loss of a kiss." I by no means approve any of these proceedings, which manifested both the insolence of Alexander on the present occasion and the churlish nature of Callisthenes. But I think that, so far as regards himself, it would have been quite sufficient if he had given his opinion discreetly, magnifying as much as possible the exploits of the king, with whom no one thought it a dishonour to associate. Therefore I consider that not without reason Callisthenes became odious to Alexander on account of the unseasonable freedom of speech in which he indulged,[1] as well as from the egregious fatuity of his conduct. I surmise that this was the reason why such easy credit was given to those who accused him of participating in the conspiracy formed against Alexander by his pages, and to those also who affirmed that they had been incited to engage in the conspiracy by him alone. The facts of this conspiracy were as follows:—

CHAPTER XIII.

Conspiracy of the Pages.

It was a custom introduced by Philip, that the sons of those Macedonians who had enjoyed high office, should, as soon as they reached the age of puberty, be selected to attend the king's court. These youths were entrusted with the general attendance on the king's person and the protection of his body while he was asleep. Whenever the king rode out, some of them received the horses from the grooms, and brought them to him, and others assisted him to mount in the Persian fashion. They were

---

[1] *Ammianus* (xviii. 3) says: "Ignorans profecto vetus Aristotelis sapiens dictum, qui Callisthenem sectatorem et propinquum suum ad regem Alexandrum mittens, ei saepe mandabat, ut quam rarissime et jucunde apud hominem loqueretur, vitae potestatem et necis in acie linguae portantem."

also companions of the king in the emulation of the chase.[1] Among these youths was Hermolaus, son of Sopolis, who seemed to be applying his mind to the study of philosophy, and to be cultivating the society of Callisthenes for this purpose. There is current a tale about this youth to the effect that in the chase, a boar rushed at Alexander, and that Hermolaus anticipated him by casting a javelin at the beast, by which it was smitten and killed. But Alexander, having lost the opportunity of distinguishing himself by being too late in the assault, was indignant with Hermolaus, and in his wrath ordered him to receive a scourgiug in sight of the other pages; and also deprived him of his horse. This Hermolaus, being chagrined at the disgrace he had incurred, told Sostratus, son of Amyntas, who was his equal in age and intimate confidential friend, that life would be insupportable to him unless he could take vengeance upon Alexander for the affront. He easily persuaded Sostratus to join in the enterprise, since he was fondly attached to him. They gained over to their plans Antipater, son of Asclepiodorus, viceroy of Syria, Epimenes son of Arseas, Anticles son of Theocritus, and Philotas son of Carsis the Thracian. They therefore agreed to kill the king by attacking him in his sleep, on the night when the nocturnal watch came round to Antipater's turn. Some say that Alexander accidentally happened to be drinking until day-break; but Aristobulus has given the following account: A Syrian woman, who was under the inspiration of the deity, used to follow Alexander about. At first she was a subject of mirth to Alexander and his courtiers; but when all that she

---

[1] Cf. *Curtius* (viii. 21); Aelian (*Varia Historia*, xiv. 49). After the battle of Pydna, where the Romans conquered the Macedonians, the *pueri regii* followed the defeated king Perseus to the sanctuary at Samothrace, and never quitted him till he surrendered to the Romans. See *Livy*, xlv. 6.

said in her inspiration was seen to be true, he no longer treated her with neglect, but she was allowed to have free access to him both by night and day, and she often took her stand near him even when he was asleep. And indeed on that occasion, when he was withdrawing from the drinking-party she met him, being under the inspiration of the deity at the time, and besought him to return and drink all night. Alexander, thinking that there was something divine in the warning, returned and went on drinking; and thus the enterprise of the pages fell through.[1] The next day, Epimenes son of Arseas, one of those who took part in the conspiracy, spoke of the undertaking to Charicles son of Menander, who had become his confidential friend; and Charicles told it to Eurylochus, brother of Epimenes. Eurylochus went to Alexander's tent and related the whole affair to Ptolemy son of Lagus, one of the confidential body-guards. He told Alexander, who ordered those whose names had been mentioned by Eurylochus to be arrested. These, being put on the rack, confessed their own conspiracy, and mentioned the names of certain others.

CHAPTER XIV.

Execution of Callisthenes and Hermolaus.

Aristobulus says that the youths asserted it was Callisthenes who instigated them to make the daring attempt; and Ptolemy says the same.[2] Most writers, however, do

---

[1] For this use of *διαπίπτειν*, cf. Aristophanes (*Knights*, 695); *Polybius* (v. 26, 16); *διαπεσούσης αὐτῷ τῆς ἐπιβουλῆς*.

[2] Alexander wrote to Craterus, Attalus, and Alcetas, that the pages, though put to the torture, asserted that no one but themselves was privy to the conspiracy. In another letter, written to Antipater the regent of Macedonia, he says that the pages had been stoned to death by the Macedonians, but that he himself would punish the Sophist, and those who sent him out, and those who harboured in their cities

not agree with this, but represent that Alexander readily believed the worst about Callisthenes, from the hatred which he already felt towards him, and because Hermolaus was known to be exceedingly intimate with him. Some authors have also recorded the following particulars:—that Hermolaus was brought before the Macedonians, to whom he confessed that he had conspired against the king's life, because it was no longer possible for a free man to bear his insolent tyranny. He then recounted all his acts of despotism, the illegal execution of Philotas, the still more illegal one of his father Parmenio and of the others who were put to death at that time, the murder of Clitus in a fit of drunkenness, his assumption of the Median garb, the introduction of the ceremony of prostration, which had been planned and not yet relinquished, and the drinking-bouts and lethargic sleep arising from them, to which he was addicting himself.[1] He said that, being no longer able to bear these things, he wished to free both himself and the other Macedonians. These same authors say that Hermolaus himself and those who had been arrested with him were stoned to death by those who were present. Aristobulus says that Callisthenes was carried about with the army bound with fetters, and afterwards died a natural death; but Ptolemy, son of Lagus, says that he was stretched upon the rack and then hanged.[2] Thus not even did these authors, whose narratives are very trustworthy, and who at the time were in intimate association with Alexander,

---

conspirators against him. Aristotle had sent Callisthene out. Alexander refers to him and the Athenians. See Plutarch (*Alex.*, 55).

[1] Cf. *Arrian* (vii. 29).

[2] *Curtius* (viii. 29) says that Alexander afterwards repented of his guilt in murdering the philosopher. His tragical death excited great indignation among the ancient philosophers. See Seneca (*Naturales Quaestiones*, vi. 23); Cicero (*Tusc. Disput.*, iii. 10), speaking of Theophrastus, the friend of Callisthenes.

give accounts consistent with each other of events so well known, and the circumstances of which could not have escaped their notice. Other writers have given many various details of these same proceedings which are inconsistent with each other; but I think I have written quite sufficient on this subject. Though these events took place shortly after the death of Clitus,[1] I have described them among those which happened to Alexander in reference to that General, because, for the purposes of narrative, I consider them very intimately connected with each other.

CHAPTER XV.

Alliance with the Scythians and Chorasmians.

Another embassy from the European Scythians came to Alexander with the envoys whom he had despatched to those people; for the king who was reigning over them at the time when he sent these envoys, happened to die, and his brother was reigning in his stead. The object of the embassy was to state that the Scythians were willing to do whatsoever Alexander commanded. They were also bringing to him from their king the gifts which among them are deemed most valuable. They said their monarch was willing to give his daughter to Alexander in marriage, in order to confirm the friendship and alliance with him; but if Alexander himself deigned not to marry the princess of the Scythians, then he was willing at any rate to give the daughters of the viceroys of the Scythian territory and of the other mighty men throughout the country of Scythia to the most faithful of Alexander's officers. He also sent word that he would come in person if bidden, in order to hear from Alexander's own mouth what his orders were. At this time

---

[1] We find from chapter xxii. that these events occurred at Bactra.

also came Pharasmanes, king of the Chorasmians,[1] to Alexander with 1,500 horsemen, who affirmed that he dwelt on the confines of the nations of the Colchians and the women called Amazons,[2] and promised, if Alexander was willing to march against these nations in order to subjugate the races in this district whose territories extended to the Euxine Sea, to act as his guide through the mountains and to supply his army with provisions. Alexander then gave a courteous reply to the men who had come from the Scythians, and one that was adapted to the exigencies of that particular time; but said that he had no need of a Scythian wedding. He also commended Pharasmanes and concluded a friendship and alliance with him, saying that at present it was not convenient for him to march towards the Euxine Sea. After introducing Pharasmanes as a friend to Artabazus the Persian, to whom he had intrusted the government of the Bactrians,[3] and to all the other viceroys who were his neighbours, he sent him back to his own abode. He said that his mind at that time was engrossed by the desire of conquering the Indians; for when he had subdued them, he should possess the whole of Asia. He added that when Asia was in his power he would return to Greece, and thence make an expedition with all his naval and military forces to the eastern extremity of the Euxine Sea through the Hellespont and Propontis.[4] He desired Pharasmanes to reserve the fulfilment of his present promises until then.

---

[1] The Chorasmians were a people who inhabited the country near the lower part of the river Oxus, between the Caspian and Aral Seas.

[2] This mythical race of warlike females is said to have come from the Caucasus and to have settled near the modern Trebizond, their original abode being in Colchis. Cf. *Arrian* (vii. 13); *Strabo* (xi. 5); *Diod.* (xvii. 77); *Curt.* (vi. 19); *Justin* (xii. 3); Homer (*Iliad*, iii. 189); Aeschylus (*Eumenides*, 655); *Herod* (iv. 110–116; ix. 27).

[3] See iii. 29 supra.

[4] Propontis means the sea *before the Pontus*. Compare Ovid (*Tristia*, i. 10, 31):—"Quaque tenent *Ponti* Byzantia littora *fauces*."

Alexander then returned to the river Oxus, with the intention of advancing into Sogdiana, because news was brought that many of the Sogdianians had fled for refuge into their strongholds and refused to submit to the viceroy whom he had placed over them. While he was encamping near the river Oxus, a spring of water and near it another of oil rose from the ground not far from Alexander's own tent. When this prodigy was announced to Ptolemy, son of Lagus, the confidential body-guard, he told Alexander, who offered the sacrifices which the prophets directed on account of the phenomenon. Aristander affirmed that the spring of oil was the sign of labours; but it also signified that after the labours there would be victory.

CHAPTER XVI.

Subjugation of Sogdiana.—Revolt of Spitamenes.

He therefore crossed the river with a part of his army and entered Sogdiana, leaving Polysperchon, Attalus, Gorgias, and Meleager there among the Bactrians, with instructions to guard the land, to prevent the barbarians of that region from making any revolutionary change, and to reduce those who had already rebelled. He divided the army which he had with him into five parts; the first of which he put under the command of Hephaestion, the second under that of Ptolemy, son of Lagus, the confidential body-guard; over the third he put Perdiccas; Coenus and Artabazus commanded the fourth brigade for him, while he himself took the fifth division and penetrated into the land towards Maracanda.[1] The others also advanced as each found it practicable, reducing by force some of those who had fled for refuge into the

---

[1] We learn, from *Curtius* (viii. 3), that it was at this place that Clitus was murdered.

strongholds, and capturing others who surrendered to them on terms of capitulation. When all his forces reached Maracanda, after traversing the greater part of the land of the Sogdianians, he sent Hephaestion away to plant colonies in the cities of Sogdiana. He also sent Coenus and Artabazus into Scythia, because he was informed that Spitamenes had fled for refuge thither; but he himself with the rest of his army traversed Sogdiana and easily reduced all the places still held by the rebels.

While Alexander was thus engaged, Spitamenes, accompanied by some of the Sogdianian exiles, fled into the land of the Scythians called Massagetians,[1] and having collected 600 horsemen from this nation, he came to one of the forts in Bactriana. Falling upon the commander of this fort, who was not expecting any hostile demonstration, and upon those who were keeping guard with him, he destroyed the soldiers, and capturing the commander, kept him in custody. Being emboldened by the capture of this fort, a few days after he approached Zariaspa; but resolving not to attack the city, he marched away after collecting a great quantity of booty. But at Zariaspa a few of the Companion cavalry had been left behind on the score of illness, and with them Peithon, son of Sosicles,[2] who had been placed over the royal household of attendants at Zariaspa, and Aristonicus the harper. These men, hearing of the incursion of the Scythians, and having now recovered from their illness, took their arms and mounted their horses. Then collecting eighty mercenary Grecian horsemen, who had been left behind to guard Zariaspa, and some of the royal pages, they sallied forth against the Massagetians. Fall-

---

[1] These were a people dwelling to the north-east of the Caspian, who were chiefly remarkable for having defeated and killed Cyrus the Great. See *Herodotus*, i. 201–216.

[2] There were two other generals named Peithon; one the son of Agenor, and the other the son of Crateas. See *Arrian*, vi. 15, 28, etc.

ing upon the Scythians, who had no suspicion of such an event, they deprived them of all the booty at the first onset, and killed many of those who were driving it off. But as no one was in command, they returned without any regard to order: and being drawn into an ambush by Spitamenes and other Scythians, they lost seven of the Companions and sixty of the mercenary cavalry. Aristonicus the harper was also slain there, having proved himself a brave man, beyond what might have been expected of a harper. Peithon, being wounded, was taken prisoner by the Scythians.[1]

CHAPTER XVII.

Defeat and Death of Spitamenes.

When this news was brought to Craterus, he made a forced march against the Massagetians, who, when they heard that he was marching against them, fled as fast as they could towards the desert. Following them up closely, he overtook those very men and more than 1,000 other Massagetian horsemen, not far from the desert. A fierce battle ensued, in which the Macedonians were victorious. Of the Scythians, 150 horsemen were slain; but the rest of them easily escaped into the desert, for it was impossible for the Macedonians to pursue them any further. At this time, Alexander relieved Artabazus of the viceroyalty of the Bactrians, at his own request, on the ground of his advanced age; and Amyntas, son of Nicolaüs, was appointed viceroy in his stead.[2] Coenus

---

[1] *Curtius* (viii. 1) says that the name of the defeated general was Attinas.

[2] Artabazus was in his 95th year when he joined Alexander with the Grecian troops of Darius in B.C. 330. See *Curtius*, vi. 14. His viceroyalty was destined for Clitus; but on the death of that general it was conferred on Amyntas. See *Curtius*, viii. 3.

was left with his own brigade and that of Meleager, 400 of the Companion cavalry, and all the horse-archers, besides the Bactrians, Sogdianians, and others who were under the command of Amyntas. They were all under strict injunctions to obey Coenus and to winter there in Sogdiana, in order to protect the country and to arrest Spitamenes, if anyhow they might be able to draw him into an ambush, as he was wandering about during the winter. But when Spitamenes saw that every place was occupied by the Macedonians for a garrison, and that there would soon be no way of flight left open to him, he turned round against Coenus and the army with him, thinking that he would be better able to fight in this way. Coming to Bagae, a fortified place in Sogdiana, situated on the confines of the countries of the Sogdianians and the Massagetian Scythians, he easily persuaded 3,000 Scythian horsemen to join him in an invasion of Sogdiana. It is an easy matter to induce these Scythians to engage in one war after another, because they are pinched by poverty, and at the same time have no cities or settled abodes, to give them cause for anxiety about what is most dear to them. When Coenus ascertained that Spitamenes was advancing with his cavalry, he went to meet him with his army. A sharp contest ensued, in which the Macedonians were victorious, so that of the barbarian cavalry over 800 fell in the battle, while Coenus lost 25 horsemen and twelve foot-soldiers. The consequence was, that the Sogdianians who were still left with Spitamenes, as well as most of the Bactrians, deserted him in the flight, and came to Coenus to surrender. The Massagetian Scythians having met with ill-success in the battle, plundered the baggage of the Bactrians and Sogdianians who were serving in the same army as themselves, and then fled into the desert in company with Spitamenes. But when they were informed that Alexander was already on the start to march into the desert, they cut off the head of Spitamenes and sent it to him, with the hope by this deed of diverting him from pursuing them.[1]

CHAPTER XVIII.

Oxyartes Besieged in the Sogdian Rock.

Meantime Coenus returned to Alexander at Nautaca, as also did Craterus, Phrataphernes the viceroy of the Parthians, and Stasanor the viceroy of the Areians, after executing all the orders which Alexander had given them. The king then caused his army to rest around Nautaca, because it was now mid-winter; but he despatched Phrataphernes into the land of the Mardians and Tapurians to fetch Autophradates the viceroy, because, though he had often been sent for, he did not obey the summons. He also sent Stasanor into the land of the Drangians, and Atropates into Media,[2] with the appointment of viceroy over the Medes, because Oxodates seemed disaffected to him. Stamenes also he despatched to Babylon, because news came to him that Mazaeus the Babylonian governor was dead. Sopolis, Epocillus, and Menidas he sent away to Macedonia, to bring him the army up from that country. At the first appearance of spring,[3] he advanced towards the rock in Sogdiana, to which he was informed many of the Sogdianians had fled for refuge; among whom were said to be the wife and daughters of Oxyartes the Bactrian, who had deposited them for safety in that place, as if forsooth it

---

[1] *Curtius* (viii. 11 and 12) says that the wife of Spitamenes murdered him and carried his head to Alexander.

[2] The Hebrew name for Media is Madai, which means *middle-land.* The Greeks called the country Media, according to *Polybius* (v. 44), because it lies near the middle of Asia.

[3] Of the year 327 B.C.

were impregnable. For he also had revolted from Alexander. If this rock was captured, it seemed that nothing would be left to those of the Sogdianians who wished to throw off their allegiance. When Alexander approached it, he found it precipitous on all sides against assault, and that the barbarians had collected provisions for a long siege. The great quantity of snow which had fallen helped to make the approach more difficult to the Macedonians, while at the same time it kept the barbarians supplied with plenty of water. But notwithstanding all this, he resolved to assault the place; for a certain overweening and insolent boast uttered by the barbarians had thrown him into a wrathful state of ambitious pertinacity. For when they were invited to come to terms of capitulation, and it was held out to them as an inducement, that if they surrendered the place, they would be allowed to withdraw in safety to their own abodes, they burst out laughing, and in their barbaric tongue bade Alexander seek winged soldiers, to capture the mountain for him, since they had no apprehension of danger from other men.[1] He then issued a proclamation that the first man who mounted should have a reward of twelve talents,[2] the man who came next to him the second prize, and the third so on in proportion, so that the last reward should be three hundred darics [3] to the last prize-taker who reached the top. This proclamation excited the valour of the Macedonians still more, though they were even before very eager to commence the assault.

---

[1] ὤρα, akin to Latin *cura*, a poetical and Ionic word, often found in Herodotus.

[2] About £2,700.

[3] About £327. *Curtius* (vii. 41) says that the first prize was 10 talents, the second 9 talents, and the same proportion for the eight others, so that the tenth man who mounted received one talent. The stater of Darius, usually called a daricus, was a gold coin of Persia. See Smith's *Dictionary of Antiquities*.

CHAPTER XIX.

Alexander Captures the Rock and Marries Roxana.

All the men who had gained practice in scaling rocks in sieges, banded themselves together to the number of three hundred, and provided themselves with the small iron pegs with which their tents had been fastened to the ground, with the intention of fixing them into the snow, where it might be seen to be frozen hard, or into the ground, if it should anywhere exhibit itself free from snow. Tying strong ropes made of flax to these pegs, they advanced in the night towards the most precipitous part of the rock, which was also most unguarded; and fixing some of these pegs into the earth, where it made itself visible, and others into the snow where it seemed least likely to break up, they hoisted themselves up the rock, some in one place and some in another. Thirty of them perished in the ascent; and as they fell into various parts of the snows, not even could their bodies be found for burial. The rest, however, reached the top of the mountain at the approach of dawn; and taking possession of it, they waved linen flags towards the camp of the Macedonians,[1] as Alexander had directed them to do. He now sent a herald with instructions to shout to the sentries of the barbarians to make no further delay, but surrender at once; since "the winged men" had been found, and the summits of the mountain were in their possession. At the same time the herald pointed at the soldiers upon the crest of the mountain. The barbarians, being alarmed by the unexpectedness of the sight, and suspecting that the men who were occupying the peaks were more numerous than they really were, and that they were completely armed, surrendered, so frightened did they become at the sight of those few

[1] Cf. *Curtius* (vii. 43), vela, signum capti verticis.

Macedonians. The wives and children of many important men were there captured, including those of Oxyartes. This chief had a daughter, a maiden of marriageable age, named Roxana,[1] who was asserted by the men who served in Alexander's army to have been the most beautiful of all Asiatic women, with the single exception of the wife of Darius.[2] They also say that no sooner did Alexander see her than he fell in love with her; but though he was in love with her, he refused to offer violence to her as a captive, and did not think it derogatory to his dignity to marry her. This conduct of Alexander I think worthy rather of praise than blame. Moreover, in regard to the wife of Darius, who was said to be the most beautiful woman in Asia, he either did not entertain a passion for her, or else he exercised control over himself,[3] though he was young, and in the very meridian of success, when men usually act with insolence and violence. On the contrary, he acted with modesty and spared her honour, exercising a great amount of chastity, and at the same time exhibiting a very proper desire to obtain a good reputation.[4]

CHAPTER XX.

Magnanimous Treatment of the Family of Darius.

In relation to this subject there is a story current, that soon after the battle which was fought at Issus between

---

[1] Roxana and her son Alexander Aegus were put to death by Cassander, B.C. 311.

[2] Statira. She died shortly before the battle of Arbela.

[3] καρτερὸς αὑτοῦ. Cf. *Theocritus*, xv. 94, ἁμῶν καρτερός.

[4] After the capture of Damascus, Alexander married Barsine, the widow of his rival Memnon, and daughter of Artabazus. She was distinguished for her beauty and accomplishments, having received a Grecian education. By her he had a son named Heracles. See Plutarch (*Alex.*, 21). She and her son were put to death by Polysperchon, B.C. 309.

Darius and Alexander, the eunuch who was guardian of Darius's wife escaped and came to him. When Darius saw this man, his first inquiry was, whether his children, wife, and mother were alive? Ascertaining that they were not only alive, but were called queens, and enjoyed the same personal service and attention which they had been accustomed to have with Darius, he thereupon made a second inquiry, whether his wife was still chaste? When he ascertained that she remained so, he asked again whether Alexander had not offered any violence to her to gratify his lust? The eunuch took an oath and said: "O king, thy wife is just as thou didst leave her; and Alexander is the best and most chaste of men." Upon this Darius stretched his hands towards heaven and prayed as follows:—"O King Zeus,[1] to whom power has been assigned to regulate the affairs of kings among men, do thou now protect for me especially the empire of the Persians and Medes, as indeed thou didst give it to me. But if I am no longer king of Asia according to thy behest, at any rate do thou hand over my power to no other man but Alexander." Thus not even to enemies, I ween, are chaste actions a matter of unconcern. Oxyartes, hearing that his children were in the power of Alexander, and that he was treating his daughter Roxana with respect, took courage and came to him. He was held in honour at the king's court, as was natural after such a piece of good fortune.[2]

---

[1] Cf. *Herodotus*, i. 131; *Curtius*, iv. 42. The Persians called this god Ormuzd.

[2] *Curtius* (viii. 16) says that Alexander saw Roxana at a banquet given by Oxyartes in his honour.

CHAPTER XXI.

Capture of the Rock of Chorienes.

When Alexander had finished his operations among the Sogdianians, and was now in possession of the rock, he advanced into the land of the Paraetacians, because many of the barbarians were said to be holding another rock, a strongly fortified place in that country. This was called the rock of Chorienes; and to it Chorienes himself and many other chiefs had fled for refuge. The height of this rock was about twenty stades, and the circuit about sixty. It was precipitous on all sides, and there was only one ascent to it, which was narrow and not easy to mount, since it had been constructed in spite of the nature of the place. It was therefore difficult to ascend even by men in single file and when no one barred the way. A deep ravine also enclosed[1] the rock all round, so that whoever intended to lead an army up to it, must long before make a causeway of earth over this ravine in order that he might start from level ground, when he led his troops to the assault. Notwithstanding all this, Alexander undertook the enterprise. To so great a pitch of audacity had he advanced through his career of success, that he thought every place ought to be accessible to him,[2] and to be captured by him. He cut down the pines, which were very abundant and lofty all round the mountain, and made ladders of them, so that by means of them the soldiers might be able to descend into the ravine[3]; for otherwise it was impossible for them to do so. During the day-time he himself superintended the work, keeping half of his army engaged in it; and during the night his confidential body-guards, Perdiccas,

---

[1] Krüger substituted *περιεῖργε* for *περιέργει*.

[2] *βατά*. Cf. Xenophon (*Anab.*, iv. 6, 17).

[3] Arrian imitates Herodotus in the use of *ὡς* with the infinitive instead of *ὥστε*.

Leonnatus, and Ptolemy, son of Lagus, in turn with the other half of the army, divided into three parts, performed the duty which had been assigned to each for the night. But they could complete no more than twenty cubits in a day, and not quite so much in a night, though the whole army engaged in the labour; so difficult was the place to approach and so hard was the work in it. Descending into the ravine, they fastened pegs into the sharpest and narrowest part of it, distant from each other as far as was consistent with strength to support the weight of what was placed upon them. Upon these they placed hurdles made of willow and osiers, very much in the form of a bridge. Binding these together, they loaded earth above them, so that there might be an approach to the rock for the army on level ground. At first the barbarians derided, as if the attempt was altogether abortive; but when the arrows began to reach the rock, and they were unable to drive back the Macedonians, though they themselves were on a higher level, because the former had constructed screens to ward off the missiles, that they might carry on their labour under them without receiving injury, Chorienes grew alarmed at what was being done, and sent a herald to Alexander, beseeching him to send Oxyartes up to him. Alexander accordingly sent Oxyartes, who on his arrival persuaded Chorienes to entrust himself and the place to Alexander; for he told him that there was nothing which Alexander and his army could not take by storm; and as he himself had entered into an alliance of fidelity and friendship with him, he commended the king's honour and justice in high terms, adducing other examples, and above all his own case for the confirmation of his arguments. By these representations Chorienes was persuaded and came himself to Alexander, accompanied by some of his relations and companions. When he arrived, the king gave him a courteous answer to his inquiries, and retained him after pledging his fidelity and friendship. But he bade him send to the rock some of those who came down with him to order his men to surrender the place; and it was surrendered by those who had fled to it for refuge. Alexander therefore took 500 of his shield-bearing guards and went up to get a view of the rock; and was so far from inflicting any harsh treatment upon Chorienes that he entrusted that very place to him again, and made him governor of all that he had ruled before. It happened that the army suffered much hardship from the severity of the winter, a great quantity of snow having fallen during the siege; while at the same time the men were reduced to great straits from lack of provisions. But Chorienes said he would give the army food for two months; and he gave the men in every tent corn, wine, and salted meat out of the stores in the rock. When he had given them this, he said he had not exhausted even the tenth part of what had been laid up for the siege. Hence Alexander held him in still greater honour, inasmuch as he had surrendered the rock, not so much from compulsion as from his own inclination.

CHAPTER XXII.

Alexander Reaches the River Cabul, and Receives the Homage of Taxiles.

After performing this exploit, Alexander himself went to Bactra; but sent Craterus with 600 of the cavalry Companions and his own brigade of infantry as well those of Polysperchon, Attalus, and Alcetas, against Catanes and Austanes, who were the only rebels still remaining in the land of the Paraetacenians.[1] A sharp battle was fought

[1] This term is a Persian word meaning mountaineers. The tribe

with them, in which Craterus was victorious; Catanes being killed there while fighting, and Austanes being captured and brought to Alexander. Of the barbarians with them 120 horsemen and about 1,500 foot soldiers were killed. When Craterus had done this, he also went to Bactra, where the tragedy in reference to Callisthenes and the pages befell Alexander. As the spring was now over, he took the army and advanced from Bactra towards India,[1] leaving Amyntas in the land of the Bactrians with 3,500 horse, and 10,000 foot. He crossed the Caucasus[2] in ten days and arrived at the city of Alexandria, which had been founded in the land of the Parapamisadae when he made his first expedition to Bactra. He dismissed from office the governor whom he had then placed over the city, because he thought he was not ruling well. He also settled in Alexandria others from the neighbouring tribes and the soldiers who were now unfit for service in addition to the first settlers, and commanded Nicanor, one of the Companions, to regulate the affairs of the city itself. Moreover he appointed Tyriaspes viceroy of the land of the Parapamisadae and of the rest of the country as far as the river Cophen.[3] Arriving at the city of Nicaea, he offered sacrifice to Athena and then advanced towards the Cophen, sending a herald forward to Taxiles[4]

---

mentioned here lived between the rivers Oxus and Jaxartes, on the borders of Bactria and Sogdiana.

[1] *Curtius* (viii. 17) says Alexander took with him 30,000 select troops from all the conquered provinces, and that the army which he led against the Indians numbered 120,000 men.

[2] This is the Indian Caucasus, or mount Parapamisus, now called Hindu-Koosh.

[3] The Cophen is now called Cabul. Nicaea was probably on the same site as the city of Cabul. Others say it is Beghram. The Greek word *Satrapes* denotes a Persian viceroy. It is a corruption of a word meaning *court-guardian*, in the Behistûn Inscriptions written Khshatrapâ. See Rawlinson's *Herod.*, i. 192.

[4] *Curtius* (viii. 43) says that Taxiles was the title which the king of this district received. His name was Omphis.

and the other chiefs on this side the river Indus, to bid them come and meet him as each might find it convenient. Taxiles and the other chiefs accordingly did come to meet him, bringing the gifts which are reckoned of most value among the Indians. They said that they would also present to him the elephants which they had with them, twenty-five in number. There he divided his army, and sent Hephaestion and Perdiccas away into the land of Peucelaotis,[1] towards the river Indus, with the brigades of Gorgias, Clitus,[2] and Meleager, half of the Companion cavalry, and all the cavalry of the Grecian mercenaries. He gave them instructions either to capture the places on their route by force, or to bring them over on terms of capitulation; and when they reached the river Indus, to make the necessary preparations for the passage of the army. With them Taxiles and the other chiefs also marched. When they reached the river Indus they carried out all Alexander's orders. But Astes, the ruler of the land of Peucelaotis, effected a revolt, which both ruined himself and brought ruin also upon the city into which he had fled for refuge. For Hephaestion captured it after a siege of thirty days, and Astes himself was killed. Sangaeus, who had some time before fled from Astes and deserted to Taxiles, was appointed to take charge of the city. This desertion was a pledge to Alexander of his fidelity.

CHAPTER XXIII.

Battles with the Aspasians.

Alexander now took command of the shield-bearing guards, the Companion cavalry with the exception of

---

[1] A district between the rivers Indus and Attock. Its capital, Peucela, is the modern Pekheli.

[2] The brigade of Clitus still bore the name of its commander after his death. Cf. *Arrian*, vii. 14 infra.

those who had been joined with Hephaestion's division, the regiments of what were called foot-Companions, the archers, the Agrianians and the horse-lancers, and advanced with them into the land of the Aspasians, Guraeans and Assacenians.[1] Marching by a mountainous and rough road along the river called Choes,[2] which he crossed with difficulty, he ordered the main body of his infantry to follow at leisure; while he himself took all the cavalry, and 800 of the Macedonian infantry whom he mounted upon horses with their infantry shields, and made a forced march, because he had received information that the barbarians who inhabited that district had fled for safety into the mountains which extend through the land and into as many of their cities as were strong enough to resist attack. Assaulting the first of these cities which was situated on his route, he routed, at the first attack without any delay, the men whom he found drawn up in front of the city, and shut them up in it. He was himself wounded by a dart which penetrated through the breastplate into his shoulder; but the wound was only a slight one, for the breastplate prevented the dart from penetrating right through his shoulder. Leonnatus and Ptolemy, son of Lagus, were also wounded. Then he encamped near the city at the place where the wall seemed most easy to assault. At dawn on the following day the Macedonians easily forced their way through the first wall, as it had not been strongly built. The city had been surrounded with a double wall. At the second wall the barbarians stood their ground for a short time; but when the scaling ladders were now being fixed, and the defenders were being wounded with darts from all sides, they no longer stayed; but rushed through the gates out of the

---

[1] These were tribes living in the north-west of the Punjab.

[2] Probably the modern Kama, a tributary of the Cabul.

city towards the mountains. Some of them were killed in the flight, and the Macedonians, being enraged because they had wounded Alexander, slew all whom they took prisoners. Most of them, however, escaped into the mountains, because they were not far from the city. Having levelled this city with the ground, he marched to another, named Audaca, which he got possession of by capitulation. He left Craterus there with the other commanders of the infantry to capture all the remaining cities which would not yield of their own accord, and to set the affairs of the whole country in such order as he should find most convenient under the circumstances.

CHAPTER XXIV.

Operations against the Aspasians.

Alexander now took command of the shield-bearing guards, the archers, the Agrianians, the brigade of Coenus and Attalus, the royal body-guard of cavalry, about four regiments of the other Companion cavalry, and half of the horse-archers, and advanced towards the river Euaspla,[1] where the chieftain of the Aspasians was. After a long journey he arrived at the city on the second day. When the barbarians ascertained that he was approaching they set fire to the city and fled to the mountains. But Alexander followed close upon the fugitives as far as the mountains, and slaughtered many of them before they could manage to get away into the places which were difficult of access. Ptolemy, son of Lagus, observing that the leader himself of the Indians of that district was on a certain hill, and that he had some of his shield-bearing guards round him, though he had with himself far fewer men, yet he still continued to pursue him on horseback. But as the hill was difficult for his

[1] Supposed to be another name for the Choes.

horse to run up, he left it there, handing it over to one of the shield-bearing guards to lead. He then followed the Indian on foot without any delay. When the latter observed Ptolemy approaching, he turned round, and so did the shield-bearing guards with him. The Indian at close quarters struck Ptolemy on the chest through the breastplate with a long spear, but the breastplate checked the violence of the blow. Then Ptolemy, smiting right through the Indian's thigh, overthrew him, and stripped him of his arms. When his men saw their leader lying dead, they stood their ground no longer; but the men on the mountains, seeing their chieftain's corpse being carried off by the enemy, were seized with indignation, aud running down engaged in a desperate conflict over him on the hill. For Alexander himself was now on the hill with the infantry who had dismounted from the horses. These, falling upon the Indians, drove them away to the mountains after a hard struggle, and remained in possession of the corpse. Then crossing the mountains he descended to a city called Arigaeum, and found that this had been set on fire by the inhabitants, who had afterwards fled. There Craterus with his army reached him, after accomplishing all the king's orders; and because this city seemed to be built in a convenient place, he directed that general to fortify it well, and settle in it as many of the neighbouring people as were willing to live there, together with any of the soldiers who were unfit for service. He then advanced to the place where he heard that most of the barbarians of the district had fled for refuge; and coming to a certain mountain, he encamped at the foot of it. Meantime Ptolemy, son of Lagus, being sent out by Alexander on a foraging expedition, and advancing a considerable distance with a few men to reconnoitre, brought back word to the king that he had observed many more fires in the camp of the barbarians than there were in Alexander's. But the latter did not believe in the multitude of the enemy's fires. Discovering, however, that the barbarians of the district had joined their forces into one body, he left a part of his army there near the mountain, encamped as they were, and taking as many men as seemed sufficient, according to the reports he had received, as soon as they could descry the fires near at hand, he divided his army into three parts. Over one part he placed Leonnatus, the confidential body-guard, joining the brigades of Attalus and Balacrus with his own; the second division he put under the lead of Ptolemy, son of Lagus, including the third part of the royal shield-bearing guards, the brigades of Philip and Philotas, two regiments of horse-archers, the Agrianians, and half of the cavalry. The third division he himself led towards the place where most of the barbarians were visible.

CHAPTER XXV.

Defeat of the Aspasians.—The Assacenians and Guraeans Attacked.

When the enemy who were occupying the commanding heights perceived the Macedonians approaching, they descended into the plain, being emboldened by their superiority in number and despising the Macedonians, because they were seen to be few. A sharp contest ensued; but Alexander won the victory with ease. Ptolemy's men did not range themselves on the level ground, for the barbarians were occupying a hill. Wherefore Ptolemy, forming his battalions into column, led them to the point where the hill seemed most easily assailable, not surrounding it entirely, but leaving room for the barbarians to flee if they were inclined to do so. A sharp contest also ensued with these men, both from the difficult nature of the ground, and because the Indians are not like the other barbarians of this district, but are far stronger than their neighbours. These men also were driven away from the mountain by the Macedonians. In the same way did Leonnatus with the third division of the army; for his men also defeated those opposed to them. Ptolemy indeed says that all the men were captured, to a number exceeding 40,000, and that 230,000 oxen were also taken, of which Alexander picked out the finest, because they seemed to him to excel both in beauty and size, wishing to send them into Macedonia to till the soil. Thence he marched towards the land of the Assacenians; for he received news that these people had made preparations to fight him, having 20,000 cavalry, more than 30,000 infantry, and 30 elephants. When Craterus had thoroughly fortified the city, for the founding of which he had been left behind, he brought the heavier armed men of his army for Alexander as well as the military engines, in case it might be necessary to lay siege to any place. Alexander then marched against the Assacenians at the head of the Companion cavalry, the horse-archers, the brigades of Coenus and Polysperchon, the Agrianians, the light-armed troops,[1] and the archers. Passing through the land of the Guraeans, he crossed the river Guraeus,[2] which gives its name to the land, with difficulty, both on account of its depth, and because its current is swift, and the stones in the river being round caused those who stepped upon them to stumble.[3] When the barbarians perceived Alexander approaching, they durst not take their stand for a battle in close array, but dispersed one by one to their various cities with the determination of preserving these by resolute fighting.

---

[1] καὶ τοὺς ψιλοὺς. The usual reading is τοὺς χιλίους, 1,000 *Agrianians.*

[2] A tributary of the Cophen, probably what is now called the Lundye, running parallel with the Kama.

[3] Cf. *Livy*, xxi. 31:—"Amnis saxa glareosa volvens, nihil stabile nec tutum ingredienti praebet."

CHAPTER XXVI.

SIEGE OF MASSAGA.

In the first place Alexander led his forces against Massaga,[1] the largest of the cities in that district; and when he was approaching the walls, the barbarians being emboldened by the mercenaries whom they had obtained from the more distant Indians to the number of 7,000, when they saw the Macedonians pitching their camp, advanced against them with a run. Alexander, seeing that the battle was about to be fought near the city, was anxious to draw them further away from their walls, so that if they were put to rout, as he knew they would be, they might not be able easily to preserve themselves by fleeing for refuge into the city close at hand. When therefore he saw the barbarians running out, he ordered the Macedonians to turn round and retreat to a certain hill distant something about seven stades from the place where he had resolved to encamp. The enemy being emboldened, as if the Macedonians had already given way, rushed upon them with a run and with no kind of order. Bnt when the arrows began to reach them, Alexander at once wheeled round at the appointed signal, and led his plalanx against them with a run. His horse-lancers, Agrianians, and archers first ran forward and engaged with the barbarians, while he himself led the phalanx in regular order. The Indians were alarmed at this unexpected manœuvre, and as soon as the battle became a hand-to-hand conflict, they gave way and fled into the city. About 200 of them were killed, and the rest were shut up within the walls. Alexander then led his phalanx up to the wall, from which he was soon after slightly wounded in the ankle with an arrow.

---

[1] This was the capital of the Assacenians. *Curtius* (viii. 37) calls it Mazagae, and describes its strong position.

On the next day he brought up his military engines and easily battered down a piece of the wall; but the Indians so gallantly kept back the Macedonians who were trying to force an entrance where the breach had been made, that he recalled the army for this day. But on the morrow the Macedonians themselves made a more vigorous assault, and a wooden tower was drawn up to the walls, from which the archers shot at the Indians, and missiles were hurled from the military engines which repulsed them to a great distance. But not even thus were they able to force their way within the wall. On the third day he led the phalanx near again, and throwing a bridge from a military engine over to the part of the wall where the breach had been made, by this he led up the shield-bearing guards, who had captured Tyre for him in a similar way.[1] But as many were urged on by their ardour, the bridge received too great a weight, and was snapped asunder, so that the Macedonians fell with it. The barbarians, seeing what was taking place, raised a great shout, and shot at them from the wall with stones, arrows, and whatever else any one happened to have at hand, or whatever any one could lay hold of at the time. Others issued forth by the small gates which they had between the towers in the wall, and at close quarters struck the men who had been thrown into confusion by the fall.

CHAPTER XXVII.

Sieges of Massaga and Ora.

Alexander now sent Alcetas with his own brigade to recover the men who had been severely wounded, and to recall to the camp those who were assailing the enemy. On the fourth day he brought up another bridge against

---

[1] See Bk. ii. 23 supra.

the wall in like manner upon another military engine. The Indians, as long as the ruler of the place survived, defended themselves gallantly; but when he was struck and killed with a missile hurled from an engine, and as some of their number had fallen in the siege, which had gone on without any cessation, while most of them were wounded and unfit for service, they sent a herald to Alexander. He was glad to preserve the lives of brave men; so he came to terms with the Indian mercenaries on this condition, that they should be admitted into the ranks with the rest of his army and serve as his soldiers. They therefore came out of the city with their arms, and encamped by themselves upon a hill which was facing the camp of the Macedonians; but they resolved to arise by night and run away to their own abodes, because they were unwilling to take up arms against the other Indians. When Alexander received intelligence of this, he placed the whole of his army round the hill in the night, and intercepting them in the midst of their flight, cut them to pieces. He then took the city by storm, denuded as it was of defenders; and captured the mother and daughter of Assacenus.[1] In the whole siege five-and-twenty of Alexander's men were killed. Thence he despatched Coenus to Bazira,[2] entertaining an opinion that the inhabitants would surrender, when they heard of the capture of Massaga. He also despatched Attalus, Alcetas, and Demetrius the cavalry officer to another city, named Ora, with instructions to blockade it until he himself arrived. The men of this city made a sortie against the forces of Alcetas; but the Macedonians easily routed them, and drove them into the city

---

[1] *Curtius* (viii. 37, 38) says that the name of the queen was Cleophis, and that after the surrender she gained Alexander's favour. He also informs us that the king died just before Alexander's arrival.

[2] Probably Bajour, north-west of Peshawur. The position of Ora cannot be fixed.

within the wall. But affairs at Bazira were not favourable to Coenus, for the inhabitants showed no sign of capitulating, trusting to the strength of the place, because not only was it situated on a lofty eminence, but it was also thoroughly fortified all round. When Alexander learnt this, he started off to Bazira; but ascertaining that some of the neighbouring barbarians were about to get into the city of Ora by stealth, being despatched thither by Abisares[1] for that very purpose, he first marched to Ora. He ordered Coenus to fortify a certain strong position to serve as a basis of operations against the city of Bazira, and then to come to him with the rest of his army, after leaving in that place a sufficient garrison to restrain the men in the city from enjoying the free use of their land. But when the men of Bazira saw Coenus departing with the larger part of his army, they despised the Macedonians, as not being able to contend with them, and sallied forth into the plain. A sharply contested battle ensued, in which 500 of the barbarians fell, and over seventy were taken prisoners. But the rest, fleeing for refuge into the city,[2] were now more securely shut off from the country by the men in the fort. The siege of Ora proved an easy matter to Alexander, for he no sooner attacked the walls than at the first assault he got possession of the city, and captured the elephants which had been left there.

CHAPTER XXVIII.

Capture of Bazira.—Advance to the Rock of Aornus.

When the men in Bazira heard this news, despairing of

[1] This was the king of the Indian mountaineers. See *Arrian*, v. 8 infra.

[2] On the ground of *ἐν τῇ πόλει ξυμφυγόντες* not being classical Greek, Krüger has substituted *ἐν τῇ πόλει ξυμπεθευγότες*, and Sintenis *εἰς τὴν πόλιν ξυμφυγόντες*. No one however ought to expect Arrian to be free from error, writing, as he did, in the middle of the second century of the Christian era.

their own affairs, they abandoned the city about the middle of the night, and fled to the rock as the other barbarians were doing. For all the inhabitants deserted the cities and began to flee to the rock which is in their land, and is called Aornus.[1] For stupendous is this rock in this land, about which the current report is, that it was found impregnable even by Heracles, the son of Zeus. I cannot affirm with confidence either way, whether the Theban, Tyrian, or Egyptian Heracles[2] penetrated into India or not; but I am rather inclined to think that he did not penetrate so far; for men are wont to magnify the difficulty of difficult enterprises to such a degree as to assert that they would have been impracticable even to Heracles. Therefore, I am inclined to think, that in regard to this rock the name of Heracles was mentioned simply to add to the marvellousness of the tale. The circuit of the rock is said to be about 200 stades (*i.e.* about twenty-three miles), and its height where it is lowest, eleven stades (*i.e.*, about a mile and a quarter). There was only one ascent, which was artificial and difficult; on the summit of the rock there was abundance of pure water, a spring issuing from the ground, from which the water flowed; and there was also timber, and sufficient good arable land for 1,000 men to till.[3] When Alexander heard this, he was seized with a vehement desire to capture this mountain also, especially on account of the legend which was current

---

[1] This seems to be the Greek translation of the native name, meaning the place to which no bird can rise on account of its height. Cf. *Strabo*, xv. 1. This mountain was identified by Major Abbot, in 1854, as Mount Mahabunn, near the right bank of the Indus, about 60 miles above its confluence with the Cabul.

[2] Cf. *Arrian*, ii. 16 supra.

[3] *Curtius* (viii. 39) says that the river Indus washed the base of the rock, and that its shape resembled the *meta* or goal in a race-course, which was a stone shaped like a sugar-loaf. Arrian's description is more likely to be correct as he took it from Ptolemy, one of Alexander's generals.

about Heracles. He then made Ora and Massaga fortresses to keep the land in subjection, and fortified the city of Bazira. Hephaestion and Perdiccas also fortified for him another city, named Orobatis, and leaving a garrison in it marched towards the river Indus. When they reached that river they at once began to carry out Alexander's instructions in regard to bridging it. Alexander then appointed Nicanor, one of the Companions, viceroy of the land on this side the river Indus; and in the first place leading his army towards that river, he brought over on terms of capitulation the city of Peucelaotis, which was situated not far from it. In this city he placed a garrison of Macedonians, under the command of Philip, and then reduced to subjection some other small towns situated near the same river, being accompanied by Cophaeus and Assagetes, the chieftains of the land. Arriving at the city of Embolima,[1] which was situated near the rock Aornus, he left Craterus there with a part of the army, to gather as much corn as possible into the city, as well as all the other things requisite for a long stay, so that making this their base of operations, the Macedonians might be able by a long siege to wear out the men who were holding the rock, supposing it were not captured at the first assault. He then took the bowmen, the Agrianians, and the brigade of Coenus, and selecting the lightest as well as the best-armed men from the rest of the phalanx, with 200 of the Companion cavalry and 100 horse-bowmen, he advanced to the rock. This day he encamped where it appeared to him convenient; but on the morrow he approached a little nearer to the rock, and encamped again.

---

[1] Near mount Mahabunn are two places called Umb and Balimah, the one in the valley of the river and the other on the mountain above it. See Major Abbot's *Gradus ad Aornon.*

CHAPTER XXIX.

Siege of Aornus.

At this juncture some of the natives came to him, and surrendering themselves, offered to lead him to the part of the rock where it could be most easily assailed, and from which it would be easy for him to capture the place. With these he sent Ptolemy, son of Lagus, the confidential body-guard, in command of the Agrianians and the other light-armed troops, together with picked men from the shield-bearing guards. He gave this officer instructions, as soon as he had got possession of the place, to occupy it with a strong guard, and signal to him that it was held. Ptolemy proceeded along a road which was rough and difficult to pass, and occupied the position without the knowledge of the barbarians. After strengthening his position with a stockade and a ditch all round, he raised a beacon from the mountain, whence it was likely to be seen by Alexander. The flame was at once seen, and on the following day the king led his army forward; but as the barbarians disputed his advance, he could do nothing further on account of the difficult nature of the ground. When the barbarians perceived that Alexander could not make an assault, they turned round and attacked Ptolemy, and a sharp battle ensued between them and the Macedonians, the Indians making great efforts to demolish the stockade, and Ptolemy to preserve his position. But the barbarians, getting the worst of it in the skirmish, withdrew as the night came on. Alexander now selected from the Indian deserters a man who was not only devoted to him but acquainted with the locality,[1] and sent him by night to Ptolemy, carrying a letter, in which it was written that as soon as the king attacked the rock,

[1] *δαήμων*, a poetical word. Cf. Homer (*Odyssey*, viii. 159).

Ptolemy was to come down the mountain upon the barbarians, and not be contented with holding his position in guard; so that the Indians, being assailed from both sides at once, might be in perplexity what course to pursue. Accordingly, starting from his camp at daybreak, he led his army up the path by which Ptolemy had ascended by stealth, entertaining the opinion that if he could force his way in this direction and join his forces with those of Ptolemy, the work would no longer be difficult for him; and so it turned out. For until midday a smart battle was kept up between the Indians and the Macedonians, the latter striving to force a way of approach, and the former hurling missiles at them as they ascended. But as the Macedonians did not relax their efforts, advancing one after another, and those who were in advance rested till their comrades came up, after great exertions they gained possession of the pass early in the afternoon, and formed a junction with Ptolemy's forces. As the whole army was now united, Alexander led it thence against the rock itself. But the approach to it was still impracticable. Such then was the result of this day's labours. At the approach of the dawn he issued an order that each soldier individually should cut 100 stakes; and when this had been done he heaped up a great mound against the rock, beginning from the top of the hill where they had encamped. From this mound he thought the arrows as well as the missiles launched from the military engines would be able to reach the defenders of the rock. Every one in the army assisted him in this work of raising the mound; while he himself superintended it, as an observer, not only commending the man who completed his task with zeal and alacrity, but also chastising him who was dilatory in the pressing emergency.

CHAPTER XXX.

Capture of Aornus.—Arrival at the Indus.

On the first day his army constructed the mound the length of a stade; and on the following day the slingers shooting at the Indians from the part already finished, assisted by the missiles which were hurled from the military engines, repulsed the sallies which they made against the men who were constructing the mound. He went on with the work for three days without intermission, and on the fourth day a few of the Macedonians forcing their way occupied a small eminence which was on a level with the rock. Without taking any rest, Alexander went on with the mound, being desirous of connecting his artificial rampart with the eminence which the few men were now occupying for him. But then the Indians, being alarmed at the indescribable audacity of the Macedonians, who had forced their way to the eminence, and seeing that the mound was already united with it, desisted from attempting any longer to resist. They sent their herald to Alexander, saying that they were willing to surrender the rock, if he would grant them a truce. But they had formed the design of wasting the day by continually delaying the ratification of the truce, and of scattering themselves in the night with the view of escaping one by one to their own abodes. When Alexander discovered this plan of theirs, he allowed them time to commence their retreat, and to remove the guard which was placed all round the place. He remained quiet until they began their retreat; then taking 700 of the body-guards and shield-bearing infantry, he was the first to scale the rock at the part of it abandoned by the enemy; and the Macedonians ascended after him, one in one place another in another, drawing each other up. These men at the concerted signal turned themselves upon the retreating barbarians, and killed many of them in their flight.

Others retreating with panic terror perished by leaping down the precipices; and thus the rock which had been inexpugnable to Heracles was occupied by Alexander. He offered sacrifice upon it, and arranged a fort, committing the superintendence of the garrison to Sisicottus, who long before had deserted from the Indians to Bessus in Bactra, and after Alexander had acquired possession of the country of Bactra, entered his army and appeared to be eminently trustworthy.

He now set out from the rock and invaded the land of the Assacenians; for he was informed that the brother of Assacenus, with his elephants and many of the neighbouring barbarians had fled into the mountains in this district. When he arrived at the city of Dyrta,[1] he found none of the inhabitants either in it or in the land adjacent. On the following day he sent out Nearchus and Antiochus, the colonels of the shield-bearing guards, giving the former the command of the Agrianians and the light-armed troops,[2] and the latter the command of his own regiments and two others besides. They were despatched both to reconnoitre the locality and to try if they could capture some of the barbarians anywhere in order to get information about the general affairs of the country; and he was especially anxious to learn news of the elephants. He now directed his march towards the river Indus,[3] the army going in advance to make

---

1 Probably Dyrta was at the point where the Indus issues from the Hindu-Koosh.

2 Gronovius first introduced καὶ before τοὺς ψιλούς.

3 The name Indus is derived from the Sanscrit appellation *Sindhu*, from a root *Syandh*, meaning *to flow*. The name Indians, or Sindians, was originally applied only to the dwellers on the banks of this river. *Hindustan* is a Persian word meaning the country of the Hindus or Sindus. Compare the modern Sinde, in the north-west of India, which contains the lower course of the Indus. In Hebrew India was called Hodu, which is a contraction of Hondu, another form of Hindu. See Esther i. 1; viii. 9. Krüger changed ὡδοποιεῖτο into ὡδοποίει.

a road for him, as otherwise this district would have been impassable. Here he captured a few of the barbarians, from whom he learnt that the Indians of that land had fled for safety to Abisares, but that they had left their elephants there to pasture near the river Indus. He ordered these men to show him the way to the elephants. Many of the Indians are elephant-hunters, and these Alexander kept in attendance upon him in high honour, going out to hunt the elephants in company with them. Two of these animals perished in the chase, by leaping down a precipice, but the rest were caught and being ridden by drivers were marshalled with the army. He also as he was marching along the river lighted upon a wood the timber of which was suitable for building ships; this was cut down by the army, and ships were built for him, which were brought down the river Indus to the bridge, which had long since been constructed by Hephaestion and Perdiccas at his command.

BOOK V.

CHAPTER I.

ALEXANDER AT NYSA.

IN this country, lying between the rivers Cophen and Indus, which was traversed by Alexander, the city of Nysa[1] is said to be situated. The report is, that its foundation was the work of Dionysus, who built it after he had subjugated the Indians.[2] But it is impossible to determine who this Dionysus[3] was, and at what time, or from what quarter he led an army against the Indians. For I am unable to decide whether the Theban Dionysus, starting from Thebes or from the Lydian Tmolus[4] came into India at the head of an army, and after traversing the territories of so many warlike nations, unknown to the Greeks of that time, forcibly subjugated none of them except that of the Indians. But I do not think we ought to make a minute examination of the legends which were promulgated in ancient times about the divinity; for things which are not credible to the man who examines them according to the rule of probability, do not appear to be wholly incredible, if one adds the

---

[1] This city was probably on the site of Jelalabad.

[2] ἐπεί τε. This is the only place where Arrian uses this Ionic form for the simple ἐπεί.

[3] The Indians worship a god Homa, the personification of the intoxicating soma juice. This deity corresponds to the Greek Dionysus or Bacchus.

[4] The slopes of this mountain were covered with vines. See Ovid (*Fasti*, ii. 313; *Metamorphoses*, xi. 86); Vergil (*Georgics*, ii. 98); *Pliny*, xiv. 9.

divine agency to the story. When Alexander came to Nysa the citizens sent out to him their president, whose name was Acuphis, accompanied by thirty of their most distinguished men as envoys, to entreat Alexander to leave their city free for the sake of the god. The envoys entered Alexander's tent and found him seated in his armour still covered with dust from the journey, with his helmet on his head, and holding his spear in his hand. When they beheld the sight they were struck with astonishment, and falling to the earth remained silent a long time. But when Alexander caused them to rise, and bade them be of good courage, then at length Acuphis began thus to speak: "The Nysaeans beseech thee, O king, out of respect for Dionysus, to allow them to remain free and independent; for when Dionysus had subjugated the nation of the Indians, and was returning to the Grecian sea, he founded this city from the soldiers who had become unfit for military service, and were under his inspiration as Bacchanals, so that it might be a monument both of his wandering and of his victory, to men of after times; just as thou also hast founded Alexandria near mount Caucasus, and another Alexandria in the country of the Egyptians. Many other cities thou hast already founded, and others thou wilt found hereafter, in the course of time, inasmuch as thou hast achieved more exploits than Dionysus. The god indeed called the city Nysa, and the land Nysaea after his nurse Nysa. The mountain also which is near the city he named Meros (*i.e.* thigh), because, according to the legend, he grew in the thigh of Zeus. From that time we inhabit Nysa, a free city, and we ourselves are independent, conducting our government with constitutional order. And let this be to thee a proof that our city owes its foundation to Dionysus; for ivy, which does not grow in the rest of the country of India, grows among us."

CHAPTER II.

ALEXANDER AT NYSA.

ALL this was very pleasant to Alexander to hear; for he wished that the legend about the wandering of Dionysus should be believed, as well as that Nysa owed its foundation to that deity, since he had himself reached the place where Dionysus came, and had even advanced beyond the limits of the latter's march. He also thought that the Macedonians would not decline still to share his labours if he advanced further, from a desire to surpass the achievements of Dionysus. He therefore granted the inhabitants of Nysa the privilege of remaining free and independent; and when he inquired about their laws, he commended them because the government was in the hands of the aristocracy. He required them to send 300 of their horsemen to accompany him, and to select and send 100 of the aristocrats who presided over the government of the State, who also were 300 in number. He ordered Acuphis to make the selection, and appointed him governor of the land of Nysaea. When Acuphis heard this, he is said to have smiled at the speech; whereupon Alexander asked him why he laughed. Acuphis replied:—"How, O king, could a single city deprived of 100 of its good men be still well governed? But if thou carest for the welfare of the Nysaeans, lead with thee the 300 horsemen, and still more than that number if thou wishest: but instead of the hundred of the best men whom thou orderest me to select lead with thee double the number of the others who are bad, so that when thou comest here again the city may appear[1] in the same good order in which it now is." By these remarks he persuaded Alexander; for he thought he

[1] φανείη. Arrian does not comply with the Attic rule, that the subjunctive should follow the principal tenses in the leading sentence. Cf. v. 6, 6; 7, 5; vii. 7, 5; 15, 2.

was speaking with prudence. So he ordered them to send the horsemen to accompany him, but no longer demanded the hundred select men, nor indeed others in their stead. But he commanded Acuphis to send his own son and his daughter's son to accompany him. He was now seized with a strong desire of seeing the place where the Nysaeans boasted to have certain memorials of Dionysus. So he went to Mount Merus with the Companion cavalry and the foot guard, and saw the mountain, which was quite covered with ivy and laurel and groves thickly shaded with all sorts of timber, and on it were chases of all kinds of wild animals.[1] The Macedonians were delighted at seeing the ivy, as they had not seen any for a long time; for in the land of the Indians there was no ivy, even where they had vines. They eagerly made garlands of it, and crowned themselves with them, as they were, singing hymns in honour of Dionysus, and invoking the deity by his various names.[2] Alexander there offered sacrifice to Dionysus, and feasted in company with his companions.[3] Some authors have also stated, but I do not know if any one will believe it, that many of the distinguished Macedonians in attendance upon him, having crowned themselves with ivy, while they were engaged in the invocation of the deity, were seized with the inspiration of Dionysus, uttered cries of Evoi in honour of the god, and acted as Bacchanals.[4]

---

1 Cf. Pliny (*Nat. Hist.*, vi. 23; viii. 60; xvi. 62). The ordinary reading is *ἄλση παντοῖα· καὶ ἰδεῖν σύσκιον*. For this Krüger has proposed *ἄλση παντοίᾳ ὕλῃ σύσκια*.

2 The other names of Dionysus were: Bacchus, Bromius, Evius, Iacchus, Lenaeus, Lyaeus. The Romans called him Liber.

3 *Curtius* (viii. 36) says that the Macedonians celebrated Bacchanalia for the space of ten days on this mountain.

4 The 1st aor. pass. *ἐσχέθην* is found only in Arrian and Plutarch. Cf. vii. 22, 2 infra.

CHAPTER III.

INCREDULITY OF ERATOSTHENES.—PASSAGE OF THE INDUS.

ANY one who receives these stories may believe or disbelieve them as he pleases. But I do not altogether agree with Eratosthenes the Cyrenaean,[1] who says that everything which was attributed to the divine agency by the Macedonians was really said to gratify Alexander by their excessive eulogy. For he says that the Macedonians, seeing a cavern in the land of the Parapamisadians,[2] and hearing a certain legend which was current among the natives, or themselves forming a conjecture, spread the report that this forsooth was the cave where Prometheus had been bound, that an eagle frequented it to feast on his inward parts, that when Heracles arrived there he killed the eagle and set Prometheus free from his bonds. He also says that by their account the Macedonians transferred Mount Caucasus from the Euxine Sea to the eastern parts of the earth, and the land of the Parapamisadians to that of the Indians;[3] calling what was really Mount Parapamisus by the name of Caucasus, in order to enhance Alexander's glory, seeing that he forsooth had gone over the Caucasus. He adds, that when they saw in India itself some oxen marked with the brand of a club, they concluded from this that Heracles had penetrated into India. Eratosthenes also disbelieves the similar tale of the wandering of Dionysus. Let me leave the stories about these matters undecided as far as I am concerned.

When Alexander arrived at the river Indus, he found a bridge made over it by Hephaestion, and two thirty-

---

[1] The celebrated Geographer and Mathematician, who was born B.C. 276 and died about B.C. 196. His principal work was one on geography, which was of great use to Strabo. None of his works are extant. He was made president of the Alexandrian library, B.C. 236.

[2] Cf. Arrian (*Indica*, v. 11).

[3] The earliest mention of India which has descended to our times is in Aeschylus (*Supplices*, 284).

oared galleys, besides many smaller craft.[1] He moreover found that 200 talents of silver,[2] 3,000 oxen, above 10,000 sheep for sacrificial victims, and thirty elephants had arrived as gifts from Taxiles the Indian; 700 Indian horsemen also arrived from Taxiles as a reinforcement, and that prince sent word that he would surrender to him the city of Taxila,[3] the largest town between the rivers Indus and Hydaspes.[4] Alexander there offered sacrifice to the gods to whom he was in the habit of sacrificing, and celebrated a gymnastic and horse contest near the river. The sacrifices were favourable to his crossing.

CHAPTER IV.

Digression about India.

The following are statements about the river Indus which are quite unquestionable, and therefore let me record them. The Indus is the largest of all the rivers in Asia and Europe, except the Ganges,[5] which is also an Indian river. It takes its rise on this side mount Parapamisus, or Caucasus, and discharges its water into the Great Sea which lies near India in the direction of the south wind. It has two mouths, both of which outlets are full of shallow pools like the five outlets of the Ister (or Danube).[6] It forms a Delta in the land of

---

[1] Arrian frequently uses the Ionic and old Attic word, σμικρός.

[2] About £480,000.

[3] Alexander probably crossed the Indus near Attock. The exact site of Taxila cannot be fixed.

[4] The Hydaspes is now called Jelum, one of the five great tributaries of the Indus.

[5] Herodotus considered the Danube the largest river in the world as known to him, and the Dnieper the largest of all rivers except the Danube and the Nile. See *Herodotus*, iv. 48–53.

[6] "Amnis Danubius sexaginta navigabiles paene recipiens fluvios, septem ostiis erumpit in mare. Quorum primum est Peuce insula supra dicta, ut interpretata sunt vocabula Graeco sermone, secundum Naracu-

the Indians resembling that of Egypt[1]; and this is called Pattala in the Indian language. The Hydaspes, Acesines, Hydraotes, and Hyphasis are also Indian rivers,[2] and far exceed the other rivers of Asia in size; but they are not only smaller but much smaller than the Indus, just as that river itself is smaller than the Ganges. Indeed Ctesias[3] says (if any one thinks his evidence to be depended upon), that where the Indus is narrowest, its banks are forty stades apart; where it is broadest, 100 stades; and most of it is the mean between these breadths.[4] This river Indus Alexander crossed at day-break with his army into the country of the Indians; concerning whom, in this history I have described neither what laws they enjoy, nor what strange animals their land produces, nor how many and what sort of fish and water-monsters are produced by the Indus, Hydaspes, Ganges, or the other rivers of India. Nor have I described the ants which dig up the gold for them,[5] nor the guardian griffins, nor any of the other tales that have been composed rather to amuse than to be received as

---

stoma, tertium Calonstoma, quartum Pseudostoma: nam Boreonstoma ac deinde Sthenostoma longe minora sunt caeteris: septimum ingens te palustri specie nigrum."—*Ammianus* (xxii. 8, 44). *Pliny* (iv. 24) says that the Danube has six mouths, the names of which he gives.

[1] The Indus does not rise in the Parapamisus, but in the Himalayas. It has two principal mouths, but there are a number of smaller ones. Ptolemy said there were seven. The Delta is between 70 and 80 miles broad. "Delta, a triquetrae litterae forma hoc vocabulo signatius adpellata."—*Ammianus*, xxii. 15.

[2] The territory included by the Indus and its four affluents is now called Punjab, a Persian word meaning *five rivers*.

[3] Ctesias was the Greek physician of Artaxerxes Mnemon. He wrote a history of Persia and a book on India. His works are only preserved in meagre abridgement by Photius. Aristotle says that he was false and untrustworthy (*Hist. of Animals*, viii. 27; *De Generatione Animalium*, ii. 2). Subsequent research has proved Ctesias to be wrong and Herodotus generally right in the many statements in which they are at variance.

[4] The fact is, that the Indus is nowhere more than 20 stades, or 2¼ miles broad.

[5] See *Strabo*, xv. 1; xvi. 4; *Herod.*, iii. 102, with Dean Blakesley's note.

the relation of facts; since the falsity of the strange stories which have been fabricated about India cannot be exposed by any one.[1] However, Alexander and those who served in his army exposed the falsity of most of these tales; but there were even some of these very men who fabricated other stories. They proved that the Indians whom Alexander visited with his army, and he visited many tribes of them, were destitute of gold; and also that they were by no means luxurious in their mode of living. Moreover, they discovered that they were tall in stature, in fact as tall as any men throughout Asia, most of them being five cubits in height, or a little less. They were blacker than the rest of men, except the Ethiopians[2]; and in war they were far the bravest of all the races inhabiting Asia at that time. For I cannot with any justice compare the race of the ancient Persians with those of India, though at the head of the former Cyrus, son of Cambyses, set out and deprived the Medes of the empire of Asia, and subdued many other races partly by force and partly by voluntary surrender on their own part. For at that time the Persians were a poor people and inhabitants of a rugged land, having laws and customs very similar to the Laconian discipline.[3] Nor am I able with certainty to conjecture whether the defeat sustained by the Persians in the Scythian land was due to the difficult nature of the country invaded or to some other error on the part of Cyrus, or whether the Persians were really inferior in warlike matters to the Scythians of that district.

---

[1] *οὐδαμῶν* is the Ionic form for *οὐδένων*.

[2] The Greek name *Αἴθιοψ* means *sun-burnt*. The Hebrew name for Aethiopia is Cush (black). In ancient Egyptian inscriptions it is called *Keesh*. It is the country now called Abyssinia. Aethiopas vicini sideris vapore torreri, adustisque similes gigni, barba et capillo vibrato, non est dubium. (*Pliny*, ii. 80).

[3] Cf. Xenophon (*Cyropaedia*, vii. 5, 67).

CHAPTER V.

Mountains and Rivers of Asia.

But of the Indians I shall treat in a distinct work,[1] giving the most credible accounts which were compiled by those who accompanied Alexander in his expedition, as well as by Nearchus,[2] who sailed right round the Great Sea which is near India. Then I shall add what has been compiled by Megasthenes[3] and Eratosthenes, two men of distinguished authority. I shall describe the customs peculiar to the Indians and the strange animals which are produced in the country, as well as the voyage itself in the external sea. But now let me describe so much only as appears to me sufficient to explain Alexander's achievements. Mount Taurus divides Asia, beginning from Mycale, the mountain which lies opposite the island of Samos; then, cutting through the country of the Pamphylians and Cilicians, it extends into Armenia. From this country it stretches into Media and through the land of the Parthians and Chorasmians. In Bactria it unites with mount Parapamisus, which the Macedonians who served in Alexander's army called Caucasus, in order, as it is said, to enhance their king's glory; asserting that he went even beyond the Caucasus with his victorious arms. Perhaps it is a fact that this mountain range is a continuation of the other Caucasus in Scythia, as the Taurus[4] is of the same. For this reason I have on a previous occasion called this range Caucasus, and by the same

---

[1] Called the *Indica*, a valuable little work in the Ionic dialect, still existing. [2] Nearchus left an account of his voyage, which is not now extant. Arrian made use of it in writing the *Indica*. See that work, chapters xvii. to lxiii.

[3] Megasthenes was sent with the Plataean Dēimachus, by Seleucus Nicator, the king of Syria and one of Alexander's generals, as ambassador to Sandracotus, king of the country near the Ganges. He wrote a very valuable account of India in four books.

[4] *Taurus* is from the old root *tor* meaning *high*, another form of which is *dor*. Hence Dorians = highlanders.

name I shall continue to call it in the future. This Caucasus extends as far as the Great Sea which lies in the direction of India and the East. Of the rivers in Asia worth consideration which take their rise from the Taurus and Caucasus, some have their course turned towards the north, discharging themselves either into the lake Maeotis,[1] or into the sea called Hyrcanian, which in reality is a gulf of the Great Sea.[2] Others flow towards the south, namely, the Euphrates, Tigres, Indus, Hydaspes, Acesines, Hydraotes, Hyphasis, and all those that lie between these and the river Ganges. All these either discharge their water into the sea, or disappear by pouring themselves out into marshes, as the river Euphrates [3] does.

CHAPTER VI.

General Description of India.

Whoever arranges the position of Asia in such a way that it is divided by the Taurus and the Caucasus from the west wind to the east wind, will find that these two very large divisions are made by the Taurus itself, one of which is inclined towards the south and the south wind, and the other towards the north and the north wind. Southern Asia again may be divided into four parts, of which Eratosthenes and Megasthenes make India the

---

[1] The ancient geographers thought that the Jaxartes bifurcated, part of it forming the Tanaïs, or Don, and flowing into the lake Maeotis, or Sea of Azov; and the other part falling into the Hyrcanian, or Caspian Sea. The Jaxartes and Oxus flow into the Sea of Aral, but the ancients thought that they fell into the Caspian, as there is indeed evidence to prove that they once did. *Hyrcania* is the Greek form of the old Persian *Virkâna*, that is *Wolf's Land.* It is now called Gurgân.

[2] *Herodotus* (i. 203) states decidedly that the Caspian is an inland sea. *Strabo* (xi. 1), following Eratosthenes, says that it is a gulf of the Northern Ocean.

[3] The Euphrates, after its junction with the Tigres, flows through the marshes of Lamlum, where its current moves less than a mile an hour.

largest. The latter author lived with Sibyrtius,[1] the viceroy of Arachosia, and says that he frequently visited Sandracotus, king of the Indians.[2] These authors say that the smallest of the four parts is that which is bounded by the river Euphrates and extends to our inland sea. The other two lying between the rivers Euphrates and Indus are scarcely worthy to be compared with India, if they were joined together. They say that India is bounded towards the east and the east wind as far as the south by the Great Sea, towards the north by mount Caucasus, as far as its junction with the Taurus; and that the river Indus cuts it off towards the west and the north-west wind, as far as the Great Sea. The greater part of it is a plain, which, as they conjecture, has been formed by the alluvial deposits of the rivers; just as the plains in the rest of the earth lying near the sea are for the most part due to the alluvial action of the rivers taken singly. Consequently, the names by which the countries are called were attached in ancient times to the rivers. For instance, a certain plain was called after the Hermus, which rises in the country of Asia from the mountain of Mother Dindymene,[3] and after flowing past the Aeolian city of Smyrna discharges its water into the sea. Another Lydian plain is named after the Caÿster, a Lydian river; another from the Caïcus in Mysia; and the Carian plain, extending as far as the Ionian city of Miletus, is named from the Maeander. Both Herodotus and Hecataeus[4] the his-

---

[1] Cf. *Arrian*, vi. 27 infra.

[2] Probably the Chandragupta of the Sanscrit writers. He conquered from the Macedonians the Punjab and the country as far as the Hindu-Koosh. He reigned about 310 B.C.

[3] Mount Dindymus, now called Murad Dagh, was sacred to Cybele, the mother of the gods, who was hence called Dindymene.

[4] Hecataeus of Miletus died about B.C. 476. He wrote a work upon Geography, and another on History. His works were well known to Herodotus but only fragments survive.

torians (unless the work about the Egyptian country is by another person, and not by Hecataeus) in like manner call Egypt a gift of the river[1]; and Herodotus has shown by no uncertain proofs that such is the case[2]; so that even the country itself perhaps received its name from the river. For that the river which both the Egyptians and men outside Egypt now name the Nile, was in ancient times called Aegyptus, Homer is sufficient to prove; since he says that Menelaus stationed his ships at the outlet of the river Aegyptus.[3] If therefore single rivers by themselves, and those not large ones, are sufficient to form an extensive tract of country, while flowing forward into the sea, since they carry down slime and mud from the higher districts whence they derive their sources, surely it is unbecoming to exhibit incredulity about India, how it has come to pass that most of it is a plain, which has been formed by the alluvial deposits of its rivers. For if the Hermus, the Caÿster, the Caïcus, the Maeander, and all the other[4] rivers of Asia which discharge their waters into the midland sea were all put together, they would not be worthy of comparison for volume of water with one of the Indian rivers. Not only do I mean the Ganges, which is the largest, and with which neither the water of the Egyptian Nile nor the Ister flowing through Europe is worthy to compare; but if all those rivers were mingled together they would not even then become equal to the river Indus, which is a large river as soon as it issues from its springs, and after receiving fifteen rivers,[5] all larger than those in the province of Asia, discharges its water

---

[1] See *Herodotus*, ii. 5. [2] See *Herodotus*, ii. 10–34.

[3] See Homer's *Odyssey*, iv. 477, 581. In Hebrew the name for Egypt is *Mitsraim* (dark-red). In form the word is dual, evidently in reference to the division of the country by the Nile. The native name was *Chem*, meaning *black*, probably on account of the blackness of the alluvial soil.

[4] ἄλλοι is Abicht's reading instead of πολλοί.

[5] Arrian, in his *Indica*, chap. 4, gives the names of these rivers.

into the sea, retaining its own name and absorbing those of its tributaries. Let these remarks which I have made about India suffice for the present, and let the rest be reserved for my "Description of India."

CHAPTER VII.

Method of Bridging Rivers.

How Alexander constructed his bridge over the river Indus, is explained neither by Aristobulus nor Ptolemy, authors whom I usually follow; nor am I able to form a decided opinion whether the passage was bridged with boats, as the Hellespont was by Xerxes and the Bosporus and the Ister were by Darius,[1] or whether he made a continuous bridge over the river. To me it seems probable that the bridge was made of boats; for the depth of the water would not have admitted of the construction of a regular bridge, nor could so enormous a work have been completed in so short a time.[2] If the passage was bridged with boats, I cannot decide whether the vessels being fastened together with ropes and moored in a row were sufficient to form the bridge, as Herodotus the Halicarnassian says the Hellespont was bridged, or whether the work was effected in the way in which the bridge upon the Ister and that upon the Celtic Rhine[3] are made by the Romans, and in the way in which they bridged the Euphrates and Tigres, as often as necessity

---

[1] See *Herodotus*, vii. 33–36; iv. 83, 97, 133–141. *Bosporus* = Oxford. The name was applied to the Straits of Constantinople, and also to those of Yenikale, the former being called the Thracian and the latter the Cimmerian Bosporus. Cf. Aeschylus (*Prom.*, 734). Ad Bosporos duos, vel bubus meabili transitu; unde nomen ambobus (*Pliny*, vi. 1).

[2] *Diodorus* (xvii. 86) says that Alexander crossed on a bridge of boats. Cf. *Strabo*, p. 698; *Curtius*, viii. 34.

[3] There was another river called Rhenus, a tributary of the Po, now called the Reno. It was called Rhenus Bononiensis, being near Bononia or Bologna.

compelled them. However, as I know myself, the Romans find the quickest way of making a bridge to be with vessels; and this method I shall on the present occasion explain, because it is worth describing. At a preconcerted signal they let the vessels loose down the stream, not with their prows forward, but as if backing water.[1] As might naturally be expected, the stream carries them down, but a skiff furnished with oars holds them back, until it settles them in the place assigned to them. Then pyramidal wicker-baskets made of willow, full of unhewn stones, are let down into the water from the prow of each vessel, in order to hold it up against the force of the stream. As soon as any one of these vessels has been held fast, another is in the same way moored with its prow against the stream, distant from the first as far as is consistent with their supporting what is put upon them. On both of them are placed pieces of timber with sharp ends projecting out, on which cross-planks are placed to bind them together; and so proceeds the work through all the vessels which are required to bridge the river. At each end of this bridge firmly fixed gangways are thrown forward,[2] so that the approach may be safer for the horses and beasts of burden, and at the same time to serve as a bond to the bridge. In a short time the whole is finished with a great noise and bustle; but yet discipline is not relaxed while the work is going on. In each vessel the exhortations of the overseers to the men, or their censures of sluggishness, neither prevent the orders being heard nor impede the rapidity of the work.[3]

---

[1] *αἱ πρύμναν κρουόμεναι.* For this nautical term compare *Thucydides*, i. 51; *Herodotus*, viii. 84; *Diodorus*, xi. 18; Aristophanes, *Wasps*, 399. *κατὰ ῥοῦν* is Krüger's reading for the usual *κατὰ πόρον*.

[2] The explanation of this passage given in Liddell and Scott's *Lexicon*, sub voce *κλῖμαξ*, is evidently incorrect, as there is nothing about a chariot in the original.

[3] Compare the description of Cæsar's bridge over the Rhine (*Gallic War*, iv. 17).

CHAPTER VIII.

March from the Indus to the Hydaspes.

This has been the method of constructing bridges, practised by the Romans from olden times; but how Alexander laid a bridge over the river Indus I cannot say, because those who served in his army have said nothing about it. But I should think that the bridge was made as near as possible as I have described, or if it were effected by some other contrivance so let it be. When Alexander had crossed to the other side of the river Indus, he again offered sacrifice there, according to his custom.[1] Then starting from the Indus, he arrived at Taxila, a large and prosperous city, in fact the largest of those situated between the rivers Indus and Hydaspes. He was received in a friendly manner by Taxiles, the governor of the city, and by the Indians of that place; and he added to their territory as much of the adjacent country as they asked for. Thither also came to him envoys from Abisares, king of the mountaineer Indians, the embassy including the brother of Abisares as well as the other most notable men. Other envoys also came from Doxareus, the chief of the province, bringing gifts with them. Here again at Taxila Alexander offered the sacrifices which were customary for him to offer, and celebrated a gymnastic and equestrian contest. Having appointed Philip, son of Machatas, viceroy of the Indians of that district, he left a garrison in Taxila, as well as the soldiers who were invalided by sickness, and then marched towards the river Hydaspes.

---

1 The place where Alexander crossed the Indus was probably at its junction with the Cophen or Cabul river, near Attock. Before he crossed he gave his army a rest of thirty days, as we learn from *Diodorus*, xvii. 86. From the same passage we learn that a certain king named Aphrices with an army of 20,000 men and 15 elephants, was killed by his own men and his army joined Alexander.

For he was informed that Porus,[1] with the whole of his army was on the other side of that river, having determined either to prevent him from making the passage, or to attack him while crossing. When Alexander ascertained this, he sent Coenus, son of Polemocrates, back to the river Indus, with instructions to cut in pieces all the vessels which he had prepared for the passage of that river, and to bring them to the river Hydaspes. Coenus cut the vessels in pieces and conveyed them thither, the smaller ones being cut into two parts, and the thirty-oared galleys into three. The sections were conveyed upon waggons, as far as the bank of the Hydaspes; and there the vessels were fixed together again, and seen as a fleet upon that river. Alexander took the forces which he had when he arrived at Taxila, and the 5,000 Indians under the command of Taxiles and the chiefs of that district, and marched towards the same river.

CHAPTER IX.

Porus obstructs Alexander's Passage.

Alexander encamped on the bank of the Hydaspes, and Porus was seen with all his army and his large troop of elephants lining the opposite bank.[2] He remained to guard the passage at the place where he saw Alexander had encamped; and sent guards to all the other parts of the river which were easily fordable, placing officers over each detachment, being resolved to obstruct the passage of the Macedonians. When Alexander saw this,

---

[1] The kingdom of Porus lay between the Hydaspes and Acesines, the district now called Bari-doab with Lahore as capital. It was conquered by Lords Hardinge and Gough in 1849.

[2] *Diodorus* (xvii. 87) says that Porus had more than 50,000 infantry, about 3,000 cavalry, more than 1,000 chariots, and 130 elephants. *Curtius* (viii. 44) says he had about 30,000 infantry, 300 chariots, and 85 elephants.

he thought it advisable to move his army in various directions, to distract the attention of Porus, and render him uncertain what to do. Dividing his army into many parts, he led some of his troops now in one direction and now in another, at one time ravaging the enemy's country, at another looking out for a place where the river might appear easier for him to ford it. The rest of his troops he entrusted[1] to his different generals, and sent them about in many directions. He also conveyed corn from all quarters into his camp from the land on this side the Hydaspes, so that it might be evident to Porus that he had resolved to remain quiet near the bank until the water of the river subsided in the winter, and afforded him a passage in many places. As his vessels were sailing up and down the river, and skins were being filled with hay, and the whole bank appeared to be covered in one place with cavalry and in another with infantry, Porus was not allowed to keep at rest, or to bring his preparations together from all sides to any one point if he selected this as suitable for the defence of the passage. Besides at this season all the Indian rivers were flowing with swollen and turbid waters and with rapid currents; for it was the time of year when the sun is wont to turn towards the summer solstice.[2] At this season incessant and heavy rain falls in India; and the snows on the Caucasus, whence most of the rivers have their sources, melt and swell their streams to a great degree. But in the winter they again subside, become small and clear, and are fordable in certain places, with the exception of the Indus, Ganges, and perhaps one or two others. At any rate the Hydaspes becomes fordable.

---

[1] *ἐπιτρέψας* is Krüger's reading instead of *ἐπιτάξας*.

[2] About the month of May. See chap. 12 infra; also *Curtius*, viii. 45, 46. *Strabo* (xv. 1) quotes from Aristobulus describing the rainy season at the time of Alexander's battle with Porus at the Hydaspes.

CHAPTER X.

Alexander and Porus at the Hydaspes.

Alexander therefore spread a report that he would wait for that season of the year, if his passage was obstructed at the present time; but yet all the time he was waiting in ambush to see whether by rapidity of movement he could steal a passage anywhere without being observed. But he perceived that it was impossible for him to cross at the place where Porus himself had encamped near the bank of the Hydaspes, not only on account of the multitude of his elephants, but also because his large army, arranged in order of battle and splendidly accoutred, was ready to attack his men as they emerged from the water. Moreover he thonght that his horses would not be willing to mount the opposite bank, because the elephants would at once fall upon them and frighten them both by their aspect and trumpeting; nor even before that would they remain upon the inflated hides during the passage of the river; but when they looked across and saw the elephants they would become frantic and leap into the water. He therefore resolved to steal a crossing by the following manœuvre:—In the night he led most of his cavalry along the bank in various directions, making a clamour and raising the battle-cry in honour of Enyalius.[1] Every kind of noise was raised, as if they were making all the preparations necessary for crossing the river. Porus also marched along the river at the head of his elephants opposite the places where the clamour was heard, and Alexander thus gradually got him into the habit of leading his men along opposite the noise. But when this occurred frequently, and there was merely a clamour and a raising of the battle-cry, Porus no longer continued to move about to meet the

[1] Cf. *Arrian*, i. 14 supra.

expected advance of the cavalry; but perceiving that his fear had been groundless,[1] he kept his position in the camp. However he posted his scouts at many places along the bank. When Alexander had brought it about that the mind of Porus no longer entertained any fear of his nocturnal attempts, he devised the following stratagem.

CHAPTER XI.

ALEXANDER'S STRATAGEM TO GET ACROSS.

THERE was in the bank of the Hydaspes, a projecting headland, where the river makes a remarkable bend. It was densely covered by a grove,[2] containing all sorts of trees; and over against it in the river was an island full of trees and without a foot-track, on account of its being uninhabited. Perceiving that this island was right in front of the headland, and that both the spots were woody and adapted to conceal his attempt to cross the river, he resolved to convey his army over at this place. The headland and island were 150 stades distant from his great camp.[3] Along the whole of the bank, he posted sentries, separated as far as was consistent with keeping each other in sight, and easily hearing when any order should be sent along from any quarter. From all sides also during many nights clamours were raised and fires were burnt. But when he had made up his mind to undertake the passage of the river, he openly prepared his measures for crossing opposite the camp. Craterus had been left behind at the camp with his own division of cavalry, and the horsemen from the Arachotians and Parapamisadians, as well as the brigades of Alcetas and Polysperchon from the phalanx of the

---

[1] ἀλλὰ κενόν is Krüger's reading, instead of ἀλλ' ἐκεῖνον.

[2] ἄλσει is Abicht's reading for εἴδει.

[3] About 17 miles.

Macedonian infantry, together with the chiefs of the Indians dwelling this side of the Hyphasis, who had with them 5,000 men. He gave Craterus orders not to cross the river before Porus moved off with his forces against them, or before he ascertained that Porus was in flight and that they were victorious.[1] "If however," said he, "Porus should take only a part of his army and march against me, and leave the other part with the elephants in his camp, in that case do thou also remain in thy present position. But if he leads all his elephants with him against me, and a part of the rest of his army is left behind in the camp, then do thou cross the river with all speed. For it is the elephants alone," said he, "which render it impossible for the horses to land on the other bank. The rest of the army can easily cross."

CHAPTER XII.

Passage of the Hydaspes.

Such were the injunctions laid upon Craterus. Between the island and the great camp where Alexander had left this general, he posted Meleager, Attalus, and Gorgias, with the Grecian mercenaries, cavalry and infantry, giving them instructions to cross in detachments, breaking up the army as soon as they saw the Indians already involved in battle. He then picked the select body-guard called the Companions, as well as the cavalry regiments of Hephaestion, Perdiccas, and Demetrius, the cavalry from Bactria, Sogdiana, and Scythia, and the Daan horse-archers; and from the phalanx of infantry the shield-bearing guards, the brigades of Clitus and Coenus, with the archers and Agrianians, and made a secret march, keeping far away from the bank of the river,

---

[1] This use of πρὶν with infinitive after negative clauses, is contrary to Attic usage.

in order not to be seen marching towards the island and headland, from which he had determined to cross. There the skins were filled in the night with the hay which had been procured long before, and they were tightly stitched up. In the night a furious storm of rain occurred, by which his preparations and attempt to cross were rendered still more unobserved, since the noise of the thunder and the storm drowned with its din the clatter of the weapons and the noise which arose from the orders given by the officers. Most of the vessels, the thirty-oared galleys included with the rest, had been cut in pieces by his order and conveyed to this place, where they had been fixed together again[1] and hidden in the wood. At the approach of daylight, both the wind and the rain calmed down; and the rest of the army went over opposite the island, the cavalry mounting upon the skins, and as many of the foot soldiers as the boats would receive getting into them. They went so secretly that they were not observed by the sentinels posted by Porus, before they had already got beyond the island and were only a little way from the other bank.

CHAPTER XIII.

Passage of the Hydaspes.

Alexander himself embarked in a thirty-oared galley and went over, accompanied by Perdiccas, Lysimachus, the confidential body-guards, Seleucus, one of the Companions, who was afterwards king,[2] and half of the shield-bearing guards; the rest of these troops being conveyed in

---

[1] The perf. pass. *πέπηγμαι* is used by Arrian and Dionysius, but by Homer and the Attic writers the form used is *πέπηγα*. *Doric*, *πέπαγα*.

[2] Seleucus Nicator, the most powerful of Alexander's successors, became king of Syria and founder of the dynasty of the Seleucidae, which came to an end in B.C. 79.

other galleys of the same size. When the soldiers got beyond the island, they openly directed their course to the bank; and when the sentinels perceived that they had started, they at once rode off to Porus as fast as each man's horse could gallop. Alexander himself was the first to land, and he at once took the cavalry as they kept on landing from his own and the other thirty-oared galleys, and drew them up in proper order. For the cavalry had received orders to land first; and at the head of these in regular array he advanced. But through ignorance of the locality he had effected a landing on ground which was not a part of the mainland, but an island, a large one indeed and where from the fact that it was an island, he more easily escaped notice. It was cut off from the rest of the land by a part of the river where the water was shallow. However, the furious storm of rain, which lasted the greater part of the night, had swelled the water so much that his cavalry could not find out the ford; and he was afraid that he would have to undergo another labour in crossing as great as the first. But when at last the ford was found, he led his men through it with much difficulty; for where the water was deepest, it reached higher than the breasts of the infantry; and of the horses only the heads rose above the river.[1] When he had also crossed this piece of water, he selected the choice guard of cavalry, and the best men from the other cavalry regiments, and brought them up from column into line on the right wing.[2] In front of all the cavalry he posted the horse-archers, and placed next to the cavalry in front of the other infantry the royal shield-bearing guards under the command of Seleucus. Near these he placed the royal foot-guard, and next to

---

[1] For this use of ὅσον, cf. Homer (*Iliad*, ix. 354); *Herodotus*, iv. 45; Plato (*Gorgias*, 485 A; *Euthydemus*, 273 A).

[2] Compare the passage of the Rhone by Hannibal. (See *Livy*, xxi. 26–28; *Polybius*, iii. 45, 46.)

these the other shield-bearing guards, as each happened at the time to have the right of precedence. On each side, at the extremities of the phalanx, his archers, Agrianians and javelin-throwers were posted.

CHAPTER XIV.

The Battle at the Hydaspes.

Having thus arranged his army, he ordered the infantry to follow at a slow pace and in regular order, numbering as it did not much under 6,000 men; and because he thought he was superior in cavalry, he took only his horse-soldiers, who were 5,000 in number, and led them forward with speed. He also instructed Tauron, the commander of the archers, to lead them on also with speed to back up the cavalry. He had come to the conclusion that if Porus should engage him with all his forces, he would easily be able to overcome him by attacking with his cavalry, or to stand on the defensive until his infantry arrived in the course of the action; but if the Indians should be alarmed at his extraordinary audacity in making the passage of the river and take to flight, he would be able to keep close to them in their flight, so that the slaughter of them in the retreat being greater, there would be only a slight work left for him. Aristobulus says that the son of Porus arrived with about sixty chariots, before Alexander made his later passage from the large island, and that he could have hindered Alexander's crossing (for he made the passage with difficulty even when no one opposed him); if the Indians had leaped down from their chariots and assaulted those who first emerged from the water. But he passed by with the chariots and thus made the passage quite safe for Alexander; who on reaching the bank discharged his horse-archers against the Indians in the chariots, and these were easily put to rout, many of them being wounded. Other writers say that a battle took place between the Indians who came with the son of Porus and Alexander at the head of his cavalry, that the son of Porus came with a greater force, that Alexander himself was wounded by him, and that his horse Bucephalas, of which he was exceedingly fond, was killed, being wounded like his master by the son of Porus. But Ptolemy, son of Lagus, with whom I agree, gives a different account. This author also says that Porus despatched his son, but not at the head of merely sixty chariots; nor is it indeed likely that Porus hearing from his scouts that either Alexander himself or at any rate a part of his army had effected the passage of the Hydaspes, would despatch his son against him with only sixty chariots. These indeed were too many to be sent out as a reconnoitring party, and not adapted for speedy retreat; but they were by no means a sufficient force to keep back those of the enemy who had not yet got across, as well as to attack those who had already landed. Ptolemy says that the son of Porus arrived at the head of 2000 cavalry and 120 chariots; but that Alexander had already made even the last passage from the island before he appeared.

CHAPTER XV.

Arrangements of Porus.

Ptolemy also says that Alexander in the first place sent the horse-archers against these, and led the cavalry himself, thinking that Porus was approaching with all his forces, and that this body of cavalry was marching in front of the rest of his army, being drawn up by him as the vanguard. But as soon as he had ascertained with accuracy the number of the Indians, he immediately made a rapid charge upon them with the cavalry around him. When they perceived that Alexander himself and the body of cavalry around him had made the assault, not in line of battle regularly formed, but by squadrons, they gave way; and 400 of their cavalry, including the son of Porus, fell in the contest. The chariots also were captured, horses and all, being heavy and slow in the retreat, and useless in the action itself on account of the clayey ground. When the horsemen who had escaped from this rout brought news to Porus that Alexander himself had crossed the river with the strongest part of his army, and that his son had been slain in the battle, he nevertheless could not make up his mind what course to take, because the men who had been left behind under Craterus were seen to be attempting to cross the river from the great camp which was directly opposite his position. However, at last he preferred to march against Alexander himself with all his army, and to come into a decisive conflict with the strongest division of the Macedonians, commanded by the king in person. But nevertheless he left a few of the elephants together with a small army there at the camp to frighten the cavalry under Craterus from the bank of the river. He then took all his cavalry to the number of 4,000 men, all his chariots to the number of 300, with 200 of his elephants and 30,000 choice infantry, and marched against Alexander. When he found a place where he saw there was no clay, but that on account of the sand the ground was all level and hard, and thus fit for the advance and retreat of horses, he there drew up his army. First he placed the elephants in the front, each animal being not less than a plethrum[1] apart, so that they might be extended in the front before the whole of the phalanx of infantry, and produce terror everywhere among Alexander's cavalry. Besides he thought that none of the enemy would have the audacity to push themselves into the spaces between

[1] 100 Greek and 101 English feet.

the elephants, the cavalry being deterred by the fright of their horses; and still less would the infantry do so, it being likely they would be kept off in front by the heavy-armed soldiers falling upon them, and trampled down by the elephants wheeling round against them. Near these he had posted the infantry, not occupying a line on a level with the beasts, but in a second line behind them, only so far distant that the companies of foot might be pushed forward a short distance into the spaces between them. He had also bodies of infantry standing beyond the elephants on the wings; and on both sides of the infantry he had posted the cavalry, in front of which were placed the chariots on both wings of his army.

CHAPTER XVI.

Alexander's Tactics.

Such was the arrangement which Porus made of his forces. As soon as Alexander observed that the Indians were drawn up in order of battle, he stopped his cavalry from advancing farther, so that he might take up the infantry as it kept on arriving; and even when the phalanx in quick march had effected a junction with the cavalry, he did not at once draw it out and lead it to the attack, not wishing to hand over his men exhausted with fatigue and out of breath, to the barbarians who were fresh and untired. On the contrary, he caused his infantry to rest until their strength was recruited, riding along round the lines to inspect them.[1] When he had surveyed the arrangement of the Indians, he resolved not to advance against the centre, in front of which the elephants had been posted, and in the gaps between them a dense phalanx of men; for he was alarmed at the very arrangements which Porus had made here with that express design. But as he was superior in the number

[1] See Donaldson's *New Cratylus*, sec. 178.

of his cavalry, he took the greater part of that force, and marched along against the left wing of the enemy for the purpose of making an attack in this direction. Against the right wing he sent Coenus with his own regiment of cavalry and that of Demetrius, with instructions to keep close behind the barbarians when they, seeing the dense mass of cavalry opposed to them, should ride out to fight them. Seleucus, Antigenes, and Tauron were ordered to lead the phalanx of infantry, but not to engage in the action until they observed[1] the enemy's cavalry and phalanx of infantry thrown into disorder by the cavalry under his own command. But when they came within range of missiles, he launched the horse-archers, 1000 in number, against the left wing of the Indians, in order to throw those of the enemy who were posted there into confusion by the incessant storm of arrows and by the charge of the horses. He himself with the Companion cavalry marched along rapidly against the left wing of the barbarians, being eager to attack them in flank while still in a state of disorder, before their cavalry could be deployed.

CHAPTER XVII.

Defeat of Porus.

Meantime the Indians had collected their cavalry from all parts, and were riding along, advancing out of their position to meet Alexander's charge. Coenus also appeared with his men in their rear, according to his instructions. The Indians, observing this, were compelled to make the line of their cavalry face both ways[2]; the largest and best part against Alexander, while the rest wheeled round against Coenus and his forces. This therefore at once threw the ranks as well as the decisions of the Indians

[1] πρὶν κατίδωσιν. In Attic, πρὶν ἄν is the regular form with the subjunctive; but in Homer and the Tragic writers ἄν is often omitted.

[2] Cf. Arrian's *Tactics*, chap. 29.

into confusion. Alexander, seeing his opportunity, at the very moment the cavalry was wheeling round in the other direction, made an attack on those opposed to him with such vigour that the Indians could not sustain the charge of his cavalry, but were scattered and driven to the elephants, as to a friendly wall, for refuge. Upon this, the drivers of the elephants urged forward the beasts against the cavalry; but now the phalanx itself of the Macedonians was advancing against the elephants, the men casting darts at the riders and also striking the beasts themselves, standing round them on all sides. The action was unlike any of the previous contests; for wherever the beasts could wheel round, they rushed forth against the ranks of infantry and demolished the phalanx of the Macedonians, dense as it was. The Indian cavalry also, seeing that the infantry were engaged in the action, rallied again and advanced against the Macedonian cavalry. But when Alexander's men, who far excelled both in strength and military discipline, got the mastery over them the second time, they were again repulsed towards the elephants and cooped up among them. By this time the whole of Alexander's cavalry had collected into one squadron, not by any command of his, but having settled into this arrangement by the mere effect of the struggle itself; and wherever it fell upon the ranks of the Indians they were broken up with great slaughter. The beasts being now cooped up into a narrow space, their friends were no less injured by them than their foes, being trampled down in their wheeling and pushing about. Accordingly there ensued a great slaughter of the cavalry, cooped up as it was in a narrow space around the elephants. Most of the keepers of the elephants had been killed by the javelins, and some of the elephants themselves had been wounded, while others no longer kept apart in the battle on account of their sufferings or from being destitute of keepers. But, as if frantic with pain, rushing forward at friends and foes alike, they pushed about, trampled down and killed them in every kind of way. However, the Macedonians retired whenever they were assailed, for they rushed at the beasts in a more open space, and in accordance with their own plan; and when they wheeled round to return, they followed them closely and hurled javelins at them; whereas the Indians retreating among them were now receiving greater injury from them. But when the beasts were tired out, and they were no longer able to charge with any vigour, they began to retire, facing the foe like ships backing water, merely uttering a shrill piping sound. Alexander himself surrounded the whole line with his cavalry, and gave the signal that the infantry should link their shields together so as to form a very densely closed body, and thus advance in phalanx. By this means the Indian cavalry, with the exception of a few men, was quite cut up in the action; as was also the infantry, since the Macedonians were now pressing upon them from all sides. Upon this, all who could do so turned to flight through the spaces which intervened between the parts of Alexander's cavalry.

CHAPTER XVIII.

Losses of the Combatants.—Porus Surrenders.

At the same time Craterus and the other officers of Alexander's army who had been left behind on the bank of the Hydaspes crossed the river, when they perceived that Alexander was winning a brilliant victory. These men, being fresh, followed up the pursuit instead of Alexander's exhausted troops, and made no less a slaughter of the Indians in their retreat. Of the Indians little short of 20,000 infantry and 3,000 cavalry were killed in this battle.[1] All their chariots were broken

[1] *Diodorus* (xvii. 89) says that more than 12,000 Indians were killed in this battle, over 9,000 being captured, besides 80 elephants.

to pieces; and two sons of Porus were slain, as were also Spitaces, the governor of the Indians of that district, the managers of the elephants and of the chariots, and all the cavalry officers and generals of Porus's army. All the elephants which were not killed there, were captured. Of Alexander's forces, about 80 of the 6,000 foot-soldiers who were engaged in the first attack, were killed; 10 of the horse-archers, who were also the first to engage in the action; about 20 of the Companion cavalry, and about 200 of the other horsemen fell.[1] When Porus, who exhibited great talent in the battle, performing the deeds not only of a general but also of a valiant soldier, observed the slaughter of his cavalry, and some of his elephants lying dead, others destitute of keepers straying about in a forlorn condition, while most of his infantry had perished, he did not depart as Darius the Great King did, setting an example of flight to his men; but as long as any body of Indians remained compact in the battle, he kept up the struggle. But at last, having received a wound on the right shoulder, which part of his body alone was unprotected during the battle, he wheeled round. His coat of mail warded off the missiles from the rest of his body, being extraordinary both for its strength and the close fitting of its joints, as it was afterwards possible for those who saw him to observe. Then indeed he turned his elephant round and began to retire. Alexander, having seen that he was a great man and valiant in the battle, was very desirous of saving his life. He accordingly sent first to him Taxiles the Indian; who rode up as near to the elephant which was carrying Porus as seemed to him safe, and bade him stop the beast, assuring him that it was no longer possible for him to flee, and bidding him listen to Alex-

[1] According to Diodorus there fell of the Macedonians 280 cavalry and more than 700 infantry. Plutarch (*Alex.* 60) says that the battle lasted eight hours.

ander's message. But when he saw his old foe Taxiles, he wheeled round and was preparing to strike him with a javelin; and he would probably have killed him, if he had not quickly driven his horse forward out of the reach of Porus before he could strike him. But not even on this account was Alexander angry with Porus; but he kept on sending others in succession; and last of all Meroës an Indian, because he ascertained that he was an old friend of Porus. As soon as the latter heard the message brought to him by Meroës, being at the same time overcome by thirst, he stopped his elephant and dismounted from it. After he had drunk some water and felt refreshed, he ordered Meroës to lead him without delay to Alexander; and Meroës led him thither.[1]

CHAPTER XIX.

Alliance with Porus.—Death of Bucephalas.

When Alexander heard that Meroes was bringing Porus to him, he rode in front of the line with a few of the Companions to meet Porus; and stopping his horse, he admired his handsome figure and his stature,[2] which reached somewhat above five cubits. He was also surprised that he did not seem to be cowed in spirit,[3] but advanced to meet him as one brave man would meet another brave man, after having gallantly struggled in defence of his own kingdom against another king. Then indeed Alexander was the first to speak, bidding him say what treatment he would like to receive. The report goes that Porus replied: "Treat me, O Alexander, in a kingly way!" Alexander being pleased at the expres-

[1] *Curtius* (viii. 50, 51) represents Porus sinking half dead, and being protected to the last by his faithful elephant. *Diodorus* (xvii. 88) agrees with him.

[2] Cf. *Curtius*, viii. 44; *Justin*, xii. 8.

[3] Cf. *Arrian*, ii. 10 supra. *δεδουλωμένος τῇ γνώμῃ*. The Scholiast on *Thucydides* iv. 34, explains this by *τεταπεινωμένος φόβῳ*.

sion, said: "For my own sake, O Porus, thou shalt be thus treated; but for thy own sake do thou demand what is pleasing to thee!" But Porus said that everything was included in that. Alexander, being still more pleased at this remark, not only granted him the rule over his own Indians, but also added another country to that which he had before, of larger extent than the former.[1] Thus he treated the brave man in a kingly way, and from that time found him faithful in all things. Such was the result of Alexander's battle with Porus and the Indians living beyond the river Hydaspes, which was fought in the archonship of Hegemon at Athens, in the month Munychion[2] (18 April to 18 May, 326 B.C.).

Alexander founded two cities, one where the battle took place, and the other on the spot whence he started to cross the river Hydaspes; the former he named Nicaea,[3] after his victory over the Indians, and the latter Bucephala in memory of his horse Bucephalas, which died there, not from having been wounded by any one, but from the effects of toil and old age; for he was about thirty years old, and quite worn out with toil.[4] This Bucephalas had shared many hardships and incurred many dangers with Alexander during many years, being ridden by none but the king, because he rejected all other riders. He was both of unusual size and generous in mettle. The head of an ox had been engraved upon him as a distinguishing mark, and according to some

---

[1] Cf. Plutarch (*Alex.*, 60); *Curtius*, viii. 51.

[2] *Diodorus* (xvii. 87) says that the battle was fought in the archonship of Chremes at Athens.

[3] Nicaea is supposed to be Mong and Bucephala may be Jelalpur. See *Strabo*, xv. 1.

[4] Cf. Plutarch (*Alex.*, 61). Schmieder says that Alexander could not have broken in the horse before he was sixteen years old. But since at this time he was in his twenty-ninth year he would have had him thirteen years. Consequently the horse must have been at least seventeen years old when he acquired him. Can any one believe this? Yet Plutarch also states that the horse was thirty years old at his death.

this was the reason why he bore that name; but others say, that though he was black he had a white mark upon his head which bore a great resemblance to the head of an ox. In the land of the Uxians this horse vanished from Alexander, who thereupon sent a proclamation throughout the country that he would kill all the inhabitants, unless they brought the horse back to him. As a result of this proclamation it was immediately brought back. So great was Alexander's attachment to the horse, and so great was the fear of Alexander entertained by the barbarians.[1] Let so much honour be paid by me to this Bucephalas for the sake of his master.

CHAPTER XX.

Conquest of the Glausians.—Embassy from Abisares.—Passage of the Acesines.

When Alexander had paid all due honours to those who had been killed in the battle, he offered the customary sacrifices to the gods in gratitude for his victory, and celebrated a gymnastic and horse contest upon the bank of the Hydaspes at the place where he first crossed with his army.[2] He then left Craterus behind with a part of the army, to erect and fortify the cities which he was founding there; but he himself marched against the Indians conterminous with the dominion of Porus. According to Aristobulus the name of this nation was Glauganicians; but Ptolemy calls them Glausians. I am quite indifferent which name it bore. Alexander traversed their land with half the Companion cavalry, the picked men from each phalanx of the infantry, all the horse-bowmen, the Agrianians, and the archers. All the

---

[1] *Curtius* (vi. 17) says this occurred in the land of the Mardians; whereas Plutarch (*Alex.*, 44) says it happened in Hyrcania.

[2] *Diodorus* (xvii. 89), says Alexander made a halt of 30 days after this battle.

inhabitants came over to him on terms of capitulation; and he thus took thirty-seven cities, the inhabitants of which, where they were fewest, amounted to no less than 5,000, and those of many numbered above 10,000. He also took many villages, which were no less populous than the cities. This land also he granted to Porus to rule; and sent Taxiles back to his own abode after affecting a reconciliation between him and Porus. At this time arrived envoys from Abisares,[1] who told him that their king was ready to surrender himself and the land which he ruled. And yet before the battle which was fought between Alexander and Porus, Abisares intended to join his forces with those of the latter. On this occasion he sent his brother with the other envoys to Alexander, taking with them money and forty elephants as a gift. Envoys also arrived from the independent Indians, and from a certain other Indian ruler named Porus.[2] Alexander ordered Abisares to come to him as soon as possible, threatening that unless he came he would see him arrive with his army at a place where he would not rejoice to see him. At this time Phrataphernes, viceroy of Parthia and Hyrcania, came to Alexander at the head of the Thracians who had been left with him. Messengers also came from Sisicottus, viceroy of the Assacenians, to inform him that those people had slain their governor and revolted from Alexander. Against these he despatched Philip and Tyriaspes with an army, to arrange and set in order the affairs of their land.

He himself advanced towards the river Acesines.[3]

---

[1] Cf. *Arrian*, v. 8 supra, where an earlier embassy from Abisares is mentioned.

[2] *Strabo* (xv. 1) says that this Porus was a cousin of the Porus captured by Alexander.

[3] This is the Chenab. See Arrian (*Indica*, iii.), who says that where it joins the Indus it is 30 stades broad.

Ptolemy, son of Lagus, has described the size of this river alone of those in India, stating that where Alexander crossed it with his army upon boats and skins, the stream was rapid and the channel was full of large and sharp rocks, over which the water being violently carried seethed and dashed. He says also that its breadth amounted to fifteen stades; that those who went over upon skins had an easy passage; but that not a few of those who crossed in the boats perished there in the water, many of the boats being wrecked upon the rocks and dashed to pieces. From this description then it would be possible for one to come to a conclusion by comparison, that the size of the river Indus has been stated not far from the fact by those who think that its mean breadth is forty stades, but that it contracts to fifteen stades where it is narrowest and therefore deepest; and that this is the width of the Indus in many places. I come then to the conclusion that Alexander chose a part of the Acesines where the passage was widest, so that he might find the stream slower than elsewhere.

CHAPTER XXI.

Advance Beyond the Hydraotes.

After crossing the river,[1] he left Coenus with his own brigade there upon the bank, with instructions to superintend the passage of the part of the army which had been left behind for the purpose of collecting[2] corn and other supplies from the country of the Indians which was already subject to him. He now sent Porus away to his own abode, commanding him to select the most warlike

---

[1] *Diodorus* (xvii. 95) says that Alexander received a reinforcement from Greece at this river of more than 30,000 infantry and nearly 6,000 cavalry; also suits of armour for 25,000 infantry, and 100 talents of medical drugs.

[2] Μέλλειν is usually connected with the future infinitive; but Arrian frequently uses it with the present.

of the Indians and take all the elephants he had and come to him. He resolved to pursue the other Porus, the bad one, with the lightest troops in his army, because he was informed that he had left the land which he ruled and had fled. For this Porus, while hostilities subsisted between Alexander and the other Porus, sent envoys to Alexander offering to surrender both himself and the land subject to him, rather out of enmity to Porus than from friendship to Alexander. But when he ascertained that the former had been released, and that he was ruling over another large country in addition to his own, then, fearing not so much Alexander as the other Porus, his namesake, he fled from his own land, taking with him as many of his warriors as he could persuade to share his flight. Against this man Alexander marched, and arrived at the Hydraotes,[1] which is another Indian river, not less than the Acesines in breadth, but less in swiftness of current. He traversed the whole country as far as the Hydraotes, leaving garrisons in the most suitable places, in order that Craterus and Coenus might advance with safety, scouring most of the land for forage. Then he despatched Hephaestion into the land of the Porus who had revolted, giving him a part of the army, comprising two brigades of infantry, his own regiment of cavalry with that of Demetrius and half of the archers, with instructions to hand the country over to the other Porus, to subdue any independent tribes of Indians which dwelt near the banks of the river Hydraotes, and to give them also into the hands of Porus to rule. He himself then crossed the river Hydraotes, not with difficulty, as he had crossed the Acesines. As he was advancing into the country beyond the Hydraotes, it happened that most of the people yielded themselves up on terms of capitulation; but some came to meet him with

[1] Now called the Ravi.

arms, while others who tried to escape he captured and forcibly reduced to obedience.

CHAPTER XXII.

Invasion of the Land of the Cathaeans.

Meantime he received information that the tribe called Cathaeans and some other tribes of the independent Indians were preparing for battle, if he approached their land; and that they were summoning to the enterprise all the tribes conterminous with them who were in like manner independent. He was also informed that the city, Sangala by name,[1] near which they were thinking of having the struggle, was a strong one. The Cathaeans themselves were considered very daring and skilful in war; and two other tribes of Indians, the Oxydracians and Mallians, were in the same temper as the Cathaeans. For a short time before it happened that Porus and Abisares had marched against them with their own forces and had roused many other tribes of the independent Indians to arms, but were forced to retreat without effecting anything worthy of the preparations they had made. When Alexander was informed of this, he made a forced march against the Cathaeans, and on the second day after starting from the river Hydraotes he arrived at a city called Pimprama, inhabited by a tribe of Indians named Adraistaeans, who yielded to him on terms of capitulation. Giving his army a rest the next day, he advanced on the third day to Sangala, where the Cathaeans and the other neighbouring tribes had assembled and marshalled themselves in front of the city upon a hill which was not precipitous on all sides. They had posted their waggons all round this hill and were

[1] Sangala is supposed to be Lahore; but probably it lay some distance from that city, on the bank of the Chenab.

encamping within them in such a way that they were surrounded by a triple palisade of waggons. When Alexander perceived the great number of the barbarians and the nature of their position, he drew up his forces in the order which seemed to him especially adapted to his present circumstances, and sent his horse-archers at once without any delay against them, ordering them to ride along and shoot at them from a distance; so that the Indians might not be able to make any sortie, before his army was in proper array, and that even before the battle commenced they might be wounded within their stronghold. Upon the right wing he posted the guard of cavalry and the cavalry regiment of Clitus; next to these the shield-bearing guards, and then the Agrianians. Towards the left he had stationed Perdiccas with his own regiment of cavalry, and the battalions of foot Companions. The archers he divided into two parts and placed them on each wing. While he was marshalling his army, the infantry and cavalry of the rear-guard came up. Of these, he divided the cavalry into two parts and led them to the wings, and with the infantry which came up he made the ranks of the phalanx more dense and compact. He then took the cavalry which had been drawn up on the right, and led it towards the waggons on the left wing of the Indians; for here their position seemed to him more easy to assail, and the waggons had not been placed together so densely.

CHAPTER XXIII.

Assault upon Sangala.

As the Indians did not run out from behind the waggons against the advancing cavalry, but mounted upon them and began to shoot from the top of them, Alexander, perceiving that it was not the work for cavalry, leaped down from his horse, and on foot led the phalanx of infantry against them. The Macedonians without difficulty forced the Indians from the first row of waggons; but then the Indians, taking their stand in front of the second row, more easily repulsed the attack, because they were posted in denser array in a smaller circle. Moreover the Macedonians were attacking them likewise in a confined space, while the Indians were secretly creeping under the front row of waggons, and without regard to discipline were assaulting their enemy through the gaps left between the waggons as each man found a chance.[1] But nevertheless even from these the Indians were forcibly driven by the phalanx of infantry. They no longer made a stand at the third row, but fled as fast as possible into the city and shut themselves up in it. During that day Alexander with his infantry encamped round the city, as much of it, at least, as his phalanx could surround; for he could not with his camp completely encircle the wall, so extensive was it. Opposite the part unenclosed by his camp, near which also was a lake, he posted the cavalry, placing them all round the lake, which he discovered to be shallow. Moreover, he conjectured that the Indians, being terrified at their previous defeat, would abandon the city in the night; and it turned out just as he had conjectured; for about the second watch of the night most of them dropped down from the wall, but fell in with [2] the sentinels of cavalry. The foremost of them were cut to pieces by these; but the men behind them perceiving that the lake was guarded all round, withdrew into the city again. Alexander now surrounded the city with a double stockade, except in the part where

---

[1] Compare Cæsar (*Bell. Gall.*, i. 26): pro vallo carros objecerant et e loco superiore in nostros venientes tela conjiciebant, et nonnulli inter carros rotasque mataras ac tragulas subjiciebant nostrosque vulnerabant.

[2] ἐγκυρεῖν is an epic and Ionic word rarely used in Attic; but found frequently in *Herodotus*, *Homer*, *Hesiod*, and *Pindar*.

the lake shut it in, and round the lake he posted more perfect guards. He also resolved to bring military engines up to the wall, to batter it down. But some of the men in the city deserted to him, and told him that the Indians intended that very night to steal out of the city and escape by the lake, where the gap in the stockade existed. He accordingly stationed Ptolemy, son of Lagus, there, giving him three regiments of the shield-bearing guards, all the Agrianians, and one line of archers, pointing out to him the place where he especially conjectured the barbarians would try to force their way. "When thou perceivest the barbarians forcing their way here," said he, "do thou, with the army obstruct their advance, and order the bugler to give the signal. And do you, O officers, as soon as the signal has been given, each being arrayed in battle order with your own men, advance towards the noise, wherever the bugle summons you. Nor will I myself withdraw from the action."

CHAPTER XXIV.

Capture of Sangala.

Such were the orders he gave; and Ptolemy collected there as many waggons as he could from those which had been left behind in the first flight, and placed them athwart, so that there might seem to the fugitives in the night to be many difficulties in their way; and as the stockade had been knocked down, or had not been firmly fixed in the ground, he ordered his men to heap up a mound of earth in various places between the lake and the wall. This his soldiers effected in the night. When it was about the fourth watch,[1] the barbarians, just as Alexander had been informed, opened the gates towards

[1] The Greeks had only three watches; but Arrian is speaking as a Roman.

the lake, and made a run in that direction. However they did not escape the notice of the guards there, nor that of Ptolemy, who had been placed behind them to render aid. But at this moment the buglers gave him the signal, and he advanced against the barbarians with his army fully equipped and drawn up in battle array. Moreover the waggons and the stockade which had been placed in the intervening space, were an obstruction to them. When the bugle sounded and Ptolemy attacked them, killing the men as they kept on stealing out through the waggons, then indeed they were driven back again into the city; and in their retreat 500 of them were killed. In the meanwhile Porus arrived, bringing with him the elephants that were left to him, and 5,000 Indians. Alexander had constructed his military engines and they were being led up to the wall; but before any of it was battered down, the Macedonians took the city by storm, digging under the wall, which was made of brick, and placing scaling ladders against it all round. In the capture 17,000 of the Indians were killed, and above 70,000 were captured, besides 300 chariots and 500 cavalry. In the whole siege a little less than 100 of Alexander's army were killed; but the number of the wounded was greater than the proportion of the slain, being more than 1,200, among whom were Lysimachus, the confidential bodyguard, and other officers. After burying the dead according to his custom, Alexander sent Eumenes, the secretary,[1] with 300 cavalry to the two cities which had joined

[1] Eumenes, of Cardia in Thrace, was private secretary to Philip and Alexander. After the death of the latter, he obtained the rule of Cappadocia, Paphlagonia, and Pontus. He displayed great ability both as a general and statesman; but was put to death by Antigonus in B.C. 316, when he was 45 years of age. Being a Greek, he was disliked by the Macedonian generals, from whom he experienced very unjust treatment. It is evident from the biographies of him written by Plutarch and Cornelius Nepos, that he was one of the most eminent men of his era.

Sangala in revolt, to tell those who held them about the capture of Sangala, and to inform them that they would receive no harsh treatment from Alexander if they stayed there and received him as a friend; for no harm had happened to any of the other independent Indians who had surrendered to him of their own accord. But they had become frightened, and had abandoned the cities and were fleeing; for the news had already reached them that Alexander had taken Sangala by storm. When Alexander was informed of their flight he pursued them with speed; but most of them were too quick for him, and effected their escape, because the pursuit began from a distant starting-place. But all those who were left behind in the retreat from weakness, were seized by the army and killed, to the number of about 500. Then, giving up the design of pursuing the fugitives any further, he returned to Sangala, and razed the city to the ground. He added the land to that of the Indians who had formerly been independent, but who had then voluntarily submitted to him. He then sent Porus with his forces to the cities which had submitted to him, to introduce garrisons into them; whilst he himself, with his army, advanced to the river Hyphasis,[1] to subjugate the Indians beyond it. Nor did there seem to him any end of the war, so long as anything hostile to him remained.

CHAPTER XXV.

The Army Refuses to Advance.—Alexander's Speech to the Officers.

It was reported that the country beyond the river Hyphasis was fertile, and that the men were good agri-

---

[1] Now called the Beas, or Bibasa. Strabo calls it Hypanis, and Pliny calls it Hypasis.

culturists, and gallant in war; and that they conducted their own political affairs in a regular and constitutional manner. For the multitude was ruled by the aristocracy, who governed in no respect contrary to the rules of moderation. It was also stated that the men of that district possessed a much greater number of elephants than the other Indians, and that those men were of very great stature, and excelled in valour. These reports excited in Alexander an ardent desire to advance farther; but the spirit of the Macedonians now began to flag, when they saw the king raising one labour after another, and incurring one danger after another. Conferences were held throughout the camp, in which those who were the most moderate bewailed their lot, while others resolutely declared that they would not follow Alexander any farther, even if he should lead the way. When he heard of this, before the disorder and pusillanimity of the soldiers should advance to a great degree, he called a council of the officers of the brigades and addressed them as follows:—"O Macedonians and Grecian allies, seeing that you no longer follow me into dangerous enterprises with a resolution equal to that which formerly animated you, I have collected you together into the same spot, so that I may either persuade you to march forward with me, or may be persuaded by you to return. If indeed the labours which you have already undergone up to our present position seem to you worthy of disapprobation, and if you do not approve of my leading you into them, there can be no advantage in my speaking any further. But, if as the result of these labours, you hold possession of Ionia,[1] the Hellespont, both the

[1] In the Hebrew Bible Javan denotes the Ionian race of Greeks, and then the Greeks in general (Gen. x. 2, 4; Isa. lxvi. 19; Ezek. xxvii. 13; Joel iii. 6; Zech. ix. 13). In Dan. viii. 21, x. 20, xi. 2, Javan stands for the kingdom of Alexander the Great, comprising Macedonia as well as Greece. The form of the name *Javan* is closely connected with the

Phrygias, Cappadocia, Paphlagonia, Lydia, Caria, Lycia, Pamphylia, Phoenicia, Egypt together with Grecian Libya, as well as part of Arabia, Hollow Syria, Syria between the rivers,[1] Babylon, the nation of the Susians, Persia, Media, besides all the nations which the Persians and the Medes ruled, and many of those which they did not rule, the land beyond the Caspian Gates, the country beyond the Caucasus, the Tanais, as well as the land beyond that river, Bactria, Hyrcania, and the Hyrcanian Sea; if we have also subdued the Scythians as far as the desert; if, in addition to these, the river Indus flows through our territory, as do also the Hydaspes, the Acesines, and the Hydraotes, why do ye shrink from adding the Hyphasis also, and the nations beyond this river, to your empire of Macedonia? Do ye fear that your advance will be stopped in the future by any other barbarians? Of whom some submit to us of their own accord, and others are captured in the act of fleeing, while others, succeeding in their efforts to escape, hand over to us their deserted land, which we add to that of our allies, or to that of those who have voluntarily submitted to us.

CHAPTER XXVI.

ALEXANDER'S SPEECH (*continued*).

"I, FOR my part, think, that to a brave man there is no end to labours except the labours themselves, provided

---

Greek *Ion*, which originally had a digamma, *Ivon*. Pott says that it means *the young*, in opposition to the *Graikoi*, the old. According to Aristotle (*Meteorologica*, i. 14) the Hellenes were originally called Graikoi. Cf. Sanscrit, *jewan*; Zend, *jawan*; Latin, *juvenis*; English, *young*.

[1] Coele-Syria, or the Hollow Syria, was the country between the ranges of Libanus and Antilibanus. Syria between the rivers is usually called by its Greek name of Mesopotamia. It is the Padan Aram of the Bible. Cappadocia embraced the whole north-eastern part of the peninsula of Asia Minor. Slaves were procured from this region. See Horace (*Epistles*, i. 6, 39); *Persius*, vi. 77. The name *Pamphylia* is from πᾶν and φυλή, because of the mixed origin of the inhabitants.

they lead to glorious achievements. But if any one desires to hear what will be the end to the warfare itself, let him learn that the distance still remaining before we reach the river Ganges and the Eastern Sea is not great; and I inform you that the Hyrcanian Sea will be seen to be united with this, because the Great Sea encircles the whole earth. I will also demonstrate both to the Macedonians and to the Grecian allies, that the Indian Gulf is confluent with the Persian, and the Hyrcanian Sea with the Indian Gulf. From the Persian Gulf our expedition will sail round into Libya as far as the Pillars of Heracles.[1] From the pillars all the interior of Libya [2] becomes ours, and so the whole of Asia [3] will belong to us, and the limits of our empire, in that direction, will be those which God has made also the limits of the earth. But, if we now return, many warlike nations are left unconquered beyond the Hyphasis as far as the Eastern Sea, and many besides between these and Hyrcania in the direction of the north wind, and not far from these the Scythian races. Wherefore, if we go back, there is reason to fear that the races which are now held in subjection, not being firm in their allegiance, may be excited to revolt by those who are not yet subdued. Then our

---

[1] Cf. Arrian (*Anabasis*, vii. 1; *Indica*, 43). *Herodotus* (iv. 42) says that Pharaoh Neco sent a Phoenician expedition from the Red Sea, which circumnavigated Africa and returned by the Straits of Gibraltar, or the Pillars of Hercules. The Carthaginian Hanno is said to have sailed from Cadiz to the extremity of Arabia. See Pliny (*Historia Naturalis*, ii. 67; v. 1). *Herodotus* (iv. 43) says that the Carthaginians asserted they had sailed round Africa. There is a Greek translation of Hanno's *Periplus* still extant. As to the Pillars of Hercules, see Aelian (*Varia Historia*, v. 3). They are first mentioned by Pindar (*Olym.* iii. 79; *Nem.* iii. 36).

[2] The interior of Africa, from the Straits of Gibraltar to Egypt, and from the Mediterranean to the then unexplored South.

[3] Arrian, like many other ancient writers, includes Africa, or Libya, as a part of Asia. The boundaries were the Eastern Sea and the Atlas Mountains. Cf. *Arrian*, iii. 30; vii. 1 and 30. The name Asia first occurs in Homer (*Iliad*, ii. 461), in reference to the marsh about the Caÿster, and was thence gradually extended over the whole continent.

many labours will prove to have been in vain; or it will be necessary for us to incur over again fresh labours and dangers, as at the beginning. But, O Macedonians and Grecian allies, stand firm! Glorious are the deeds of those who undergo labour and run the risk of danger; and it is delightful to live a life of valour and to die leaving behind immortal glory. Do ye not know that our ancestor[1] reached so great a height of glory as from being a man to become a god, or to seem to become one, not by remaining in Tiryns[2] or Argos, or even in the Peloponnese or at Thebes? The labours of Dionysus were not few, and he was too exalted a deity to be compared with Heracles. But we, indeed, have penetrated into regions beyond Nysa[3]; and the rock of Aornus, which Heracles was unable to capture, is in our possession. Do ye also add the parts of Asia still left unsubdued to those already acquired, the few to the many. But what great or glorious deed could we have performed, if, sitting at ease in Macedonia, we had thought it sufficient to preserve our own country without any labour, simply repelling the attacks of the nations on our frontiers, the Thracians, Illyrians, and Triballians, or even those Greeks who were unfriendly to our interests? If, indeed, without undergoing labour and being free from danger I were acting as your commander, while you were undergoing labour and incurring danger, not without reason would you be growing faint in spirit and resolution, because you alone would be sharing the labours, while procuring the rewards of them for others. But now the labours are common to you and me, we have an equal share of the dangers, and the rewards are open to the free competition of all. For the land is yours, and you act as its viceroys. The greater part also of the

---

[1] Heracles, from whom the Macedonian kings claimed to be descended.

[2] Hence Hercules is called Tirynthius. (Virgil, *Aeneid*, vii. 662; viii. 228).

[3] See chap. 1 of this book.

money now comes to you; and when we have traversed the whole of Asia, then, by Zeus, not merely having satisfied your expectations, but having even exceeded the advantages which each man hopes to receive, those of you who wish to return home I will send back to their own land, or I will myself lead them back; while those who remain here, I will make objects of envy to those who go back."[1]

CHAPTER XXVII.

The Answer of Coenus.

When Alexander had uttered these remarks, and others in the same strain, a long silence ensued, for the auditors neither had the audacity to speak in opposition to the king without constraint, nor did they wish to acquiesce in his proposal. Hereupon, he repeatedly urged any one who wished it, to speak, if he entertained different views from those which he had himself expressed. Nevertheless the silence still continued a long time; but at last, Coenus, son of Polemocrates, plucked up courage and spoke as follows[2]:—"O king, inasmuch as thou dost not wish to rule Macedonians by compulsion, but sayest thou wilt lead them by persuasion, or yielding to their persuasion wilt not use violence towards them, I am going to make a speech, not on my own behalf and that of my colleagues here present, who are held in greater honour than the other soldiers, and most of us have already carried off the rewards of our labours, and from our preeminence are more zealous than the rest to serve thee in all things; but I am going to speak on behalf of the bulk of the army. On behalf of this army I am not going to say what may be gratifying to the men, but what I consider to be both advantageous to thee at present, and safest for the future. I feel it incumbent upon me not

---

[1] Cf. Xenophon (*Anab.*, i. 7, 4). [2] Cf. *Curtius*, ix. 12.

to conceal what I think the best course to pursue, both on account of my age, the honour paid to me by the rest of the army at thy behest, and the boldness which I have without any hesitation displayed up to the present time in incurring dangers and undergoing labours. The more numerous and the greater the exploits have been, which were achieved by thee as our commander, and by those who started from home with thee, the more advantageous does it seem to me that some end should be put to our labours and dangers. For thou thyself seest how many Macedonians and Greeks started with thee, and how few of us have been left. Of our number thou didst well in sending back home the Thessalians at once from Bactra, because thou didst perceive that they were no longer eager to undergo labours.[1] Of the other Greeks, some have been settled as colonists in the cities which thou hast founded; where they remain not indeed all of them of their own free will. The Macedonian soldiers and the other Greeks who still continued to share our labours and dangers, have either perished in the battles, become unfit for war on account of their wounds, or been left behind in the different parts of Asia. The majority, however, have perished from disease, so that few are left out of many; and these few are no longer equally vigorous in body, while in spirit they are much more exhausted. All those whose parents still survive, feel a great yearning to see them once more; they feel a yearning after their wives and children, and a yearning for their native land itself; which it is surely pardonable for them to yearn to see again with the honour and dignity they have acquired from thee, returning as great men, whereas they departed small, and as rich men instead of being poor. Do not lead us now against our will; for thou wilt no longer find us the same men in

[1] *Arrian* (iii. 19) says that the Thessalians were sent back from Ecbatana.

regard to dangers, since free-will will be wanting to us in the contests. But, rather, if it seem good to thee, return to thy own land, see thy mother, regulate the affairs of the Greeks, and carry to the home of thy fathers these victories so many and great. Then start afresh on another expedition, if thou wishest, against these very tribes of Indians situated towards the east; or, if thou wishest, into the Euxine Sea [1]; or else against Carchedon and the parts of Libya beyond the Carchedonians.[2] It is now thy business to manage these matters; and the other Macedonians and Greeks will follow thee, young men in place of old, fresh men in place of exhausted ones, and men to whom warfare has no terrors, because up to the present time they have had no experience of it; and they will be eager to set out, from hope of future reward. The probability also is, that they will accompany thee with still more zeal on this account, when they see that those who in the earlier expedition shared thy labours and dangers have returned to their own abodes as rich men instead of being poor, and renowned instead of being obscure as they were before. Self-control in the midst of success is the noblest of all virtues, O king! For thou hast nothing to fear from enemies, while thou art commanding and leading such an army as this; but the visitations of the deity are unexpected, and consequently men can take no precautions against them."

CHAPTER XXVIII.

ALEXANDER RESOLVES TO RETURN.

WHEN Coenus had concluded this speech, loud applause was given to his words by those who were present; and the fact that many even shed tears, made it still more

---

[1] *Pontus Euxinus* antea ab inhospitali feritate *Axenos* appellatus (*Pliny*, vi. 1).

[2] The Latin name Carthago and the Greek Carchedon were corruptions of the Phoenician Carth-Hadeshoth, the "new city."

evident that they were disinclined to incur further hazards, and that return would be delightful to them. Alexander then broke up the conference, being annoyed at the freedom of speech in which Coenus indulged, and the hesitation displayed by the other officers. But the next day he called the same men together again in wrath, and told them that he intended to advance farther, but would not force any Macedonian to accompany him against his will; that he would have those only who followed their king of their own accord; and that those who wished to return home were at liberty to return and carry back word to their relations that they were come back, having deserted their king in the midst of his enemies. Having said this, he retired into his tent, and did not admit any of the Companions on that day, or until the third day from that, waiting to see if any change would occur in the minds of the Macedonians and Grecian allies, as is wont to happen as a general rule among a crowd of soldiers, rendering them more disposed to obey. But on the contrary, when there was a profound silence throughout the camp, and the soldiers were evidently annoyed at his wrath, without being at all changed by it, Ptolemy, son of Lagus, says that he none the less offered sacrifice there for the passage of the river, but the victims were unfavourable to him when he sacrificed. Then indeed he collected the oldest of the Companions and especially those who were friendly to him, and as all things indicated the advisability of returning, he made known to the army that he had resolved to march back again.

CHAPTER XXIX.

Alexander Recrosses the Hydraotes and Acesines.

Then they shouted as a mixed multitude would shout when rejoicing; and most of them shed tears of joy.

Some of them even approached the royal tent, and prayed for many blessings upon Alexander; because by them alone he suffered himself to be conquered. Then he divided the army into brigades, and ordered twelve altars to be prepared, equal in height to very large towers, and in breadth much larger than towers, to serve as thank-offerings to the gods who had led him so far as a conqueror, and also to serve as monuments of his own labours.[1] When the altars were completed, he offered sacrifice upon them according to his custom, and celebrated a gymnastic and equestrian contest. After adding the country as far as the river Hyphasis to the dominion of Porus, he marched back to the Hydraotes. Having crossed this river, he continued his return march to the Acesines, where he found the city which Hephaestion had been ordered to fortify, quite built. In this city he settled as many of the neighbouring people as volunteered to live in it, as well as those of the Grecian mercenaries who were now unfit for military service; and then began to make the necessary preparations for a voyage down the river into the Great Sea. At this time Arsaces, the ruler of the land bordering on that of Abisares, and the brother of the latter, with his other relations, came to Alexander, bringing the gifts which are reckoned most valuable among the Indians, including some elephants from Abisares, thirty in number. They declared that Abisares himself was unable to come on account of illness; and with these men the ambassadors sent by Alexander to Abisares agreed. Readily believing that such was the case, he granted that prince the privilege of ruling his own country as his viceroy, and placed Arsaces also under his power. After arranging what tribute they were

---

[1] *Pliny* (vi. 21), says that Alexander erected the altars on the farther bank of the Hyphasis, whereas Arrian, Diodorus, and Plutarch say they were on this side of the river. *Curtius* (ix. 13) does not specify the side of the river.

to pay, he again offered sacrifice near the river Acesines. He then crossed that river again, and came to the Hydaspes, where he employed the army in repairing the damage caused to the cities of Nicaea and Bucephala by the rain, and put the other affairs of the country in order.

BOOK VI.

CHAPTER I.

PREPARATIONS FOR A VOYAGE DOWN THE INDUS.

ALEXANDER now resolved to sail down the Hydaspes to the Great Sea, after he had prepared on the banks of that river many thirty-oared galleys and others with one and a half bank of oars, as well as a number of vessels for conveying horses, and all the other things requisite for the easy conveyance of an army on a river. At first he thought he had discovered the origin of the Nile, when he saw crocodiles in the river Indus, which he had seen in no other river except the Nile,[1] as well as beans growing near the banks of the Acesines of the same kind as those which the Egyptian land produces.[2] This conjecture was confirmed when he heard that the Acesines falls into the Indus. He thought the Nile rises somewhere or other in India, and after flowing through an extensive tract of desert country loses the name of Indus there; but afterwards when it begins to flow again through the inhabited land, it is called Nile both by the Aethiopians of that district and by the Egyptians, and

[1] *Herodotus* (iv. 44) says that the Indus is the only river besides the Nile which produces crocodiles. He does not seem to have known the Ganges.

[2] This was the *Nelumbium speciosum*, the Egyptian bean of Pythagoras the Lotus of the Hindus, held sacred by them. It is cultivated and highly valued in China, where it is eaten. The seeds are the shape and size of acorns.

finally empties itself into the Inner Sea.[1] In like manner Homer made the river Egypt give its name to the country of Egypt.[2] Accordingly when he wrote to Olympias about the country of India, after mentioning other things, he said that he thought he had discovered the sources of the Nile, forming his conclusions about things so great from such small and trivial premisses. However, when he had made a more careful inquiry into the facts relating to the river Indus, he learned the following details from the natives:—That the Hydaspes unites its water with the Acesines, as the latter does with the Indus, and that they both yield up their names to the Indus; that the last-named river has two mouths, through which it discharges itself into the Great Sea; but that it has no connection with the Egyptian country. He then removed from the letter to his mother the part he had written about the Nile.[3] Planning a voyage down the rivers as far as the Great Sea, he ordered ships for this purpose to be prepared for him. The crews of his ships were fully supplied from the Phoenicians, Cyprians, Carians, and Egyptians who accompanied the army.

CHAPTER II.

Voyage down the Hydaspes.

At this time Coenus, who was one of Alexander's most faithful Companions, fell ill and died, and the king buried him with as much magnificence as circumstances allowed. Then collecting the Companions and the Indian envoys who had come to him, he appointed Porus king of the part of India which had already been conquered, seven

---

[1] *I.e.* the Mediterranean.

[2] See *Arrian*, v. 6 supra. The native name of Egypt was *Chem* (black). Compare Vergil (*Georgic.* iv. 291):—Viridem Aegyptum *nigrâ* fecundat arenâ. Usque coloratis amnis devexus ab Indis.

[3] This use of ἀμφί with the dative is instead of the Attic περί with the genitive or accusative.

nations in all, containing more than 2,000 cities. After this he made the following distribution of his army.[1] With himself he placed on board the ships all the shield-bearing guards, the archers, the Agrianians, and the body-guard of cavalry.[2] Craterus led a part of the infantry and cavalry along the right bank of the Hydaspes, while along the other bank Hephaestion advanced at the head of the most numerous and efficient part of the army, including the elephants, which now numbered about 200. These generals were ordered to march as quickly as possible to the place where the palace of Sopeithes was situated,[3] and Philip, the viceroy of the country beyond the Indus[4] extending to Bactria, was ordered to follow them with his forces after an interval of three days. He sent the Nysaean cavalry back to Nysa.[5] The whole of the naval force was under the command of Nearchus; but the pilot of Alexander's ship was Onesicritus, who, in the narrative which he composed of Alexander's campaigns, falsely asserted that he was admiral, while in reality he was only a pilot.[6] According to Ptolemy, son of Lagus, whose statements I chiefly follow, the entire number of the ships was about eighty thirty-oared galleys; but the whole number of vessels, including the horse transports and boats, and all the other river craft, both those previously plying on the rivers and those built at that time, fell not far short of 2,000.[7]

---

[1] Plutarch (*Alex.* 66) informs us that Alexander's army numbered 120,000 infantry and 15,000 cavalry. Cf. Arrian (*Indica*, 19).

[2] Arrian, in the *Indica* (chap. 19), says that Alexander embarked with 8,000 men.

[3] *Strabo* (xv. 1) says that the realm of Sopeithes was called Cathaia.

[4] As Alexander was at this time east of the Indus, the expression, "beyond the Indus," means west of it.

[5] Cf. *Arrian*, v. 2 supra.

[6] Only fragments of this narrative are preserved. *Strabo* (xv. 1) says that the statements of Onesicritus are not to be relied upon.

[7] *Curtius* (ix. 13) and *Diodorus* (xvii. 95) say that there were 1,000 vessels. Arrian (*Indica*, 19) says there were 800. Krüger reads χιλίων in this passage instead of the common reading δισχιλίων.

CHAPTER III.

Voyage down the Hydaspes (*continued*).

When he had made all the necessary preparations the army began to embark at the approach of the dawn; while according to custom he offered sacrifice to the gods and to the river Hydaspes, as the prophets directed.[1] When he had embarked he poured a libation into the river from the prow of the ship out of a golden goblet, invoking the Acesines as well as the Hydaspes, because he had ascertained that it is the largest of all the rivers which unite with the Hydaspes, and that their confluence was not far off. He also invoked the Indus, into which the Acesines flows after its junction with the Hydaspes. Moreover he poured out libations to his forefather Heracles, to Ammon,[2] and the other gods to whom he was in the habit of sacrificing, and then he ordered the signal for starting seawards to be given with the trumpet. As soon as the signal was given they commenced the voyage in regular order; for directions had been given at what distance apart it was necessary for the baggage vessels to be arranged, as also for the vessels conveying the horses and for the ships of war; so that they might not fall foul of each other by sailing down the channel at random. He did not allow even the fast-sailing ships to get out of rank by outstripping the rest. The noise of the rowing was never equalled on any other occasion, inasmuch as it proceeded from so many ships rowed at the same time; also the shouting of the boatswains giving the time for beginning and stopping the stroke of the oars, and the clamour of the rowers, when keeping time all together with the

---

[1] From Arrian (*Indica*, 18) we learn that he sacrificed to his country gods, and to Poseidon, Amphitrite, the Nereids, the Ocean, as well as to the three rivers. Cf. i. 11, supra.

[2] Cf. iii. 3 supra.

dashing of the oars, made a noise like a battle-cry. The banks of the river also, being in many places higher than the ships, and collecting the sound into a narrow space, sent back to each other an echo which was very much increased by its very compression. In some parts too the groves of trees on each side of the river helped to swell the sound, both from the solitude and the reverberation of the noise. The horses which were visible on the decks of the transports struck the barbarians who saw them with such surprise that those of them who were present at the starting of the fleet accompanied it a long way from the place of embarkation. For horses had never before been seen on board ships in the country of India; and the natives did not call to mind that the expedition of Dionysus into India was a naval one. The shouting of the rowers and the noise of the rowing were heard by the Indians who had already submitted to Alexander, and these came running down to the river's bank and accompanied him singing their native songs. For the Indians have been eminently fond of singing and dancing since the time of Dionysus and those who under his bacchic inspiration traversed the land of the Indians with him.[1]

CHAPTER IV.

Voyage down the Hydaspes into the Acesines.

Sailing thus, he stopped on the third day at the spot where he had instructed Hephaestion and Craterus to encamp on opposite banks of the river at the same place. Here he remained two days, until Philip with the rest of the army came up with him. He then sent this general with the men he brought with him to the river Acesines, with orders to march along the bank of that river. He

[1] Cf. Arrian (*Indica*, 7).

also sent Craterus and Hephaestion off again with instructions how they were to conduct the march. But he himself continued his voyage down the river Hydaspes, the channel of which is nowhere less than twenty stades broad. Mooring his vessels near the banks wherever he could, he received some of the Indians dwelling near into allegiauce by their voluntary surrender, while he reduced by force those who came into a trial of strength with him. Then he sailed rapidly towards the country of the Mallians and Oxydracians, having ascertained that these tribes were the most numerous and the most warlike of the Indians in that region; and having been informed that they had put their wives and children for safety into their strongest cities, with the resolution of fighting a battle with him, he made the voyage with the greater speed with the express design of attacking them before they had arranged their plans, and while there was still lack of preparation and a state of confusion among them. Thence he made his second start, and on the fifth day reached the junction of the Hydaspes and Acesines. Where these rivers unite, one very narrow river is formed out of the two; and on account of its narrowness the curreut is swift. There are also prodigious eddies in the whirling stream, and the water rises in waves and plashes exceedingly, so that the noise of the swell of waters is distinctly heard by people while they are still far off. These things had previously been reported to Alexander by the natives, and he had told his soldiers; and yet, when his army approached the junction of the rivers, the noise made by the stream produced so great an impression upon them that the sailors stopped rowing, not from any word of command, but because the very boatswains who gave the time to the rowers became silent from astonishment and stood aghast at the noise.

CHAPTER V.

Voyage down the Acesines.

When they came near the junction of the rivers, the pilots passed on the order that the men should row as hard as possible to get out of the narrows, so that the ships might not fall into the eddies and be overturned by them, but might by the vigorous rowing overcome the whirlings of the water. Being of a round form, the merchant vessels which happened to be whirled round by the current received no damage from the eddy, but the men who were on board were thrown into disorder and fright. For being kept upright by the force of the stream itself, these vessels settled again into the onward course. But the ships of war, being long, did not emerge so scatheless from the whirling current, not being raised aloft in the same way as the others upon the plashing swell of water. These ships had two ranks of oars on each side, the lower oars being only a little out of the water. These vessels getting athwart in the eddies, their oars could not be raised aloft in proper time and were consequently caught by the water and came into collision with each other. Thus many of the ships were damaged; two indeed fell foul of each other and were destroyed, and many of those sailing in them perished.[1] But when the river widened out, there the current was no longer so rapid, and the eddies did not whirl round with so much violence. Alexander therefore moored his fleet on the right bank, where there was a protection from the force of the stream and a roadstead for the ships. A certain promontory also in the river jutted out conveniently for collecting the wrecks. He preserved the lives of the men

---

[1] Cf. *Curtius* (ix. 15); *Diodorus* (xvii. 97). The latter says that Alexander offered sacrifice to the gods for having escaped the greatest danger, and having contested with a river like Achilles.

who were still being conveyed upon them; and when he had repaired the damaged ships, he ordered Nearchus to sail down the river until he reached the confines of the nation called Mallians. He himself made an inroad into the territories of the barbarians who would not yield to him, and after preventing them from succouring the Mallians, he again formed a junction with the naval armament.[1] Hephaestion, Craterus, and Philip had already united their forces here. Alexander then transported the elephants, the brigade of Polysperchon, the horse-archers, and Philip with his army, across the river Hydaspes, and instructed Craterus to lead them. He sent Nearchus with the fleet with orders to set sail three days before the army started. He divided the rest of his army into three parts, and ordered Hephaestion to go five days in advance, so that if any should flee before the men under his own command and go rapidly forward they might fall in with Hephaestion's brigade and thus be captured. He also gave a part of the army to Ptolemy, son of Lagus, with orders to follow him after the lapse of three days, so that all those who fled from him and turned back again might fall in with Ptolemy's brigade. He ordered those in advance to wait, when they arrived at the confluence of the rivers Acesines and Hydraotes, until he himself came up; and he instructed Craterus and Ptolemy also to form a junction with him at the same place.

CHAPTER VI.

Campaign against the Mallians.

He then took the shield-bearing guards, the bowmen, the Agrianians, Peithon's brigade of men, who were

---

[1] According to *Diodorus* (xvii. 96) and *Curtius* (ix. 14) Alexander here made an expedition against the Sibi; defeated an army of 40,000 Indians, and captured the city of Agallassa.

called foot Companions, all the horse bowmen and half the cavalry Companions, and marched through a tract of country destitute of water against the Mallians, a tribe of the independent Indians.[1] On the first day he encamped near a small piece of water which was about 100 stades distant from the river Acesines. Having dined there and caused his army to rest a short time, he ordered every man to fill whatever vessel he had with water. After travelling the remaining part of that day and all the ensuing night a distance of about 400 stades, he at daybreak reached the city into which many of the Mallians had fled for refuge. Most of them were outside the city and unarmed, supposing that Alexander would never come against them through the waterless country. It was evident that he led his army by this route for this very reason, because it was difficult to lead an army this way, and consequently it appeared incredible to the enemy that he would lead his forces in this direction. He therefore fell upon them unexpectedly, and killed most of them without their even turning to defend themselves, since they were unarmed. He cooped the rest up in the city, and posted his cavalry all round the wall, because the phalanx of infantry had not yet[2] come up with him. He thus made use of his cavalry in place of a stockade. As soon as the infantry arrived, he sent Perdiccas with his own cavalry regiment and that of Clitus, as well as the Agrianians, against another city of the Mallians, whither many of the Indians of that region had fled for refuge. He ordered Perdiccas to blockade the men in the city, but not to commence the action until he himself should arrive, so that none might escape from this city and carry news to the rest of the bar-

---

[1] The chief city of the Mallians is the modern Mooltan.

[2] Μήπω. In later writers μή is often used where the Attic writers would use οὐ.

barians that Alexander was already approaching. He then began to assault the wall; but the barbarians abandoned it, finding that they were no longer able to defend it, since many had been killed in the capture, and others had been rendered unfit for fighting on account of their wounds. Fleeing for refuge into the citadel, they defended themselves for some time from a position commanding from its height and difficult of access. But as the Macedonians pressed on vigorously from all sides, and Alexander himself appeared now in this part of the action and now in that, the citadel was taken by storm, and all the men who had fled into it for refuge were killed, to the number of 2,000. Perdiccas also reached the city to which he had been despatched and found it deserted; but learning that the inhabitants had fled from it not long before, he made a forced march on the track of the fugitives. The light-armed troops followed him as quickly as they could on foot, so that he took and massacred as many of the fugitives as could not outstrip him and flee for safety into the river-marshes.

CHAPTER VII.

Campaign against the Mallians (*continued*).

After dining and causing his men to rest until the first watch of the night, Alexander marched forward; and travelling a great distance through the night, he arrived at the river Hydraotes[1] at daybreak. There he ascertained that most of the Mallians had already crossed the river; but coming upon those who were still in the act of crossing, he slew many of them in their passage. Having crossed with them in pursuit without any delay by the same ford, he kept close up with those who had out-

[1] Strabo and Curtius call this river Hyarotis.

stripped him in their retreat. Many also of these he slew; some he took prisoners; but the majority of them escaped into a place strong by nature and made more so by fortifications. When the infantry reached him, Alexander despatched Peithon against the men in the fortress, giving him the command of his own brigade of infantry and two regiments of cavalry. These, attacking the place, took it at the first assault, and made slaves of all those who had fled thither for safety, at least as many of them as had not perished in the attack. After accomplishing this, Peithon returned again to the camp. Alexander in person led his forces against a certain city of the Brachmans,[1] because he ascertained that some of the Mallians had fled for refuge into it. When he reached it, he led his phalanx in serried ranks close up to the wall on all sides. The enemy seeing that their walls were being undermined, and being themselves repulsed by the missiles, abandoned the walls, and having fled for safety into the citadel, began to defend themselves from thence. A few Macedoniaus having rushed in with them, turning round and drawing together into a close body, drove some of them back and killed five-and-twenty of them in their retreat. Hereupon Alexander ordered the scaling-ladders to be placed against the citadel on all sides, and the wall to be undermined; and when one of the towers, being undermined, fell down, and a part of the wall between two towers was breached, and thus rendered the citadel more accessible to assault in this quarter, he was seen to be the first man to scale the wall and get hold of it. The other Macedonians seeing him were ashamed of themselves and mounted the ladders in various places. The citadel was soon in their possession. Some of the Indians began to set fire to

---

[1] The Brachmans, or Brahmins, were a religious caste of Indians. The name was sometimes used for the people whose religion was Brahminism. Cf. Arrian (*Indica*, 11); *Strabo*, xv. 1; p. 713 ed. *Casaubon*.

the houses, and being caught in them were killed; but most of them were slain fighting. About 5,000 in all were killed; and on account of their valour, only a few were taken prisoners.

CHAPTER VIII.

Defeat of the Mallians at the River Hydraotes.

Having remained there one day to give his army rest, he advanced on the morrow against the other Mallians. He found the cities abandoned, and ascertained that the men had fled into the desert. There he again gave the army one day's rest, and on the next day sent Peithon and Demetrius the cavalry general back to the river, in command of their own troops, giving them in addition as many battalions of the light-armed infantry as were sufficient for the enterprise. Their instructions were to go along the bank of the river, and if they met any of those who had fled for safety into the woods, of which there were many near the river's bank, to kill all who refused to surrender. Peithon and Demetrius captured many of these in the woods and killed them. He himself led his forces against the largest city of the Mallians, whither he was informed many from the other cities had taken refuge. But this also the Indians abandoned when they heard that Alexander was marching against it. Crossing the river Hydraotes, they remained with their forces drawn up upon its bank, because it was high, and they thought they could obstruct Alexander's passage. When he heard this, he took all the cavalry which he had with him, and went to the part of the river where he was informed that the Mallians had drawn themselves up for battle; and the infantry was ordered to follow. When he reached the river and beheld the enemy drawn up on the opposite bank, he made no delay, but instantly plunged into the ford with the cavalry alone. When they saw that he was now in the middle of the river, though they were drawn up ready for battle, they withdrew from the bank with all speed; and Alexander followed them with his cavalry alone. But when the Indians perceived only cavalry, they wheeled round and fought with desperate valour, being about 50,000 in number. When Alexander perceived that their phalanx was densely compact, and that his own infantry was absent, he rode right round their army and made charges upon them, but did not come to close fighting with them. Meanwhile the archers, the Agrianians and the other battalions of light-armed infantry, being picked men whom he was leading with him, arrived, and his phalanx of infantry was seen not far off. As all kinds of danger were threatening them at once, the Indians now wheeled round again and began to flee with headlong speed into the strongest of their adjacent cities; but Alexander followed them and slew many, while those who escaped into the city were cooped up within it. At first indeed he surrounded the city with the horse-soldiers as they came up from the march; but when the infantry arrived, he encamped all round the wall for this day, because not much of it was left for making the assault, and his army had been exhausted, the infantry by the long march, and the cavalry by the uninterrupted pursuit, and especially by the passage of the river.

CHAPTER IX.

Storming of the Mallian Stronghold.

On the following day, dividing the army into two parts, he himself assaulted the wall at the head of one, and Perdiccas led on the other. Upon this the Indians did not wait to receive the attack of the Macedonians, but abandoned the walls of the city and fled for safety into the citadel. Alexander and his troops therefore split open a small gate, and got within the city long before the others; for those who had been put under Perdiccas were behind time, having experienced difficulty in scaling the walls, as most of them did not bring ladders, thinking that the city had been captured, when they observed that the walls were deserted by the defenders. But when the citadel was seen to be still in the possession of the enemy, and many of them were observed drawn up in front of it to repel attacks, some of the Macedonians tried to force an entry by undermining the wall, and others by placing scaling ladders against it, wherever it was practicable to do so. Alexander, thinking that the men who carried the ladders were too slow, snatched one from a man who was carrying it, placed it against the wall, and began to mount it, crouching under his shield. After him mounted Peucestas, the man who carried the sacred shield which Alexander took from the temple of the Trojan Athena and used to keep with him, and have it carried before him in all his battles.[1] After Peucestas, by the same ladder ascended Leonnatus the confidential body-guard; and up another ladder went Abreas, one of the soldiers who received double pay for distinguished services.[2] The king was now near the battlement of the wall, and leaning his shield against it was pushing some of the Indians within the fort, and had cleared that part of the wall, by killing others with his sword. The shield-bearing guards becoming very anxious for the king's safety, pushed each other with ardour up the same ladder and broke it; so that those who were already mounting fell down and made the ascent impracticable for the rest. Alexander then, standing upon the wall, was being assailed all round from the adjacent towers; for none of the Indians dared approach him. He was also being assailed by the men in the city, who were throwing darts at him from no great distance; for a mound of earth happened to have been heaped up

---

[1] Cf. *Arrian* i. 11 supra.

[2] The Romans called these men *duplicarii*. See *Livy*, ii. 59; vii. 37.

there opposite the wall. Alexander was conspicuous both by the brightness of his weapons and by his extraordinary display of audacity. He therefore perceived that if he remained where he was, he would be incurring danger without being able to perform anything at all worthy of consideration; but if he leaped down within the fort he might perhaps by this very act strike the Indians with terror, and if he did not, but should only thereby be incurring danger, at any rate he would die not ignobly after performing great deeds of valour worthy of recollection by men of after times.[1] Forming this resolution, he leaped down from the wall into the citadel; where, supporting himself against the wall, he struck with his sword and killed some of the Indians who came to close quarters with him, including their leader, who rushed upon him too boldly. Another man who approached him he kept in check by hurling a stone at him, and a third in like manner. Those who advanced nearer to him he again kept off with his sword; so that the barbarians were no longer willing to approach him, but standing round him cast at him from all sides whatever any one happened to have or could get hold of at the time.

CHAPTER X.

Alexander Dangerously Wounded.

Meantime Peucestas and Abreas, the soldier entitled to double pay, and after them Leonnatus, being the only men who happened to have scaled the wall before the ladders were broken, had leaped down and were fighting in front of the king. Abreas, the man entitled to double pay, fell there, being shot with an arrow in the forehead. Alexander himself also was wounded with an arrow under the breast through his breastplate into the chest, so that

---

[1] *τοῖς ἔπειτα πυθέσθαι.* Cf. Homer (*Iliad*, xxii. 305; ii. 119).

Ptolemy says air was breathed out from the wound together with the blood. But although he was faint with exhaustion, he defended himself, as long as his blood was still warm. But the blood streaming out copiously and without ceasing at every expiration of breath, he was seized with a dizziness and swooning, and bending over fell upon his shield. After he had fallen Peucestas defended him, holding over him in front the sacred shield brought from Troy; and on the other side he was defended by Leonnatus. But both these men were themselves wounded, and Alexander was now nearly fainting away from loss of blood. For the Macedonians had experienced great difficulty in the assault also on this account, because those who saw Alexander being shot at upon the wall and then leaping down into the citadel within, in their ardour arising from fear lest their king should meet with any mishap by recklessly exposing himself to danger, broke the ladders. Then some began to devise one plan and others another to mount upon the wall, as well as they could in their state of embarrassment, some fixing pegs into the wall, which was made of earth, and suspending themselves from these hoisted themselves up with difficulty by their means; others got up by mounting one upon the other. The first man who got up threw himself down from the wall into the city, and so on in succession; and when they saw the king lying there on the ground they all raised a loud lamentation and howl of grief. Now ensued a desperate conflict around his fallen body, one Macedonian after another holding his shield in front of him. In the meantime some of the soldiers having shivered in pieces the bar by which the gate in the space of wall between the towers was secured, entered the city a few at the time; while others, inasmuch as a gap had been made in the gate, put their shoulders under it and forced it into the space inside the wall, and thus laid the citadel open in that quarter.

CHAPTER XI.

Alexander Wounded.

Hereupon some of them began to kill the Indians, all of whom they slew, sparing not even a woman or child. Others carried off the king, who was lying in a faint condition, upon his shield; and they could not yet tell whether he was likely to survive. Some authors have stated that Critodemus, a physician of Cos, an Asclepiad by birth,[1] made an incision into the injured part and drew the weapon out of the wound. Other authors say that as there was no physician present at the critical moment, Perdiccas, the confidential body-guard, at Alexander's bidding, made an incision with his sword into the wounded part and removed the weapon. On its removal there was such a copious effusion of blood that Alexander swooned again; and the effect of the swoon was, that the effusion of blood was stanched.[2] Many other things concerning this catastrophe have been recorded by the historians; and Rumour having received the statements as they were given by the first falsifiers of the facts, still preserves them even to our times, nor will she desist from handing the falsehoods on to others also in regular succession, unless a stop is put to it by this history.[3] For example, the common account is, that this calamity befell Alexander among the Oxydracians; whereas, it really occurred among the Mallians, an independent tribe

---

[1] *Curtius* (ix. 22) calls the physician Critobulus. Near the city of Cos stood the Asclepiēum, or temple of Asclepius, to whom the island was sacred, and from whom the chief family, the Asclepiadae, claimed descent. Curtius says:—Igitur patefacto latius vulnere, et spiculo evolso, ingens vis sanguinis manare coepit, linquique animo rex, et caligine oculis offusa, veluti moribundus extendi.

[2] Cf. Plutarch (*Alex.* 63); *Diodorus* (xvii. 98, 99); *Curtius* (ix. 18–23); *Justin* (xii. 9).

[3] As to Fame, or Rumour, see Homer (*Iliad*, ii. 93; *Odyss.* xxiv. 412); Hesiod (*Works and Days*, 758–762); Vergil (*Aeneid*, iv. 173–190); Ovid (*Met.* xii. 39–63); Statius (*Theb.* ii. 426).

of Indians; the city belonged to the Mallians,[1] and the men who wounded him were Mallians. These people, indeed, had resolved to join their forces with the Oxydracians and then to make a desperate struggle; but he forestalled them by marching against them through the waterless country, before any aid could reach them from the Oxydracians, or they could render any help to the latter. Moreover, the common account is, that the last battle fought with Darius was near Arbela, at which battle he fled and did not desist from flight until he was arrested by Bessus and put to death at Alexander's approach; just as the battle before this was at Issus, and the first cavalry battle near the Granicus. The cavalry battle did really take place near the Granicus, and the next battle with Darius near Issus; but those authors who make Arbela most distant say that it is 600[2] stades distant from the place where the last battle between Alexander and Darius was fought, while those who make it least distant, say that it is 500 stades off. Moreover, Ptolemy and Aristobulus say that the battle was fought at Gaugamela near the river Bumodus. But as Gaugamela was not a city, but only a large village, the place is not celebrated, nor is the name pleasing to the ear; hence, it seems to me, that Arbela, being a city, has carried off the glory of the great battle. But if it is necessary to consider that this engagement took place near Arbela, being in reality so far distant from it, then it is allowable to say that the sea-battle fought at Salamis occurred near the isthmus[3] of the Corinthians, and that fought at Artemisium, in Euboea, occurred near Aegina or Sunium. Moreover, in regard to those who covered Alexander with their shields in his peril, all agree that Peucestas did so; but they no longer

[1] *Curtius* (ix. 18) says it was the town of the Oxydracians.

[2] Nearly 70 miles.

[3] *Isthmus* is from the same root as *ἰέναι*, *to go*, and thus means a *passage*. Pindar (*Isthmia*, iv. 34) calls it the "bridge of the sea."

agree in regard to Leonnatus or Abreas, the soldier in receipt of double pay for his distinguished services. Some say that Alexander, having received a blow on the head with a piece of wood, fell down in a fit of dizziness; and that having risen again he was wounded with a dart through the corselet in the chest. But Ptolemy, son of Lagus, says that he received only this wound in the chest. However, in my opinion, the greatest error made by those who have written the history of Alexander is the following. There are some who have recorded[1] that Ptolemy, son of Lagus, in company with Peucestas, mounted the ladder with Alexander; that Ptolemy held his shield over him when he lay wounded, and that he was called Soter (the preserver) on that account.[2] And yet Ptolemy himself has recorded that he was not even present at this engagement, but was fighting battles against other barbarians at the head of another army. Let me mention these facts as a digression from the main narrative, so that the correct account of such great deeds and calamities may not be a matter of indifference to men of the future.[3]

CHAPTER XII.

Anxiety of the Soldiers about Alexander.

While Alexander was remaining in this place until his wound was cured, the first news which reached the camp from which he had set out to attack the Mallians was

---

[1] We learn from *Curtius* (ix. 21) that the authors who stated that Ptolemy was present in this battle were Clitarchus and Timagenes. From the history of the former, who was a contemporary of Alexander, Curtius mainly drew the materials for his history of Alexander.

[2] Ptolemy received this appellation from the Rhodians whom he relieved from the assaults of Demetrius. The grateful Rhodians paid him divine honours as their preserver, and he was henceforward known as Ptolemy Soter. B.C. 304. See *Pausanias*, i. 8, 6.

[3] The word ἀταλαίπωρος is used in a similar way by *Thucydides*, i. 20, 4.

that he had died of the wound; and at first there arose a sound of lamentation from the entire army, as one man handed the rumour on to another. When they ceased their lamentation, they became spiritless, and felt perplexed as to the man who was to become the leader of the army; for many of the officers seemed to have stood in equal rank and merit, both in the opinion of Alexander and in that of the Macedonians. They were also in a state of perplexity how to get back in safety to their own country, being quite enclosed by so many warlike nations, some of whom had not yet submitted, and who they conjectured would fight stoutly for their freedom; while others would no doubt revolt as soon as they were relieved of their fear of Alexander. Besides, they seemed at that time to be in the midst of impassable rivers, and all things appeared to them uncertain and impracticable now that they were bereft of Alexander. But when at length the news came that he was still alive, they with difficulty acquiesced in it; and did not yet believe that he was likely to survive. Even when a letter came from the king, saying that he was coming down to the camp in a short time, this did not appear to most of them worthy of credit, on account of their excessive fear; for they conjectured that the letter was concocted by his confidential body-guards and generals.

CHAPTER XIII.

Joy of the Soldiers at Alexander's Recovery.

When Alexander became acquainted with this, for fear some attempt at a revolution might be made in the army, he had himself conveyed, as soon as it could be done with safety, to the bank of the river Hydraotes, and placed in a boat to sail down the river. For the camp was at the confluence of the Hydraotes and Acesines, where Hephaestion was at the head of the army, and Nearchus of the fleet. When the ship bearing the king approached the camp, he ordered the tent covering to be removed from the stern, that he might be visible to all. But they were still incredulous, thinking, forsooth, that Alexander's corpse was being conveyed on the vessel; until at length he stretched out his hand to the multitude, when the ship was nearing the bank. Then the men raised a cheer, lifting their hands, some towards the sky and others to the king himself. Many even shed involuntary tears at the unexpected sight. Some of the shield-bearing guards brought a litter for him when he was conveyed out of the ship; but he ordered them to fetch his horse. When he was seen again mounting his horse, the whole army re-echoed with loud clapping of hands, so that the banks of the river and the groves near them reverberated with the sound. On approaching his tent he dismounted from his horse, so that he might be seen walking. Then the men came near, some on one side, others on the other, some touching his hands, others his knees, others only his clothes. Some only came close to get a sight of him, and went away having chanted his praise, while others threw garlands upon him, or the flowers which the country of India supplied at that season of the year. Nearchus says that some of his friends incurred his displeasure, reproaching him for exposing himself to danger in the front of the army in battle; which they said was the duty of a private soldier, and not that of the general.[1] It seems to me that Alexander was offended at these remarks, because he knew that they were correct, and that he deserved the censure. However, like those who are

---

[1] *Curtius* (ix. 24) says that Craterus was deputed by the officers to make this representation to the king, and that he was backed up by Ptolemy and the rest.

mastered by any other pleasure, he had not sufficient self-control to keep aloof from danger, through his impetuosity in battle and his passion for glory. Nearchus also says that a certain old Boeotian, whose name he does not mention, perceiving that Alexander was offended at the censures of his friends and was looking sullenly at them, came near him, and speaking in the Boeotian dialect, said: "O Alexander, it is the part of heroes to perform great deeds!" and repeated a certain Iambic verse, the purport of which is, that the man who performs anything great is destined also to suffer.[1] This man was not only acceptable to Alexander at the time, but was afterwards received into his more intimate acquaintance.

CHAPTER XIV.

Voyage down the Hydraotes and Acesines into the Indus.

At this time arrived envoys from the Mallians who still survived, offering the submission of the nation; also from the Oxydracians came both the leaders of the cities and the governors of the provinces, accompanied by the other 150 most notable men, with full powers to make a treaty, bringing the gifts which are considered most valuable among the Indians, and also, like the Mallians, offering the submission of their nation. They said that their error in not having sent an embassy to him before was pardonable, because they excelled other races in the desire to be free and independent, and their freedom had been secure from the time Dionysus came into India until Alexander came; but if it seemed good to him, inasmuch as there was a general report that

---

[1] This line is a fragment from one of the lost tragedies of Aeschylus: δράσαντι γάρ τι καὶ παθεῖν ὀφείλεται.

he also was sprung from gods, they were willing to receive whatever viceroy he might appoint, pay the tribute decreed by him, and give him as many hostages as he might demand. He therefore demanded the thousand best men of the nation, whom he might hold as hostages, if he pleased; and if not, that he might keep them as soldiers in his army, until he had finished the war which he was waging against the other Indians. They accordingly selected the thousand best and tallest men of their number, and sent them to him, together with 500 chariots and charioteers, though these were not demanded. Alexander appointed Philip viceroy over these people and the Mallians who were still surviving. He sent back the hostages to them, but retained the chariots. When he had satisfactorily arranged these matters, since many vessels had been built during the delay arising from his being wounded,[1] he embarked 1,700 of the cavalry Companions, as many of the light-armed troops as before, and 10,000 infantry, and sailed a short distance down the river Hydraotes. But when that river mingled its waters with the Acesines, the latter giving its name to the united stream, he continued his voyage down the Acesines, until he reached its junction with the Indus. For these four large rivers,[2] which are all navigable, discharge their water into the river Indus, though each does not retain its distinct name. for the Hydaspes discharges itself into the Acesines, and after the junction the whole stream forms what is called the Acesines. Again this same river unites with the Hydraotes, and after absorbing this river, still retains its own name. After this the Acesines takes in the

---

[1] *Curtius* (ix. 23) says that he was cured of his wound in seven days. *Diodorus* (xvii. 99) says that it took many days.

[2] Arrian does not mention the Sutledj, which is the fifth of the rivers of the Punjab. *Pliny* (vi. 21) calls it Hesidrus; *Ptolemy* (vii. 1) calls it Zaradrus.

Hyphasis, and finally flows into the Indus under its own name; but after the junction it yields its name to the Indus. From this point I have no doubt that the Indus proceeds 100 stades,[1] and perhaps more, before it is divided so as to form the Delta; and there it spreads out more like a lake than a river.

CHAPTER XV.

Voyage down the Indus to the Land of Musicanus.

There, at the confluence of the Acesines and Indus, he waited until Perdiccas with the army arrived, after having routed on his way the independent tribe of the Abastanians.[2] Meantime, he was joined by other thirty-oared galleys and trading vessels which had been built for him among the Xathrians, another independent tribe of Indians who had yielded to him. From the Ossadians, who were also an independent tribe of Indians, came envoys to offer the submission of their nation. Having fixed the confluence of the Acesines and Indus as the limit of Philip's viceroyalty, he left with him all the Thracians and as many men from the infantry regiments as appeared to him sufficient to provide for the security of the country. He then ordered a city to be founded there at the very junction of the two rivers, expecting that it would become large and famous among men.[3] He also ordered a dockyard to be made there. At this time

---

[1] About 12 miles. Ita se findente Nilo ut triquestram terrae figuram efficiat. Ideo multi Graecae literae vocabulo Delta appellavere Aegyptum (*Pliny*, v. 9).

[2] This tribe dwelt between the Acesines and the Indus. *Diodorus* (xvii. 102) calls them Sambastians; while *Curtius* (ix. 30) calls them Sabarcians. The Xathrians and Ossadians dwelt on the left bank of the Indus.

[3] We find from *Curtius* (ix. 31) and *Diodorus* (xvii. 102) that the name of this was Alexandria. It is probably the present Mittun.

the Bactrian Oxyartes, father of his wife Roxana, came to him, to whom he gave the viceroyalty over the Parapamisadians, after dismissing the former viceroy, Tiryaspes, because he was reported to be exercising his authority improperly.[1] Then he transported Craterus with the main body of the army and the elephants to the left bank of the river Indus, both because it seemed easier for a heavy-armed force to march along that side of the river, and the tribes dwelling near were not quite friendly. He himself sailed down to the capital of the Sogdians; where he fortified another city, made another dockyard, and repaired his shattered vessels. He appointed Oxyartes viceroy, and Peithon general of the land extending from the confluence of the Indus and Acesines as far as the sea, together with all the coast-land of India. He then again despatched Craterus with his army through the country of the Arachotians and Drangians; and himself sailed down the river into the dominions of Musicanus, which was reported to be the most prosperous part of India. He advanced against this king because he had not yet come to meet him to offer the submission of himself and his land, nor had he sent envoys to seek his alliance. He had not even sent him the gifts which were suitable for a great king, or asked any favour from him. He accelerated his voyage down the river to such a degree that he succeeded in reaching the confines of the land of Musicanus before he had even heard that Alexander had started against him. Musicanus was so greatly alarmed that he went as fast as he could to meet him, bringing with him the gifts valued most highly among the Indians, and taking all his elephants. He offered to surrender both his nation and himself, at the same time acknow-

---

[1] *Curtius* (ix. 31) calls this satrap Terioltes, and says he was put to death. His appointment as viceroy is mentioned by *Arrian* (iv. 22 supra).

ledging his error, which was the most effectual way with Alexander for any one to get what he requested. Accordingly for these considerations Alexander granted him an indemnity for his offences. He also granted him the privilege of ruling the city and country, both of which Alexander admired. Craterus was directed to fortify the citadel in the capital; which was done while Alexander was still present. A garrison was also placed in it, because he thought the place suitable for keeping the circumjacent tribes in subjection.

CHAPTER XVI.

Campaign against Oxycanus and Sambus.

Then he took the archers, Agrianians, and cavalry sailing with him, and marched against the governor of that country, whose name was Oxycanus,[1] because he neither came himself nor did envoys come from him, to offer the surrender of himself and his land. At the very first assault he took by storm the two largest cities under the rule of Oxycanus; in the second of which that prince himself was captured. The booty he gave to his army, but the elephants he led with himself. The other cities in the same land surrendered to him as he advanced, nor did any one turn to resist him; so cowed in spirit[2] had all the Indians now become at the thought of Alexander and his fortune. He then marched back against Sambus, whom he had appointed viceroy of the mountaineer Indians and who was reported to have fled, because he learned that Musicanus had been pardoned by Alexander and was ruling over his own land. For he was at war with Musicanus.

---

[1] This king is called Porticanus by *Curtius* (ix. 31), *Diodorus* (xvii. 102), and *Strabo* (xv. 1).

[2] An expression imitated from *Thucydides* (iv. 34). Cf. *Arrian*, ii. 10; v. 19; where the same words are used of Darius and Porus.

But when Alexander approached the city which the country of Sambus held as its metropolis, the name of which was Sindimana, the gates were thrown open to him at his approach, and the relations of Sambus reckoned up his money and went out to meet him, taking with them the elephants also. They assured him that Sambus had fled, not from any hostile feeling towards Alexander, but fearing on account of the pardon of Musicanus.[1] He also captured another city which had revolted at this time, and slew as many of the Brachmans[2] as had been instigators of this revolt. These men are the philosophers of the Indians, of whose philosophy, if such it may be called, I shall give an account in my book descriptive of India.[3]

CHAPTER XVII.

Musicanus Executed.—Capture of Patala.

Meantime he was informed that Musicanus had revolted. He despatched the viceroy, Peithon, son of Agenor, with a sufficient army against him, while he himself marched against the cities which had been put under the rule of Musicanus. Some of these he razed to the ground, reducing the inhabitants to slavery; and into others he introduced garrisons and fortified the citadels. After accomplishing this, he returned to the camp and fleet. By this time Musicanus had been captured by Peithon, who was bringing him to Alexander. The king ordered him to be hanged in his own country, and with him as many of the Brachmans as had instigated him to the revolt. Then came to him the ruler of the land of the Patalians,[4]

---

[1] *Diodorus* (xvii. 102) says that Sambus escaped beyond the Indus with thirty elephants.

[2] See note, page 327 supra.

[3] The *Indica*, a valuable work still existing. See chapters x. and xi. of that book.

[4] These people inhabited the Delta of the Indus, which is now called Lower Scinde. Their capital, Patala, is the modern Tatta.

who said that the Delta formed by the river Indus was still larger than the Egyptian Delta.[1] This man surrendered to him the whole of his own land and entrusted both himself and his property to him. Alexander sent him away again in possession of his own dominions, with instructions to provide whatever was needful for the reception of the army. He then sent Craterus into Carmania with the brigades of Attalus, Meleager, and Antigenes, some of the archers, and as many of the Companions and other Macedonians as, being now unfit for military service, he was despatching to Macedonia by the route through the lands of the Arachotians and Zarangians. To Craterus he also gave the duty of leading the elephants; but the rest of the army, except the part of it which was sailing with himself down to the sea, he put under the command of Hephaestion. He transported Peithon with the cavalry-lancers and Agrianians to the opposite bank of the Indus, not the one along which Hephaestion was about to lead the army. Peithon was ordered to collect men to colonize the cities which had just been fortified, and to form a junction with the king at Patala, after having settled the affairs of the Indians of that region, if they attempted any revolutionary proceedings. On the third day of his voyage, Alexander was informed that the governor of the Patalians[2] had collected most of his subjects and was going away by stealth, having left his land deserted. For this reason Alexander sailed down the river with greater speed than before[3]; and when he arrived at Patala, he found both the country and the city deserted by the inhabitants and tillers of the soil. He however despatched the light-

---

[1] Cf. Arrian (*Indica*, ii.).

[2] *Curtius* (ix. 34) calls this king Moeris.

[3] Aristobulus, as quoted by *Strabo* (xv. 1), said that the voyage down the Indus occupied ten months, the fleet arriving at Patala about the time of the rising of Sirius, or July, 325 B.C.

ost troops in his army in pursuit of the fugitives; and when some of them were captured, he sent them away to the rest, bidding them be of good courage and return, for they might inhabit the city and till the country as before. Most of them accordingly returned.

CHAPTER XVIII.

Voyage down the Indus.

After instructing Hephaestion to fortify the citadel in Patala, he sent men into the adjacent country, which was waterless, to dig wells and to render the land fit for habitation. Certain of the native barbarians attacked these men, and falling upon them unawares slew some of them; but having lost many of their own men, they fled into the desert. The work was therefore accomplished by those who had been sent out, another army having joined them, which Alexander had despatched to take part in the work, when he heard of the attack of the barbarians. Near Patala the water of the Indus is divided into two large rivers, both of which retain the name of Indus as far as the sea. Here Alexander constructed a harbour and dockyard; and when his works had advanced towards completion he resolved to sail down as far as the mouth of the right branch of the river.[1] He gave Leonnatus the command of 1,000 cavalry and 8,000 heavy and light-armed infantry, and sent him to march through the island of Patala opposite the naval expedition; while he himself took the fastest sailing vessels, having one and a half bank of oars, all the thirty-oared galleys, and some of the boats, and began to sail down the right branch of the river. The Indians of that region had fled, and conse-

---

[1] The right arm of the Indus is now called the Buggaur, and the left Sata.

quently he could get no pilot for the voyage, and the navigation of the river was very difficult. On the day after the start a storm arose, and the wind blowing right against the stream made the river hollow [1] and shattered the hulls of the vessels violently, so that most of his ships were injured, and some of the thirty-oared galleys were entirely broken up. But they succeeded in running them aground before they quite fell to pieces in the water; and others were therefore constructed. He then sent the quickest of the light-armed troops into the land beyond the river's bank and captured some Indians, who from this time piloted him down the channel. But when they arrived at the place where the river expands, so that where it was widest it extended 200 stades, a strong wind blew from the outer sea, and the oars could hardly be raised in the swell; they therefore took refuge again in a canal into which his pilots conducted them.

CHAPTER XIX.

Voyage down the Indus into the Sea.

While their vessels were moored here, the phenomenon of the ebb and flow of the tide in the great sea occurred, so that their ships were left upon dry ground. This caused Alexander and his companions no small alarm, inasmuch as they were previously quite unacquainted with it. But they were much more alarmed when, the time coming round again, the water approached and the hulls of the vessels were raised aloft.[2] The ships which it caught settled in the mud were raised aloft without any damage,

---

[1] *I.e.* caused a heavy swell of waters. Cf. *Apollonius Rhodius*, ii. 595; *Polybius*, i. 60, 6. This wind was the south-west monsoon.

[2] Cf. *Curtius* (ix. 35, 36); Caesar (*Bell. Gall.* iv. 29). τὰ σκάφη ἐμετεωρίζοντο. Arrian does not comply with the Attic rule, that the plural neuter should take a verb in the singular. Compare ii. 20, 8; v. 17, 6 and 7; etc.

and floated again without receiving any injury; but those that had been left on the drier land and had not a firm settlement, when an immense compact wave advanced, either fell foul of each other or were dashed against the land and thus shattered to pieces. When Alexander had repaired these vessels as well as his circumstances permitted, he sent some men on in advance down the river in two boats to explore the island at which the natives said he must moor his vessels in his voyage to the sea. They told him that the name of the island was Cilluta.[1] As he was informed that there were harbours in this island, that it was a large one and had plenty of water in it, he made the rest of his fleet put in there; but he himself with the best sailing ships advanced beyond, to see if the mouth of the river afforded an easy voyage out into the open sea. After advancing about 200 stades from the first island, they descried another which was quite out in the sea. Then indeed they returned to the island in the river; and having moored his vessels near the extremity of it, Alexander offered sacrifice to those gods to whom he said he had been directed by Ammon to sacrifice. On the following day he sailed down to the other island which was in the deep sea; and having come to shore here also, he offered other sacrifices to other gods and in another manner. These sacrifices he also offered according to the oracular instructions of Ammon. Then having gone beyond the mouths of the river Indus, he sailed out into the open sea, as he said, to discover if any land lay anywhere near in the sea; but in my opinion, chiefly that he might be able to say that he had navigated the great outer sea of India. There he sacrificed some bulls to Poseidon and cast them into the sea; and having poured out a libation after the sacrifice, he threw the goblet and

[1] Plutarch (*Alex.* 66) says that Alexander called the island Scillustis; but others called it Psiltucis. He also says that the voyage down the rivers to the sea took seven months.

bowls, which were golden, into the deep as thankofferings, praying the god to escort safely for him the fleet, which he intended to despatch to the Persian Gulf and the mouths of the Euphrates and Tigres.[1]

CHAPTER XX.

Exploration of the Mouths of the Indus.

Returning to Patala, he found that the citadel had been fortified and that Peithon had arrived with his army, having accomplished everything for which he was despatched. He ordered Hephaestion to prepare what was needful for the fortification of a naval station and the construction of dockyards; for he resolved to leave behind here a fleet of many ships near the city of Patala, where the river Indus divides itself into two streams. He himself sailed down again into the Great Sea by the other mouth of the Indus, to ascertain which branch of the river is easier to navigate. The mouths of the river Indus are about 1800 stades distant from each other.[2] In the voyage down he arrived at a large lake in the mouth of the river, which the river makes by spreading itself out; or perhaps the waters of the surrounding district draining into it make it large, so that it very much resembles a gulf of the sea.[3] For in it were seen fish like those in the sea, larger indeed than those in our sea. Having moored his ships then in this lake, where the pilots directed, he left there most of the soldiers and all the boats with Leonnatus; but he himself with the thirty-oared galleys and the vessels with one and a half row of oars passed beyond the mouth of the Indus, and ad-

---

[1] In regard to this expedition, see *Arrian*, vii. 20 infra.

[2] About 200 miles. Arrian here follows the statement of Nearchus. Aristobulus said that the distance was 1,000 stades. See *Strabo*, xv. 1.

[3] See *Curtius*, ix. 38. This lake has disappeared.

vancing into the sea also this way, ascertained that the outlet of the river on this side (*i.e.* the west) was easier to navigate than the other. He moored his ships near the shore, and taking with him some of the cavalry went along the sea-coast three days' journey, exploring what kind of country it was for a coasting voyage, and ordering wells to be dug, so that the sailors might have water to drink. He then returned to the ships and sailed back to Patala; but he sent a part of his army along the sea-coast to effect the same thing, instructing them to return to Patala when they had dug the wells. Sailing again down to the lake, he there constructed another harbour and dockyard; and leaving a garrison for the place, he collected sufficient food to supply the army for four months, as well as whatever else he could procure for the coasting voyage.

CHAPTER XXI.

Campaign against the Oritians.

The season of the year was then unfit for voyaging; for the periodical winds prevailed, which at that season do not blow there from the north, as with us, but from the Great Sea, in the direction of the south wind.[1] Moreover it was reported that there the sea was fit for navigation after the beginning of winter, from the setting of the Pleiades[2] until the winter solstice; for at that season mild breezes usually blow from the land, drenched as it has been with great rains; and these winds are convenient on a coasting voyage both for oars and sails.

[1] These periodical winds are the southerly monsoon of the Indian Ocean. Cf. Arrian (*Indica*, 21).

[2] This occurs at the beginning of November. The Romans called the Pleiads *Vergiliae*. Cf. *Pliny* (ii. 47, 125): Vergiliarum occasus hiemem inchoat, quod tempus in III. Idus Novembres incidere consuevit. Also *Livy* (xxi. 35, 6): Nivis etiam casus, occidente jam sidère Vergiliarum, ingentem terrorem adjecit.

Nearchus, who had been placed in command of the fleet, waited for the coasting season; but Alexander, starting from Patala, advanced with all his army as far as the river Arabius.[1] He then took half of the shield-bearing guards and archers, the infantry regiments called foot Companions, the guard of the Companion cavalry, a squadron of each of the other cavalry regiments, and all the horse-bowmen, and turned away thence on the left towards the sea to dig wells, so that there might be abundance of them for the fleet sailing along on the coasting voyage; and at the same time to make an unexpected attack upon the Oritians,[2] a tribe of the Indians in this region, which had long been independent. This he meditated doing because they had performed no friendly act either to himself or his army. He placed Hephaestion in command of the forces left behind. The Arabitians,[3] another independent tribe dwelling near the river Arabius, thinking that they could not cope with Alexander in battle, and yet being unwilling to submit to him, fled into the desert when they heard that he was approaching. But crossing the river Arabius, which was both narrow and shallow, and travelling by night through the greater part of the desert, he came near the inhabited country at daybreak. Then ordering the infantry to follow him in regular line, he took the cavalry with him, dividing it into squadrons, that it might occupy a very large part of the plain, and thus marched into the land of the Oritians. All those who turned to

---

[1] This river, which is now called the Purally, is about 120 miles west of the mouth of the Indus. It is called Arabis by Arrian (*Indica*, 21); and Arbis by *Strabo* (xv. 2).

[2] These were a people of Gadrosia, inhabiting a coast district nearly 200 miles long in the present Beloochistan. Cf. Arrian (*Indica*, 22 and 25); *Pliny*, vi. 23.

[3] The Arabitians dwelt between the Indus and the Arabius; the Oritians were west of the latter river.

defend themselves were cut to pieces by the cavalry, and many of the others were taken prisoners. He then encamped near a small piece of water; but when Hephaestion formed a junction with him, he advanced farther. Arriving at the largest village of the tribe of the Oritians, which was called Rhambacia,[1] he commended the place and thought that if he colonized a city there it would become great and prosperous. He therefore left Hephaestion behind to carry out this project.[2]

CHAPTER XXII.

March through the Desert of Gadrosia.

Again he took half of the shield-bearing guards and Agrianians, the guard of cavalry and the horse-bowmen, and marched forward to the confines of the Gadrosians and Oritians, where he was informed that the passage was narrow, and the Oritians were drawn up with the Gadrosians and were encamping in front of the pass, with the purpose of barring Alexander's passage. They had indeed marshalled themselves there; but when it was reported that he was already approaching, most of them fled from the pass, deserting their guard. The chiefs of the Oritians, however, came to him, offering to surrender both themselves and their nation. He instructed these to collect the multitude of their people together and send them to their own abodes, since they were not about to suffer any harm. Over these people he placed Apollophanes as viceroy, and with him he left Leonnatus the confidential body-guard in Ora,[3] at the head of all the Agrianians, some of the bowmen and cavalry, and the rest of the Grecian mercenary infantry and cavalry. He

---

1 Rhambacia was probably at or near Haur.

2 According to *Diodorus* (xvii. 104) the city was called Alexandria.

3 Ora was the name of the district inhabited by the Oritians.

instructed him to wait until the fleet had sailed round the land, to colonize the city, and to regulate the affairs of the Oritians so that they might pay the greater respect to the viceroy. He himself, with the main body of the army (for Hephaestion had arrived at the head of the men who had been left behind), advanced into the land of the Gadrosians by a route most of which was desert. Aristobulus says that in this desert many myrrh-trees grew, larger than the ordinary kind; and that the Phoenicians, who accompanied the army for trafficking, gathered the gum of myrrh, and loading the beasts of burden, carried it away.[1] For there was a great quantity of it, inasmuch as it exuded from large stems and had never before been gathered. He also says that this desert produces many odoriferous roots of nard,[2] which the Phoenicians likewise gathered; but much of it was trampled down by the army, and a sweet perfume was diffused far and wide over the land by the trampling; so great was the abundance of it. In the desert there were also other kinds of trees, one of which had foliage like that of the bay-tree, and grew in places washed by the waves of the sea. These trees were on ground which was left dry by the ebb-tide; but when the water advanced they looked as if they had grown in the sea. Of others the roots were always washed by the sea, because they grew in hollow places, from which the water could not retire; and yet the trees were not destroyed by the sea. Some of these trees in this region were even thirty cubits high. At that season they happened to be in bloom; and the flower was very much like the white violet,[3] but the perfume was far superior to that of the latter. There was also another thorny stalk growing out of the earth, the thorn on which was

---

[1] Cf. Pliny (*Nat. Hist.* xii. 33–35).

[2] Cf. *Strabo* (xv. 2); Pliny (*Nat. Hist.* xii. 26).

[3] Probably the snow-flake.

so strong that, piercing the clothes of some men just riding past, it pulled the horseman down from his horse rather than be itself torn off the stalk. It is also said that when hares run past these bushes, the thorns cling to their fur; and thus these animals are caught, as birds are with bird-lime, or fish with hooks. However they were easily cut through with steel; and when the thorns are cut the stalk gives forth much juice, still more abundantly than fig-trees do in the springtime, and more pungent.[1]

CHAPTER XXIII.

March through the Desert of Gadrosia.

Thence Alexander marched through the land of the Gadrosians, by a difficult route, which was also destitute of all the necessaries of life; and in many places there was no water for the army. Moreover they were compelled to march most of the way by night, and a great distance from the sea. However he was very desirous of coming to the part of the country along the sea, both to see what harbours were there, and to make what preparations he could on his march for the fleet, either by employing his men in digging wells, or by making arrangements somewhere for a market and anchorage. But the part of the country of the Gadrosians near the sea was entirely desert. He therefore sent Thoas, son of Mandrodorus, with a few horsemen down to the sea, to reconnoitre and see if there happened to be any haven anywhere near, or whether there was water or any other of the necessaries of life not far from the sea. This man returned and reported that he found some fishermen upon the shore living in stifling huts, which were made

---

[1] This is the well-known catechu, obtained chiefly from the Acacia Catechu. The liquid gum is called kuth or cutch in India.

by putting together mussel-shells, and the back-bones of fishes were used to form the roofs.[1] He also said that these fishermen used little water, obtaining it with difficulty by scraping away the gravel, and that what they got was not at all fresh. When Alexander reached a certain place in Gadrosia, where corn was more abundant, he seized it and placed it upon the beasts of burden; and marking it with his own seal, he ordered it to be conveyed down to the sea. But while he was marching to the halting stage nearest to the sea, the soldiers paying little regard to the seal, the guards made use of the corn themselves, and gave a share of it to those who were especially pinched with hunger. To such a degree were they overcome by their misery that after mature deliberation they resolved to take account of the visible and already impending destruction rather than the danger of incurring the king's wrath, which was not before their eyes and still remote. When Alexander ascertained the necessity which constrained them so to act, he pardoned those who had done the deed. He himself hastened forward to collect from the land all he could for victualling the army which was sailing round with the fleet; and sent Cretheus the Callatian[2] to convey the supplies to the coast. He also ordered the natives to grind as much corn as they could and convey it down from the interior of the country, together with dates[3] and sheep for sale to the soldiers. Moreover he sent Telephus, one of the confidential Companions, down to another place on the coast with a small quantity of ground corn.

---

[1] These people were called Ichthyophagi, or Fish-eaters. They are described by Arrian (*Indica*, 29); *Curtius*, ix. 40; *Diodorus*, xvii. 105; Pliny (*Nat. Hist.* vi. 25, 26); Plutarch (*Alex.* 66); *Strabo*, xv. 2. They occupied the sea-coast of Gadrosia, or Beloochistan. Cf. Alciphron (*Epistolae*, i. 1, 2).

[2] A man of Callatis, a town on the Black Sea in Thrace, originally colonized by the Milesians.

[3] Cf. *Herodotus*, i. 193.

CHAPTER XXIV.

MARCH THROUGH GADROSIA.

HE then advanced towards the capital of the Gadrosians, which was named Pura[1]; and he arrived there in sixty days after starting from Ora. Most of the historians of Alexander's reign assert that all the hardships which his army suffered in Asia were not worthy of comparison with the labours undergone here. Nearchus alone asserts that Alexander pursued this route, not from ignorance of the difficulty of the journey, but because he heard that no one had ever hitherto passed that way with an army and emerged in safety from the desert, except Semiramis, when she fled from India. The natives said that even she emerged with only twenty men of her army; and that Cyrus, son of Cambyses, escaped with only seven of his men.[2] For they say that Cyrus also marched into this region for the purpose of invading India, but that he did not effect his retreat before losing the greater part of his army, from the desert and the other difficulties of this route. When Alexander received this information he was seized with a desire of excelling Cyrus and Semiramis. Nearchus says that he turned his march this way, both for this reason and at the same time for the purpose of conveying provisions near the fleet. The scorching heat and lack of water destroyed a great part of the army, and especially the beasts of burden; most of which perished from thirst and some of them even from the depth and heat of the sand, because it had been thoroughly scorched

---

[1] Pura was near the borders of Carmania, probably at Bampur. The name means *town*.

[2] Cf. *Strabo*, xv. 2; *Diodorus*, ii. 19, 20. According to Megasthenes, Semiramis died before she could carry out her intended invasion of India. See Arrian (*Indica*, 5). Neither Herodotus nor Ctesias mentions an invasion of India by Cyrus; and according to Arrian (*Indica*, 9), the Indians expressly denied that Cyrus attacked them.

by the sun. For they met with lofty ridges of deep sand, not closely pressed and hardened, but such as received those who stepped upon it just as if they were stepping into mud, or rather into untrodden snow. At the same time too the horses and mules suffered still more, both in going up and coming down the hills, from the unevenness of the road as well as from its instability. The length of the marches between the stages also exceedingly distressed the army; for the lack of water often compelled them to make the marches of unusual length.[1] When they travelled by night on a journey which it was necessary to complete, and at daybreak came to water, they suffered no hardship at all; but if, while still on the march, on account of the length of the way, they were caught by the heat, then they did indeed suffer hardships from the blazing sun, being at the same time oppressed by unassuageable thirst.[2]

CHAPTER XXV.

Sufferings of the Army.

The soldiers killed many of the beasts of burden of their own accord; for when provisions were lacking, they came together, and slaughtered most of the horses and mules. They ate the flesh of these, and said that they had died of thirst or had perished from the heat. There was no one who divulged the real truth of their conduct, both on account of the men's distress and because all alike were implicated in the same offence. What was being done had not escaped Alexander's notice; but he saw that the best cure for the present state of affairs would be to pretend to be ignorant of it, rather than to

[1] Strabo says that some of these marches extended 200, 400, and even 600 stades; most of the marching being done in the night. Krüger substitutes ξυμμέτρους for ξύμμετρος οὖσα.

[2] Cf. *Thucydides*, ii. 49, 3.

permit it as a thing known to himself. The consequence was, that it was no longer easy to convey the soldiers who were suffering from disease, or those who were left behind on the roads on account of the heat, partly from the want of beasts of burden and partly because the men themselves were knocking the waggons to pieces, not being able to draw them on account of the depth of the sand. They did this also because in the first stages they were compelled on this account to go, not by the shortest routes, but by those which were easiest for the carriages. Thus some were left behind along the roads on account of sickness, others from fatigue or the effects of the heat, or from not being able to bear up against the drought; and there was no one either to show them the way or to remain and tend them in their sickness. For the expedition was being made with great urgency; and the care of individual persons was necessarily neglected in the zeal displayed for the safety of the army as a whole. As they generally made the marches by night, some of the men were overcome by sleep on the road; afterwards rousing up again, those who still had strength followed upon the tracks of the army; but only a few out of many overtook the main body in safety. Most of them perished in the sand, like men shipwrecked on the sea.[1] Another calamity also befell the army, which greatly distressed men, horses, and beasts of burden; for the country of the Gadrosians is supplied with rain by the periodical winds, just as that of the Indians is; not the plains of Gadrosia, but only the mountains where the clouds are carried by the wind and are dissolved into rain without passing beyond the summits of the mountains. On one occasion, when the army bivouacked, for the sake of its water, near a small brook which was a winter torrent, about the second watch of

[1] Cf. Xenophon (*Anab.* vii. 5, 13); Homer (*Odyss.* vii. 283).

the night the brook which flowed there was suddenly swelled by the rains in the mountains which had fallen unperceived by the soldiers. The torrent advanced with so great a flood as to destroy most of the wives and children of the men who followed the army, and to sweep away all the royal baggage as well as all the beasts of burden still remaining. The soldiers, after great exertions, were hardly able to save themselves together with their weapons, many of which they lost beyond recovery. When, after enduring the burning heat and thirst, they lighted upon abundance of water, many of them perished from drinking to excess, not being able to check their appetite for it. For this reason Alexander generally pitched his camp, not near the water itself, but at a distance of about twenty stades from it, to prevent the men and beasts from pressing in crowds into the river and thus perishing, and at the same time to prevent those who had no control over themselves from fouling the water for the rest of the army by stepping into the springs or streams.

CHAPTER XXVI.

Alexander's Magnanimous Conduct.

Here I have resolved not to pass over in silence the most noble deed perhaps ever performed by Alexander, which occurred either in this land or, according to the assertion of some other authors, still earlier, among the Parapamisadians.[1] The army was continuing its march through the sand, though the heat of the sun was already

[1] *Curtius* (vii. 20) mentions a similar act of magnanimity as having occurred on the march in pursuit of Bessus through the desert to the river Oxus. Plutarch (*Alex.* 42) says it was when Alexander was pursuing Darius; Frontinus (*Strategematica*, i. 7, 7) says it was in the desert of Africa; *Polyaemus* (iv. 3, 25) relates the anecdote without specifying where the event occurred. μετεξέτεροι is an Ionic form very frequently used by Herodotus.

scorching, because it was necessary to reach water before halting. They were far on the journey, and Alexander himself, though oppressed with thirst, was nevertheless with great pain and difficulty leading the army on foot, so that his soldiers, as is usual in such a case, might more patiently bear their hardships by the equalization of the distress. At this time some of the light-armed soldiers, starting away from the army in quest of water, found some collected in a shallow cleft, a small and mean spring. Collecting this water with difficulty, they came with all speed to Alexander, as if they were bringing him some great boon. As soon as they approached the king, they poured the water into a helmet and carried it to him. He took it, and commending the men who brought it, immediately poured it upon the ground in the sight of all. As a result of this action, the entire army was re-invigorated to so great a degree that any one would have imagined that the water poured away by Alexander had furnished a draught to every man. This deed beyond all others I commend as evidence of Alexander's power of endurance and self-control, as well as of his skill in managing an army. The following adventure also occurred to the army in that country. At last the guides declared that they no longer remembered the way, because the tracks of it had been rendered invisible by the wind blowing the sand over them. Moreover, in the deep sand which had been everywhere reduced to one level, there was nothing by which they could conjecture the right way, not even the usual trees growing along it, nor any solid hillock rising up; and they had not practised themselves in making journeys by the stars at night or by the sun in the daytime, as sailors do by the constellations of the Bears—the Phoenicians by the Little Bear, and other men by the Greater Bear.[1] Then

[1] Compare note on page 146.

at length Alexander perceived that it was necessary for him to lead the way by declining to the left; and taking a few horsemen with him he advanced in front of the army. But when the horses even of these were exhausted by the heat, he left most of these men behind, and rode away with only five men and found the sea. Having scraped away the shingle on the sea-beach, he found water fresh and pure, and then went and fetched the whole army. For seven days they marched along the sea-coast, supplying themselves with water from the shore. Thence he led his expedition into the interior, for now the guides knew the way.

CHAPTER XXVII.

March through Carmania.—Punishment of Viceroys.

When he arrived at the capital of Gadrosia, he there gave his army a rest. He deposed Apollophanes from the viceroyalty,[1] because he discovered that he had paid no heed to his instructions. Thoas was appointed viceroy over the people of this district; but as he fell ill and died, Sibyrtius succeeded to the office. The same man had also lately been appointed by Alexander viceroy of Carmania; but now the rule over the Arachotians and Gadrosians was given to him, and Tlepolemus, son of Pythophanes, received Carmania. The king was already advancing into Carmania, when news was brought to him that Philip, the viceroy of the country of the Indians, had been plotted against by the mercenaries and treacherously killed; but that Philip's Macedonian bodyguards had caught some of the murderers in the very act and others afterwards, and had put them to death. When he had ascertained this, he sent a letter into India to Eudemus and Taxiles, ordering them to administer

---

[1] This man had been placed over the Oritians. See page 351 supra.

the affairs of the land which had previously been subordinated to Philip until he could send a viceroy for it. When he arrived in Carmania, Craterus effected a junction with him, bringing with him the rest of the army and the elephants. He also brought Ordanes, whom he had arrested for revolting and trying to effect a revolution.[1] Thither also came Stasanor, the viceroy of the Areians[2] and Zarangians, accompanied by Pharismanes, son of Phrataphernes, the viceroy of the Parthians and Hyrcanians. There came also the generals who had been left with Parmenio over the army in Media, Cleander, Sitalces, and Heracon, bringing with them the greater part of their army. Both the natives and the soldiers themselves brought many accusations against Cleander and Sitalces, as for example, that the temples had been pillaged by them, old tombs rifled, and other acts of injustice, recklessness, and tyranny perpetrated against their subjects. As these charges were proved,[3] he put them to death, in order to inspire others who might be left as viceroys, governors, or prefects of provinces with the fear of suffering equal penalties with them if they swerved from the path of duty.[4] This was one of the chief means by which Alexander kept in subordination the nations which he had conquered in war or which had voluntarily submitted to him, though they were so many in number and so far distant from each other; because under his regal sway it was not allowed

[1] *Curtius* (ix. 41) says that Craterus sent a messenger to the king, to say that he was holding in chains two Persian nobles, Ozines and Zeriaspes, who had been trying to effect a revolt.

[2] The Areians were famed for their skill as professional mourners. See Aeschylus (*Choëphorae*, 423). For the origin of the name see Donaldson (*New Cratylus*, sect. 81.)

[3] ἐξηλέγχθη is substituted by Sintenis for the common reading ἐξηγγέλθη.

[4] According to *Curtius* (x. 1), Cleander and his colleagues were not slain, but put into prison; whereas 600 of the soldiers who had been the agents of their cruelty were put to death. Curtius says Cleander was spared for having killed Parmenio with his own hand. Cf. iii. 26 supra.

that those who were ruled should be unjustly treated by those who ruled. At that time Heracon was acquitted of the charge, but soon after, being convicted by the men of Susa of having pillaged the temple in that city, he also suffered punishment. Stasanor and Phrataphernes came to Alexander bringing a multitude of beasts of burden and many camels, when they learnt that he was marching by the route to Gadrosia, conjecturing that his army would suffer the very hardships which it did suffer. Therefore these men arrived just at the very time they were required, as also did their camels and beasts of burden. For Alexander distributed all these animals to the officers man by man, to all the various squadrons and centuries of the cavalry, and to the various companies of the infantry, as their number allowed him.

CHAPTER XXVIII.

Alexander in Carmania.

Certain authors have said (though to me the statement seems incredible) that Alexander led his forces through Carmania lying extended with his Companions upon two covered waggons joined together, the flute being played to him; and that the soldiers followed him wearing garlands and sporting. Food was provided for them, as well as all kinds of dainties which had been brought together along the roads by the Carmanians. They say that he did this in imitation of the Bacchic revelry of Dionysus, because a story was told about that deity, that after subduing the Indians he traversed the greater part of Asia in this manner and received the appellation of Thriambus.[1] For the same reason the processions in

---

[1] The *thriambus* was a hymn to Bacchus, sung in festal processions in his honour. It was also used as a name of that deity, as we learn from *Diodorus*, iv. 5. It was afterwards used as synonymous with the Roman *triumphus*, by Polybius, Dionysius, and Plutarch.

honour of victories after war were called *thriambi*. This has been recorded neither by Ptolemy, son of Lagus, nor by Aristobulus, son of Aristobulus, nor by any other writer whose testimony on such points any one would feel to be worthy of credit. It is sufficient therefore for me to record it as unworthy of belief.[1] But as to what I am now going to describe I follow the account of Aristobulus. In Carmania Alexander offered sacrifices to the gods as thank-offerings for his victory over the Indians, and because his army had been brought in safety out of Gadrosia. He also celebrated a musical and gymnastic contest. He then appointed Peucestas one of his confidential body-guards, having already resolved to make him viceroy of Persis. He wished him, before being appointed to the viceroyalty, to experience this honour and evidence of confidence, as a reward for his exploit among the Mallians. Up to this time the number of his confidential body-guards had been seven:—Leonnatus, son of Anteas, Hephaestion, son of Amyntor, Lysimachus, son of Agathocles, Aristonous, son of Pisaeus, these four being Pellaeans; Perdiccas, son of Orontes, from Orestis, Ptolemy, son of Lagus, and Peithon, son of Crateas, the Heordaeans. Peucestas, who had held the shield over Alexander, was now added to them as an eighth. At this time Nearchus, having sailed round the coast of Ora and Gadrosia and that of the Ichthyophagi, put into port in the inhabited part of the coastland of Carmania,[2] and going up thence into the interior with a few men he reported to Alexander the particulars of the voyage which he had made along the coasts of the external sea. Nearchus was then sent down to the sea again to sail round as far as the country of Susiana, and the outlets of the river

---

[1] The Bacchanalian procession through Carmania is described by *Curtius* (ix. 42); Plutarch (*Alex.* 67); and *Diodorus* (xvii. 106).

[2] *Diodorus* (xvii. 106) says that the port into which Nearchus put was called Salmus.

Tigres.[1] How he sailed from the river Indus to the Persian Sea and the mouth of the Tigres, I shall describe in a separate book, following the account of Nearchus himself.[2] For he also wrote a history of Alexander in Greek. Perhaps I shall be able to compose this narrative in the future, if inclination and the divine influence urge me to it. Alexander now ordered Hephaestion to march into Persis[3] from Carmania along the sea-shore with the larger division of the army and the beasts of burden, taking with him also the elephants; because, as he was making the expedition in the season of winter,[4] the part of Persis near the sea was warm and possessed abundant supplies of provisions.

CHAPTER XXIX.

Alexander in Persis.—Tomb of Cyrus Repaired.

He himself then marched to Pasargadae in Persis, with the lightest of his infantry, the Companion cavalry and a part of the archers; but he sent Stasanor down to his own land.[5] When he arrived at the confines of Persis, he found that Phrasaortes was no longer viceroy, for he

---

[1] *ἐκπεριπλεύσοντα.* The Attic future of *πλέω* is *πλεύσομαι.* *πλεύσω* is only found in Polybius and the later writers.

[2] See Arrian (*Indica*, 18–43).

[3] The name for Persia and the Persians in the Hebrew Bible, is Paras. Cyrus is called Koresh (the sun) in Hebrew; in the cuneiform inscriptions the name is Khurush. Cambyses is called Ahasuerus in Ezra iv. 6; and Smerdis the Magian is the Artaxerxes who was induced by the Samaritans to forbid the further building of the temple (Ezra iv. 7–24). The Ahasuerus of the Book of Esther is probably Xerxes. Artaxerxes the Long-handed was the patron of Ezra and Nehemiah (Ezra vii. 11–28; Neh. ii. 1–9, etc). "Darius the Persian," mentioned in Neh. xii. 22, was probably Darius Codomannus, who was conquered by Alexander. The province of Susiana, previously called Elymais, appears in the Hebrew under the name of Eilam or Elam. Persis is still called Fars.

[4] B.C. 325.

[5] Aria. See chap. 27 supra.

happened to have died of disease while Alexander was still in India. Orxines was managing the affairs of the country, not because he had been appointed ruler by Alexander, but because he thought it his duty to keep Persia in order for him, as there was no other ruler.[1] Atropates, the viceroy of Media, also came to Pasargadae, bringing Baryaxes, a Mede, under arrest, because he had assumed the upright head-dress and called himself king of the Persians and Medes.[2] With Baryaxes he also brought those who had taken part with him in the attempted revolution and revolt. Alexander put these men to death.

He was grieved by the outrage committed upon the tomb of Cyrus, son of Cambyses; for according to Aristobulus, he found it dug through and pillaged. The tomb of the famous Cyrus was in the royal park at Pasargadae, and around it a grove of all kinds of trees had been planted. It was also watered by a stream, and high grass grew in the meadow. The base of the tomb itself had been made of squared stone in the form of a rectangle. Above there was a stone building surmounted by a roof, with a door leading within, so narrow that even a small man could with difficulty enter, after suffering much discomfort.[3] In the building lay a golden coffin, in which the body of Cyrus had been buried, and by the side of the coffin was a couch, the feet of which were of gold wrought with the hammer. A carpet of Babylonian tapestry with purple rugs formed the bedding; upon it were also a Median coat with sleeves and other tunics of Babylonian manufacture. Aristobulus adds that Median trousers and robes dyed the colour of

---

[1] *Curtius* (x. 4) says Orxines was descended from Cyrus.

[2] See iii. 25 supra.

[3] Cf. *Strabo*, xv. 3, where a description of this tomb is given, derived from Onesicritus, the pilot of Alexander. See Dean Blakesley's note on *Herodotus* i. 214.

hyacinth were also lying upon it, as well as others of purple and various other colours; moreover there were collars, sabres, and earrings of gold and precious stones soldered together, and near them stood a table. On the middle of the couch lay the coffin[1] which contained the body of Cyrus. Within the enclosure, near the ascent leading to the tomb, there was a small house built for the Magians who guarded the tomb; a duty which they had discharged ever since the time of Cambyses, son of Cyrus, son succeeding father as guard. To these men a sheep and specified quantities of wheaten flour and wine were given daily by the king; and a horse once a month as a sacrifice to Cyrus. Upon the tomb an inscription in Persian letters had been placed, which bore the following meaning in the Persian language: "O man, I am Cyrus, son of Cambyses, who founded the empire of the Persians, and was king of Asia. Do not therefore grudge me this monument." As soon as Alexander had conquered Persia, he was very desirous of entering the tomb of Cvrus; but he found that everything else had been carried off except the coffin and couch. They had even maltreated the king's body; for they had torn off the lid of the coffin and cast out the corpse. They had tried to make the coffin itself of smaller bulk and thus more portable, by cutting part of it off and crushing part of it up; but as their efforts did not succeed, they departed, leaving the coffin in that state. Aristobulus says that he was himself commissioned by Alexander to restore the tomb for Cyrus, to put in the coffin the parts of the body still preserved, to put the lid on, and to restore the parts of the coffin which had been defaced. Moreover he was instructed to stretch the couch tight with bands, and to deposit all the other things which used to lie there for ornament, both resembling the

[1] Just a few lines above, Arrian says that the couch was by the side of the coffin.

former ones and of the same number. He was ordered also to do away with the door, building part of it up with stone and plastering part of it over with cement; and finally to put the royal seal upon the cement. Alexander arrested the Magians who were the guards of the tomb, and put them to the torture to make them confess who had done the deed; but in spite of the torture they confessed nothing either about themselves or any other person. In no other way were they proved to have been privy to the deed; they were therefore released by Alexander.[1]

CHAPTER XXX.

Peucestas Appointed Viceroy of Persis.

Thence he proceeded to the royal palace of the Persians, which he had on a former occasion himself burnt down, as I have previously related, expressing my disapprobation of the act[2]; and on his return Alexander himself did not commend it. Many charges were brought by the Persians against Orxines, who ruled them after the death of Phrasaortes. He was convicted of having pillaged temples and royal tombs, and of having unjustly put many of the Persians to death. He was therefore hanged by men acting under Alexander's orders[3]; and Peucestas the confidential body-guard was appointed viceroy of Persis. The king placed special confidence in him both for other reasons, and especially on account of his exploit

[1] Cf. *Ammianus*, xxiii. 6, 32, 33. The Magi were the priests of the religion of Zoroaster, which was professed by the Medes and Persians. Their Bible was the Avesta, originally consisting of twenty-one books, only one of which, the twentieth (Vendidad), is still extant.

[2] See iii. 18 supra.

[3] According to *Curtius* (x. 4, 5) Orxines was not only innocent, but was very devoted and attached to Alexander. The favourite eunuch, Bagoas, poisoned the king's mind against him, and suborned other accusers against him. He was condemned unheard.

among the Mallians, where he braved the greatest dangers and helped to save Alexander's life. Besides this, he did not refuse to accommodate himself to the Asiatic mode of living; and as soon as he was appointed to the position of viceroy of Persis, he openly assumed the native garb, being the only man among the Macedonians who adopted the Median dress in preference to the Grecian.[1] He also learnt to speak the Persian language correctly, and comported himself in all other respects like a Persian. For this conduct he was not only commended by Alexander, but the Persians also were highly delighted with him, for preferring their national customs to those of his own forefathers.

---

[1] Purpura et nitor corporis, ornatusque Persicus multo auro multisque gemmis.—Cicero (*de Senectute*, 17).

BOOK VII.

CHAPTER I.

Alexander's Plans.—The Indian Philosophers.

When Alexander arrived at Pasargadae and Persepolis,[1] he was seized with an ardent desire to sail down the Euphrates and Tigres[2] to the Persian Sea, and to see the mouths of those rivers as he had already seen those of the Indus as well as the sea into which it flows. Some authors[3] also have stated that he was meditating a voyage round the larger portion of Arabia, the country of the Ethiopians, Libya (*i.e.* Africa), and Numidia beyond Mount Atlas to Gadeira (*i.e.* Cadiz),[4] inward into our sea

---

[1] Pasargadae was the ancient capital of Cyrus, but Persepolis was that of the later kings of Persia. The tomb of Cyrus has been discovered at Murghab; consequently Parsagadae was on the banks of the river Cyrus, N.E. of Persepolis. The latter city was at the junction of the Araxes and Medus. Its extensive ruins are called Chel-Minar, "the forty columns."

[2] The Tigris rises in Armenia, and joins the Euphrates ninety miles from the sea, the united stream being then called Shat-el-Arab. In ancient times the two rivers had distinct outlets. In the Hebrew the Tigris is called Chiddekel, *i.e. arrow*. The Greek name Tigres is derived from the Zend *Tighra*, which comes from the Sanscrit *Tig*, to sharpen. Its present name is Dijleh. The respective lengths of the Euphrates and Tigris are 1,780 and 1,146 miles.

[3] Among these were *Curtius* (x. 3); *Diodorus* (xviii. 4); and Plutarch (*Alex.*, 68).

[4] Gadeira or Gades was a Phoenician colony. The name is from the Hebrew גָּדֵר, *a fence*. Cf. *Pliny* (iv. 36); appellant Poeni *Gadir* ita Punica lingua *septum* significante. Also Avienus (*Ora Maritima*, 268): Punicorum lingua conseptum locum *Gaddir* vocabat. According to *Pliny* (v. 1), Suetonius Paulinus was the first Roman general who crossed the Atlas Mountains.

(*i.e.* the Mediterranean); thinking that after he had subdued both Libya and Carchedon (*i.e.* Carthage), he might with justice be called king of all Asia.[1] For he said that the kings of the Persians and Medes called themselves Great Kings without any right, since they did not rule the larger part of Asia. Some say that he was meditating a voyage thence into the Euxine Sea, to Scythia and the Lake Maeotis (*i.e.* the Sea of Azov); while others assert that he intended to go to Sicily and the Iapygian Cape,[2] for the fame of the Romans spreading far and wide was now exciting his jealousy. For my own part I cannot conjecture with any certainty what were his plans; and I do not care to guess. But this I think I can confidently affirm, that he meditated nothing small or mean; and that he would never have remained satisfied with any of the acquisitions he had made, even if he had added Europe to Asia, or the islands of the Britons to Europe; but would still have gone on seeking for unknown lands beyond those mentioned. I verily believe that if he had found no one else to strive with, he would have striven with himself. And on this account I commend some of the Indian philosophers, who are said to have been caught by Alexander as they were walking in the open meadow where they were accustomed to spend their time.[3] At the sight of him and his army they did nothing else but stamp with their feet on the earth, upon which they were stepping. When he asked them by means of interpreters what was the meaning of their action, they replied as follows: "O king Alexander, every man possesses as much of the earth as this upon which we have stepped; but thou being only a man like the rest of us, except in being meddlesome and arrogant, art come over so great a part of the earth from thy own

[1] See note 3, page 309.

[2] Now called Capo di Leuca, the south-eastern point of Italy.

[3] Cf. Arrian (*Indica*, 11).

land, giving trouble both to thyself and others.[1] And yet thou also wilt soon die, and possess only as much of the earth as is sufficient for thy body to be buried in."

CHAPTER II.

Alexander's Dealings with the Indian Sages.

On this occasion Alexander commended both the words and the men who spoke them; but nevertheless he did just the opposite to that which he commended. When also in the Isthmus he met Diogenes of Sinope, lying in the sun, standing near him with his shield-bearing guards and foot Companions, he asked if he wanted anything. But Diogenes said that he wanted nothing else, except that he and his attendants would stand out of the sunlight. Alexander is said to have expressed his admiration of Diogenes's conduct.[2] Thus it is evident that Alexander was not entirely destitute of better feelings; but he was the slave of his insatiable ambition. Again, when he arrived at Taxila and saw the naked sect of Indian philosophers, he was exceedingly desirous that one of these men should live with him; because he admired their power of endurance.[3] But the oldest of the philosophers, Dandamis by name, of whom the others were disciples, refused to come himself to Alexander, and would not allow the others to do so.[4] He is said to have replied that he was himself a son of Zeus, if Alexander was[5]; and that he wanted nothing from him, because he

---

[1] Cf. Alciphron (*Epistolae*, i. 30, 1), with Bergler and Wagner's notes.

[2] This must have occurred B.C. 336. See Plutarch (*Alex.* 14); Cicero (*Tusculanae Disputationes*, v. 32). Alexander said: "If I were not Alexander, I should like to be Diogenes." Cf. *Arrian*, i. 1; Plutarch (*de Fortit. Alex.*, p. 331).

[3] Cf. *Strabo*, xv. 1.

[4] Strabo calls this sage Mandanis.

[5] Strabo says, Alexander's messengers summoned Mandanis to the son of Zeus.

was quite contented with what he had. And besides he said that he saw his attendants wandering over so much of the land and sea to no advantage, and that there was no end to their many wanderings. Therefore he had no desire that Alexander should give him anything which was in his own possession, nor on the other hand was he afraid that he should be excluded from anything which Alexander ruled over. For while he lived the country of India, which produces the fruits in their season, was sufficient for him; and when he died he should be released from the body, an unsuitable associate. Alexander then did not attempt to force him to come with him, considering that the man was free to do as he pleased. But Megasthenes has recorded that Calanus, one of the philosophers of this region, who had very little power over his desires, was induced to do so; and that the philosophers themselves reproached him, for having deserted the happiness existing among them, and serving another lord instead of the God.[1]

CHAPTER III.

Self-sacrifice of the Indian Calanus.

This I have recorded, because in a history of Alexander it is necessary also to speak of Calanus; for when he was in the country of Persis his health became delicate, though he had never before been subject to illness.[2] Accordingly, not being willing to lead the life of a man in infirm health, he told Alexander that in such circum-

[1] Plutarch (*Alex.*, 65) says this philosopher's name was Sphines; but the Greeks called him Calanus, because when he met them, instead of using the word χαῖρε in greeting them, he said καλέ. The same author says that he was persuaded to come to Alexander by Taxiles. See also *Strabo* (xv. 1).

[2] *Strabo* (xv. 1) says that the voluntary death of Calanus occurred at Pasargadae; Aelian (*Varia Historia*, v. 6) says it was at Babylon; but *Diodorus* (xvii. 107) says it happened at Susa, which statement is confirmed by the fact of Nearchus being seemingly present.

stances he thought it best for him to put an end to his existence, before he came into experience of any disease which might compel him to change his former mode of living. For a long time the king tried to dissuade him; however, when he saw that he was not to be overcome, but would find some other way of release, if this were not yielded to him, he ordered a funeral pyre to be heaped up for him, in the place where the man himself directed, and gave instructions that Ptolemy, son of Lagus, the confidential body-guard, should have the charge of it. They say that a solemn procession, consisting both of horses and men, advanced before him, some of the latter being armed and others carrying all kinds of incense for the pyre. They also say that they were carrying gold and silver goblets and royal apparel; and because he was unable to walk through illness, a horse was prepared for him. However, not being able to mount the horse, he was conveyed stretched out upon a litter, crowned with a garland after the custom of the Indians, and singing in the Indian language. The Indians say that he sang hymns to the gods and eulogiums on his countrymen.[1] Before he ascended the funeral-pyre he presented the horse which he should himself have mounted, being a royal steed of the Nisaean breed,[2] to Lysimachus, one of those who attended him to learn his philosophy. He distributed among his other disciples the goblets and rugs which Alexander had ordered to be cast into the pyre as an honour to him. Then mounting the pyre he lay down upon it in a becoming manner, and was visible to the whole army. To Alexander the spectacle appeared unseemly, as it was being exhibited at the cost of a friend; but to the rest it was a cause of wonder that he did not move any part of his body in the fire.[3] As

[1] Cf. Arrian (*Indica*, 10).

[2] Cf. *Arrian*, vii. 13 infra; and *Herodotus*, vii. 40.

[3] Cf. Cicero (*Tusc. Disput.* v. 27).

soon as the men to whom the duty had been assigned set fire to the pyre, Nearchus says the trumpets sounded, in accordance with Alexander's order, and the whole army raised the war-cry as it was in the habit of shouting when advancing to battle. The elephants also chimed in with their shrill and warlike cry, in honour of Calanus. Authors upon whom reliance may be placed, have recorded these and such-like things, facts of great import to those who are desirous of learning how steadfast and immovable a thing the human mind is in regard to what it wishes to accomplish.

CHAPTER IV.

Marriages between Macedonians and Persians.

At this time Alexander sent Atropates away to his own viceroyalty,[1] after advancing to Susa; where he arrested Abulites and his son Oxathres, and put them to death on the ground that they were governing the Susians badly.[2] Many outrages upon temples, tombs, and the subjects themselves had been committed by those who were ruling the countries conquered by Alexander in war; because the king's expedition into India had taken a long time, and it was not thought credible that he would ever return in safety from so many nations possessing so many elephants, going to his destruction beyond the Indus, Hydaspes, Acesines, and Hyphasis.[3] The calamities that befell him among the Gadrosians were still greater inducements to those acting as viceroys in this region to be free from apprehension of his return to his dominions.

---

[1] Media. See vi. 29 supra.

[2] Oxathres was killed by Alexander himself with a sarissa, or long Macedonian pike. See Plutarch (*Alex.* 68), who calls him Oxyartes.

[3] For this use of φθείρομαι, cf. Aristophanes (*Plutus*, 610); *Alciphron*, i. 13, 3; with Bergler's note.

Not only so, but Alexander himself is said to have become more inclined at that time to believe accusations which were plausible in every way, as well as to inflict very severe punishment upon those who were convicted even of small offences, because with the same disposition he thought they would be likely to perform great ones.[1]

In Susa also he celebrated both his own wedding and those of his companions. He himself married Barsine, the eldest daughter of Darius,[2] and according to Aristobulus, besides her another, Parysatis, the youngest daughter of Ochus.[3] He had already married Roxana, daughter of Oxyartes the Bactrian.[4] To Hephaestion he gave Drypetis, another daughter of Darius, and his own wife's sister; for he wished Hephaestion's children to be first cousins to his own. To Craterus he gave Amastrine, daughter of Oxyartes the brother of Darius; to Perdiccas, the daughter of Atropates, viceroy of Media; to Ptolemy the confidential body-guard, and Eumenes the royal secretary, the daughters of Artabazus, to the former Artacama, and to the latter Artonis. To Nearchus he gave the daughter of Barsine and Mentor; to Seleucus the daughter of Spitamenes the Bactrian. Likewise to the rest of his Companions he gave the choicest daughters of the Persians and Medes, to the number of eighty. The weddings were celebrated after the Persian manner, seats being placed in a row for the bridegrooms; and after the banquet the brides

---

[1] Cf. *Curtius*, x. 5.

[2] She was also called Statira. See *Diodorus*, xvii. 107; Plutarch (*Alex.*, 70). She is called Arsinoe by Photius.

[3] "By these two marriages, Alexander thus engrafted himself upon the two lines of antecedent Persian kings. Ochus was of the Achaemenid family, but Darius Codomannus, father of Statira, was not of that family; he began a new lineage. About the overweening regal state of Alexander, outdoing even the previous Persian kings, see *Pylarchus apud Athenaeum*, xii. p. 539."—*Grote.*

[4] See p. 242.

came in and seated themselves, each one near her own husband. The bridegrooms took them by the right hand and kissed them; the king being the first to begin, for the weddings of all were conducted in the same way. This appeared the most popular thing which Alexander ever did; and it proved his affection for his Companions. Each man took his own bride and led her away; and on all without exception Alexander bestowed dowries.[1] He also ordered that the names of all the other Macedonians who had married any of the Asiatic women should be registered. They were over 10,000 in number; and to these Alexander made presents on account of their weddings.

CHAPTER V.

The Soldiers Rewarded.

He now thought it a favourable opportunity to liquidate the debts of all the soldiers who had incurred them[2]; and for this purpose he ordered that a register should be made of how much each man owed, in order that they might receive the money. At first only a few registered their names, fearing that this was being instituted as a test by Alexander, to discover which of the soldiers found their pay insufficient for their expenses, and which of them were extravagant in their mode of living. When he was informed that most of them were not registering their names, but that those who had borrowed money on bonds were concealing the fact, he reproached them for their distrust of him. For he said that it was not right either that the king should deal otherwise than sincerely

---

[1] Cf. Aelian (*Varia Historia*, viii. 7). A copious account of this celebrated marriage feast is given in *Athenaeus*, xii. p. 538.

[2] Cf. *Curtius*, x. 8.

with his subjects, or that any of those ruled by him should think that he would deal otherwise than sincerely with them. Accordingly, he had tables placed in the camp with money upon them; and he appointed men to manage the distribution of it. He ordered the debts of all who showed a money-bond to be liquidated without the debtors' names being any longer registered. Consequently, the men believed that Alexander was dealing sincerely with them; and the fact that they were not known was a greater pleasure to them than the fact that they ceased to be in debt. This presentation to the army is said to have amounted to 20,000 talents.[1] He also gave presents to particular individuals, according as each man was held in honour for his merit or valour, if he had become conspicuous in crises of danger. Those who were distinguished for their personal gallantry he crowned with golden chaplets:—first, Peucestas, the man who had held the shield over him; second, Leonnatus, who also had held his shield over him, and moreover had incurred dangers in India and won a victory in Ora.[2] For he had posted himself with the forces left with him against the Oritians and the tribes living near them, who were trying to effect a revolution, and had conquered them in battle. He also seemed to have managed other affairs in Ora with great success. In addition to these, he crowned Nearchus for his successful voyage round the coast from the land of the Indians through the Great Sea; for this officer had now arrived at Susa. Besides these three, he crowned Onesicritus, the pilot of the royal ship; as well as Hephaestion and the rest of the confidential bodyguards.

---

[1] About £4,600,000. *Justin*, xii. 11, agrees with Arrian; but *Diodorus* (xvii. 109); Plutarch (*Alex.*, 70); *Curtius* (x. 8) say 10,000 talents.

[2] Cf. *Curtius* (ix. 41); *Arrian* (vi. 22) supra.

CHAPTER VI.

An Army of Asiatics Trained under the Macedonian Discipline.

The viceroys from the newly-built cities and the rest of the territory subdued in war came to him, bringing with them youths just growing into manhood to the number of 30,000, all of the same age, whom Alexander called Epigoni (successors).[1] They were accoutred with Macedonian arms, and exercised in military discipline after the Macedonian system. The arrival of these is said to have vexed the Macedonians, who thought that Alexander was contriving every means in his power to free himself from his previous need of their services. For the same reason also the sight of his Median dress was no small cause of dissatisfaction to them; and the weddings celebrated in the Persian fashion were displeasing to most of them, even including some of those who married, although they had been greatly honoured by the king putting himself on the same level with them in the marriage ceremony. They were offended at Peucestas, the viceroy of Persis, on account of his Persianizing both in dress and in speech, because the king was delighted by his adopting the Asiatic customs. They were disgusted that the Bactrian, Sogdianian, Arachotian, Zarangian, Arian, and Parthian horsemen, as well as the Persian horsemen called the Evacae, were distributed among the squadrons of the Companion cavalry; as many of them at least as were seen to excel in reputation, fineness of stature, or any other good quality; and that a fifth cavalry division was added to these troops, not composed entirely of foreigners; but the whole body of cavalry was increased in number, and men were picked

[1] The Epigoni, or Afterborn, were the sons of the seven chiefs who fell in the first war against Thebes. See Herodotus, Pindar, Sophocles, etc.

from the foreigners and put into it. Cophen, son of Artabazus, Hydarnes and Artiboles, sons of Mazaeus, Sisines and Phradasmenes, sons of Phrataphernes, viceroy of Parthia and Hyrcania, Histanes, son of Oxyartes and brother of Alexander's wife, Roxane, as well as Autobares and his brother Mithrobaeus were picked out and enrolled among the foot-guard in addition to the Macedonian officers. Over these Hystaspes the Bactrian was placed as commander; and Macedonian spears were given to them instead of the barbarian javelins which had thongs attached to them.[1] All this offended the Macedonians, who thought that Alexander was becoming altogether Asiatic in his ideas, and was holding the Macedonians themselves as well as their customs in a position of contempt.[2]

CHAPTER VII.

Navigation of the Tigres.

Alexander now ordered Hephaestion to lead the main body of the infantry as far as the Persian Sea, while he himself, his fleet having sailed up into the land of Susiana, embarked with the shield-bearing guards and the body-guard of infantry; and having also put on board a few of the cavalry Companions, he sailed down the river Eulaeus to the sea.[3] When he was near the

---

[1] For this *mesanculon* see Gellius (*Noctes Atticae*, x. 25); *Polybius*, xxiii. 1, 9; Euripides (*Phoenissae*, 1141; *Andromache*, 1133); *Alciphron*, iii. 36.

[2] It was at this time that Harpalus, viceroy of Babylon, having squandered a great deal of the treasure committed to his charge, became frightened at the return of Alexander, and fled to Greece with 50,000 talents and 6,000 mercenary troops. See *Diodorus*, xvii. 108.

[3] The Eulaeus is now called Kara Su. After joining the Coprates it was called Pasitigris. It formerly discharged itself into the Persian Gulf, but now into the Shat-el-Arab, as the united stream of the Euphrates and Tigris is now called. In Dan. viii. 2, 16, it is called Ulai. Cf. *Pliny*, vi. 26, 31; xxxi. 21.

place where the river discharges itself into the deep, he left there most of his ships, including those which were in need of repair, and with those especially adapted for fast sailing he coasted along out of the river Eulaeus through the sea to the mouth of the Tigres. The rest of the ships were conveyed down the Eulaeus as far as the canal which has been cut from the Tigres into the Eulaeus, and by this means they were brought into the Tigres. Of the rivers Euphrates and Tigres which enclose Syria between them, whence also its name is called by the natives Mesopotamia,[1] the Tigres flows in a much lower channel than the Euphrates, from which it receives many canals; and after taking up many tributaries and its waters being swelled by them, it falls into the Persian Sea.[2] It is a large river and can be crossed on foot nowhere as far as its mouth,[3] inasmuch as none of its water is used up by irrigation of the country. For the land through which it flows is more elevated than its water, and it is not drawn off into canals or into another river, but rather receives them into itself. It is nowhere possible to irrigate the land from it. But the Euphrates flows in an elevated channel, and is everywhere on a level with the land through which it passes. Many canals have been made from it, some of which are always kept flowing, and from which the inhabitants on both banks supply themselves with water; others the people make only when requisite to irrigate the land, when they are in need of water from drought.[4] For this country is usually free from rain. The consequence is, that the

---

[1] The Greeks and Romans sometimes speak of Mesopotamia as a part of Syria, and at other times they call it a part of Assyria. The Hebrew and native name of this country was Aram Naharaim, or "Syria of the two rivers."

[2] The Tigris now falls into the Euphrates.

[3] Cf. *Arrian*, iii. 7, supra; *Curtius*, iv. 37.

[4] Cf. *Strabo*, xvi. 1; *Herodotus*, i. 193; *Ammianus*, xxiv. 3, 14.

Euphrates at last has only a small volume of water, which disappears into a marsh. Alexander sailed over the sea round the shore of the Persian Gulf lying between the rivers Eulaeus and Tigres; and thence he sailed up the latter river as far as the camp where Hephaestion had settled with all his forces. Thence he sailed again to Opis, a city situated on that river.[1] In his voyage up he destroyed the weirs which existed in the river, and thus made the stream quite level. These weirs had been constructed by the Persians, to prevent any enemy having a superior naval force from sailing up from the sea into their country. The Persians had had recourse to these contrivances because they were not a nautical people; and thus by making an unbroken succession of weirs they had rendered the voyage up the Tigres a matter of impossibility. But Alexander said that such devices were unbecoming to men who are victorious in battle; and therefore he considered this means of safety unsuitable for him; and by easily demolishing the laborious work of the Persians, he proved in fact that what they thought a protection was unworthy of the name.

CHAPTER VIII.

THE MACEDONIANS OFFENDED AT ALEXANDER.

WHEN he arrived at Opis, he collected the Macedonians and announced that he intended to discharge from the army those who were useless for military service either from age or from being maimed in the limbs; and he said he would send them back to their own abodes. He

[1] Probably this city stood at the junction of the Tigris with the Physcus, or Odorneh. See Xenophon (*Anab.* ii. 4, 25); *Herodotus*, i. 189; *Strabo*, (xvi. 1) says that Alexander made the Tigris navigable up to Opis.

also promised to give those who went back as much as would make them special objects of envy to those at home and arouse in the other Macedonians the wish to share similar dangers and labours. Alexander said this, no doubt, for the purpose of pleasing the Macedonians; but on the contrary they were, not without reason, offended by the speech which he delivered, thinking that now they were despised by him and deemed to be quite useless for military service. Indeed, throughout the whole of this expedition they had been offended at many other things; for his adoption of the Persian dress, thereby exhibiting his contempt for their opinion, caused them grief, as did also his accoutring the foreign soldiers called Epigoni in the Macedonian style, and the mixing of the alien horsemen among the ranks of the Companions. Therefore they could not remain silent and control themselves, but urged him to dismiss all of them from his army; and they advised him to prosecute the war in company with his father, deriding Ammon by this remark. When Alexander heard this (for at that time he was more hasty in temper than heretofore, and no longer, as of old, indulgent to the Macedonians from having a retinue of foreign attendants), leaping down from the platform with his officers around him, he ordered the most conspicuous of the men who had tried to stir up the multitude to sedition to be arrested. He himself pointed out with his hand to the shield-bearing guards those whom they were to arrest, to the number of thirteen; and he ordered these to be led away to execution.[1] When the rest, stricken with terror, became silent, he mounted the platform and spoke as follows:—

---

[1] Cf. *Justin* (xii. 11); *Diodorus* (xvii. 109); *Curtius* (x. 10, 11). These authors put the punishment of the ringleaders after the speech instead of before.

CHAPTER IX.

Alexander's Speech.

"The speech which I am about to deliver will not be for the purpose of checking your start homeward, for, so far as I am concerned, you may depart wherever you wish; but because I wish you to know what kind of men you were originally and how you have been transformed since you came into our service. In the first place, as is reasonable, I shall begin my speech from my father Philip. For he found you vagabonds and destitute of means, most of you clad in hides, feeding a few sheep up the mountain sides, for the protection of which you had to fight with small success against Illyrians, Triballians, and the border Thracians.[1] Instead of the hides he gave you cloaks to wear, and from the mountains he led you down into the plains, and made you capable of fighting the neighbouring barbarians, so that you were no longer compelled to preserve yourselves by trusting rather to the inaccessible strongholds than to your own valour. He made you colonists of cities, which he adorned with useful laws and customs; and from being slaves and subjects, he made you rulers over those very barbarians by whom you yourselves, as well as your property, were previously liable to be plundered and ravaged. He also added the greater part of Thrace to Macedonia, and by seizing the most conveniently situated places on the sea-coast, he spread abundance over the land from commerce, and made the working of the mines a secure employment.[2] He made you rulers over the Thessalians,

---

[1] Thracians mean *mountaineers;* Hellenes, *warriors;* Dorians, *highlanders;* Ionians, *coast-men;* and Aeolians, *mixed men.* See Donaldson (*New Cratylus*, sect. 92).

[2] The gold and silver mines at Mount Pangaeon near Philippi brought Philip a yearly revenue of more than 1,000 talents (*Diodorus*, xvi. 8). *Herodotus* (v. 17) says that the silver mines at Mount Dysorum brought a talent every day to Alexander, father of Amyntas.

of whom you had formerly been in mortal fear[1]; and by humbling the nation of the Phocians, he rendered the avenue into Greece broad and easy for you, instead of being narrow and difficult.[2] The Athenians and Thebans, who were always lying in wait to attack Macedonia, he humbled to such a degree,—I also then rendering him my personal aid in the campaign,[3]—that instead of paying tribute to the former[4] and being vassals to the latter,[5] those States in their turn procure security to themselves by our assistance. He penetrated into the Peloponnese, and after regulating its affairs, was publicly declared commander-in-chief of all the rest of Greece in the expedition against the Persian, adding this glory not more to himself than to the commonwealth of the Macedonians. These were the advantages which accrued to you from my father Philip; great indeed if looked at by themselves, but small if compared with those you have obtained from me. For though I inherited from my father only a few gold and silver goblets, and there were not even sixty talents in the treasury, and though I found myself charged with a debt of 500 talents owing by Philip,[6] and I was obliged myself to borrow 800 talents in addition to these, I started from the country which could not decently support you, and forthwith laid open to you the passage of the Hellespont, though at that time the Persians held the sovereignty of the sea. Having overpowered the viceroys of Darius

---

[1] This is a Demosthenic expression. See *De Falsa Legatione*, 92; and *I. Philippic*, 45.

[2] B.C. 346.

[3] He here refers to his own part in the victory of Chaeronea, B.C. 336. See *Diodorus*, xvi. 86; Plutarch (*Alex.* 9).

[4] This fact is attested by Demosthenes (*De Haloneso*, 12).

[5] The Thebans under Pelopidas settled the affairs of Macedonia, and took young Philip to Thebes as a hostage, B.C. 368.

[6] About £122,000. Cf. Plutarch (*Alex.* 15); *Curtius*, x. 10.

ith my cavalry, I added to your empire the whole of nia,[1] the whole of Aeolis, both Phrygias [2] and Lydia, id I took Miletus by siege. All the other places I ained by voluntary surrender, and I granted you the rivilege of appropriating the wealth found in them. The ches of Egypt and Cyrene, which I acquired with- it fighting a battle, have come to you. Coele-Syria, alestine, and Mesopotamia are your property. Babylon, actra, and Susa are yours. The wealth of the Lydians, ie treasures of the Persians, and the riches of the idians are yours; and so is the External Sea. You are iceroys, you are generals, you are captains. What then ave I reserved to myself after all these labours, except iis purple robe and this diadem? [3] I have appropriated othing myself, nor can any one point out my treasures, xcept these possessions of yours or the things which I m guarding on your behalf. [4] Individually, however, have no motive to guard them, since I feed on the ame fare as you do, and I take only the same amount f sleep. Nay, I do not think that my fare is as good s that of those among you who live luxuriously; and I now that I often sit up at night to watch for you, that ou may be able to sleep.

---

[1] Ἴων is the Hebrew Javan without the vowel points. In the Persian ame for the Greeks Ἰάονες, one of these vowels appear. See Aeschylus *Persae*, 178, 562).

[2] Larger Phrygia formed the western part of the great central table-land f Asia Minor. Smaller Phrygia was also called Hellespontine Phrygia, ecause it lay near the Hellespont. See *Strabo*, xii. 8.

[3] A blue band worked with white, which went round the tiara of the 'ersian kings.

[4] Cf. *Ammianus*, xxv. 4, 15: "(Julianus) id aliquoties praedicans, lexandrum Magnum, ubi haberet thesauros interrogatum, apud amicos enevole respondisse."

CHAPTER X.

Alexander's Speech (*continued*).

"But some one may say, that while you endured toil and fatigue, I have acquired these things as your leader without myself sharing the toil and fatigue. But who is there of you who knows that he has endured greater toil for me than I have for him? Come now! whoever of you has wounds, let him strip and show them, and I will show mine in turn; for there is no part of my body, in front at any rate, remaining free from wounds; nor is there any kind of weapon used either for close combat or for hurling at the enemy, the traces of which I do not bear on my person. For I have been wounded with the sword in close fight, I have been shot with arrows, and I have been struck with missiles projected from engines of war; and though oftentimes I have been hit with stones and bolts of wood for the sake of your lives, your glory, and your wealth, I am still leading you as conquerors over all the land and sea, all rivers, mountains, and plains. I have celebrated your weddings with my own, and the children of many of you will be akin to my children. Moreover I have liquidated the debts of all those who had incurred them, without inquiring too closely for what purpose they were contracted, though you receive such high pay, and carry off so much booty whenever there is booty to be got after a siege. Most of you have golden crowns, the eternal memorials of your valour and of the honour you receive from me. Whoever has been killed, has met with a glorious end and has been honoured with a splendid burial. Brazen statues of most of the slain have been erected at home,[1] and their parents are held in honour, being released from all public service and from taxation. But no one of you

[1] Cf. *Arrian*, i. 16 supra.

has ever been killed in flight under my leadership. And now I was intending to send back those of you who are unfit for service, objects of envy to those at home; but since you all wish to depart, depart all of you! Go back and report at home that your king Alexander, the conqueror of the Persians, Medes, Bactrians, and Sacians[1]; the man who has subjugated the Uxians, Arachotians, and Drangians; who has also acquired the rule of the Parthians, Chorasmians, and Hyrcanians, as far as the Caspian Sea; who has marched over the Caucasus, through the Caspian Gates; who has crossed the rivers Oxus and Tanais, and the Indus besides, which has never been crossed by any one else except Dionysus; who has also crossed the Hydaspes, Acesines, and Hydraotes, and who would have crossed the Hyphasis, if you had not shrunk back with alarm; who has penetrated into the Great Sea by both the mouths of the Indus; who has marched through the desert of Gadrosia, where no one ever before marched with an army; who on his route acquired possession of Carmania and the land of the Oritians, in addition to his other conquests, his fleet having in the meantime already sailed round the coast of the sea which extends from India to Persia—report that when you returned to Susa you deserted him and went away, handing him over to the protection of conquered foreigners. Perhaps this report of yours will be both glorious to you in the eyes of men and devout forsooth in the eyes of the gods. Depart!"

CHAPTER XI.

Reconciliation between Alexander and his Army.

Having thus spoken, he leaped down quickly from the platform, and entered the palace, where he paid no atten-

[1] It is supposed that the Saxones, *i.e.* Sacasuna, *sons of the Sacae*, originated from this nation.

tion to the decoration of his person, nor was any of his Companions admitted to see him. Not even on the morrow was any one of them admitted to an audience; but on the third day he summoned the select Persians within, and among them he distributed the commands of the brigades, and made the rule that only those whom he had proclaimed his kinsmen,[1] should have the honour of saluting him with a kiss.[2] But the Macedonians who heard the speech were thoroughly astonished at the moment, and remained there in silence near the platform; nor when he retired did any of them accompany the king, except his personal Companions and the confidential body-guards. Though they remained, most of them had nothing to do or say; and yet they were unwilling to retire. But when the news was reported to them about the Persians and Medes, that the military commands were being given to Persians, that the foreign soldiers were being selected and divided into companies, that a Persian footguard, Persian foot Companions, a Persian regiment of men with silver shields,[3] as well as the cavalry Companions, and another royal regiment of cavalry distinct from these, were being called by Macedonian names, they were no longer able to restrain themselves; but running in a body to the palace, they cast their weapons there in front of the gates as a sign of supplication to the king. Standing in front of the gates, they shouted, beseeching to be allowed to enter, and saying that they were willing to surrender the men who had been the instigators of the disturbance on that occasion, and those who

---

[1] At the Persian court, *kinsman* was a title bestowed by the king as a mark of honour. Curtius says they were 15,000 in number. Cf. *Diodorus*, xvi. 50; Xenophon (*Cyropaedia*, i. 4, 27; ii. 2, 31).

[2] As to this Persian custom, see Xenophon (*Agesilaus*, v. 4; *Cyropaedia* i. 4, 27).

[3] Cf. *Justin*, xii. 7; Plutarch (*Eumenes*, 16); *Curtius*, viii. 17; *Livy* xxxvii. 40; *Polybius*, v. 79, 4.

had begun the clamour. They also declared they would not retire from the gates either day or night, unless Alexander would take some pity upon them. When he was informed of this, he came out without delay; and seeing them lying on the ground in humble guise, and hearing most of them lamenting with loud voice, tears began to flow also from his own eyes. He made an effort to say something to them, but they continued their importunate entreaties.[1] At length one of them, Callines by name, a man conspicuous both for his age and because he was captain of the Companion cavalry, spoke as follows:—"O king, what grieves the Macedonians is, that thou hast already made some of the Persians kinsmen to thyself, and that Persians are called Alexander's kinsmen, and have the honour of saluting thee with a kiss; whereas none of the Macedonians have as yet enjoyed this honour." Then Alexander interrupting him, said:—"But all of you without exception I consider my kinsmen, and so from this time I shall call you." When he had said this, Callines advanced and saluted him with a kiss, and so did all those who wished to salute him. Then they took up their weapons and returned to the camp, shouting and singing a song of thanksgiving to Apollo. After this Alexander offered sacrifice to the gods to whom it was his custom to sacrifice, and gave a public banquet, over which he himself presided, with the Macedonians sitting around him; and next to them the Persians; after whom came the men of the other nations, honoured for their personal rank or for some meritorious action. The king and his guests drew wine from the same bowl and poured out the same libations, both the Grecian prophets and the Magians commencing the ceremony. He prayed for

---

[1] *ἔμενον λιπαροῦντες.* The more usual construction would be *ἐλιπάρουν μένοντες.* Cf. *Herodotus*, ix. 45 (*λιπαρέετε μένοντες*); iii. 51 (*ἐλιπάρεε ἱστορέων*).

other blessings, and especially that harmony and community of rule might exist between the Macedonians and Persians. The common account is, that those who took part in this banquet were 9,000 in number, that all of them poured out one libation, and after it sang a song of thanksgiving to Apollo.[1]

CHAPTER XII.

Ten Thousand Macedonians Sent Home with Craterus.—Disputes between Antipater and Olympias.

Then those of the Macedonians who were unfit for service on account of age or any other misfortune, went back of their own accord, to the number of about 10,000. To these Alexander gave the pay not only for the time which had already elapsed, but also for that which they would spend in returning home. He also gave to each man a talent in addition to his pay.[2] If any of them had children by Asiatic wives, he ordered them to leave them behind with him, lest they should introduce into Macedonia a cause of discord, taking with them children by foreign women who were of a different race from the children whom they had left behind at home born of Macedonian mothers. He promised to take care that they should be brought up as Macedonians, educating them not only in general matters but also in the art of war. He also undertook to lead them into Macedonia when they arrived at manhood, and hand them over to their fathers. These uncertain and obscure promises were made to them as they were departing; and he thought he was giving a most indubitable proof of the friendship and

---

[1] The paean was sung, not only before and after battle, but also after a banquet, as we see from this passage and from Xenophon (*Symposium*, ii. 1).

[2] About £240.

affection he had for them by sending with them, as their guardian and the leader of the expedition, Craterus, the man most faithful to him, and whom he valued equally with himself.[1] Then, having saluted them all, he with tears dismissed them likewise weeping from his presence. He ordered Craterus[2] to lead these men back, and when he had done so, to take upon himself the government of Macedonia, Thrace, and Thessaly, and to preside over the freedom of the Greeks. He also ordered Antipater to bring to him the Macedonians of manly age as successors to those who were being sent back. He despatched Polysperchon also with Craterus, as his second in command, so that if any mishap befell Craterus on the march (for he was sending him back on account of the weakness of his health), those who were going might not be in need of a general.[3] A secret report was also going about that Alexander was now overcome by his mother's accusations of Antipater, and that he wished to remove him from Macedonia.[4] This report was current among those who thought that royal actions are more worthy of honour in proportion to their secrecy, and who were inclined to impute what is worthy of belief to a bad motive rather

---

1 Literally "with his own head," an Homeric expression. We learn from Plutarch (*Eumenes*, 6), that Craterus was a great favourite with the Macedonians because he opposed Alexander's Asiatic innovations. See also Plutarch (*Alexander*, 47); *Diodorus*, xvii. 114:—*Κράτερον μὲν γὰρ εἶναι φιλοβασιλέα, Ἡφαιστίωνα δὲ φιλαλέξανδρον.*

2 The use of *κελεύειν* with the dative, is in imitation of Homer. Cf. i. 26, 3 supra.

3 We learn from Diodorus (xviii. 4) that when Alexander died, Craterus had got no farther than Cilicia on his return journey. He had with him a paper of written instructions, among which were projects for building an immense fleet in Phoenicia and the adjacent countries for conveying an expedition against the Carthaginians and the other western nations as far as the pillars of Hercules; for the erection of magnificent temples, and for the transportation of people from Europe into Asia and from Asia into Europe. Alexander's generals put these projects aside, as too vast for any one but Alexander himself.

4 Cf. *Curtius*, x. 31.

than to attribute it to the real one; a course to which they were led by appearances and their own depravity. But probably this sending for Antipater was not designed for his dishonour, but rather to prevent any unpleasant consequences to Antipater and Olympias from their quarrel which he might not himself be able to rectify. For they were incessantly writing to Alexander, the former saying that the arrogance, acerbity, and meddlesomeness of Olympias was exceedingly unbecoming to the king's mother; insomuch that Alexander was related to have used the following remark in reference to the reports which he received about his mother:—that she was exacting from him a heavy house-rent for the ten months.[1] The queen wrote that Antipater was overweeningly insolent in his pretensions and in the service of his court, no longer remembering the one who had appointed him, but claiming to win and hold the first rank[2] among the Macedonians and Greeks. These slanderous reports about Antipater appeared to have more weight with Alexander, since they were more formidable in regard to the regal dignity. However no overt act or word of the king was reported, from which any one could infer that Antipater was in any way less in favour with him than before.[3]

---

[1] The Greeks reckoned according to the lunar months, and therefore they talked of ten months instead of nine as the period of gestation. Cf. *Herodotus*, vi. 63; Aristophanes (*Thesmoph.* 742); Menander (*Plocion*, fragment 3); Plautus (*Cistell*, i. 3, 15); Terence (*Adelphi*, iii. 4, 29).

[2] For this expression, cf. *Dion Cassius*, xlii. 57; Homer (*Iliad*, 23, 538); *Pausanias*, vii. 10, 2; *Herodotus*, viii. 104.

[3] Here there is a gap in the manuscripts of Arrian, which probably contained an account of the flight of Harpalus, the viceroy of Babylon, with the treasures committed to his care, and also a description of the dispute between Hephaestion and Eumenes. See *Photius* (codex 92).

CHAPTER XIII.

THE NISAEAN PLAIN.—THE AMAZONS.

IT is said that Hephaestion much against his will yielded to this argument and was reconciled to Eumenes, who on his part wished to settle the dispute.[1] In this journey[2] Alexander is said to have seen the plain which was devoted to the royal mares. Herodotus says that the plain itself was named Nisaean, and that the mares were called Nisaean[3]; adding that in olden times there were 150,000 of these horses. But at this time Alexander found not many above 50,000; for most of them had been carried off by robbers. They say that Atropates, the viceroy of Media, gave him a hundred women, saying that they were of the race of Amazons.[4] These had been equipped with the arms of male horsemen, except that they carried axes instead of spears and targets instead of shields. They also say that they had the right breast smaller than the left, and that they exposed it in battle. Alexander dismissed them from the army, that no attempt to violate them might be made by the Macedonians or

---

[1] Cf. Plutarch (*Eumenes*, 2).

[2] The march was from Opis to Media, as we see from the next chapter.

[3] Cf. *Herodotus* (iii. 106; vii. 40); *Strabo*, xi. 7 and 14; *Diodor.* xvii. 110; *Ammianus*, xxiii. 6. Sir Henry Rawlinson says: "With Herodotus, who was most imperfectly acquainted with the geography of Media, originated the error of transferring to that province the Nisea (Nesá) of Khorassan, and all later writers either copied or confounded his statement. Strabo alone has escaped from the general confusion. In his description we recognise the great grazing plains of Khawah, Alishtar, Huru, Sílakhur, Burburud, Japalak, and Feridun, which thus stretch in a continuous line from one point to another along the southern frontiers of Media." Alexander probably visited the westernmost of these pastures which stretch from Behistun to Ispahan along the mountain range. The form διαρπαγῆναι is used only by the later writers for διαρπασθῆναι.

[4] Cf. *Strabo*, xi. 5; *Diodorus*, xvii. 77; *Curtius*, vi. 19; *Justin*, xii. 3; *Arrian*, iv. 15; Homer (*Iliad*, iii. 189); Aeschylus (*Eumenides*, 655); Hippocrates (*De Aere, Aquis, et Locis*, p. 553).

barbarians; and he ordered them to carry word to their queen that he was coming to her in order to procreate children by her.[1] But this story has been recorded neither by Aristobulus nor Ptolemy, nor any other writer who is a trustworthy authority on such matters. I do not even think that the race of Amazons was surviving at that time; for before Alexander's time they were not mentioned even by Xenophon,[2] who mentions the Phasians, Colchians, and all the other barbaric races which the Greeks came upon, when they started from Trapezus or before they marched down to Trapezus. They would certainly have fallen in with the Amazons if they were still in existence. However it does not seem to me credible that this race of women was altogether fictitious, because it has been celebrated by so many famous poets. For the general account is, that Heracles marched against them and brought the girdle of their queen Hippolyte into Greece.[3] The Athenians also under Theseus were the first to conquer and repulse these women as they were advancing into Europe[4]; and the battle of the Athenians and Amazons has been painted by Micon,[5] no less than that of the Athenians and Persians. Herodotus also has frequently written about these women[6]; and so have the Athenian writers who have honoured the men who perished in war with funeral orations. They have men-

---

[1] The queen is called Thalestris by Diodorus and Curtius.

[2] This is a mistake, for Xenophon does mention the Amazons in the *Anabasis* (iv. 4, 16). For Trapezus and the Phasians see his *Anabasis* (iv. 8, 22; v. 6, 36.)

[3] See *Diodorus*, iv. 16. This was one of the twelve labours of Hercules.

[4] See Plutarch (*Theseus*, 26).

[5] "The Battle of the Amazons" was a celebrated painting in the Stoa Poecile at Athens, executed by Micon, son of Phanichus, a contemporary of Polygnotus about B.C. 460. Cf. Aristophanes (*Lysistrata*, 678): "Look at the Amazons whom Micon painted on horseback fighting with the men." See also *Pausanias* (i. 15; viii. 11).

[6] Cf. *Herodotus*, iv. 110–117; ix. 27.

tioned the exploit of the Athenians against the Amazons as one of their special glories.[1] If therefore Atropates showed any equestrian women to Alexander, I think he must have shown him some other foreign women trained in horsemanship, and equipped with the arms which were said to be those of the Amazons.[2]

CHAPTER XIV.

Death of Hephaestion.

In Ecbatana Alexander offered sacrifice according to his custom, for good fortune; and he celebrated a gymnastic and musical contest. He also held drinking parties with his Companions. At this time Hephaestion fell sick; and they say that the stadium was full of people on the seventh day of his fever, for on that day there was a gymnastic contest for boys. When Alexander was informed that Hephaestion was in a critical state, he went to him without delay, but found him no longer alive.[3] Different authors have given different accounts of Alexander's grief on this occasion; but they agree in this, that his grief was great. As to what was done in honour of Hephaestion, they make diverse statements, just as each writer was actuated by good-will or envy towards him, or even towards Alexander himself. Of the authors who have made these reckless statements, some seem to me to have thought that whatever Alexander said or did

---

[1] See Isocrates (*Panegyricus*, 19); Lysias (*Oratio Funebris*, near the beginning).

[2] *Strabo* (xi. 5) declined to believe in the existence of the Amazons altogether. However, even Julius Caesar spoke of them as having once ruled over a large part of Asia. See Suetonius (*Life of Julius Caesar*, 22). Eustathius, on *Dionysius Periegetes*, p. 110, derives the name *Amazones* from ά, *not*, and *μᾶζα*, *barley-bread*:—διὸ καὶ 'Αμαζόνες ἐκαλοῦντο οἷα μὴ μάζαις ἀλλὰ κρέασι θηρίων ἐπιστρεφόμεναι. This is not the usual derivation of the word.

[3] Cf. Plutarch (*Alex.* 72); *Diodorus* (xvii. 110).

to show his excessive grief for the man who was the dearest to him in the world, redounds to his own honour; whereas others seem to have thought that it rather tended to his disgrace, as being conduct unbecoming to any king and especially to Alexander. Some say that he lay prostrate on his companion's body for the greater part of that day, bewailing him and refusing to depart from him, until he was forcibly carried away by his Companions. Others that he lay upon the body the whole day and night. Others again say that he hanged the physician Glaucias, for having indiscreetly given the medicine[1]; while others affirm that he, being a spectator of the games, neglected Hephaestion, who was filled with wine. That Alexander should have cut off his hair in honour of the dead man, I do not think improbable, both for other reasons and especially from a desire to imitate Achilles, whom from his boyhood he had an ambition to rival.[2] Others also say that Alexander himself at one time drove the chariot on which the body was borne; but this statement I by no means believe. Others again affirm that he ordered the shrine of Asclepius in Ecbatana to be razed to the ground; which was an act of barbarism, and by no means in harmony with Alexander's general behaviour, but rather in accordance with the arrogance of Xerxes in his dealings with the deity, who is said to have let fetters down into the Hellespont, in order to punish it forsooth.[3] But the following statement, which has been recorded, does not seem to me entirely beyond the range of probability:—that when Alexander was marching to Babylon, he was met on the road by many embassies from Greece, among which were some Epidaurian envoys, who obtained

---

[1] Plutarch makes this statement.

[2] See Homer (*Iliad*, xxiii. 141, 152); *Arrian* (i. 12).

[3] See *Herodotus* (vii. 35). Xerxes means *the venerable king*. Cf. *Herod.*, vi. 98. See Donaldson's *New Cratylus*, sections 161, 479.

from him their requests.[1] He also gave them an offering to be conveyed to Asclepius, adding this remark:—"Although Asclepius has not treated me fairly, in not saving the life of my Companion, whom I valued equally with my own head."[2] It has been stated by most writers that he ordered honours to be always paid to Hephaestion as a hero; and some say that he even sent men to Ammon's temple to ask the god if it were allowable to offer sacrifice to Hephaestion as a god; but Ammon replied that it was not allowable. All the authorities, however, agree as to the following facts:—that until the third day after Hephaestion's death, Alexander neither tasted food nor paid any attention to his personal appearance, but lay on the ground either bewailing or silently mourning; that he also ordered a funeral pyre to be prepared for him in Babylon at the expense of 10,000 talents; some say at a still greater cost[3]; that a decree was published throughout all the barbarian territory for the observance of a public mourning.[4] Many of Alexander's Companions dedicated themselves and their arms to the dead Hephaestion in order to show their respect to him; and the first to begin the artifice was Eumenes, whom we a short time ago mentioned as having been at variance with him.[5] This he did that Alexander might not think he was pleased at Hephaestion's death. Alexander did not appoint any one else to be commander of the Companion cavalry in the place of Hephaestion, so that the name of that general might not perish from the brigade; but that division of cavalry was still called Hephaestion's and the

---

[1] Epidaurus in Argolis was celebrated as the chief seat of the worship of Aesculapius.

[2] This is an Homeric expression, meaning *myself*.

[3] Equal to £2,300,000. Plutarch (*Alex.* 72) agrees with Arrian. *Diodorus* (xvii. 115) and *Justin* (xii. 12) say 12,000 talents.

[4] Cf. Aelian (*Varia Historia*, vii. 8); *Diodorus* (xvii. 114, 115); Plutarch (*Alex.* 72, 75; *Eumenes*, 2; *Pelopidas*, 34).

[5] See p. 392, note 3.

figure made from Hephaestion went in front of it. He also resolved to celebrate a gymnastic and musical contest, much more magnificent than any of the preceding, both in the multitude of competitors and in the amount of money expended upon it. For he provided 3,000 competitors in all; and it is said that these men a short time after also competed in the games held at Alexander's own funeral.

CHAPTER XV.

Subjugation of the Cossaeans.—Embassies from Distant Nations.

The mourning was prolonged for many days; and as he was now beginning to recall himself from it, under such circumstances his Companions had less difficulty in rousing him to action. Then at length he made an expedition against the Cossaeans,[1] a warlike race bordering on the territory of the Uxians. They are mountaineers, inhabiting strong positions in separate villages. Whenever a force approached them, they were in the habit of retiring to the summits of their mountains, either in a body or separately as each man found it practicable; and thus they escaped, making it difficult for those who attacked them with their forces to come near them. After the enemy's departure, they used to turn themselves again to marauding, by which occupation they supported themselves. But Alexander subdued this race, though he marched against them in the winter; for neither winter nor ruggedness of ground

---

[1] Cossaea was a district on the north-east of Susiana, which the Persian kings never subdued, but purchased the quiet of the inhabitants by paying them tribute. It is supposed to be the Cush of the Old Testament. *Diodorus* (xvii. 111) says that Alexander completed his conquest of the Cossaeans in forty days. Plutarch (*Alex.* 72) says he called the massacre of the Cossaeans his offering to the manes of Hephaestion.

was any impediment either to him or to Ptolemy, son of Lagus, who led a part of the army in the campaign against them. Thus no military enterprise which Alexander undertook was ever unsuccessful. As he was marching back to Babylon, he was met by embassies from the Libyans, who congratulated him and crowned him as conqueror of the kingdom of Asia.[1] From Italy also came Bruttians, Lucanians, and Tyrrhenians[2] as envoys, for the same purpose. The Carthaginians are said to have sent an embassy to him at this time[3]; and it is also asserted that envoys came to request his friendship from the Ethiopians, the Scythians of Europe, the Gauls, and Iberians—nations whose names were heard and their accoutrements seen then for the first time by Greeks and Macedonians. They are also said to have entrusted to Alexander the duty of settling their disputes with each other. Then indeed it was especially evident both to himself and to those about him that he was lord of all the land and sea.[4] Of the men who have written the history of Alexander, Aristus and Asclepiades[5] alone say that the Romans also sent an embassy to him, and that when he met their embassy, he predicted something of the future power of Rome, observing both the attire of the men, their love of labour, and their devotion to freedom. At the same time he made urgent inquiries about their political constitution. This incident I have recorded neither as certainly authentic nor as altogether incredible; but none of the Roman writers have made

---

[1] Cf. *Livy*, vii. 37, 38; *Pliny*, xxii. 4; *Justin*, xii. 13.

[2] The Romans called these people Etruscans.

[3] *Justin* (xxi. 6) says that the Carthaginians sent Hamilcar to learn Alexander's real designs against them, under the pretence of being an exile offering his services.

[4] Cf. *Diodorus*, xvii. 113.

[5] Aristus was a man of Salamis in Cyprus. Neither his work nor that of Asclepiades is extant. Aristus is mentioned by *Athenaeus* (x. 10) and *Strabo* (lib. xv.).

any mention of this embassy having been despatched to Alexander; nor of those who have written an account of Alexander's actions, has either Ptolemy, son of Lagus, or Aristobulus mentioned it. With these authors I am generally inclined to agree. Nor does it seem likely that the Roman republic, which was at that time remarkable for its love of liberty, would send an embassy to a foreign king, especially to a place so far away from their own land, when they were not compelled to do so by fear or any hope of advantage, being possessed as they were beyond any other people by hatred to the very name and race of despots.[1]

CHAPTER XVI.

Exploration of the Caspian.—The Chaldaean Soothsayers.

After this, Alexander sent Heraclides, son of Argaeus, into Hyrcania in command of a company of shipwrights, with orders to cut timber from the Hyrcanian mountains and with it to construct a number of ships of war, some without decks and others with decks after the Grecian fashion of ship-building.[2] For he was very desirous of discovering with what sea the one called the Hyrcanian or Caspian unites; whether it communicates with the water of the Euxine Sea, or whether the Great Sea comes right round from the Eastern Sea, which is near India and flows up into the Hyrcanian Gulf; just as he had discovered that the Persian Sea, which was called the Red Sea, is really a gulf of the Great Sea.[3] For the

---

[1] *Livy* (ix. 18) says he does not think the contemporary Romans even knew Alexander by report.

[2] These are what Hirtius (*Bell. Alex.* 11) calls "naves apertas et constratas."

[3] See p. 155, note 6.

sources of the Caspian Sea had not yet been discovered, although many nations dwell around it, and navigable rivers discharge their waters into it. From Bactria, the Oxus, the largest of Asiatic rivers, those of India excepted, discharges itself into this sea[1]; and through Scythia flows the Jaxartes.[2] The general account is, that the Araxes also, which flows from Armenia, falls into the same sea.[3] These are the largest; but many others flow into these, while others again discharge themselves directly into this sea. Some of these were known to those who visited these nations with Alexander; others are situated towards the farther side of the gulf, as it seems, in the country of the Nomadic Scythians, a district which is quite unknown.

When Alexander had crossed the river Tigres with his army and was marching to Babylon, he was met by the Chaldaean philosophers[4]; who, having led him away from his Companions, besought him to suspend his march to that city. For they said that an oracular declaration had been made to them by the god Belus, that his entrance into Babylon at that time would not be for his good. But he answered their speech with a line from the poet Euripides to this effect: "He the best prophet is that guesses well."[5] But said the Chaldaeans:—"O king, do not at any rate enter the city looking towards the west,

---

[1] See p. 199, note 1. *Strabo* (xi. 7) says that Aristobulus declared the Oxus to be the largest river which he had seen except those in India.

[2] See p. 198, note 3. The Oxus and Jaxartes really flow into the Sea of Aral, or the Palus Oxiana, which was first noticed by *Ammianus Marcellinus* (xxiii. 6, 59) in the 4th century A.D. Ptolemy, however, mentions it as a small lake, and not as the recipient of these rivers. Cf. *Pliny*, vi. 18.

[3] The Araxes, or Aras, joins the Cyrus, or Kour, and falls into the Caspian Sea. It is now called Kizil-Ozan, or Yellow River. Its Hebrew name is Chabor (2 Kings xvii. 6). Pontem indignatus Araxes (Vergil, *Aeneid*, viii. 728). See Aeschylus (*Prometheus*, 736), Dr. Paley's note.

[4] As to the Chaldaeans, see Cicero (*De Div.*, i. 1) and *Diod.* (ii. 29–31).

[5] This is a verse from one of the lost tragedies of Euripides. It is

nor leading the army advancing in that direction; but rather go right round towards the east." But this did not turn out to be easy for him, on account of the difficulty of the ground; for the deity was leading him to the place where entering he was doomed soon to die. And perhaps it was better for him to be taken off in the very acme of his glory as well as of the affection entertained for him by men, before any of the vicissitudes natural to man befell him. Probably this was the reason Solon advised Croesus to look at the end of a long life, and not before pronounce any man happy.[1] Yea indeed, Hephaestion's death had been no small misfortune to Alexander; and I think he would rather have departed before it occurred than have been alive to experience it; no less than Achilles, as it seems to me, would rather have died before Patroclus than have been the avenger of his death.

CHAPTER XVII.

The Advice of the Chaldees Rejected.

But he had a suspicion that the Chaldaeans were trying to prevent his entrance into Babylon at that time with reference rather to their own advantage than to the declaration of the oracle. For in the middle of the city of the Babylonians was the temple of Belus,[2] an edifice very great in size, constructed of baked bricks which

---

also quoted by Cicero (*De Divin.*, ii. 5): Est quidam Graecus vulgaris in hanc sententiam versus; bene qui conjiciet, vatem hunc perhibebo optimum.

[1] See *Herodotus* (i. 32); Plutarch (*Solon*, 27).

[2] See p. 171, note 3. *Herodotus* (i. 181) gives a description of this temple, which he says existed in his time. *Strabo* (xvi. 1) agrees with Arrian that it was said to have been destroyed by Xerxes. He also says that Alexander employed 10,000 men in clearing away the rubbish of the ruins. Professor Sayce and others adduce this passage of Arrian to prove that Herodotus is not to be trusted even when he says he had seen the places and things which he describes. The words of Herodotus are ἐς

were cemented together with bitumen. This temple had been razed to the ground by Xerxes, when he returned from Greece; as were also all the other sacred buildings of the Babylonians. Some say that Alexander had formed the resolution to rebuild it upon the former foundations; and for this reason he ordered the Babylonians to carry away the mound. Others say that he intended to build a still larger one than that which formerly existed.[1] But after his departure, the men who had been entrusted with the work prosecuted it without any vigour, so that he determined to employ the whole of his army in completing it. A great quantity of land as well as gold had been dedicated to the god Belus by the Assyrian kings; and in olden times the temple was kept in repair and sacrifices were offered to the god. But at that time the Chaldaeans were appropriating the property of the god, since nothing existed upon which the revenues could be expended. Alexander suspected that they did not wish him to enter Babylon for this reason, for fear that in a short time the temple would be finished, and they should be deprived of the gains accruing from the money. And yet, according to Aristobulus, he was willing to yield to their persuasions so far at least as to change the direction of his entry into the city. For this purpose, on the first day he encamped near the river Euphrates; and on the next day he marched along the bank, keeping the river on

---

ἐμὲ τοῦτο ἔτι ἐόν, meaning, not that he had himself seen the temple, but that it existed *till his time*. In chap. 183 he expressly states that he did not see other things which he is describing, but that he derived his information from the Chaldaeans. He was about twenty years of age when Xerxes was assassinated. It must not be forgotten that Strabo and Arrian lived five or six hundred years after Xerxes. The veracity of Strabo is never doubted; yet in his description of Babylon this author speaks of the walls and hanging gardens as if they were still in existence, though not expressly saying so.

[1] Cf. *Arrian*, iii. 16 supra.

his right hand, with the intention of passing beyond the part of the city turned towards the west, and there wheeling round to lead his army towards the east. But on account of the difficulty of the ground he could not march with his army in this direction; because if a man who is entering the city from the west, here changes his direction eastward, he comes upon ground covered with marshes and shoals. Thus, partly by his own will and partly against his will, he disobeyed the god.

CHAPTER XVIII.

Predictions of Alexander's Death.

Moreover Aristobulus has recorded the following story. Apollodorus the Amphipolitan, one of Alexander's Companions, was general of the army which the king left with Mazaeus, the viceroy of Babylon.[1] When he joined his forces with the king's on the return of the latter from India, and observed that he was severely punishing the viceroys who had been placed over the several countries, he sent to his brother Peithagoras and asked him to divine about his safety. For Peithagoras was a diviner who derived his knowledge of the future from the inspection of the inward parts of animals. This man sent back to Apollodorus, inquiring of whom he was so especially afraid, as to wish to consult divination. The latter wrote back: "The king himself and Hephaestion." Peithagoras therefore in the first place offered sacrifice with reference to Hephaestion. But as there was no lobe visible upon the liver of the sacrificial victim,[2] he stated this fact in a letter, which he sealed and sent to his brother from Babylon to Ecbatana, explaining that there was no reason at all to be afraid

---

[1] See *Arrian*, iii. 16 supra.

[2] Cf. Philostratus (*Life of Apollonius*, viii. 7, 5).

of Hephaestion, for in a short time he would be out of their way. And Aristobulus says that Apollodorus received this epistle only one day before Hephaestion died. Then Peithagoras again offered sacrifice in respect to Alexander, and the liver of the victim consulted in respect to him was also destitute of a lobe. He therefore wrote to Apollodorus to the same purport about Alexander as about Hephaestion. Apollodorus did not conceal the information sent to him, but told Alexander, in order the more to show his good-will to the king, if he urged him to be on his guard lest some danger might befall him at that time. And Aristobulus says that the king commended Apollodorus, and when he entered Babylon, he asked Peithagoras what sign he had met with, to induce him to write thus to his brother. He said that the liver of the victim sacrificed for him was without a lobe. When Alexander asked what the sign portended, he said that it was a very disastrous one. The king was so far from being angry with him, that he even treated him with greater respect, for telling him the truth without any disguise. Aristobulus says that he himself heard this story from Peithagoras; and adds that the same man acted as diviner for Perdiccas and afterwards for Antigonus, and that the same sign occurred for both. It was verified by fact; for Perdiccas lost his life leading an army against Ptolemy,[1] and Antigonus was killed in the battle fought by him at Ipsus against Seleucus and Lysimachus.[2] Also concerning Calanus, the Indian philosopher, the following story has been recorded. When he was going to the funeral pyre to die, he gave the parting salutation to all his other companions; but he refused to approach Alexander to

---

[1] Perdiccas was killed by his own troops at Memphis, B.C. 321. See *Diodorus*, xviii. 36.

[2] The battle of Ipsus was fought B.C. 301. See Plutarch (*Demetrius*, 29).

give him the salutation, saying he would meet him at Babylon and there salute him. At the time indeed this remark was treated with neglect; but afterwards, when Alexander had died at Babylon, it came to the recollection of those who had heard it, and they thought forsooth that it was a divine intimation of Alexander's approaching end.

CHAPTER XIX.

EMBASSIES FROM GREECE.—FLEET PREPARED FOR INVADING ARABIA.

As he was entering Babylon, he was met by embassies from the Greeks; but for what purpose each embassy was sent has not been recorded.[1] To me indeed it seems probable that most of them came to crown and eulogize him on account of his victories, especially the Indian ones, as well as to say that the Greeks rejoiced at his safe return from India. It is said that he greeted these men with the right hand, and after paying them suitable honour sent them back. He also gave the ambassadors permission to take with them all the statues of men and images of gods and the other votive offerings which Xerxes had carried off from Greece to Babylon, Pasargadae, Susa, or any other place in Asia. In this way it is said that the brazen statues of Harmodius and Aristogeiton,[2] as well as the monument of the Celcaean Artemis, were carried back to Athens.[3]

Aristobulus says that he found at Babylon the fleet with Nearchus, which had sailed from the Persian Sea up the river Euphrates; and another which had been conveyed

---

[1] *Diodorus* (xvii. 113) says that embassies came from the Carthaginians, Liby-Phoenicians, Greeks, Macedonians, Illyrians, Thracians, and Gauls.

[2] Cf. *Arrian*, iii. 16 supra.

[3] The name Athens is said to have been derived from the worship of Athena. See Euripides (*Ion*, 8): Πόλις τῆς χρυσολόγχου Παλλάδος κεκλημένη. Attica is ἀττική or ἀκτικὴ γῆ, the "promontory land."

from Phoenicia, consisting of two Phoenician quinqueremes, three quadriremes, twelve triremes, and thirty triacontors. These had been taken to pieces and conveyed to the river Euphrates from Phoenicia to the city of Thapsacus. There they were joined together again and sailed down to Babylon. The same writer says that he cut down the cypresses in Babylonia and with them built another fleet; for in the land of the Assyrians these trees alone are abundant, but of the other things necessary for ship-building this country affords no supply. A multitude of purple-fishers and other sea-faring men came to him from Phoenicia and the rest of the sea-board to serve as crews for the ships and perform the other services on board. Near Babylon he made a harbour by excavation large enough to afford anchorage to 1,000 ships of war; and adjoining the harbour he made dockyards. Miccalus the Clazomenian[1] was despatched to Phoenicia and Syria with 500 talents[2] to enlist some men and to purchase others who were experienced in nautical affairs. For Alexander designed to colonize the sea-board near the Persian Gulf, as well as the islands in that sea. For he thought that this land would become no less prosperous than Phoenicia. He made these preparations of the fleet to attack the main body of the Arabs,[3] under the pretext that they were the only barbarians of this region who had not sent an embassy to him or done anything else becoming their position and showing respect to him. But the truth was, as it seems to me, that Alexander was insatiably ambitious of acquiring fresh territory.[4]

---

[1] Clazomenae was an Ionian city on the Gulf of Smyrna, celebrated as the birthplace of Anaxagoras. It is now called Kelisman.

[2] About £1,200,000. [3] The Hebrew name for Arabia is Arâb (wilderness). In Gen. xxv. 6 it is called the "East country," and in Gen. xxix. 1 the "Land of the Sons of the East."

[4] Cf. *Arrian*, v. 26; vii. 1 and 15 supra.

CHAPTER XX.

Description of Arabia.—Voyage of Nearchus.

The common report is, that he heard that the Arabs venerated only two gods, Uranus and Dionysus[1]; the former because he is visible and contains in himself the heavenly luminaries, especially the sun, from which emanates the greatest and most evident benefit to all things human; and the latter on account of the fame he acquired by his expedition into India. Therefore he thought himself quite worthy to be considered by the Arabs as a third god, since he had performed deeds by no means inferior to those of Dionysus. If then he could conquer the Arabs, he intended to grant them the privilege of conducting their government according to their own customs, as he had already done to the Indians. The fertility of the land was a secret inducement to him to invade it; because he heard that the people obtained cassia from the lakes, and myrrh and frankincense from the trees; that cinnamon was cut from the shrubs, and that the meadows produce spikenard without any cultivation.[2] As to the size of the country, he was informed that the seaboard of Arabia was not less in extent than that of India; that near it lie many islands; that in all parts of the country there were harbours sufficiently commodious to provide anchorage for his fleet, and that it supplied sites for founding cities, which would become flourishing. He was also informed that there were two islands in the sea facing the mouth of the Euphrates, the first of which was not far from the place where the waters of that river are discharged into the sea, being about 120 stades[3]

---

[1] Cf. *Herodotus*, iii. 8.

[2] Cf. *Herodotus*, ii. 40, 86; iii. 110–112; *Strabo*, xvi. 4; Pliny (*Nat. Hist.* xii.).

[3] About 17 miles.

distant from the shore and the river's mouth. This is the smaller of the two, and was densely covered with every kind of timber. In it was also a temple of Artemis, around which the inhabitants themselves spent their lives. The island was devoted to the use of wild goats and stags, which were allowed to range at large as being dedicated to Artemis. It was unlawful to chase them unless any one wished to offer sacrifice to the goddess; and for this purpose alone it was lawful to chase them. Aristobulus says that Alexander ordered this island to be called Icarus, after the island so named in the Aegean Sea,[1] on which, as the report goes, Icarus, son of Daedalus fell, when the wax, by which the wings had been fastened to him, melted. For he did not fly near the earth, according to his father's injunctions, but senselessly flying far aloft, he allowed the sun to soften and loosen the wax. Icarus left his name to the island and the sea, the former being called Icarus and the latter the Icarian. The other island was said to be distant from the mouth of the Euphrates about a day and night's voyage for a ship running before the breeze. Its name was Tylus[2]; it was large and most of it neither rugged nor woody, but suitable for producing cultivated fruits and all things in due season. Some of this information was imparted to Alexander by Archias, who was sent with a triacontor to investigate the course of the coasting voyage to Arabia, and who went as far as the island of Tylus, but durst not pass beyond that point. Androsthenes[3] was despatched with another triacontor and sailed to a part of the peninsula of Arabia. Hieron of

---

[1] One of the Sporades, west of Samos, now called Nikaria. Cf. Horace (*Carm.*, iv. 2, 2) and Ovid (*Fasti*, iv. 28).

[2] Called Tyrus by *Strabo* (xvi. 3). It is now called Bahrein, and is celebrated for pearl fisheries.

[3] A fragment of the work of Androsthenes descriptive of his voyage is preserved by *Athenaeus* (iii. p. 936).

Soli the pilot also received a triacontor from Alexander and advanced farthest of those whom he despatched to this region; for he had received instructions to sail round the whole Arabian peninsula as far as the Arabian Gulf near Egypt over against Heroopolis.[1] Although he coasted along the country of the Arabs to a great distance, he durst not go as far as he was ordered; but returning to Alexander he reported that the size of the peninsula was marvellous, being only a little smaller than the country of the Indians, and its extremity projected far into the Great Sea.[2] Nearchus indeed in his voyage from India had seen this stretching out a little, before he turned aside into the Persian Gulf, and he was almost induced to cross over to it. The pilot Onesicritus thought they ought to have gone thither; but Nearchus says that he himself prevented it, so that after sailing right round the Persian Gulf he might be able to give a report to Alexander that he had accomplished the voyage on which he had sent him. For Nearchus said he had not been despatched to navigate the Great Sea, but to explore the land bordering on the sea, to find out what men inhabit it, to discover the harbours and rivers in it, to ascertain the customs of the people, and to see if any of the country was fertile and if any was sterile. This was the reason why Alexander's naval expedition returned in safety; for if it had sailed beyond the deserts of Arabia, it would not have returned in safety. This is said also to have been the reason why Hieron turned back.[3]

---

[1] Probably Ramses. Its ruins are at Abu-Kesheb.

[2] Probably the projection now called Ras-al-Had.

[3] Cf. Arrian (*Indica*, 32).

CHAPTER XXI.

Description of the Euphrates and the Pállacopas.

While the triremes were being built for him, and the harbour near Babylon was being excavated, Alexander sailed from Babylon down the Euphrates to what was called the river Pallacopas, which is distant from Babylon about 800 stades.[1] This Pallacopas is not a river rising from springs, but a canal cut from the Euphrates. For that river flowing from the Armenian mountains,[2] proceeds within its banks in the season of winter, because its water is scanty; but when the spring begins to make its appearance, and especially just before the summer solstice, it pours along with mighty stream and overflows its banks into the Assyrian country.[3] For at that season the snow upon the Armenian mountains melts and swells its water to a great degree; and as its stream flows high above the level of the country, it would flow over the land if some one had not furnished it with an outlet along the Pallacopas and turned it aside into the marshes and pools, which, beginning from this canal, extend as far as the country contiguous to Arabia. Thence it spreads out far and wide into a shallow lake, from which it falls into the sea by many invisible mouths. After the snow has melted, about the time of the setting of the Pleiades, the Euphrates flows with a small stream; but none the less the greater part of it discharges itself into the pools along the Pallacopas. Unless, therefore, some one

---

[1] About 90 miles. This canal fell into the Persian Gulf at Teredon. No trace of it now remains.

[2] The Hebrew name for Armenia is Ararat (2 Kings xix. 37; Isa. xxxvii. 38; Jer. li. 27).

[3] The country called Assyria by the Greeks is called Asshur (level) in Hebrew. In Gen. x. 11 the foundation of the Assyrian kingdom is ascribed to Nimrod; for the verse ought to be translated: "He went forth from that land into Asshur." Hence in Micah v. 6, Assyria is called the "land of Nimrod."

had dammed up the Pallacopas again, so that the water might be turned back within the banks and carried down the channel of the river, it would have drained the Euphrates into itself, and consequently the Assyrian country would not be watered by it. But the outlet of the Euphrates into the Pallacopas was dammed up by the viceroy of Babylonia with great labour (although it was an easy matter to construct the outlet), because the ground in this region is slimy and most of it mud, so that when it has once received the water of the river it is not easy to turn it back. But more than 10,000 Assyrians were engaged in this labour even until the third month. When Alexander was informed of this, he was induced to confer a benefit upon the land of Assyria. He determined to shut up the outlet where the stream of the Euphrates was turned into the Pallacopas. When he had advanced about thirty stades, the earth appeared to be somewhat rocky, so that if it were cut through and a junction made with the old canal along the Pallacopas, on account of the hardness of the soil, it would not allow the water to percolate, and there would be no difficulty in turning it back at the appointed season. For this purpose he sailed to the Pallacopas, and then continued his voyage down that canal into the pools towards the country of the Arabs. There seeing a certain admirable site, he founded a city upon it and fortified it. In it he settled as many of the Grecian mercenaries as volunteered to remain, and such as were unfit for military service by reason of age or wounds.

CHAPTER XXII.

An Omen of Alexander's Approaching Death.

Having thus proved the falsity of the prophecy of the Chaldaeans, by not having experienced any unpleasant fortune in Babylon,[1] as they had predicted, but having marched out of that city without suffering any mishap, he grew confident in spirit and sailed again through the marshes, having Babylon on his left hand. Here a part of his fleet lost its way in the narrow branches of the river through want of a pilot, until he sent a man to pilot it and lead it back into the channel of the river. The following story is told. Most of the tombs of the Assyrian kings had been built among the pools and marshes.[2] When Alexander was sailing through these marshes, and, as the story goes, was himself steering the trireme, a strong gust of wind fell upon his broad-brimmed Macedonian hat, and the fillet which encircled it. The hat, being heavy, fell into the water; but the fillet, being carried along by the wind, was caught by one of the reeds growing near the tomb of one of the ancient kings.[3] This incident itself was an omen of what was about to occur, and so was the fact that one of the sailors[4] swam off towards the fillet and snatched it from the reed. But he did not carry it in his hands, because it would have been wetted while he was swimming; he therefore put it round his own head and thus conveyed it to the king. Most of the biographers of Alexander say that

---

[1] The Hebrew name for Babylon is Babel, *i.e.* Bab-Bel, *court of Bel:* porta vel aula, civitas Beli (*Winer*). In Jer. xxv. 26; li. 41, it is called Sheshach, which Jewish commentators, followed by Jerome, explain by the Canon Atbash, *i.e.* after the alphabet put in an inverted order. According to this rule the word Babel, which is the Hebrew name of Babylon, would be written Sheshach. Sir Henry Rawlinson, however, says it was the name of a god after whom the city was named; and the word has been found among the Assyrian inscriptions representing a deity.

[2] The perfect passive *δεδόμημαι* is equivalent to the Epic and Ionic form *δέδμημαι.*

[3] *σχεθῆναι.* See p. 268, note 4.

[4] *τῶν τὶς ναυτῶν.* This position of *τὶς* is an imitation of the usage in Ionic prose. Cf. *Herod.* i. 85; *τῶν τὶς Περσέων.* See *Liddell and Scott*, sub voce *τὶς.* Cf. *Arrian*, ii. 26, 4; vi. 9, 3; vii. 3, 4; 22, 5; 24, 2.

the king presented him with a talent as a reward for his zeal, and then ordered his head to be cut off; as the prophets had directed him not to permit that head to be safe which had worn the royal fillet. However, Aristobulus says that the man received a talent; but afterwards also received a scourging for placing the fillet round his head. The same author says that it was one of the Phoenician sailors who fetched the fillet for Alexander; but there are some who say it was Seleucus, and that this was an omen to Alexander of his death and to Seleucus of his great kingdom. For that of all those who succeeded to the sovereignty after Alexander, Seleucus became the greatest king, was the most kingly in mind, and ruled over the greatest extent of land after Alexander himself, does not seem to me to admit of question.[1]

CHAPTER XXIII.

The Army Recruited from the Persians.—Hephaestion's Memory Honoured.

When he returned to Babylon he found that Peucestas had arrived from Persis, bringing with him 20,000 Persians, as well as many Cossaeans and Tapurians, because these races were reported to be the most warlike of those bordering on Persis. Philoxenus also came to him, bringing an army from Caria; Menander, with another from Lydia, and Menidas with the cavalry which had been put under his command.[2] At the same time arrived embassies from Greece, the members of which, with crowns upon their own heads, approached Alexander and crowned him with golden crowns, as if forsooth they came to him as special envoys deputed to pay him divine

---

[1] Cf. *Arrian* v. 13 supra. [2] Cf. *Arrian*, iii. 6; iv. 18.

honours; and his end was not far off. Then he commended the Persians for their great zeal towards him, which was shown by their obedience to Peucestas in all things, and Peucestas himself for the prudence which he had displayed in ruling them. He distributed these foreign soldiers among the Macedonian ranks in the following way. Each company was led by a Macedonian decurion, and next to him was a Macedonian receiving double pay for distinguished valour; and then came one who received ten staters,[1] who was so named from the pay he received, being less than that received by the man with double pay, but more than that of the men who were serving as soldiers without holding a position of honour. Next to these came twelve Persians, and last in the company another Macedonian, who also received the pay of ten staters; so that in each company there were twelve Persians and four Macedonians, three of whom received higher pay, and the fourth was in command of the company.[2] The Macedonians were armed in their hereditary manner; but of the Persians some were archers, while others had javelins furnished with straps, by which they were held.[3] At this time Alexander often reviewed his fleet, had many sham-fights with his triremes and quadriremes in the river, and contests both for rowers and pilots, the winners receiving crowns.

Now arrived the special envoys whom he had despatched to Ammon to inquire how it was lawful for him to honour Hephaestion. They told him that Ammon said it was lawful to offer sacrifice to him as to a hero. Rejoicing at the response of the oracle, he paid respect to him as a hero from that time. He also despatched a letter to Cleomenes, who was a bad man and had committed many

---

[1] The Macedonian stater was worth about £1 3*s.* 6*d.*

[2] Cf. Arrian (*Tactics*, 12, 11).

[3] Cf. *Arrian*, p. 379, note 1.

acts of injustice in Egypt.[1] For my own part I do not blame him for his friendship to Hephaestion and for his recollection of him even when dead; but I do blame him for many other acts. For the letter commanded Cleomenes to prepare chapels for the hero Hephaestion in the Egyptian Alexandria, one in the city itself and another in the island of Pharos, where the tower is situated.[2] The chapels were to be exceedingly large and to be built at lavish expense. The letter also directed that Cleomenes should take care that Hephaestion's name should be attached to them; and moreover that his name should be engraved on all the legal documents with which the merchants entered into bargains with each other.[3] These things I cannot blame, except that he made so much ado about matters of trifling moment. But the following I must blame severely: "If I find," said the letter, "the temples and chapels of the hero Hephaestion in Egypt well completed, I will not only pardon you any crimes you may have committed in the past, but in the future you shall suffer no unpleasant treatment from me, however great may be the crimes you have committed." I cannot commend this message sent from a great king to a man who was ruling a large country and many people, especially as the man was a wicked one.[4]

---

[1] We read in the speech of Demosthenes against Dionysiodorus (1285), that Cleomenes and his partisans enriched themselves by monopolizing the exportation of corn from Egypt. Cf. *Arrian*, iii. 5 supra.

[2] This island is mentioned by Homer (*Odyssey*, iv. 355). Alexander constructed a mole seven stades long from the coast to the island, thus forming the two harbours of Alexandria. See *Strabo*, xvii. 1. The island is chiefly famous for the lofty tower built upon it by Ptolemy Philadelphus, for a lighthouse. Cf. Caesar (*De Bello Civili*, iii. 112); *Ammianus*, xxii. 16.

[3] Consult Lucian (*Calumniae non temere credendum*, 17).

[4] After Alexander's death Cleomenes was executed by Ptolemy, who received Egypt as his share of the great king's dominions.

CHAPTER XXIV.

Another Omen of Alexander's Death.

But Alexander's own end was now near. Aristobulus says that the following occurrence was a prognostication of what was about to happen. He was distributing the army which came with Peucestas from Persia, and that which came with Philoxenus and Menander from the sea,[1] among the Macedonian lines, and becoming thirsty he retired from his seat and thus left the royal throne empty. On each side of the throne were couches with silver feet, upon which his personal Companions were sitting. A certain man of obscure condition (some say that he was even one of the men kept under guard without being in chains), seeing the throne and the couches empty, and the eunuchs standing round the throne (for the Companions also rose up from their seats with the king when he retired), walked through the line of eunuchs, ascended the throne, and sat down upon it.[2] According to a Persian law, they did not make him rise from the throne; but rent their garments and beat their breasts and faces as if on account of a great evil.

When Alexander was informed of this, he ordered the man who had sat upon his throne to be put to the torture, with the view of discovering whether he had done this according to a plan concerted by a conspiracy. But the man confessed nothing, except that it came into his mind at the time to act thus. Even more for this reason the diviners explained that this occurrence boded no good to him. A few days after this, after offering to the gods the customary sacrifices for good success, and certain others also for the purpose of divination, he was feasting with

---

[1] *I.e.* the Mediterranean.

[2] *Diodorus* (xvii. 116) and Plutarch (*Alex.*, 73) say that he was a bound prisoner. The latter says his name was Dionysius, and that he was a Messenian.

his friends, and was drinking far into the night.[1] He is also said to have distributed the sacrificial victims as well as a quantity of wine to the army throughout the companies and centuries. There are some who have recorded that he wished to retire after the drinking party to his bed-chamber; but Medius, at that time the most influential of the Companions, met him and begged him to join a party of revellers at his residence, saying that the revel would be a pleasant one.

CHAPTER XXV.

Alexander Seized with Fever.

The Royal Diary gives the following account,[2] to the effect that he revelled and drank at the dwelling of Medius; then rose up, took a bath, and slept; then again supped at the house of Medius and again drank till far into the night. After retiring from the drinking party he took a bath; after which he took a little food and slept there, because he already felt feverish. He was carried out upon a couch to the sacrifices, in order that he might offer them according to his daily custom. After performing the sacred rites he lay down in the banqueting hall until dusk. In the meantime he gave instructions to the officers about the expedition and voyage, ordering those who were going on foot to be ready on the fourth day, and those who were going to sail with him to be ready to sail on the fifth day. From

---

[1] Plutarch (*Alex.*, 75) and *Justin* (xii. 13) say that he gave a banquet to Nearchus the admiral, and that, as he was leaving it, he was invited to the revel by Medius the Thessalian. Cf. *Diodorus*, xvii. 117.

[2] We learn from *Athenaeus* (x. p. 434 B) that this Court Journal was kept by the royal secretary, Eumenes, afterwards so famous, and by the historian, Diodotus of Erythrae. As to the last days of Alexander, cf. Plutarch (*Alex.*, 76, 77).

this place he was carried upon the couch to the river, where he embarked in a boat and sailed across the river to the park. There he again took a bath and went to rest.

On the following day he took another bath and offered the customary sacrifices. He then entered a tester bed, lay down, and chatted with Medius. He also ordered his officers to meet him at daybreak. Having done this he ate a little supper and was again conveyed into the tester bed. The fever now raged the whole night without intermission. The next day he took a bath; after which he offered sacrifice, and gave orders to Nearchus and the other officers that the voyage should begin on the third day. The next day he bathed again and offered the prescribed sacrifices. After performing the sacred rites, he did not yet cease to suffer from the fever. Notwithstanding this, he summoned the officers and gave them instructions to have all things ready for the starting of the fleet. In the evening he took a bath, after which he was very ill. The next day he was transferred to the house near the swimming-bath, where he offered the prescribed sacrifices. Though he was now very dangerously ill, he summoned the most responsible of his officers and gave them fresh instructions about the voyage. On the following day he was with difficulty carried out to the sacrifices, which he offered; and none the less gave other orders to the officers about the voyage. The next day, though he was now very ill, he offered the prescribed sacrifices. He now gave orders that the generals should remain in attendance in the hall,[1] and that the colonels and captains should remain before the gates. But being now altogether in a dangerous state,

---

[1] Cf. *Curtius*, ix. 23: Mos erat principibus amicorum et custodibus corporis excubare ante praetorium, quotiens adversa regi valetudo incidisset.

he was conveyed from the park into the palace. When his officers entered the room, he knew them indeed, but could no longer utter a word, being speechless. During the ensuing night and day and the next night and day he was in a very high fever.

CHAPTER XXVI.

Alexander's Death.

Such is the account given in the Royal Diary. In addition to this, it states that the soldiers were very desirous of seeing him; some, in order to see him once more while still alive; others, because there was a report that he was already dead, imagined that his death was being concealed by the confidential body-guards, as I for my part suppose. Most of them through grief and affection for their king forced their way in to see him. It is said that when his soldiers passed by him he was unable to speak; yet he greeted each of them with his right hand, raising his head with difficulty and making a sign with his eyes. The Royal Diary also says that Peithon, Attalus, Demophon, and Peucestas, as well as Cleomenes, Menidas, and Seleucus, slept in the temple of Serapis,[1] and asked the god whether it would be better and more desirable for Alexander to be carried into his temple, in order as a suppliant to be cured by him. A voice issued from the god saying that he was not to be carried into the temple, but that it would be better for him to remain where he was. This answer was reported by the Companions; and soon after Alexander died, as if forsooth this were now

[1] Serāpis, or more correctly Sarapis, was an Egyptian deity, whose worship was introduced into Greece in the time of the Ptolemies. His worship was introduced into Rome, with that of Isis, in the time of Sulla. *Strabo* (xvii. 1) gives an account of his cultus in the celebrated temple at Canobus. The Serapeum at Alexandria, which contained the famous library, is described by *Ammianus*, xxii. 16.

the better thing. Neither Aristobulus nor Ptolemy has given an account differing much from the preceding. Some authors, however, have related that his Companions asked him to whom he left his kingdom; and that he replied: "To the best."[1] Others say, that in addition to this remark, he told them that he saw there would be a great funeral contest held in his honour.[2]

CHAPTER XXVII.

Rumour that Alexander was Poisoned.

I am aware that many other particulars have been related by historians concerning Alexander's death, and especially that poison was sent for him by Antipater, from the effects of which he died.[3] It is also asserted that the poison was procured for Antipater by Aristotle, who was now afraid of Alexander on account of Callisthenes.[4] It is said to have been conveyed by Cassander, the son of Antipater,[5] some recording that he conveyed it in the hoof of a mule, and that his younger brother Iollas gave it to the king.[6] For this man was the royal cup-bearer,

---

1 *I.e.* the most valiant.

2 To decide who was to succeed to his power. Cf. *Curtius*, x. 14; *Diodorus*, xvii. 117; *Justin*, xii. 15.

3 Cf. *Curtius*, x. 31; *Diodorus*, xvii. 117, 118; *Justin*, xii. 13. Plutarch (*Alex.*, 77) asserts that nothing was said about Alexander's being poisoned, until six years after, when Olympias, the enemy of Antipater, set the charge afloat.

4 See *Arrian*, iv. 10 supra.

5 Cassander was afterwards king of Macedonia and Greece. He put Olympias, Roxana, and her son Alexander Aegus to death, and bribed Polysperchon to put Barsine and her son Hercules to death. He died of dropsy, B.C. 297.

6 Cf. *Pausanias*, xviii. 4; *Curtius*, x. 31; Plutarch (*Alex.*, 77). The ancients called the poison, "the water of Styx"; it was obtained from Nonacris in the north of Arcadia, near which the river Styx took its origin. *Justin* (xii. 14) says: Cujus veneni tanta vis fuit, ut non aere, non ferro, non testa contineretur, nec aliter ferri nisi in ungula equi

and he happened to have received some affront from Alexander a short time before his death. Others have stated that Medius, being a lover of Iollas, took part in the deed; for he it was who induced the king to hold the revel. They say that Alexander was seized with an acute paroxysm of pain over the wine-cup, on feeling which he retired from the drinking bout.[1] One writer has not even been ashamed to record that when Alexander perceived he was unlikely to survive, he was going out to throw himself into the river Euphrates, so that he might disappear from men's sight, and leave among the men of after-times a more firmly-rooted opinion that he owed his birth to a god, and had departed to the gods. But as he was going out he did not escape the notice of his wife Roxana, who restrained him from carrying out his design. Whereupon he uttered lamentations, saying that she forsooth envied him the complete glory of being thought the offspring of the god. These statements I have recorded rather that I may not seem to be ignorant that they have been made, than because I consider them worthy of credence or even of narration.

CHAPTER XXVIII.

Character of Alexander.

Alexander died in the hundred and fourteenth Olympiad,

---

potuerit. Pliny (*Hist. Nat.*, xxx. 53) says: Ungulas tantum mularum repertas, neque aliam ullam materiam quae non perroderetur a veneno Stygis aquae, cum id dandum Alexandro magno Antipater mitteret, dignum memoria est, magna Aristotelis infamia excogitatum.

[1] *Diodorus* (xvii. 117) states that after drinking freely, Alexander swallowed the contents of a large goblet, called the cup of Heracles, and was immediately seized with violent pain. This statement, however, is contradicted by Plutarch. It seems from the last injunction of Calanus, the Indian philosopher, that it was considered the right thing to drink to intoxication at the funeral of a friend. See Plutarch (*Alex.*, 69).

in the archonship of Hegesias at Athens.[1] According to the statement of Aristobulus, he lived thirty-two years, and had reached the eighth month of his thirty-third year. He had reigned twelve years and these eight months.[2] He was very handsome in person, and much devoted to exertion, very active in mind, very heroic in courage, very tenacious of honour, exceedingly fond of incurring danger, and strictly observant of his duty to the gods. In regard to the pleasures of the body, he had perfect self-control; and of those of the mind, praise was the only one of which he was insatiable. He was very clever in recognising what was necessary to be done, even when it was still a matter unnoticed by others; and very successful in conjecturing from the observation of facts what was likely to occur. In marshalling, arming, and ruling an army, he was exceedingly skilful; and very renowned for rousing the courage of his soldiers, filling them with hopes of success, and dispelling their fear in the midst of danger by his own freedom from fear. Therefore even what he had to do in secret he did with the greatest boldness. He was also very clever in getting the start of his enemies, and snatching from them their advantages by secretly forestalling them, before any one even feared what was about to happen. He was likewise very steadfast in keeping the agreements and settlements which he made, as well as very secure from being entrapped by deceivers. Finally, he was very sparing in the expenditure of money for the gratification of his own pleasures; but he was exceedingly bountiful in spending it for the benefit of his associates.

---

[1] June, 323 B.C.

[2] Ptolemy took the embalmed body of Alexander to Egypt, and placed it in Memphis, but removed it a few years after to Alexandria. See *Curtius*, x. 31. Cf. Aelian (*Varia Historia*, xii. 64; xiii. 29).

CHAPTER XXIX.

Apology for Alexander's Errors.

That Alexander should have committed errors in his conduct from quickness of temper or from wrath,[1] and that he should have been induced to comport himself like the Persian monarchs to an immoderate degree, I do not think remarkable if we fairly consider both his youth [2] and his uninterrupted career of good fortune; likewise that kings have no associates in pleasure who aim at their best interests, but that they will always have associates urging them to do wrong. However, I am certain that Alexander was the only one of the ancient kings who, from nobility of character, repented of the errors which he had committed. The majority of men, even if they have become conscious that they have committed an error, make the mistake of thinking that they can conceal their sin by defending their error as if it had been a just action. But it seems to me that the only cure for sin is for the sinner to confess it, and to be visibly repentant in regard to it. Thus the suffering will not appear altogether intolerable to those who have undergone unpleasant treatment, if the person who inflicted it confesses that he has acted dishonourably; and this good hope for the future is left to the man himself, that he will never again commit a similar sin, if he is seen to be vexed at his former errors. I do not think that even his tracing his origin to a god was a great error on Alexander's part, if it was not perhaps merely a device to induce his subjects to show him reverence.[3] Nor does he seem to

---

[1] Cf. *Diodorus*, xvii. 4; ἡ ὀξύτης τοῦ νεανίσκου.

[2] Cf. *Curtius*, x. 18: Gloriae laudisque, ut justo major cupido, ita ut juveni et in tantis admittenda rebus.

[3] Plutarch (*Alex.*, 28) attributes the same motive to Alexander in representing himself to be the son of Zeus. *Livy* (ix. 18) says: Referre in tanto rege piget superbam mutationem vestis et desideratas humi

me to have been a less renowned king than Minos, Aeacus, or Rhadamanthus, to whom no insolence is attributed by the men of old, because they traced their origin to Zeus. Nor does he seem at all inferior to Theseus or Ion, the former being the reputed son of Poseidon, and the latter of Apollo. His adoption of the Persian mode of dressing also seems to me to have been a political device in regard to the foreigners, that the king might not appear altogether an alien to them; and in regard to the Macedonians, to show them that he had a refuge from their rashness of temper and insolence. For this reason I think, he mixed the Persian royal guards, who carried golden apples at the end of their spears,[1] among the ranks of the Macedonians, and the Persian peers [2] with the Macedonian body-guards. Aristobulus also asserts that Alexander used to have long drinking parties, not for the purpose of enjoying the wine, as he was not a great wine-drinker, but in order to exhibit his sociality and friendly feeling to his Companions.[3]

CHAPTER XXX.

Eulogy of Alexander.

Whoever therefore reproaches Alexander as a bad man, let him do so; but let him first not only bring before his mind all his actions deserving reproach, but also gather

jacentium adulationes, etiam victis Macedonibus graves, nedum victoribus; et foeda supplicia, et inter vinum et epula, caedes amicorum et vanitatem ementiendae stirpis. Consult the whole of the interesting passage in *Livy*, ix. 17–19. See also Aelian (*Varia Historia*, ii. 19; v. 12; ix. 37).

[1] Cf. *Herodotus*, vii. 41; *Arrian*, iii. 11 supra.

[2] Xenophon (*Cyropaedia*, vii. 5, 85) says that the Persian Equals-in-Honour, or Peers, spent their time about the Court.

[3] Cf. *Arrian*, iv. 14 supra; *Justin*, ix. 8; *Athenaeus*, x. p. 434 B; Aelian (*Varia Historia*, iii. 23; ix. 3; xii. 26).

into one view all his deeds of every kind. Then, indeed, let him reflect who he is himself, and what kind of fortune he has experienced; and then consider who that man was whom he reproaches as bad, and to what a height of human success he attained, becoming without any dispute king of both continents,[1] and reaching every place by his fame; while he himself who reproaches him is of smaller account, spending his labour on petty objects, which, however, he does not succeed in effecting, petty as they are. For my own part, I think there was at that time no race of men, no city, nor even a single individual to whom Alexander's name and fame had not penetrated. For this reason it seems to me that a hero totally unlike any other human being could not have been born without the agency of the deity. And this is said to have been revealed after Alexander's death by the oracular responses, by the visions which presented themselves to various people, and by the dreams which were seen by different individuals. It is also shown by the honour paid to him by men up to the present time, and by the recollection which is still held of him as more than human. Even at the present time, after so long an interval, other oracular responses in his honour have been received by the nation of the Macedonians. In relating the history of Alexander's achievements, there are some things which I have been compelled to censure; but I am not ashamed to admire Alexander himself. Those actions I have branded as bad, both from a regard to my own veracity, and at the same time for the benefit of mankind.[2] For this

---

[1] Europe and Asia. Arrian reckoned Libya, or Africa, as a part of Asia. See iii. 30; v. 26; vii. 1.

[2] Dr. Leonhard Schmitz says:—"Arrian is in this work one of the most excellent writers of his time, above which he is raised by his simplicity and his unbiassed judgment. Great as his merits thus are as an historian, they are yet surpassed by his excellence as an historical critic. His Anabasis is based upon the most trustworthy historians among the con-

reason I think that I undertook the task of writing this history not without the divine inspiration.

THE END OF THE HISTORY OF ALEXANDER'S DEEDS.

---

temporaries of Alexander, such as Ptolemy, Aristobulus, which two he chiefly followed, Diodotus of Erythrae, Eumenes of Cardia, Nearchus of Crete, and Megasthenes; and his sound judgment as to who deserved credit, justly led him to reject such authors as Onesicritus, Callisthenes, and others. No one at all acquainted with this work of Arrians can refuse his assent to the opinion of Photius (p. 73; comp. Lucian, *Alex.*, 2), that Arrian was the best among the numerous historians of Alexander. One of the great merits of the work, independent of those already mentioned, is the clearness and distinctness with which he describes all military movements and operations, the drawing up of the armies for battle, and the conduct of battles and sieges.' In all these respects the Anabasis is a masterly production, and Arrian shows that he himself possessed a thorough practical knowledge of military affairs. He seldom introduces speeches, but wherever he does he shows a profound knowledge of man; and the speech of Alexander to his rebellious soldiers, and the reply of Coenus, as well as some other speeches, are masterly specimens of oratory. Everything, moreover, which is not necessary to make his narrative clear is carefully avoided." See Smith's *Dictionary of Greek and Roman Biography*.

INDEX OF PROPER NAMES.

(*The numbers refer to the pages.*)

Abastanians, 340.
Abbot, 258.
Abdalonymus, 116.
Abdēra, 37.
Abian Scythians, 205.
Abicht, 213, 276, 283.
Abisares, 257, 264, 279, 298, 301, 315.
Aboukir, 142.
Abreas, 330–334.
Abūlites, 172, 173, 374.
Abȳdus, 37.
Abyssinia, 272.
Acĕsinēs, 271, 274, 298–300, 308, 315–325, 336, 339–341, 374, 387.
Achaeans, Port of, 37.
Achaemenids, 375.
Achilles, 38, 39, 139, 323, 396, 402.
Achilleus, 150.
Achmetha, 179.
Acropolis of Athens, 49, 173.
Acropolis of Sardis, 50.
Acūphis, 266–268.
Ada, 65, 66.
Addaeus, 63, 64.
Admētus, 131–133.
Adōnis, 116.
Adraistaeans, 301.
Aeacus, 226, 425.
Aeacidae, 138.
Aegae, 36.
Aegean Sea, 110, 408.
Aegina, 334.
Aegospotami, 31, 57.
Aegyptus, 276, 318.
Aeolis and Aeolians, 53, 71, 186, 383, 385.
Aeschines, 91, 113, 150.
Aeschȳlus, 149, 269, 338.
Aesculapius, 88, 397.
Aetolians, 26, 34.
Afghanistan, 155, 191.
Africa, 108, 203, 309.
Agallassa, 324.
Agamemnon, 37.
Agatho, 44, 164.
Agēnor, 133.
Agēsilaüs, 110.
Agis III., 109, 110, 173.
Agis the Argive, 223.
Agrianians, 11, 18, 19, 21, 23, *et passim.*
Ahasuerus, 364.
Aithiops, 272.
Alani, 2, 4.
Albanians, 155, 161, 164.
Albion, 125.
Alcetas, 246, 255, 256, 283.
Alcias, 77.
Alcmēna, 117, 145.
Alēian Plain, 89.
Alexander I., 33, 383.
Alexander the Great, *passim.*
Alexander Aegus, 242, 421.
Alexander, son of Aëropus, 27, 51, 68.
Alexander the Epirote, 152.
Alexandrīa, 141, 142, 143, 197, 206, 210, 247, 266, 340, 351, 416, 420, 423.
Alinda, 66.
Alpes, 125.
Amānic Gates, 91.
Amastrinē, 375.
Amathūs, 129.
Amazons, 234, 393–395.
Ambracia, 119.
Ammianus, 80, 106, 203, 229, 270, 271, 385, 401.
Amminaspes, 185.

Ammōn, 144-148, 223, 320, 347, 382, 397, 415.
Amphiaraüs, 89.
Amphilochians, 119.
Amphilochus, 89.
Amphīon, 30.
Amphipolis, 10, 12, 13, 37, 98, 107.
Amphitrītē, 320.
Amphoterus, 70, 144, 150.
Amyntas of Macedon, 19, 66.
Amyntas, son of Antiochus, 51, 69, 90, 91, 107, 109.
Amyntas, son of Andromenes, 29, 43, 50, 59, 162, 173, 174, 177, 188, 190, 192, 195.
Amyntas, son of Arrhabaeus, 40, 43-45, 59, 74, 95.
Amyntas, son of Nicolaüs, 237, 238, 247.
Amyntas the Theban, 25.
Anaxagoras, 407.
Anaxarchus, 222-226.
Anaxippus, 191, 192.
Anchialus, 87, 88.
Ancyra, 84.
Androcles, 129.
Andromachus, 127, 150, 162, 192, 210, 213-215.
Andronīcus, 189, 191.
Androsthenes, 409.
Anicētus, 134.
Antaeus, 145.
Antalcidas, 79, 80.
Anteas, 363.
Anthemūs, 98.
Antibēlus, 182.
Anticles, 230.
Antigĕnes, 291, 344.
Antigŏnē, 193.
Antigŏnus, 76, 88, 305, 405.
Anti-Libănus, 125, 156, 308.
Antiochus, 97, 149, 263.
Antipater, 26, 36, 43, 81, 102, 105, 109, 148, 162, 173, 231, 391, 392, 421.
Antipater, son of Asclepiodōrus, 230.
Antiphilus, 105.
Antoninus Pius, 2.
Aornus, 199, 258-263, 310.
Apelles, 48, 53, 88.
Aphrices, 279.
Apis, 142.
Apollo, 148, 196, 204, 389, 390, 425.
Apollodōrus, 171, 404, 405.
Apollonia, 40, 98.
Apollonides, 144.
Apollonius, 149.
Apollonius Rhodius, 56, 346.
Apollophanes, 351, 360.
Arab, 407.
Arabia and Arabians, 135, 140, 149, 172, 308, 309, 369, 407-412.
Arabian Gulf, 410.
Arabitians, 350.
Arabius River, 349, 350.
Arachotia and Arachotians, 155, 161, 183, 197, 275, 283, 341, 344, 360, 378, 387.
Arădus, 108, 111.
Aral Sea, 198, 199, 202, 234, 274, 401.
Aram, 87, 107, 156, 380.
Arărat, 411.
Arātus, 88.
Araxes, 177, 401.
Arbēla, 13, 98, 156-171, 334.
Arbūpales, 48.
Arcadia and Arcadians, 32, 34, 421.
Archelaüs, 36, 173, 199.
Archias, 409.
Arconnēsus, 65.
Areia and Areians, 155, 191-193, 197, 200, 216, 361, 378.
Areius River, 216.
Arēs, 45.
Arĕtes, 164, 166, 167.
Arĕtis, 46.
Argos and Argives, 51, 58, 89, 217, 224, 227.
Ariaces, 156.
Ariaspians, 196.
Arigaeum, 251.
Arimmas, 152.
Ariobarzanes, 155, 176, 177, 178, 189.
Arisbē, 40.
Aristander, 36, 70, 121, 137, 143, 154, 170, 211, 212, 235.
Aristo, 97, 162, 164, 165.
Aristobūlus, 3, 6, 83, 85, 101, 105, 145, 146, 148, 160, 193, 197, 198, 202, 209, 214, 220, 230, 231, 232, 277, 281, 297, 334, 344, 348, 351, 352, 363, 365, 366, 375, 394, 400, 404, 405, 406, 409, 414, 417, 421, 423, 425, 427.
Aristogeiton, 173, 224, 406.

Aristomēdes, 107.
Aristonīcus, 143, 144, 236, 237.
Aristonoüs, 363.
Aristophanes, 121, 152, 170, 231, 394.
Aristophon, 185.
Aristotle, 8, 18, 68, 81, 125, 223, 232, 271, 308, 421.
Aristus, 3, 399.
Armenia and Armenians, 107, 153, 155, 156, 161, 170, 171, 273, 401, 411.
Arrhabaeus, 68.
Arrhybas, 149.
Arrian, 1–5, 9, 10, 14, 20, 28, 40, 44, 49, 98, 101, 102, 119, 162, 168, 179, 202, 203, 244, 258, 265, 267, 268, 270, 273, 276, 277, 285, 304, 346, 355, 370, 392, 394, 399, 425, 426.
Arsaces, 315.
Arsames, 40, 85, 103, 189, 193, 200, 216.
Arses, 112, 113.
Arsimas, 112.
Arsinoē, 375.
Arsites, 40, 41, 48, 50.
Arta, 119.
Artabazus, 183, 189, 197, 199, 234–237, 242, 375.
Artacama, 375.
Artacoana, 192, 193.
Artaxerxes, 39, 112, 113, 192, 224, 227, 271, 364.
Artĕmis, 52, 53, 406, 409.
Artemisia, 66.
Artemisium, 334.
Artibōlēs, 379.
Artōnis, 375.
Arvad, 111.
Asander, 51, 88, 217.
Ascania Lake, 76.
Asclēpiadae, 333.
Asclēpiades, 3, 399.
Asclēpiodōrus, 148, 152, 171, 217, 230.
Asclēpius, 88, 333, 396.
Asia, 37, 38, 49, 58, 66, 91, 93, 106, 112, 114, 155, 156, 158, 178, 192, 197, 200, 203, 205, 210, 234, 242, 243, 270–272, 274, 276, 309, 369, 406, 426.
Asia Minor, 53, 59, 76, 79, 108, 151, 273, 275, 276, 308.
Aspasians, 249–251.
Aspendus, 71–73.
Assacēnians, 249, 253, 254, 263, 298.
Assacēnus, 256, 263.
Assagĕtes, 259.
Asshur, 411.
Assyria and Assyrians, 87, 89, 91, 154, 156, 172, 380, 407, 411–413.
Astes, 248.
Atbash, 413.
Athaliah, 58.
Atharrias, 64.
Athēna, 38, 49, 89, 104, 148, 247, 406.
Athenaeus, 409.
Athens and the Athenians, 1, 8, 9, 26, 31, 34, 35, 37, 49, 77, 79, 91, 105, 113, 115, 120, 150, 173, 178, 224, 227, 232, 384, 394, 406.
Atizyes, 69, 103.
Atlas Mountains, 309, 369.
Atropates, 155, 239, 365, 374, 375, 393, 395.
Attalus, 98, 163, 184, 195, 231, 235, 246, 250, 252, 256, 284, 344, 420.
Attica, 27, 406.
Attinas, 237.
Attock, 279.
Atūria, 154, 156.
Audaca, 250.
Aurelius, 2.
Austanes, 246, 247.
Autariatians, 19.
Autobares, 379.
Autophradates, 79, 80, 109–111, 117, 124, 143, 189, 190, 239.
Aven, 141.
Avienus, 118, 369.
Avon, 141.
Axenos, 15, 203, 313.
Azemilcus, 117, 133.
Azov Sea, 202, 274.
Azzah, 136.

Baal, 117, 171.
Babel, 413.
Babylon, 94, 153, 171, 172, 224, 239, 308, 372, 385, 396–420.
Babylonians, 155, 156, 161, 171, 402.
Bacchus, 221, 268, 362.

Bacchylides, 39.
Bactra, 187, 192, 196, 199, 202, 206, 233, 246, 247, 312, 385.
Bactria, 155, 183, 215, 236, 247, 263, 273, 284, 308, 319, 401.
Bactrians, 155, 161, 165, 170, 183, 192, 198, 199, 206, 234, 235, 237, 238, 378, 387.
Baetica, 118.
Bagae, 238.
Bagistanes, 182, 183.
Bagoas, 113, 367.
Bahrein, 409.
Balacrus, 76, 104, 149, 164, 165, 212, 252.
Balkan, 10.
Balkh, 187.
Bardylis, 18.
Barsaëntes, 155, 183, 185, 193.
Barsinē, 186, 242, 375, 421.
Baryaxes, 365.
Barzanes, 216.
Batis, 135–139.
Bazira, 256, 257, 259.
Beas River, 306.
Beghram, 197.
Beith-Shemesh, 141.
Beloochistan, 155, 196, 350, 354.
Bēlus, 171, 172, 401, 402, 413.
Berdes, 205.
Beroea, 151.
Bēssus, 155, 182–185, 191–202, 206, 216, 217, 263, 334.
Bianor, 107.
Bistanes, 113, 180.
Bithynia, 77, 108.
Bithynian Thracians, 77.
Boeōtarchs, 28.
Boeōtia, 26, 30.
Bospŏrus, 277.
Bottiaea, 13, 98.
Boupares, 155.
Brachmans, 327, 343.
Branchĭdae, 148, 204.
Briso, 163.
Britain, 370.
Bromius, 268.
Browne, 144.
Bruttians, 152, 399.
Būbaces, 103.
Būcĕphala, 296, 316.
Būcĕphalas, 288, 296, 297.
Būmōdus, 156, 334.
Būsiris, 145.
Byblus, 115.
Cabul, 247.
Cadiz, 108, 118, 203, 309.
Cadmēa, 25, 27, 30, 33.
Cadmus, 117.
Cadūsians, 155, 161, 180.
Caesar, 123, 278, 303, 395.
Caïcus, 275, 276.
Calanus, 149, 372–374, 405, 422.
Calas, 41, 44, 50, 51, 69, 84.
Callatis, 354.
Callicratidas, 190.
Callines, 389.
Callipolis, 88.
Callisthĕnes, 95, 101, 102, 146, 148, 222–232, 247, 421, 427.
Cambȳses, 140, 141, 226, 364.
Canōbus, 142, 420.
Caphtor, 110.
Cappadocia and Cappadocians, 2, 48, 84, 156, 161, 305, 308.
Caranus, 151, 197, 210, 214, 215, 217.
Carchēdōn, 313, 370.
Cardacĕs, 95.
Cardia, 305.
Cardūchi, 154, 172.
Caria and Carians, 58, 65, 66, 76, 88, 155, 161, 164, 186, 308, 318, 414.
Carim, 186.
Carmania, 344, 360–364, 387.
Carthage, 108, 116, 133, 309, 313, 370, 391, 399, 406.
Casdim, 172.
Caspian Gates, 179, 182, 308, 387.
Caspian Sea, 155, 161, 187, 199, 202, 234, 236, 274, 387, 400, 401.
Cassander, 19, 76, 88, 162, 242, 421.
Castor, 219.
Catanes, 246, 247.
Cathaeans, 301.
Cathaia, 319.
Catullus, 198.
Caucasus, 197–199, 202, 234, 247, 266–275, 284, 308, 387.
Caunus, 88.
Caȳster, 275, 276, 309.
Celaenae, 76.
Celts, 14, 18.
Cĕnaan, 107, 108.
Ceramīcus, 173.
Cercinītis Lake, 37.
Cĕrēth, 110.
Ceth, 109.

Chabor, 401.
Chaboras, 172.
Chaeronēa, 8, 144, 384.
Chalcedonians, 191.
Chalcis, 81.
Chaldaeans, 172, 401–403, 412.
Chandragupta, 275.
Chares, 35, 38, 102, 125, 144.
Charicles, 231.
Charidēmus, 35.
Chemi, 318.
Chenab, 298.
Chiddekel, 153.
Chios, 78, 109, 143, 144.
Choaspes, 172.
Choes, 249.
Chorasmians, 234, 273, 387.
Choriēnēs, 244–246.
Chrysippus, 88.
Cicero, 81, 84, 104, 232, 368, 401.
Cilicia, 85, 87, 88, 91, 104, 153, 173, 186, 197, 273, 391.
Cilician Gates, 84.
Cillūta, 347.
Cimōn, 72.
Citium, 109.
Cittim, 109.
Clazomĕnae, 407.
Cleander, 67, 75, 125, 163, 194, 361.
Clearchus, 39, 102, 152, 191, 227.
Cleomĕnes, 149, 415, 416, 420.
Cleōn, 224.
Cleopatra, 151, 152.
Cleophis, 256.
Clītarchus, 335.
Clītus, son of Bardylis, 18–25.
Clītus, son of Dropidas, 47, 162, 181, 195, 218-221, 232, 233, 235, 237, 248.
Cnĭdus, 88.
Coelē-Syria, 110, 156, 158, 161, 308, 385.
Coenus, 24, 43, 67, 77, 95, 131, 133, 162, 169, 177, 182, 190, 235, 236–239, 250, 256, 257, 259, 280, 284, 291, 299, 300, 311–314, 318, 427.
Coeranus, 151, 164.
Colchians, 234, 394.
Colōnae, 40.
Comēdae Mountains, 202.
Companions, 23, *et passim.*
Cŏnōn, 224.
Cōphaeus, 259.
Cōphēn, 114, 189, 379.
Cōphēn River, 247, 265.
Corē, 118.
Corinth, 9, 49, 79, 110, 334.
Corus, 53.
Cōs, 88, 109, 144, 333.
Cossaeans, 398, 414.
Crateas, 363.
Cratĕrus, 43, 44, 95, 126, 162, 175–177, 183, 188, 193, 206–209, 231, 237, 239, 246, 247, 250, 251, 253, 259, 283, 284, 289, 293, 297, 300, 319, 321, 322, 324, 337, 341–344, 361, 375, 391.
Crētē and Cretans, 58, 98, 108, 110.
Crētheus, 354.
Critodēmus, 333.
Croesus, 402.
Ctēsias, 3, 271.
Cūnaxa, 94, 102, 165.
Cūrium, 129.
Curtius, 77, 85, 96, 102, 114, 116, 139, 165, 203, 204, 219, 232, 241, 258, 333, 335, 358, 361, 419, 424.
Cush, 272, 398.
Cȳbĕlē, 275.
Cyclădēs, 80, 108.
Cydnus, 85.
Cȳmē, 71.
Cyna, 19.
Cyprus and Cyprians, 55, 108, 109, 120, 125–129, 132, 150, 318.
Cȳrēnē, 198, 385.
Cyreschăta, 207.
Cyropolis, 206, 208, 209.
Cȳrus the Elder, 84, 178, 196, 207, 208, 227, 236, 272, 355, 364, 367, 369.
Cȳrus the Younger, 39, 71, 76, 85, 87, 102.
Cyrus, camp of, 84.
Cythnus, 81.

Daans, 161, 198, 199, 284.
Dacians, 14.
Daedălus, 409.
Dăhae, 161.
Damascus, 103, 104, 114, 242.
Dammasek, 103.
Dandamis, 371, 372.
Daniel, 172, 307.
Danube, 12, 15, 270.

Darīus, 41, 48, 53, 59, 69, 79, 80, 90–114, 120, 134, 135, 140, 152–171, 179–187, 201, 211, 220, 227, 243, 277, 334, 364, 375.
Dascȳlium, 50.
Datămes, 80, 81.
Dataphernes, 200–202.
David, 110, 186.
Dēimăchus, 273.
Deinarchus, 113.
Delta, 270, 340, 343.
Delphi, 228.
Dēmādes, 34.
Dēmarātus, 47.
Dēmētrius, 76, 99, 162, 196, 228, 256, 284, 291, 300, 328, 335.
Dēmŏphōn, 420.
Dēmosthĕnēs, 35, 91, 113, 150, 175, 384, 416.
Dii, 10.
Dindȳmēnē, 275.
Dīnocrătes, 143.
Diodōrus, 28, 37, 41, 44, 48, 61, 64, 102, 116, 204, 379, 391, 422, 424.
Diŏdŏtus, 3, 418, 427.
Diogĕnes, 79, 90, 371.
Diōn Cassius, 1.
Dionȳsiodōrus, 115.
Dionȳsius of Halicarnassus, 59, 139, 285.
Dionȳsus, 117, 218, 221–225, 265–269, 310, 321, 338, 362, 387, 408.
Diophantus, 150.
Dioscūri, 218.
Diotimus, 35.
Dium, 48.
Dnieper, 270.
Doloaspis, 148.
Domitian, 2.
Don, 202, 203, 274.
Donaldson, 361, 383, 396.
Dorians, 273.
Doxareus, 279.
Drangiana and Drangians, 183, 193, 196, 239, 341, 387.
Drapsaca, 199.
Dropides, 190.
Dryden, 179.
Drypetis, 375.
Dyrta, 263.
Dysōrum, Mount, 383.
Eastern Sea, 309. 400.
Ecbătăna, 179–181, 217, 312, 395 396.
Egypt and Egyptians, 109, 118, 120, 135, 140–149, 158, 193, 266, 271, 276, 308, 317, 318, 385. 410, 416, 423.
Elaeūs, 37.
Elam, 364.
Ēlēans, 34, 77.
Elephantinē, 144.
Eleusis, 173.
Eleuthĕrae, 27.
Elimiōtis, 26.
Elymais, 364.
Embolima, 259.
England, 108.
Enȳălius, 45, 282.
Enylus, 116, 124.
Eordaea, 26, 363.
Eordaicus River. 20.
Epamīnōndas, 32.
Epardus River, 216.
Ephĕsus, 51–53.
Ephialtes, 35, 64.
Ephippus, 149.
Epictētus, 1, 2.
Epidaurians, 397.
Epigŏni, 378, 382.
Epimĕnes, 230, 231.
Epimĕnĭdēs, 110.
Ēpīrus, 19, 119.
Epocillus, 180, 216, 239.
Eratosthĕnes, 3, 269, 273, 274.
Erīgōn River, 20.
Erigyius, 151, 163, 181, 188, 189, 197.
Erythīa, 119.
Erythrae, 148.
Ethiopians, 272, 317, 369, 399.
Etruscans, 186, 399.
Etymander, 196, 216.
Euaspla River, 250.
Eubœa, 78, 81, 108. 181, 334.
Eudanĕmi, 173.
Eudēmus, 360.
Euergĕtae, 196, 216.
Eugnōstus, 149.
Eulaeus River, 107, 379. 380, 381.
Eumĕnes, 3, 43, 305, 375, 392, 397, 418, 427.
Euphrātes, 71, 91, 107, 134, 151, 153, 156, 274, 275, 277, 347, 369, 380, 381, 403, 406, 408, 411, 412, 422.

Euripĭdes, 401, 406.
Eurīpus, 81.
Europe, 14, 38, 119, 202, 203, 205, 270, 276, 370, 394, 426.
Eurybōtas, 29.
Eurylochus, 231.
Eurydĭcē, 151.
Eurymĕdōn, 72.
Eurystheus, 118, 119, 224.
Eusĕbius, 109.
Eustathius, 4, 395.
Euthycles, 114, 115.
Euxine Sea, 4, 15, 77, 94, 203, 234, 269, 313, 370, 400.
Evacae, 378.
Evius, 268.
Ewald, 149.

Fars, 364.
Frontinus, 358.
Ftah, 141, 142.

Gadeira, 203, 369.
Gadrosia, 196, 350–363, 374, 387.
Galatia, 84.
Ganges, 141, 270, 271, 274, 276, 281, 309, 317.
Gaugamēla, 156, 334.
Gauls, 14, 84, 399, 406.
Gaza, 110, 135–140, 206, 207.
Gebal, 116.
Gelo, 39.
Georgia, 155.
Geraestus, 78.
Gerostrătus, 111, 124.
Gerȳŏnēs, 118, 119.
Gesenius, 117.
Getae, 14–17.
Gibbon, 217.
Gibraltar, Straits of, 118, 203, 309.
Gizeh, 141.
Glaucias, 19–25, 162, 396.
Glaucippus, 55.
Glaucus, 171.
Glauganicians, 297.
Glausians, 297.
Gordium, 76, 77, 82.
Gordius, 82.
Gordȳaeans, 154.
Gorgias, 235, 248, 284.
Gorgons, 145.
Gough, 280.
Graikos, 308.
Granīcus, 41–49, 150, 220, 334.
Great Sea, 119, 270, 273, 274, 275, 309, 315, 317, 318, 347–349, 377, 385, 387, 400, 410.
Grecian Sea, 134, 266.
Greece, 81, 88, 93, 108, 112, 120, 142, 148, 173, 189, 234, 391, 394, 396, 406, 414, 420.
Greeks, *passim.*
Gronovius, 263.
Grote, 9, 16, 96, 103, 162, 375.
Gūraeans, 249, 253.
Gūraeus River, 253.

Hādrian, 1, 2.
Haemus, 10, 11.
Halicarnassus, 59–65, 69, 88, 109, 110, 186.
Hălys, 84.
Hamilcar, 399.
Hamley, 146.
Hannibal, 286.
Hanno, 309.
Hardinge, 280.
Harmŏdius, 173, 224, 406.
Harpălus, 151, 152, 181, 379, 392.
Hebrus, 37.
Hecataeus, 118, 275, 276.
Hecatomnus, 65.
Hector, 139.
Hēgelochus, 42, 80, 143, 144, 162.
Hēgĕmon, 296.
Hēgēsias, 139, 423.
Hēgēsistrătus, 53.
Hēliopolis, 141.
Hellanīcus, 62.
Hellēnes, 308, 383.
Hellespont, 36, 38, 234, 277, 307, 384, 396.
Heordaeans, see *Eordaea.*
Hēphaestion, 38, 85, 105, 106, 140, 169, 195, 228, 235, 236, 248, 249, 259, 264, 269, 284, 300, 315, 319, 321, 322, 324, 336, 344, 345, 348, 350–352, 363, 364, 375, 377, 379, 381, 391, 392, 395–397, 398, 402, 404, 415, 416.
Hēra, 119.
Heracles, son of Alexander, 242, 421.
Heracles or Hercules, 17, 38, 89, 104, 117–119, 121, 133, 134, 145, 150, 217, 224–227, 258, 263, 269, 310, 320, 394.
Hēracōn, 361, 362.

Hēraclīdes, 13, 162, 191, 400.
Hercules, Pillars of, 118, 203, 309, 391.
Hermolaüs, 230, 232.
Hermōtus, 40.
Hermus, 50, 275, 276.
Hērŏdŏtus, 14, 15, 58, 59, 108, 118, 141, 170, 202, 218, 226, 240, 244, 270, 271, 274–277, 286, 317, 358, 389, 392–394, 402, 413.
Hēromĕnes, 68.
Hērŏŏpŏlis, 149, 410.
Hēropythus, 52.
Hērostrătus, 52.
Hēsychius, 95.
Hidrieus, 65, 66.
Hiĕro, 39, 409, 410.
Himalayas, 271.
Hindu-Koosh, 197, 202, 263.
Hindustan, 263.
Hipparchus, 224.
Hippias, 109, 224.
Hippocrătes, 88.
Hippolўtē, 394.
Hirtius, 400.
Histanes, 379.
Hodu, 263.
Homa, 265.
Homer, 39, 45, 56, 116, 121, 141, 167, 175, 205, 218, 260, 276, 285, 286, 291, 309, 318, 331, 391, 416.
Humboldt, 108.
Hydarnes, 379.
Hydaspes, 270, 271, 274, 279–288, 293, 297, 308, 316–324, 339, 374, 387.
Hydraōtes, 271, 274, 300, 301, 308, 315, 324, 326, 328, 336, 339, 387.
Hyparna, 67.
Hypaspists, 21, *et passim*.
Hyperīdes, 35.
Hyphăsis, 24, 271, 274, 306, 308, 309, 315, 339, 374, 387.
Hyrcania and Hyrcanians, 155, 161, 181, 185, 187, 188, 191, 199, 274, 297, 308, 309, 361, 387, 400.
Hyrcanian Sea, 202, 274, 308, 309, 400.
Hystaspes, 379.

Iacchus, 118, 268.
Iapygian Cape, 370.
Iassians, 58.
Iazygians, 14.
Ibērians, 118, 119, 399.
Icarian Sea, 409.
Icărus Isle, 409.
Ichthyŏphăgi, 354, 363.
Idaean Mountains, 40, 50.
Ilium, 37, 38.
Illyria and Illyrians, 9, 19, 93, 310, 383, 406.
India, 44, 247, 258–349, 355, 360, 400, 406, 408.
Indica, the, 3, 273, 277, 343.
Indians, 155, 156, 161, 164, 167, 168, 193, 197, 199, 234, 248–349, 370–373, 385.
Indian Gulf, 309.
Indus, 156, 193, 248, 258–281, 308, 317–320, 339–345, 364, 369, 374, 387.
Iolaüs, 27.
Iollas, 421.
Iōn, 308, 385, 425.
Ionian Gulf, 18.
Ionia and Ionians, 40, 53, 54, 186, 307, 363, 385.
Iphicrătes, 66, 115, 140.
Ipsus, 53, 76, 405.
Isis, 142, 420.
Ismēnias, 224.
Isocrates, 395.
Issus, 90–104, 140, 157, 243, 334.
Ister, 12–17, 270, 276, 277.
Isthmus, 334, 371.
Italy, 152, 399.
Ivica, 108.

Javan, 307, 385.
Jaxartes, 198, 202, 247, 274, 401.
Jelalabad, 265.
Jelum, 270.
Jerome, 109, 413.
Jerusalem, 135.
Josephus, 1, 91, 109, 124.
Julian, 85, 103, 106, 385.
Juliopolis, 76.
Jupiter Ammon, 144.
Justice, 222.
Justin, 9, 31, 103, 421.

Kem, 276.
Khorasan, 155, 191.
Krüger, 99, 143, 188, 244, 257, 263, 268, 278, 281, 283, 319, 356.

Labdacus, 118.
Lacedaemonians, 9, 26, 32, 49, 113, 115, 120, 150, 173, 190, 227, 272.
Ladē, 54, 56, 57.
Lahore, 280, 301.
Läīus, 118.
Lampsacus, 40.
Langarus, 19, 20.
Lanicē, 221.
Laŏmĕdon, 151.
Lebānon, 108, 111, 122, 125, 156, 308.
Lēnaeus, 268.
Leon, 119.
Leŏnnātus, 105, 149, 228, 245, 249, 252, 253, 330–334, 345, 348, 351, 363, 377.
Leōtychĭdes, 54.
Lesbos, 78, 108, 143, 144.
Leuctra, 32.
Leugē, 98.
Liber, 268.
Lĭbya, 144, 145, 149, 203, 308, 309, 313, 369, 399, 426.
Līby-Phoenicians, 406.
Liddell and Scott, 127, 278.
Livy, 167, 210, 253, 349, 400, 424.
Lubim, 144.
Lūcanians, 152, 399.
Lūcian, 4, 6, 416, 427.
Lucullus, 71.
Lud, 186.
Lyaeus, 268.
Lўcia and Lycians, 67, 68, 80, 125, 151, 308.
Lўcidas, 148.
Lўcomēdes, 79.
Lўcūrgus, 35.
Lўcus River, 154, 169.
Lўdia and Lydians, 40, 50, 51, 152, 186, 308, 385, 414.
Lyginus, 12.
Lysander, 57.
Lysanias, 12.
Lysias, 395.
Lўsimăchus, 53, 76, 285, 305, 363, 373, 405.
Lysippus, 48.

Macedonia, 8, 9, 13, 18, 48, 49, 66, 77, 98, 112, 125, 162, 173, 174, 239, 253, 308, 310, 344, 383, 391, 405.
Macedonians, *passim.*
Madai, 239.
Maeander, 57, 275, 276.
Maeotis, Lake, 202, 203, 274, 370.
Magarsus, 89.
Magi, 366, 367, 389.
Magnesia, 58, 165.
Mahabunn Mount, 258, 259.
Malea, 78.
Mallians, 301, 322, 324–335, 338, 339.
Mallus, 89, 125.
Mandanis, 371.
Mantinēa, 32.
Maracanda, 202, 210, 213, 215, 235, 236.
Marathus, 111, 115.
Marcomanni, 14.
Mardians, 161, 164, 297.
Mareōtis, Lake, 142.
Mariamnē, 111.
Marian, Lake, 142.
Maritza, 37.
Marmarians, 67.
Marmarica, 145.
Marōnēa, 37.
Mars, 45.
Martial, 118.
Massaga, 254–256, 259.
Massăgĕtae, 2, 4, 236-238.
Mausōlus, 65.
Mavaces, 155.
Mazaces, 140, 141, 185.
Mazaeus, 152, 156, 168, 171, 239, 379, 404.
Mazarus, 173.
Mēdia and Medes, 91, 125, 155, 161, 171, 179, 180, 192, 194, 239, 272, 273, 308, 365, 374, 387, 393.
Mediterranean, 275, 276, 318, 369, 417.
Mēdius, 418–422.
Megalŏpŏlis, 173.
Megareus, 144.
Megăris, 152.
Megasthĕnes, 3, 4, 273, 274, 355, 372, 427.
Mĕlamnĭdas, 216.
Mĕlas River, 37.
Melĕăger, 17, 44, 59, 67, 77, 95, 162 176, 235, 238, 248, 284, 344.
Melkarth, 117.
Mēlos, 32.
Memnōn, 41, 46, 51, 59, 64, 78, 79, 242.

Memphis, 141, 142, 148, 150, 405, 423.
Menander, 109, 124, 152, 414, 417.
Menedēmus, 210, 215.
Menelaüs, 276.
Mĕnēs, 104, 141, 173, 181, 217.
Menĭdas, 148, 164, 165, 169, 194, 239, 414, 420.
Meniscus, 112.
Mĕnōn, 110, 197.
Menoetus, 38.
Mĕnoph, 141.
Mentor, 51, 375.
Merŏēs, 295.
Mēros Mountain, 266, 268.
Mesopotamia, 153, 156, 161, 172, 308, 380, 385.
Metellus, 48.
Methymna, 78, 143.
Miccalus, 407.
Micōn, 394.
Midas, 82.
Milētus and Milesians, 53–58, 149, 204, 275, 354, 385.
Milyas, 67.
Minōs, 110, 224, 425.
Mithraustes, 156.
Mithridates, 47, 48.
Mithrines, 50, 171.
Mithrobaeus, 379.
Mithrobūzanes, 48.
Mitylēnē, 78, 79, 80, 144.
Mitsraim, 276.
Moeris, 344.
Moerocles, 35.
Monimus, 190.
Mooltan, 325.
Moph, 41.
Muses, 36.
Musicanus, 341–343.
Mycălē, 54–57, 273.
Mycēnae, 118.
Mylasa, 59, 61.
Myndus, 59, 60, 88.
Myriandrus, 90, 92.
Mȳsia, 275.

Nabarzanes, 182, 185, 188.
Naucrătis, 149.
Nautaca, 199, 239.
Nearchus, 3, 4, 151, 217, 263, 273, 319, 324, 336, 337, 348, 349, 355, 363, 364, 372, 374, 375, 377, 406, 410, 418, 419, 427.
Nebuchadnezzar, 117.
Necho, 108, 309.
Negropont, 81.
Neilos, 141.
Neiloxĕnus, 197.
Neoptolemus, 38, 61, 138, 226.
Nĕpos, 305.
Nērēids, 38, 320.
Nervii, 61.
Nessus River, 10.
Nīcaea, 247, 296, 316.
Nīcānōr, 16, 43, 54, 56, 95, 162, 184, 192, 247, 259.
Nīcĭas, 51.
Nīcomēdia, 1, 2.
Nīcŏpŏlis, 2.
Nīcostrătus, 104.
Nile, 24, 140, 141, 144, 149, 150, 203, 270, 276, 317, 318.
Nimrod, 411.
Niphātes, 40, 48.
Nisaean Plain, 373, 393.
Nomad Libyans, or Numidians, 203, 369.
Nonacris, 421.
Noph, 141.
Nȳsa, 265–268, 310, 319.

Ocean, 320.
Ōchus, 112, 113, 116, 375.
Ocondobates, 155.
Odrysians, 164.
Oedipūs, 118.
Olympias, 8, 68, 151, 152, 223, 318, 391, 392, 421.
Ōmares, 48.
Ombrion, 149.
Omphis, 247.
On, 141.
Onchēstus, 26.
Onēsicritus, 319, 365, 377, 410, 427.
Onomas, 190.
Opis, 381.
Ōra, 256–259, 351, 355, 363, 377.
Orbelus Mountain, 10.
Orchomĕnus, 34.
Ordanes, 361.
Orestis, 363.
Ōrītians, 350–352, 377, 387.
Ormuzd, 243.
Orobatis, 259.
Orontes, 156.
Orontobates, 64, 66, 88.
Orpheus, 36.
Orxines, 365, 367.

Oscius, 12.
Ossadians, 340.
Otanes, 155.
Ovid, 15, 41, 234.
Oxathres, 155, 180, 374.
Oxiana Palus, 401.
Oxodates, 182, 239.
Ōxus, 199, 200, 202, 234, 235, 247, 274, 358, 387, 401.
Oxyartes, 199, 239–245, 340, 341, 375, 379.
Oxycanus, 342.
Oxydracians, 301, 322, 333, 338.
Ozines, 361.

Paddan-Aram, 156, 308.
Paetica, 37.
Paeonians, 18, 43, 45, 93, 97, 154, 163, 165.
Palaetyrus, 119, 122.
Palestine, 110, 135, 136, 385.
Pallacŏpas River, 411, 412.
Pamphȳlia, 67, 71, 197, 273, 308.
Pandŏsia, 152.
Panegorus, 40.
Pangaean Mountain, 37, 383.
Pantaleōn, 148.
Pantordanus, 98.
Paphlagonia and Paphlagonians, 84, 305, 308.
Paraetacae, 180, 244, 246.
Paraetŏnium, 145.
Parălus, 125, 150.
Parapamisadae, 247, 269, 283, 340, 358.
Parapamisus, 197, 270, 271, 273.
Paras, 364.
Paravaea, 26.
Parmĕnio, 12, 37, 41–43, 50, 53, 54, 67, 69, 70, 76, 84, 86, 87, 95, 96, 104, 106, 114, 135, 157–159, 163, 168, 169, 176, 178, 181, 194–196, 232, 361.
Paron, 171.
Parthia and Parthians, 155, 161, 168, 181, 182, 185, 191, 197, 216, 273, 361, 378, 387.
Pasargădae, 178, 364–369, 372, 406.
Pasicrătes, 129.
Pasitigris, 174, 379.
Patala and Patalians, 343–345, 348, 349.
Patăra, 67.
Patrŏclus, 38, 402.
Paul, St., 110.
Pausanias, 8, 51, 68, 217.
Pausippus, 190.
Peithagŏras, 404, 405.
Peithōn son of Sosicles, 236, 237.
Peithon, son of Agenor, 236, 324-328, 341, 343, 344, 348, 420.
Peithon, son of Crateas, 236, 363.
Pelagon, 52.
Pelesheth and Pelishtim, 135.
Pelina, 26.
Pēlium, 20.
Pella, 8, 20, 148, 363.
Pelopidas, 224, 384.
Peloponnēsus, 9, 51, 67, 81, 96, 125, 150, 310, 384.
Pēlūsium, 140, 141, 148.
Pēneius, 216.
Pĕrath, 107.
Percōte, 40.
Perdiccas, 17, 20, 24, 28, 29, 43, 59, 61, 95, 162, 176, 235, 244, 248, 259, 264, 284, 285, 302, 325, 326, 329, 330, 333, 340, 363, 375, 405.
Perga and Pergaĕans, 70–73.
Perinthus, 112.
Peripolus, 125.
Periplūs, the, 4.
Peroedas, 98.
Persĕpŏlis, 178, 179, 195, 367, 369.
Perseus, 145, 230.
Persian Gates, 176.
Persian Sea or Gulf, 309, 347, 364, 369, 379, 380, 381, 400, 406, 410.
Persians, 42–58, *et passim.*
Persis, 155, 173, 174, 177, 178, 185, 308, 363–368, 372, 378, 414.
Petinēs, 40, 48.
Petisis, 148.
Peucē, 12, 270.
Peucela, 248.
Peucelaōtis, 248, 259.
Peucestas, 149, 330–335, 363, 367, 368, 377, 378, 414, 415, 417, 420.
Pharasmanes, 234.
Pharismanes, 361.
Pharnabāzus, 79–81, 109, 140–144, 189.
Pharnăcēs, 48.
Pharnuches, 210, 213, 214.
Phăros, 142, 416.
Pharsalians, 163.
Phasēlis, 68, 70.

Phasians, 394.
Philēmon, 88.
Philip, 259.
Philip of Macedon, 6–9, 18, 20, 21, 24, 27, 34, 36, 68, 112, 113, 151, 219, 229, 305, 383, 384.
Philip, son of Amyntas, 43.
Philip, son of Machatas, 17, 44, 279, 298, 319, 321, 324, 339, 340, 360.
Philip, son of Menelaüs, 44, 163, 192.
Philip, the Physician, 85, 86.
Philippi, 10, 12.
Philistines, 110, 135, 136.
Philotas, son of Carsis, 230.
Philōtas, son of Parmenio, 12, 13, 21, 24, 43, 57, 62, 86, 89, 162, 177, 193–196, 200, 224, 232, 252.
Philoxĕnus, 151, 172, 414, 417.
Phisinus, 144.
Phocians, 30, 384.
Phōcĭōn, 35.
Phoenicia and Phoenicians, 55, 81, 90, 107, 108, 111, 116, 118, 120, 125–127, 132, 136, 140, 150, 151, 153, 158, 173, 308, 309, 318, 352, 359, 391, 406, 407, 414.
Phōtius, 1, 4, 271, 392, 427.
Phradasmenes, 379.
Phrasaortes, 178, 364.
Phrataphernes, 155, 188, 197, 216, 239, 298, 362, 379.
Phrygia, 40, 44, 48, 65, 67, 73, 76, 77, 82, 105, 186, 308, 385.
Pieris, 36.
Pimprama, 301.
Pinăra, 67.
Pinărus, 92, 95, 104.
Pindar, 34, 39, 177, 309, 334.
Pisidia and Pisidians, 67, 68, 73–75.
Pixōdarus, 66.
Plataeae and Plataeans, 30, 32, 138.
Plato, 181, 286.
Plautus, 108.
Pleiades, 349, 411.
Pliny, 271, 272, 277, 313, 340, 349, 369, 422.
Plutarch, 3, 6, 27, 33–35, 37, 39, 49, 92, 94, 106, 137, 268, 305, 358, 372, 396, 417, 418, 421, 424.
Pnytagŏras, 126, 129.
Polemo, 148, 149, 195.
Polyaenus, 358.
Polybĭus, 95, 101, 102, 203, 231, 239, 346, 364.
Polydămas, 194.
Polydectēs, 145.
Polydeucēs or Pollux, 219.
Polydōrus, 118.
Polyeuctus, 35.
Polysperchōn, 104, 162, 228, 235, 242, 246, 253, 283, 324, 391, 421.
Polytimētus, 213, 216.
Pompeiopolis, 88.
Pompey, 115.
Porticanus, 342.
Porus, 280–306, 315, 318.
Poseidōn, 38, 145, 320, 347, 425.
Practius River, 40.
Prasĭas, Lake, 37.
Priam, 38.
Priāpus, 40.
Proĕxes, 197.
Prŏmētheus, 269.
Propontis, 234.
Proteas, 81, 125.
Protĕsĭlāus, 37.
Protomăchus, 97.
Ptolemy the Geographer, 203, 401.
Ptolemy, son of Lagus, 3, 6, 13, 24, 28, 76, 88, 102, 103, 105, 146, 148, 151, 175, 193, 194, 196, 200–202, 209, 220, 231, 232, 235, 245, 249–253, 260, 261, 277, 288, 297, 299, 304, 305, 314, 319, 324, 332–337, 363, 373, 375, 394, 399, 405, 416, 421, 423, 427.
Ptolemy, son of Philip, 45.
Ptolemy, son of Seleucus, 66, 77, 100, 104.
Ptolemy, 63–65, 88, 95, 177, 216.
Ptolemy Philadelphus, 416.
Punjab, 249, 271.
Pūra, 355.
Purally, 349.
Pydna, 230.
Pȳrămus, 89.
Pyrrhus of Epirus, 19.
Pythagŏras, 317.
Pythodēmus, 8.

Quadi, 14.

Raamsss, 149, 410.

Rai, 182.
Ras-al-Had, 410.
Ravi, 300.
Rawlinson, 87, 393, 413.
Rawson, 146.
Red Sea, 155, 161, 309, 400.
Reno, 277.
Rha, 203.
Rhadamanthus, 425.
Rhăgae, 182.
Rhambacia, 351.
Rhĕa, 173.
Rheomithres, 40, 103.
Rhine, 141, 277.
Rhodes, 94, 125, 335.
Rhoesaces, 47.
Rhone, 153, 286.
Richard I., 136.
Rome and Romans, 1, 2, 149, 230, 277, 278, 370, 399, 400, 420.
Roxāna, 242, 243, 340, 375, 421, 422.
Rumour, 333.

Sabaces, 103, 140.
Sabictas, 84.
Sacesinians, 155, 161.
Săcians, 155, 161, 387.
Sagalassus, 74.
Salaminia, 125, 150.
Salămis, 102, 150, 334, 399.
Salmacis, 65.
Salmus, 363.
Samarcand, 202.
Samaria, 91, 150, 364.
Sambus, 342.
Sămos, 57, 273.
Samothrace, 230.
Sanballat, 91.
Sandracotus, 273, 275.
Sangaeus, 248.
Sangala, 301–306.
Sangarius River, 77.
Sardanapālus, 87.
Sardinia, 108.
Sardīs, 50, 51, 67, 171.
Sarmătians, 14.
Sarra, 117.
Satibarzanes, 155, 191–193, 197.
Satraces, 212.
Satrapes, 247.
Saurŏmătians, 14.
Saxones, 387.
Schmieder, 296.
Schmitz, 426.
Scinde, 263.
Sciōne, 32.
Scythia and Scythians, 15, 155, 161, 164, 165, 180, 192, 196, 202, 205–214, 227, 233, 234, 237, 238, 272, 273, 284, 308, 309, 370, 399, 401.
Seleucidae, 285.
Seleucus, 53, 76, 107, 273, 285, 291, 375, 405, 414, 420.
Selgians, 74.
Sĕmĕlē, 117.
Semiramis, 66, 355.
Seneca, 118, 232.
Sennacherib, 140.
Serāpis, 420.
Seriphus, 145.
Sestus, 37.
Shalmaneser, 116, 117, 121.
Shat-el-Arab, 153, 369, 379.
Sheshach, 413.
Shichor, 141.
Shushan, 172.
Sibi, 324.
Sibyrtius, 275, 360.
Sicily, 108, 370.
Sidē, 71.
Sidon, 108, 111, 116, 124–127.
Sigēum, 38.
Sigon, 111.
Sigrium, 78.
Simmias, 162, 167, 195.
Sin, 140.
Sindhu, 263.
Sindimana, 342, 343.
Sinōpe and Sinopeans, 190, 371.
Sintenis, 209, 220, 257, 361.
Siphnus, 81, 109.
Sisicottus, 263, 298.
Sisinēs, 69, 379.
Sisygambis, 105, 167, 175.
Sitacenians, 156, 161.
Sitalces, 75, 87, 98, 164, 194, 361.
Siwah, 144.
Smerdis, 364.
Smyrna, 275, 407.
Sochi, 89.
Sōcrătes, 40, 43, 45.
Sogdian Rock, 239–241.
Sogdiana and Sogdianians, 155, 199–206, 215, 235–240, 284, 378.
Sogdians, 341.
Soli, 88–90, 104, 125, 410.
Solomon, 107.

Sŏlōn, 402.
Sopeithes, 319.
Sopolis, 13, 162, 239.
Sōstrătus, 230.
Spain, 108, 118.
Sparta, 32, 39.
Sphines, 372.
Spitaces, 294.
Spitamenes, 199–202, 209, 213–215, 236–239, 375.
Spithridates, 40, 47, 48, 51.
Spŏrădēs, 88, 409.
Stamenes, 239.
Stasanor, 200, 216, 239, 361, 362, 364.
Statira, 48, 135, 242, 243.
Stiboetis, 188.
Străbo, 15, 55, 78, 108, 139, 141, 202, 269, 274, 319, 356, 371, 393, 395, 402, 420.
Străto, 111, 116.
Strȳmon, 37.
Stymphaea, 26.
Styx, 421.
Suetonius Paulinus, 369.
Sulla, 420.
Sunium, 334.
Sūsa, 171–174, 182, 362, 372, 374, 377, 385, 387, 406.
Susia, 191.
Susiana and Susianians, 155, 161, 173, 174, 308, 363, 364, 379, 398.
Sutledj, 339.
Syennĕsis, 85.
Syllium, 72.
Syria Palaestinē, 135.
Syria and Syrians, 87, 91, 140, 152, 156, 173, 285, 308, 380, 407.
Syrian Gates, 87, 89, 91, 94.
Syrmus, 12, 17.
Syrphax, 52.

Tacitus, 110.
Taenărum, 110.
Tanais, 198, 202, 203, 205, 209–211, 274, 308, 387.
Tapuria and Tapurians, 155, 161, 187, 188, 239, 414.
Tarentines, 152.
Tarshish, 118.
Tarsus, 85, 87, 89, 90.
Tartēssus, 118.
Taulantians, 19–22, 25.
Tauriscus, 151.
Tauron, 287, 291.
Taurus, 85, 151, 197, 273–275.
Taxĭla, 270, 279, 280, 371.
Taxiles, 247, 248, 270, 279, 280, 294, 298, 360, 372.
Tel-el-Kebir, 146.
Tēlĕphus, 354.
Telmissus, 36, 67, 82.
Tēmĕnus, 217.
Tempē, 216.
Tĕnĕdus, 80, 81, 143.
Tennes, 116.
Teredon, 411.
Terioltes, 341.
Termēssus, 73–75.
Thalestris, 394.
Thammuz, 116.
Thapsăcus, 71, 107, 151, 152, 406.
Thara, 183.
Thebes and Thebans, 25–34, 115, 221, 265, 310, 378, 384.
Theodectes, 68.
Theŏcrĭtus, 242.
Theophrastus, 232.
Thēra, 88, 198.
Thermopȳlae, 26.
Thēro, 39.
Thersippus, 112.
Thēseus, 394, 425.
Thessaliscus, 114, 115.
Thessaly and Thessalians, 26, 43, 67, 68, 69, 77, 87, 96, 97, 101, 163, 169, 176, 180, 200, 310, 383, 391.
Thoas, 353, 360.
Thrace and Thracians, 9–12, 15, 44, 53, 54, 69, 71, 75, 87, 93, 98, 108, 112, 148, 164, 298, 310, 340, 383, 391, 406.
Thriambus, 362.
Thūcȳdĭdēs, 12, 45, 55, 99, 295, 335.
Thymōndas, 80, 107.
Tibarēnes, 118.
Tigrēs, 107, 153, 154, 156, 274, 277, 347, 364, 369, 380, 381, 401.
Timaeus, 153, 223.
Timagenes, 335.
Timander, 63.
Timolaüs, 25.
Tiphsach, 107.
Tīryns, 310.
Tirynthius, 310.
Tissaphernes, 191.

Tlēpolĕmus, 185, 360.
Tmōlus, Mount, 265.
Tobit, 182.
Trallēs, 52, 65.
Trapĕzūs, 394.
Trebizond, 234.
Triballians, 9–17, 310, 383.
Triopium, 88.
Tripolĭs, 107, 108.
Troezēn, 59.
Troy, 332.
Tsidon, 116.
Tsor, 117.
Tubal, 119.
Tylus Island, 409.
Tyndareus, 219.
Tyre, 108, 109, 116–138, 150, 255.
Tyriaspes, 247, 298, 340.
Tyrrhenians, 399.

Ulai, 379.
Urănus, 408.
Uxians, 155, 161, 174, 175, 297, 387, 398.

Vergil, 54, 167, 186, 310, 318, 401.
Vitellius, 71.

Winer, 413.

Xanthippus, 54.
Xanthus, 67.
Xathrians, 340.
Xenophōn, 1, 39, 42, 84, 93, 94, 96, 99, 102, 159, 191, 224, 225, 227, 244, 394, 425.
Xerxēs, 37, 102, 171, 173, 204, 226, 227, 277, 364, 396, 403, 406.

Yam-Suph, 155.
Yenikale, Straits of, 277.
Yĕor, 141.

Zab, 156, 169.
Zadracarta, 188, 191.
Zaraugaeans, 193, 344, 361, 378.
Zariaspa, 206, 216, 236.
Zeleia, 41, 50.
Zeriaspes, 361.
Zeus, 36, 38, 51, 82, 89, 104, 145, 148, 219, 222, 243, 266, 371, 425.
Ziobetis, 188.
Zoroaster, 367.

Published by

Facsimile Publisher
Ashok Vihar, Delhi-110052 (India)
Website: www.facsimilepublisher.com

Distributed by

Gyan Books Pvt. Ltd.
5, Ansari Road, Daryaganj, New Delhi-110002 (India)
E-mail: books@gyanbooks.com, Website: www.gyanbooks.com

8 888000 560135